John Muir's California

North Fork

North Fork

Tuolumne

Lake Eleanor

River

Hetch Hetchy
Reserve

North Dome

Tenaya Creek

El Capitan

Half Dome

Mirror Lake

Lake
McClure

Mt. Watkins

Tenaya Lake

Mono Lake

Mt. Lyell

Mt. McClure

Mt. Ritter

**YOSEMITE
NATIONAL
PARK**

Joaquin River

River

**KING'S
CANYON
NATIONAL
PARK**

Kings

Mt. Whitney

**SEQUOIA
NATIONAL
PARK**

Kaweah River

Lake Kaweah

Kern Lake

Kern River

John Muir
Earth-planet
Universe

Published by The Word Shop, Inc.
3737 Fifth Avenue, Suite 203
San Diego, California 92103

Library of Congress Card Catalog Number 79-64178
ISBN: 0-932238-01-7

Printed in the United States of America

The
Life and Adventures
of John Muir

by James Mitchell Clarke

The
Word
Shop

Publications

Acknowledgements

I wish to thank the following for their kindness and generous help:

Paul B. Sears, the ecologist who was president of the American Association for the Advancement of Science in 1956. During our association on a book project, Dr. Sears made me responsive to the varied and increasing perils which beset our environment.
A. L. Strand, entomologist, former president of Oregon State University.
Waldo K. Lyon, Director, Arctic Submarine Laboratory, U. S. Navy Electronics Laboratory Center, San Diego, California. Dr. Lyon, who is the Navy's leading authority on Arctic ice and how to voyage beneath it, was kind enough to review the Alaska and North Arctic chapters of this book.
John Thomas Howell, Curator of Botany, the Science Museum, California Academy of Science, San Francisco.
Bryant Evans, former Science Editor, the *San Diego Union*, who read my entire manuscript and helped me with many pertinent comments and suggestions.
Victor K. McElheny, science writer, the *New York Times*, who also read the manuscript and helped me both editorially and in other ways.
H. Clair Cantelow and several other members of the California Botany Club.
Harry M. Butterfield, Professor emeritus, University of California at Davis.
A. I. Dickman, collector of oral histories at U. C. Davis.
Frederick Stansbury Clough, whose mother and aunt were friends of the Muir family.
The San Diego Public Library, especially the very competent and obliging staff of the California Room.
Ronald L. Silviera, Head of the Department of Special Collections, Library at the University of California, San Diego.
Douglas E. Davis, Editor, Forest History Society, Inc., Santa Cruz, California.
Paul C. Johnson, late author and editor of many California publications.

J. M. C.

SPECIAL ACKNOWLEDGEMENT to Martha Katt for her tremendous help in editing and coordinating production of the manuscript — and to Wayne Kempe and Lynne Foster for their equally diligent assistance.

Map design, Jeremy Crockett.
Book design consultation, Bill Byerley.

Table of Contents

Part VI   HUSBANDMAN

Part VII   ACTIVIST

Foreword

This book was written in a "cabin" overlooking a sunlit garden where, the author said, there lingered a fragrance like remembered love. The Point Loma home where James Mitchell Clarke wrote out the narrative of John Muir's pilgrimage to the wilderness, and where his wife Helen typed it all, is surrounded by such an array of lush plants and eager birds that one almost forgets the never-ending tension of human creatures who are *in* nature but not quite *of* nature.

This tension can be felt strongly in a famous painting in the Basilica of St. Francis in Assisi. In one of a score of scenes from the life of St. Francis, he is shown preaching to birds. St. Francis does not seem to be striving to dominate nature, but rather to restore a frayed contact with nature. Intently, the scene symbolizes the danger that our religious feelings could dry out and turn to dust if we failed to see ourselves as creatures among other creatures. The painting is given a special place among all the scenes in the life of St. Francis. On a May morning, as fresh sunlight sweeps down a slope of green lawn where crickets sing as they did seven hundred years ago, light is reflected from the stone floor of the Basilica doorway and shines upon the sermon to the birds.

John Muir's life was a kind of campaign, a testimony against the notion that all of nature was designed for the use of man. He was at home in, and took an ecstatic pleasure in, the world that man had not made. He felt that mankind's spirit would wither in the machine age unless people could regularly experience a world relatively untouched by human technology. He fought to preserve that natural world.

Since Muir's death in 1914, the population of the world, and of the United States, has more than doubled, thanks to technological triumphs in agriculture and public health. The massive technologies driven by the energies of coal and oil — trains, ships, cars, planes and power plants — and the gossamer linkages wrought by the telephone have eased the work of humanity and brought all peoples closer to each other.

But they do this at the price of walling off people from nature, like the denizens of Captain Nemo's submarine pushing dangerously through alien depths. In such a world, John Muir's pilgrimage becomes even more important than it was in the time when lumberjacks sawed down one of the greatest of the giant Sequoias to make a dance floor.

We need to know the sources of John Muir's passion to understand the glaciers that carved the earth, and the plants and animals living in their wake.

We need to know the experiences that carved the soul of John Muir. The best way to grasp these things is through a narrative, a story such as might be recounted night after night by a fire.

James Mitchell Clarke, himself born on a ranch at the edge of the Rockies in 1903, and also a long-time city-dweller writing for newspapers and radio, has told such a story.

Victor K. McElheny

"Books...are but piles of stones set up to show coming travelers where other minds have been...or at best smoke signals to call attention...No amount of word-making will ever make a single soul know these mountains."

Preface

The most important question the preface to this book should answer is: why should a reader today be interested in John Muir's life, which ended in 1914? One answer is that a majority of the 7,000 members of the California Historical Society recently voted Muir the greatest figure in California history. This is by no means to imply that his importance is purely local.

On the contrary, he is honored throughout the nation for opening our eyes to the supreme importance of our forests and opening many hearts to the beneficence of the wilderness. He is known as "the father of our National Park System," though the appellation would have displeased him because it leaves out the many who fought at his side to get the necessary legislation passed and is besides too narrow to suggest the many and varied accomplishments of his productive life.

The vote simply acknowledges the fact that the memory of John Muir has crossed several generation gaps and is well worth an attentive look in our time — since the life of no man or woman has the same significance for succeeding generations.

This book is a narrative which recounts the events of Muir's life in the order of their occurrence. But a narrative made up, except for a few interpretive passages, almost entirely of actions and circumstances recounted by Muir himself: observations, musings, feelings and statements he himself has given in his more than seventy articles and all-too-few books. For the rest, it consists of accounts and statements by dependable witnesses on the scene or in a position to know the facts. The book also includes a necessary amount of background data — much of it acquired since Muir's time — which makes the narrative of his life more understandable and thus more interesting.

It is true that with only the simple instruments he was able to carry on his lone-hand explorations, Muir made some errors of height and depth. These flaws, along with his unquenchable enthusiasm, were the ammunition used by his enemies to demean him as an exaggerator. His interpretations were criticized by some scientists of his generation because they were so advanced; to scientists today some of his interpretations seem old-fashioned.

But many of Muir's prophecies concerning the environment have come to pass, to our consternation. We have escaped other disasters by adopting the remedies he prescribed.

As concerns his own activities Muir was a modest and irreproachable witness. He had many adventures in which he risked his life, and in most of these he was alone. Fortunately he was in the company of a much-respected Presbyterian missionary during his most extraordinary and risky feat of mountaineering. Moreover, none of his mountain and explorer friends and companions doubted his word.

Further, Muir's interest and pleasure in the whole of nature, his delight in intellectual, as well as physical adventure, and the extraordinary range of his activities, give Muir's life a seldom-equalled richness and variety of experience — lived with humor and love.

J. M. C.

On the Graphics

The illustrations throughout the book are mostly by John Muir himself. They are sketches he jotted down as visual notes on his experiences. Some are from his journals which he carried with him on all of his expeditions. They are used here not so much to illustrate the text as to add another dimension to the reader's understanding of the range and depth of Muir's sensitivity and curiosity.

Special thanks to: The Bancroft Library, University of California at Berkeley, for the frontispiece photo and those on pages 293 and 296; the National Park Service and the Hanna Family for the Muir illustrations from the Yosemite Collection on pages 56, 60, 61, 66, 68, 70, 72, 74, 76, 78, 85, 99, 106, 117, 119, 120, 123, 127, 129, 153, 176, 247 251, 273, 274, 277 and 286; the State Historical Society of Wisconsin for the illustrations and photos on pages 25, 29, 42, 47 and 49; Laura Hough of San Diego for her illustrations on pages 43 and 159; Margaret Hough of San Diego, for her two illustrations on pages 14 and 91 and her three illustrations taken from *The Cruise of the Corwin,* by John Muir, on pages 207, 238 and 239; Allan Inglis of Edinburgh, Scotland, for his photographs on pages 13 and 16; and the Serra Museum of San Diego for their photograph on page 173.

Part I

BOY

"An adventure-loving boy...quick to accept a challenge...high-spirited, irrepressible...uncontainable."

Chapter 1
Scootchers Under the Castle

 D unbar castle was already one thousand years old when young John Muir and his bold friends played there in the 1840s. Usually the boys climbed the crumbling walls and towers. There was not much of the inside they could get into: fallen stones had filled up many of the rooms and choked the stairways. But one day when John was about nine, they found their way underneath.

The castle stands on black rocks rising out of the cold and furious North Sea that washes the east coast of Scotland. Waves had beaten against these rocks year in and year out, grinding away at them with sand and small stones. Where the waves found a soft spot, they made a sea cave that grew deeper as the years passed. Finally the sea had broken through into the lowest part of the castle — the dungeon of hallways, and cells and torture chambers carved in the solid rock.

John Muir and his friends went through the sea cave when the tide had gone out, leaving a little strip of beach. It was dark and wet-feeling down under the castle. The candle stubs that the boys carried threw light only a little way and made changing, wobbling shadows. One boy would go ahead by himself and find an adventure, then dare the others to do as he did. They called this game "scootchers."

For a while it was exciting enough just to go from room to room and touch the bones of prisoners long dead and forgotten. But then the boys came to a room below the others. It went down below the sea level outside. The ceiling had fallen in. This room was like a dark pit. The light of their candles did not reach the bottom. John Muir handed his candle to another boy and lowered himself over the edge. None of the others tried to talk him out of going. They knew it would be no use. But as the blackness closed around John, he rather wished they *had* kept him from trying this scootcher. Digging his fingers into cracks and finding footholds on little shelves, he lowered himself slowly down the rough rock wall. The other boys called to him anxiously, but he had no breath to answer. Down, down and still down. It began to seem as if there was no bottom.

At last his reaching foot found stones and rotting planks. He stood on the bottom, breathing hard and trying to stop the trembling of his muscles. The candlelight above seemed faint and far off.

"Are ye doon, Johnny?" the boys kept asking.

"Aye," said John Muir at last, and he began to climb up.

Present day Dunbar Castle ruins, Dunbar, Scotland.

It seemed a very long way. His fingers ached. His toes were bruised. He had to use his last strength to scramble up over the edge. The boys crowded around, asking questions and saying this was the best scootcher of all. None of them was willing to go into that pit. In the candlelight John Muir's blue eyes sparkled like the sea on a windy day. His red-brown hair was full of dust and cobwebs, his face dirt-smeared, and he felt just fine.

That evening a woman who worked for his family got cross with John. "Do you know where bad boys like you go?" she asked. "To hell, that's where they go!"

"Well," said John, "if I do I'll climb right out again. I was down there today and here I am."

That was John Muir for you: an adventure-loving boy with the physical equipment to enjoy such pleasures and survive them; quick to accept a challenge, even from adults, who called him a "long-tongued child" because he *would* argue and he *would* answer back; high-spirited, irrepressible — and also uncontainable. He had become adept at scaling walls and slipping through unguarded doorways to go rambling in the countryside with his friends — something which his father strictly forbade him to do for fear John would learn bad language and delinquent ways.

"The Deevil's in that boy!" his father would say when he caught John coming home from one of these adventures and laid into him with a strap or a limber cane. He stood six feet tall, weighed a hundred ninety pounds — and he hit to hurt.

Mr. Muir was entirely serious in the matter of the Devil, who was to him a living presence trying to drag human souls down into Hell's lake of eternal fire. To defeat the Devil, one must achieve what he called "the ecstasy of the Prophets," a state of religious exaltation maintained by reading the Bible — and only the Bible — thinking on eternal punishment versus salvation, and behaving at all times in a seemly manner, that is, with high seriousness at the least and, if possible, with solemnity.

John Muir's birthplace, 128 High Street, Dunbar, Scotland.

He had never permitted pictures in the high stone house of which the family occupied the two upper floors, Mr. Muir's grain and produce business occupying the lower. But when John was a little lad the family had sung together, and on special occasions Mr. Muir would get out the violin he had made for himself as a teen-ager and play the wild dance tunes of his Highland ancestors. In those early years John Muir had learned to dance and to sing the old ballads that recount the wars and fatal loves of the romantic, intransigent Scots. But now, as the calendar unrolled toward the close of the eighteen forties, he permitted only hymn-singing. Mr. Muir was advancing steadily from religious zealot toward religious fanatic. He was not more cruel than the average Dunbar father of those days, when flogging was a common form of punishment for soldiers and sailors and petty criminals. But Mr. Muir had been a sergeant in a Scotch regiment of the British Army — and he meant to be obeyed.

Mr. Muir had his virtues. At times the beauty of the natural world penetrated his gloom. He permitted his wife to grow flowers in the long, walled garden where espaliered fruit trees stood like skeletons through the long winters to become living adornments under the touch of spring. He even helped her occasionally with the gardening. A bed of lilies cultivated especially for Mrs. Muir's sister, "Aunt Rae," was the special wonder and delight of John Muir's early childhood. He dreamed of being rich enough to have such a garden himself.

Also Mr. Muir kept his promises. And he dealt fairly — to the point of cautious generosity — with his customers. His business practices, in combination with his business talents, had made him prosperous. But he shared his gains very little with his family.

For noon dinner they usually ate vegetable broth and occasionally a small piece of boiled mutton for variety. John hated the barley scones that inevitably accompanied these repasts, but ate them in a vain effort to fill himself up. Each day he ran back to school feeling almost as hungry as before. After school the Muir children had "content," made of water with a little milk and sugar mixed in, half a slice of bread without butter, and more scones; bedtime supper was a boiled potato — and still more scones. The family ate in hushed solemnity. Mr. Muir considered each meal a sacrament and permitted no laughter, no joking, no light talk.

Had it not been for Mrs. Muir, life in the tall house, unnaturally gloomy because some of the windows had been boarded up to reduce taxes (which in that time and place were levied window by window) would have been unendurable. At twenty, when she became Mrs. Muir, Ann Gilrye had loved laughter, had written verse, painted landscapes, delighted herself on long walks in the countryside. In the thirteen years of her marriage she had learned to do without all these. But she had not forgotten how to be amused and happy, or to make her own judgments and act upon them, no matter how subtly the action must be accomplished. She had, in brief, learned to conform outwardly to her husband's every wish, as a good Scotch wife was expected to do, but without losing anything of her true, central self.

Mrs. Muir expressed her thoughts and feelings by signals her seven children learned to read. A small, fleeting smile told them when she thought Mr. Muir ridiculous; a slightly raised eyebrow or a quickly smoothed frown said, "I think he's wrong." When necessary her actions in defense of her children were overt though still secret — as when she hurried John into bed when he came home late from a ramble, before his father could catch him. Through their home-made resistance movement, the eight of them managed to make life tolerable for themselves. And like oppressed people everywhere, they developed an intense loyalty and concern for one another.

From his mother John Muir learned to respond joyfully to life whenever he had a chance, however fleeting. It was through her that he learned to give and receive love.

School was, if anything, more grim than home. The masters of the "grammar school" — the upper school for boys — which John entered at age eight, went armed with a *tawse* — a sort of junior cat-o'-nine-tails consisting of a strap with thongs fastened to one end so that it would sting more, and if applied with force, cut. The boys were simply beaten into docile behavior as long as the master was in the room, and whipped into memorizing spelling, the rules of arithmetic, the sterile forms of English, French and Latin grammar and the bare bones of geography and history.

John hated school — except for the fights, boy against boy and group against group, when they re-enacted Scotland's bloody wars with rocks and snowballs, clods and bonnets weighted with sand. It was every boy's ambition to become a good fighter and join the army. But fights risked a triple penalty; for a black eye, a boy earned himself a thrashing at school and another at home.

John Muir's "old grammar school" in Dunbar, Scotland.

John endured the thrashing better than the intolerable boredom. The wastelands of memory work meant nothing to him but a performance he was forced to go through like an animal in training. At the time he felt the same way about the Bible verses and hymns his father forced him to learn at home. But the worst of it was that he did it all too easily. He could read by the time he entered primary school at the age of three. His memory was a magnet that picked up and retained almost anything toward which it was directed. By age ten he had memorized all of the New Testament and part of the Old.

School became more and more of a drag even though John tried to relieve his tedium by decorating the margins of his books with sketches of the ships he could see beyond the schoolyard wall, so close to the North Sea that, in storms, the salt spray fell like rain on playground and classroom roof.

John's escapes into the country grew to be the best times of his young life, however painful the consequences. Nature never criticized, asked nothing of him but response to her endless and beautiful variety, teaching him without his knowing he was being taught. Free among hills and fields and marshlands under the clean sky, the world man had not made seemed to take him into itself. He thought of this state as "being wild." And wildness in this sense began to compete seriously with soldiering as a longed-for way of life.

In 1848, when John was ten, news of a far wilder and more wonderful land came filtering into Dunbar, as it was filtering into every reachable part of the globe. In a place called California, men were gathering up gold by the bucketful, sifting it from the river sands, picking it out of banks with bowie knives, finding nests of nuggets under stumps. From drunken sailors to lawyers and Mormon elders, people of all kinds and classes were becoming rich overnight.

As nearly everywhere in Western Europe, the Industrial Revolution had brought poverty and suffering to Dunbar. The hand looms, until recently the tools of a thriving industry, had mostly been burned to warm the weavers — displaced by grimy factories in grimy cities — under the hedgerows where they camped. In 1848 came the Karl Marx manifesto: "Workers of the world, unite! You have nothing to lose but your chains." Instead most of them dreamed of coming to America — where gold could be obtained for the digging, and farmland for the asking.

Even people as well off as John Muir's father shared in these dreams, for America also offered freedom from the restrictions and frustations under which they chafed. John's own dreams were fed by Audubon, whose accounts of American birds, with the author's dramatic illustrations, had been introduced into his school as supplementary reading lessons. They were John Muir's first encounter with the writings of naturalists — and the only part of his Dunbar schooling he enjoyed.

Of the rest, homework gave him the least misery. It was plentiful and dull, but he did it at his grandfather's house across the street from home. Like Mr. Muir, Grandfather Gilrye was a successful merchant. But all similarity ended at this commercial point. Grandfather Gilrye was an affectionate, perceptive Scot who had plenty of time and sympathetic understanding for his grandchildren — especially young John Muir. He had taught John to read from the signs they saw on walks along the crooked, winding streets of Dunbar. He had taught John his numbers from the town clock in its squat tower — to the child a mechanical marvel which he never forgot. And Grandfather Gilrye had taken him on his first ventures into the countryside and down to the shore, encouraging him to use his eyes and ears, helping him learn to read the world about him.

Every evening John and David, his two-years-younger brother, studied in the friendly warmth of a fire in the Gilrye living room. Grandfather heard their recited lessons, and helped as needed, thus saving them many a beating and perhaps teaching them a bit. After lessons, Grandmother gave them real tea and goodies.

As they were studying on a cold February night in 1849, their father — contrary to his custom — burst into the room.

"Bairns," he announced, "you needna study your lessons the nicht. We're gang to America the morn!"

Chapter 2
To the Wilderness

In quiet resignation, with neither smiles nor tears, Mrs. Muir had made ready for their departure. She had not been consulted, but simply told that she must leave her home and parents for unknown dangers and privations half the globe away. Her husband had decided, and that was that.

Her father could not accept the decision so readily. He understood that Mr. Muir did not intend to hunt gold; that his objective was to establish a farm and enjoy the free and democratic religious climate of frontier America with other members of a relatively new sect called Disciples of Christ. But the uncertainties of clearing and planting a farm in virgin wilderness loomed darkly in Grandfather Gilrye's mind. He insisted that his daughter move into his home — the Muir's house having been sold along with the business — and stay with him until her husband had a secure and livable place ready for her. Margaret, fifteen, and the eldest of the Muir children, would remain to help her mother care for six-year-old Daniel Jr. and the two-year-old twins, Annie and Mary.

Sarah, John and David were with their father on board the bluff-bowed immigrant ship that sailed from Glasgow on the cold, misty morning of March 19, 1849.

The boys were still wild with excitement and joy; Mr. Muir was uplifted by his plans and dreams. But Sarah was a suddenly motherless girl of thirteen, now saddled with a woman's responsibilities for a demanding father and two rampageous brothers.

Cook stoves had been set up on deck under shed roofs. Sarah, who had never cooked on a stove, there being only fireplaces at home, tried to light a fire in one next morning, at about the time the ship emerged from the Firth of Clyde into the open sea. Women at neighboring stoves paused to watch her, so young and slight, the sea wind whipping wisps of blond hair around her rosy face now pinched with anxiety and the wish to cry. They saw that when Sarah's father tried to help he was as inept as Sarah herself, and that his military back was unaccustomed to bend before a stove or anything else.

The women took compassion and brought the Muirs breakfast. But the ship had begun to pitch and roll in the rising sea. Sarah suddenly clapped her hand to her mouth and disappeared below. Mr. Muir soon followed, leaving the boys, who had never felt better, more completely free than at any time in their young lives.

For several days they roamed the ship unsupervised, making friends with fellow immigrants who fed them and sailors who taught them the names of sails, the meaning of the queer-sounding orders shouted at each change of wind and some sea language to add to their already considerable stock of "bad words."

In a few days Mr. Muir staggered feebly on deck. He gave the boys some candy their mother had sent along, but otherwise paid them little attention. He was busy taking part in prayer meetings and collecting information about America. Fellow Disciples of Christ warned him that in Ontario, where he had intended to settle, it could take a whole generation to chop and burn a farm out of the dense forests. Southern Wisconsin, with its sunny openings between clumps of oak, was far more hospitable.

Meanwhile John and David had made friends with the Captain, who often invited them to his book-lined cabin and had them read aloud. He was fascinated that boys who spoke in a Scotch dialect so thick he could scarcely understand them were able not only to read English readily, but pronounce it properly.

John's special delights were the storms, when great curly-topped waves marched down to smash against the blunt bow and make the whole ship shudder. But the rough weather made the voyage hell for poor Sarah. During the entire forty-five-day crossing she never left her bunk in the bowels of the ship, down in the stinking miasma of whiskey, vomit and human wastes that had to be carried topside in slop-pails and chamber pots. All the rest of her life it made her ill to recall that experience.

The Muirs landed at New York in early April, transferred their goods to a river boat bound up-Hudson to Albany, transferred again to an Erie Canal boat that took them to Buffalo where they caught the fourth boat of the trip for the round-about voyage through Lakes Erie, Huron and Michigan to Milwaukee. Here Mr. Muir bought a ponderous kitchen stove to add to their burden of farm and home freight. Like many immigrants to little-known frontiers, Mr. Muir had brought much more than he needed, including antiquated implements and a large beam scale with nearly two hundred pounds of counterweights.

With this great load they set out westward, steering by compass over a sea of mud from which all tracks had vanished. The man Mr. Muir had hired for thirty dollars to haul them cursed the horse-killing load hourly, but they made it — stove, scale and all — to their destination, a town called Kingston in south central Wisconsin, a hundred miles from Milwaukee.

Mr. Muir wasted no time. In less than two weeks, with the help of a friendly pioneer farmer named Gray, he had selected and filed a homestead claim upon eighty acres near the Fox River, had built a log lean-to and was ready to move in with his children and goods. Meanwhile the Muirs stayed with the Grays, where Sarah had her first lessons in cooking on a stove.

Every mile of their May morning ride to the new home printed itself on John's memory as upon sensitized film. He even remembered that in his mind he had called the yoke fastened to the necks of the four white oxen "crooked stick," having never seen yokes before. It marveled him that the oxen could pull so easily so heavy a load by a single chain, swaying left and right with ponderous grace when Mr. Gray said *gee* and *haw*. Beauties and wonders unrolled throughout their plodding way; the gentle hills crowned with oaks lifting their rounded heads of tender new leaves to the spring sun; dying lakes so filled with water plants that the wagon crossed as on a trembling mat; the whir of wings and scurry of feet as birds and animals fled from the strange invaders.

To the cabin itself, the boys gave scarcely a first glance. John had spotted a bird's nest, and before the wagon stopped rolling both boys were up the tree peering at a clutch of blue-green eggs while the parent jays flew 'round their heads screaming murder.

Chapter 3
The Wild Summer

his wilderness was so far beyond the Muir boys' wildest dreams of wildness that they scarcely believed what their senses told them, except when hungry or when their father was thrashing them.

The little cabin had an open front and sat on a rise facing a marshy meadow where many springs sent rivulets oozing down to a small lake. Because of these springs Mr. Muir, who had a touch of poetry among his assortment of conflicting traits, had named their homestead "Fountain Lake Farm." One sultry evening John saw this meadow come alive with thousands of tiny glowing lights that winked on and off as they twirled and whirled as if fairies were dancing in the gloaming. He had never seen anything remotely like this, except when a fist landed in his eye. He thought the lights must be in his eyes, but when he asked his more literal brother if he saw anything unusual in the meadow, David answered: "It's all covered with shaky fire-sparks."

A Yankee whom Mr. Muir had hired to help clear the first fields was staying with them, and the boys used him as a walking encyclopedia of wilderness knowledge. "Them?" he said. "Them's only lightning bugs." And he took the boys down into the meadow where he caught a few fireflies and carried them to the now-dark cabin where they continued to glow on and off like little heart beats.

Lake and meadow also bred mosquitos, but the discomfort of their bites was all but anesthetized by the daily gifts the environment showered on them. The lake was half a mile long by a quarter mile wide, nestled among low green hills. Rushes growing in the shallow water circled the shore. Between the rushes and the hills grew a band of lilies fifty to sixty feet wide: big white ones, delicately scented, and orange lilies that reminded John of Aunt Rae's special bed in their Dunbar garden. They had seemed so precious there, and here were acres, an incredible wealth of lilies to pick or admire where they stood. On days when bright little waves leaped in the green reflections, and leaves and flowers seemed to dance with them, lake, plants and sunlight mingled in one dazzling, ever-changing light show.

If birds had a paradise of their own, John thought, it must surely be Fountain Lake Farm and its environs. The oaks and hickory trees scattered five or six to the acre made ideal nest sites and perches for the insect hunters and the hawks and owls. Tall grasses and shoots of new trees growing up in the openings provided both food and cover for the ground feeders such as bob whites and prairie chickens.

One of John's most mystifying experiences was hearing a low, booming sound which he thought, at first, must come from some strange disturbance in his head or stomach. But when he asked David if he heard anything unusual, his brother answered, "Yes, I hear something going boomp, boomp,boomp, and I'm wondering about it." Then John thought of ghosts and *bowoozies* and other spooks the housemaids used to tell about in Dunbar. It took long watching and listening before he discovered that the sounds proceeded from a ruffed grouse parading before his love.

At dusk the long-winged bullbats swooped and circled, often diving almost to the ground with a strange, bellowing sound. But the boys' favorite was the small, pugnacious kingbird, because he was such a good fighter and could whip any other bird, except maybe a sandhill crane. The male kingbirds drove off hawks by flying just above their backs and jabbing them savagely on the neck. When a kingbird tired, he sat on his victim's back and reviled him while gathering strength for a fresh attack.

Their cat became one of the boys' first teachers. As soon as her kittens were on solid food, she made regular hunting trips to supply them. Mostly she brought ground squirrels, which began to multiply as soon as the first fields were planted. But she also carried home a fair sample of the smaller animals 'round about: chipmunks and rabbits, flying squirrels and big fox squirrels.

An Indian introduced John to muskrats. One frosty morning in early fall, Watch, their small, smooth-haired dog, jumped up growling and bristling. Aware that he sensed something unusual, John trotted off with the dog to a ridge from which they looked down on a part of the lake hidden from the cabin. In the shallow water stood an Indian with spear poised over a conical mound of sedge and moss that rose above the wind-waved rushes. Driving the spear home firmly the Indian dug into the mound with his free hand and pulled out a dark-furred animal nearly two feet long, with a tail flattened for swimming. The Indian family would eat the muskrat's strong-tasting meat and the man would probably trade the hide for a drink of whiskey.

Seventeen years earlier many Wisconsin pioneers had been killed by Indians during Blackhawk's desperate war, and Sarah was frightened when they came to camp and found her alone. But the Indians came only to beg food and matches, or to sharpen their knives on the Muir's grindstone. Warfare and persecution had crushed them utterly, and they were sinking through degradation to near extinction.

The "Deevil" was still in John, and Watch bore the brunt. When the boys caught their first snapping turtle, he held it close to the solemn little dog's ear, hoping, he said, to liven him up. The strong jaws snapped and Watch ran off yowling with the turtle hanging against his side.

Pair by pair Mr. Muir bought five yoke of oxen, ideal animals for pulling the great "breaking plows" required to rip furrows through the virgin tangle of grass and tree roots that covered the oak openings. The powerful beasts also hauled lumber for the new home which carpenters were building on a commanding hill.

When ready to go on a hauling trip, Mr. Muir was not a man to be trifled with. One morning when the team was hitched he came to John demanding to know whether he had seen the ox whip. "Father," said John, "I tied it to Watch's tail and he ran off into the grass. I don't know where the whip is. It's lost."

"David, go cut me a switch!"

David departed and was gone so long that his father at last grew tired of scolding John and predicting an eternal bath in hellfire. When the boy finally came back, he handed Mr. Muir a burr-oak sapling as big around as a man's wrist and ten feet long. There was not enough room in the cabin to swing it.

"David!" roared Mr. Muir. "What do you mean by bringing me this ugly big club? I've a mind to thrash you instead of John."

David was much smarter than John when it came to avoiding whippings. He looked at the ground and said never a word. After a tense moment Mr. Muir decided that he had wasted enough time and went stamping off whipless to the wagon. He was barely out of sight before the boys had lassoed the sow and were trying to put a harness on her.

That summer Mr. Muir kept a promise he had made before they left Scotland by buying the boys an Indian pony — a bay with a black mane and tail. They called him "Jack." As soon as he could spare the time, Mr. Muir gave David and John their first, and last, riding lesson. Leading Jack up to an earth bank, he taught them how to scramble up on the pony's bare back, encouraged them to make Jack gallop and, after the first few trials, left them to learn by falling off and scrambling on again. It was a great day when John rode clear out to a bare, sandy knoll inhabited by "great gawky birds" which turned out to be sandhill cranes. "I only fell off twice!" he bragged. But it was not long before both boys could ride over the little hills and through the trees at full gallop, with neither saddle or bridle, guiding Jack by the pressure of a knee or the shifting of their weight.

When the boys had first heard they were going to America, they had promised Grandfather Gilrye cakes of maple sugar packed in a box of gold dust. The sad old man had answered: "Poor laddies! You'll find something else over the sea besides gold and sugar, bird's nests and freedom from lessons. You'll find plenty of hard, hard work!"

That time had not yet come. The first summer John's only regular job was to help Sarah with the wash on Mondays. This entailed carrying many gallons of water up from a spring, heating it on an open fire and sudsing the clothes in a great wooden tub from which the steam, impregnated with primitive soap, rose in a smog that stung their eyes. Wringing and hanging were back-breaking for slender youngsters. They were both in bad humor before they began, and they quarrelled throughout like oversize bluejays. But the shrill encounters were only a safety valve for their feelings, forgotten as soon as their eyes stopped stinging. John and Sarah loved one another.

When a field had been cleared, the men piled the heavier timber off to one side and built bonfires which John and David fed with the branches. To John those fires, with their white, glowing hearts and lurid, swirling flames, were an unforgettable delight. Mr. Muir's frequent reminders that Hell, to which his elder son would no doubt be consigned, was thousands of times hotter, made no appreciable impression.

The rest of the time the boys were free to roam the benign wilderness where even snakes seemed friendly. The feeling grew in John that the environment returned the love he gave it. Nature seemed to stream into him, wooing him to learn her bounty and her ways as the food he ate was turning into muscle and bone. Each day's treasures arrived as happiness and stored themselves like songs and poems in his extraordinary memory. Nor did he realize that the farm animals were taming his more savage impulses, implanting the belief that all living things were in some sense his brothers. He never forgot the sow's look of terror-stricken sorrow when she ran home for protection after an Indian had shot one of her piglets. And he never forgot Buck, the ingenious ox.

When the pumpkins became red-gold ornaments on the slopes where they had been planted, the Muirs fed them to the oxen. When a bull is castrated to make him an ox, he loses his ferocity but not his vigor; he becomes amiable, co-operative and sometimes a clown. Fighting bulls are admired on the farms that raise them, but oxen are loved. Nine of the ten Muir oxen, baffled by the size of pumpkins and the hardness of their shells, waited for someone to split the globes with an axe. But Buck, pawing over the pile like a boy selecting an apple, knelt down before his chosen pumpkin and crushed it with his forehead. If, John reasoned, Buck can be so different, maybe other animals are different from one another too, just as people are.

In the late fall, when frost whitened the ground in early morning and prairie chickens came pecking around the cabin like domestic fowl, the Muirs' new house was finished. It had eight rooms and was excellently constructed; the carpenters called it "a palace of a house." But the only heat was the wood-burning kitchen range and, of course, the house had no plumbing.

Sarah worked like a squirrel in nut time, making and hanging curtains, arranging the furniture brought from Scotland. Her mother and the four other Muir children were on their way. Mr. Muir set out lilac bushes and prepared flower beds in front of the house. John and David brought wildflowers for every table.

Mrs. Muir and the rest of the children arrived on a Saturday evening. In the morning Mr. Muir, who sternly opposed strolling on Sunday, signified how glad he was to have his wife with him by taking her on a walk to show all he had accomplished and watch the deer nibbling the tender young shoots of winter wheat.

Chapter 4
"You Are God's Property!"

The Muir farm was still wilderness enough for lightning-set fires to run through the tall, dry autumn grass of the oak openings and leave the ground charcoal and gray. Even the new shoots that sprang up from hickory and oak roots were burned. The fires thus kept the oak openings open, though they seemed desolate and sad when the snow first melted and the unleafed trees at the edges looked as if their lives had ended.

John, disconsolately shuffling through the ashes and wondering where his beautiful wilderness had gone, discovered to his astonishment that hairy green buds were poking up through the gray. Though the frost was not out of the ground, they shortly developed into purple windflowers two inches across. On the jag-edged ice that still clung to the lake shore, muskrats sat munching lily bulbs. From such beginnings spring came on with a rush of new growth and the rustle of returning wings. But for John Muir spring in Wisconsin would never again be the same.

Soon after his twelfth birthday, in April of 1850, his father set him to plowing one of the fields that had been cleared the year before. He had to reach up to grasp the handles and wrestle the plow at every step to keep it upright. To turn it at the end of a furrow required the help of both David and the ox. Over and over again John's laboring breath and aching muscles told him he could not go on. But his father would beat him if he quit. Moreover he was challenged. He went on plowing, repeating over and over an old Scotch phrase, "'Tis dogged that does it! 'Tis dogged that does it!"

That evening he could hardly stay awake during family prayers and stumble up to bed where he fell into the restless, troubled sleep of complete exhaustion.

As John learned to use what strength he had to greater effect, the hired men began to praise him for his straight furrows. This made John try still harder, but his increasing efficiency did not help much. His father simply laid more work on him.

After plowing came hoeing. David and Margaret and Sarah, along with John, were put to work chopping under the weeds in the corn fields and potato patches. All day long the hoes rose and fell as regularly as machines, each child in a different row so that they would not waste time talking to one another. They did not even dare go for a drink of water, for the fields were in sight of the house and their father would thrash them for leaving their work.

The second summer on the farm, Mr. Muir gave John and David a few breaks in the grinding work, usually in the long northern evenings and on Sunday afternoons. In some of this time the boys built a skiff out of planks their father provided. John had watched boats being built in Dunbar and had some idea of how to go about it, but Mr. Muir must have occasionally stopped by to give them a word of advice — though he generally left them to learn for themselves, except in Bible matters.

Rowing and drifting about the lake, John discovered, to his wonder, a new world of goggling fish and waving plants beneath the surface of the water so clear that the boys seemed to be voyaging in air. To enter that magical realm they had to learn to swim, but when they asked Mr. Muir for lessons he said, "Go to the frogs. They will teach you all you need to know."

Their efforts to imitate the frogs met with no success until John reasoned that, if these green kickers could swim under water, a boy might also. The equalized pressure automatically adjusted his body to a horizontal position and he readily reached the other side of the shallow cove where they were practicing. This method of learning to swim — for John immediately recognized what he had been doing wrong — was a great help during his first brush with imminent death.

On the Fourth of July — which was one of the two complete holidays the boys were given each year — a neighbor boy named Charlie Lawson came over to fish from the boat while the Muir boys went swimming. John decided to give Charlie a scare by swimming up on his blind side and grabbing the gunwale.

John missed, sank to the bottom, sprang up and, when he surfaced, tried to call for help. Instead he took in a strangling gulp of water and sank again. He panicked, took in more water when he rose, and might easily have drowned if he had not remembered that he could swim under water. Surfacing once more, he managed to gulp enough air to take him to shallow water.

He was so disgusted with himself for the panic and ineptitude which spoiled a rare and precious holiday that he assigned himself punishment. At the next opportunity, he rowed out to the deepest part of the lake and dove, shouting to himself, "Take that!" over and over and over again. He was never again afraid in the water and became a strong enough swimmer to pursue research aquatically when the time came.

One by one their first farm animals were taken from the Muir boys. Neighbors insisted that Watch, the long-suffering little dog, had been killing chickens. Mr. Muir finally shot him, but was not convinced of his guilt until he cut open Watch's stomach where he found the heads of eight little chickens.

Jack, the pony, enraged Mr. Muir by the way he brought home the cows. When neither John nor David turned up at sundown, Jack went for the small herd himself. Down the long, gentle slope to the barns, those cattle would come tearing, tails high and stiff, rumps bouncing in the peculiar wriggling way of frightened cows. After them came Jack, teeth bared to give any laggard bossy a nip on the behind.

One evening Mr. Muir grew so angry that he shouted to John: "Get a gun and shoot Jack before he's death to the cattle! He's got the Deevil in him!"

Heavy hearted, John went for the gun. But Mr. Muir had considered the extravagance of execution by the time he got back. Jack's life was spared, though Mr. Muir sold him soon afterward to a man who said he was going to ride him to California.

Some of the oxen were replaced by horses, the first being a team of mares named "Nell" and "Nob." Nell was an uncooperative animal with no outstanding characteristics except stubbornness. But Nob was the most intelligent, playful, affectionate horse John Muir ever knew, the most human in her responses. Nob played a major part in establishing his belief that our fellow animals have as much right to share this world as ourselves, that they were not, as most people insisted, created for man to pet, spoil, slaughter, enslave or alter without regard to the consequences for the creature itself.

When Nob was stolen by an Indian, the whole family mourned; when she was recovered a month later, they rejoiced. Nevertheless, Mr. Muir killed Nob in what he believed to be the service of the Lord.

He had become prominent in the community as a "preaching elder," one of the lay ministers on whom the Disciples of Christ relied instead of the "reverend dandies," as they called professional clergymen. The services, held in one-room schoolhouses now that the countryside was beginning to fill up, provided opportunity for farm folk to exchange news of crops and weather, babies and romances. But when the tall, austere figure of Mr. Muir, in his "Sunday blacks" and fringed shawl of Gordon plaid, stepped down from the wagon and passed among them, all chatter ceased and the congregation took its seats solemnly. The adults were impressed with Mr. Muir's forty-five minute prayers and ninety-minute sermons, though the Muir children could hardly stay awake until John discovered that chewing anemone seeds kept them bright-eyed, if not exactly reverent.

As Mr. Muir's zeal increased along with his reputation, he strove to attend every revival and other religious occasion within reach. One hot summer day, he drove Nob to the town of Portage and back in time for a meeting near Fountain Lake, a round trip of twenty-four miles over sandy roads. He pushed the willing horse hard and steadily.

When he got Nob home, she was so completely exhausted that she could neither eat nor lie down. Next morning she had symptoms that reminded John of the time he had pneumonia and his father refused to call a doctor. John bathed her head and tried to tempt her with favorite foods, but she could not swallow a mouthful, and when they turned her loose she followed John and David around pathetically as if asking help, or at least love and sympathy. After one of many dreadful spells of gasping for breath and bleeding through the mouth, she came to John with a look that wrung his heart. He bathed her head and tried to comfort her, but Nob lay down and died. All the family except Mr. Muir gathered around her, weeping.

"You are God's property!" Mr. Muir told his children, and he acted as if he were God's overseer. All his children except little Joanna, born at Fountain Lake Farm, worked like slaves. This became something of a scandal, though all the Europe-born neighbors indulged in what John Muir later called "the vice of over-industry." They cleared and planted far more land than they needed to be comfortable and struggled to keep their homes and farmyards as neat as the tiny cottages on little plots which they had left to come here. The Yankees, with generations of pioneering behind them, cultivated less land and lived better. When the noonday sun was too hot, they sat in the shade. They chopped enough firewood to keep warm in winter. Wild game and delicious wild berries, wild rice and nuts provided their luxuries, each in its season.

Mr. Muir's motives were different from those of his fellow immigrants — most of whom had some ill-defined notion of becoming rich and grand. His church was hell-bent to establish missions from Canada to Cape Town and from the factory-spawned slums of England to the waterfront of Shanghai. Money was required. Therefore when Fountain Lake became less productive under his unenlightened farming practices, he bought additional acres. The added work fell heavily upon John, as the eldest of his boys and by far the most durable.

As soon as he was tall and strong enough, his father put him to work with the heavy cradle used for harvesting wheat by hand. This implement consisted of a scythe with the blade set into a piece of hardwood that had projections along its length. These "fingers" caught the stalks in such a way that, when the reaper swung the contraption back, the wheat was laid out in an even row. This made it easier for the field hand following to gather it and bind it into sheaves.

As with plowing, John's competitive nature drove him to outstanding performance. By his mid-teens he could cut more wheat in a day than any of the men his father hired. Often Sarah or tall Margaret followed behind, binding up the sheaves. Margaret was a marvel; together they sometimes harvested six acres a day — twice the average.

During the Dog Days and Nights of August, when he rose at 4 a.m. with his nightclothes sticking to him like a wet bathing suit and spent fourteen hours seethed in his own sweat, John felt as if they were providing the staff of life to others by digging their own graves. They survived, but Margaret and Sarah never completely recovered their health. The family called John the runt, for even his sisters were taller, and believed that too hard labor too soon had stunted his growth.

Neither labor nor oppression could keep John from growing within. A pioneer farm is not like a factory farm where the plowman rides in a cloud of dust and diesel fumes over an endless geometry of cultivated fields. Nature's original creations were still on every hand, still leafing and blossoming, flying, singing, burrowing, mating, dying. All he had to do was listen to hear the lovely song of the thrush or the call of a bob-white. He had only to look up to see the incredible drama of migration, when the ducks and geese and swans flew by thousands, the passenger pigeons by literal millions, filling the whole sky. In the snowy winter woods, flying squirrels leaped from trees in which he sunk his axe and glided twenty or thirty yards to safety on another trunk. Nuthatches, which the Yankees called "Devil down-heads," wintered on the farm to cheer him with their pursuit of insects in the bark of trees they descended head first.

He had learned well his mother's teaching — to snatch every moment of pleasure that came his way. Since early childhood, responding to nature had been his greatest happiness, and it became infinitely precious now. Every fleeting observation became a treasure to examine in memory, to add to other experiences in an effort to understand, to play with — for farm work also gives one plenty of time to think, remember and imagine. So his mind grew, with no help from a school and with precious little help from books — until his fifteenth year.

Chapter 5
Poems and Inventions

To understand what effort it costs to clear virgin land, one has only to recall that a lumberjack requires at least 6,000 calories a day, as against about 3,000 for a clerk. But there were some pleasures in it for John. To keep the great breaking plow from jumping out of its furrow as it sliced through the web of roots that covered the oak-openings defied the strength of a burly man, if the share was dull or the trim imperfect. John kept his implement so sharp and well-adjusted that it stayed in the ground of its own accord. He could ride the length of every furrow standing on the cross bar.

It was grim, at six o'clock of a winter morning when the thermometer registered thirty degrees below, to stumble on aching, chilblained feet down the dark stairs from the attic room where the Muir brothers slept three in one bed. It was worse still to jam one's feet into boots frozen stiff though they had lain all night under the stove. Mr. Muir begrudged even the little time required to cut and carry enough wood to keep up the fire, though the kitchen range was the only heat in the house.

But once in the snowy woods, John enjoyed himself. He liked splitting rails because he had become good at it, and his father had abandoned axe and heavy mallet after a few days' trial. John enjoyed felling trees — having no idea as yet that trees are good for anything except boards and warm fires. There was sheer physical pleasure in swinging an axe so that it bit wood within a fraction of an inch of the selected spot — a great feeling now reserved for baseball players, golfers and tennis enthusiasts.

When he was fifteen, chopping brought John a totally unexpected fringe benefit. After the fall harvest he was made a member of a team of men and youths selected to build a "corduroy" road across a swamp in fulfillment of their community service obligation. To do this they must cut, from the forest that ringed the swamp, sufficient "tamaracks" — a species of larch whose wood is notably heavy and durable — to form a log causeway that rose above the surface of the water.

Men and youths kept dropping by to watch John work because, instead of coming to a point, the logs he cut had flat ends. He accomplished this result by driving his razor-sharp axe into the trunk horizontally, then swinging upward to send the chips flying. Only a very skillful axeman, with very strong arms and wrists, could perform this feat.

John had assembled a considerable pile of logs when he became aware that the "Twa Davies" had taken positions near him; but instead of working they were reciting poetry. These boys, a little older than John, were the sons of Scotch families more literate than most of the neighbors. Both had literary talent, and at this stage of their lives they were drunk on poetry. John had been hearing and learning ballads, hymns and Robert Burns all his life, but he had never before heard poetry recited with the feeling for cadence, sound and meaning which the Davies gave to Milton, Shakespeare and other poets whom they seemed to know by the yard.

That poetry can be a powerful pleasure, able to lift him out of the grinding drudgery of farm labor, came as a revelation to John. The Bible, most of which he had memorized because he would be beaten if he did not, became a joy as the lovely language surged once more through his head. That spring he ran down to the lake whenever he had a chance to shoot muskrats as they sat on the ice along the edge. He used the price of their hides to buy books: English classics and some then-modern poets, now forgotten. Very likely his mother contributed to these purchases. She had inherited a small income, which she kept in a black bag that never left her arm and was seldom opened except to hand out silver or gold coins to her children for the purchase of small luxuries, such as hair ribbons for the girls and linen to make Sunday shirts for the boys.

His books were treasures to John, but he could by no means buy enough to satisfy his needs. Through poetry he had become aware as by a revelation that pleasure and satisfaction could be had by reading. The more he read, the more he wanted to learn, and he began to reach for everything in sight, like a hungry teenager at a smorgasbord. He persuaded his father to buy him a higher arithmetic book and was startled to find that the elementary rules he had been forced to memorize in Scotland actually made sense. During the brief rest periods between noon and dinner and his return to the fields, he worked through the arithmetic in one summer and went on to tackle algebra, geometry and trigonometry successively. Mr. Muir was willing to buy religious books and a few historical works, as long as the word philosophy was not in the title. Other books he disapproved of but tolerated — except for novels which he considered lies of the Devil made to entrap man. So John borrowed from less restrictive neighbors and, if a book was likely to be banned, he secreted it with the help of the rest of the family.

The under-surface resistance to Mr. Muir had advanced almost to the stage of open revolt. At meals John and David mocked their father's dreadful solemnity by making grotesque faces and crossing their eyes when he was looking the other way. During Mr. Muir's absences on church affairs, which grew more and more frequent, the family became a light-hearted, fun-loving group. John's energy had become all but inexhaustible. In his father's absence his natural, high-spirited self sprang back like a sapling shaking off its weight of snow. He would unpredictably spin round the crowded kitchen where they spent their chill-weather evenings, in a jig or a wild, Highland fling.

Sometimes he would pretend to be the music instead of the dancer, puffing out his cheeks and pantomiming the kilt-waggling strut of the piper while he hummed the high, penetrating drone of bagpipes. The family sang together — and wrangled together in teasing matches and elaborate arguments like an animal family tussling and worrying as it practices the arts of hunting and war.

On quieter evenings the girls got out their embroidery. John read to them from his favorite books, most frequently the accounts of explorers whose works were then opening up the world to literate stay-at-homes. The one that meant most to John was Alexander von Humboldt (1769-1859), the first to make the so-called civilized world understand that the great treasure of South America is not Incan gold, but nature's living creations in fantastic profusion. But it was Mungo Park, explorer of Africa's Niger River, that caused John's mother to make a remark he remembered the rest of his life. When John paused, one evening when they thought Mr. Muir safely away, she looked up from her sewing and said quietly, "Maybe you will travel like Park and Humboldt some day."

Mr. Muir, arriving unexpectedly early, heard his wife and upbraided her for putting such notions into the lad's head.

By drawing on his memory of the Bible for quotations to support his logic, John began to win a few arguments from his father, but not many. When pushed, Mr. Muir called his son "a contumacious quibbler," and dismissed him. Nothing could dissuade him from buying a half section (320 acres) of virgin land six miles southeast of Fountain Lake and setting John to clearing it. The Crimean War (1854-56) — remembered chiefly for the Light Brigade and Florence Nightingale — had sent the price of wheat up spectacularly. It seemed self-evident to Mr. Muir that it was the family's duty to capitalize on this opportunity to make money for saving souls, even if it killed his children.

It very nearly killed Sarah and Margaret, for they were consigned to the grinding labor required to keep the Fountain Lake farm producing while John chopped hardwoods, grubbed out stumps, ran the breaking plow and helped build a barn and a house set among the hickory trees on top of a knoll. They called the new place "Hickory Hill Farm."

It was a six-mile walk to Hickory Hill, which reduced John's reading time to the five or ten minutes he managed to steal between the end of family worship, at eight o'clock in winter, and the moment when his father noticed his candle and ordered him to bed. One chill evening when John was wading through a volume of church history, Mr. Muir spoke to him with special irritation. "John, go to bed! I will have no irregularity in the family; you must go when the rest go and without my having to tell you!" Then, recollecting that John was reading a religious book, he softened his rebuke by adding incautiously, "If you *will* read, get up in the morning and read. You may get up as early as you like."

John had spent a hard day in the snowy woods and fell into deep sleep, though wishing with all his heart that something or someone would wake him before his father's 6 a.m. call from the foot of the stair. The wish set the curious alarm mechanism of the mind. At 1 a.m. he sprang out of bed fully awake, though he did not know the time until he had tiptoed down to the kitchen and held his candle up to the family's only clock. "Five hours to myself!" he said to the silent kitchen. "Five huge solid hours!"

He was so happy and excited, he scarcely knew what to do with this wealth of time. The cold made reading out of the question; his father would be furious if he lighted a fire. In the midst of this quandary, he recalled that he had worked out in his mind the design of a sawmill more advanced and efficient than any he had seen. On the spur of the moment, he decided to build a model. Never doubting his technical competence, for he had long been doing most of the farm's making and mending, he rushed down to the frigid cellar to search between the bins of apples and heaps of potatoes for tools and materials. He found chisels, hammer, files and a vise. But the only saw was coarse-toothed and bent. So he made a fine-tooth saw out of a piece of steel from a discarded corset. From worn-out files and wire he fashioned a pair of compasses, bradawls and punches, then set to work on his model, putting in five hours in the dark of each morning before going out to ten more of chopping in the wintry woods. Fear that his father would withdraw his permission to rise when he liked gnawed at John all the while.

It was two weeks before his father broke the solemn silence at the breakfast table by asking John what time he got up in the morning.

"At one o'clock, Father," John answered in a low, meek, guilty voice.

"And what time is that to be getting up and disturbing the whole family?"

John simply reminded his father that he had been given permission to get up any time he liked.

"I know!" said Mr. Muir with almost a groan. "I know I gave you that miserable permission. But I never imagined you would get up in the middle of the night!"

Being a man of his word, Mr. Muir said no more at this time. John finished his model, dammed a small brook to provide the power, tried it out successfully — and immediately began to work on another. On five hours sleep per night he simply grew stronger — as one of his sisters said, "savagely strong." But the older girls were being demolished by work beyond their strength.

About the time of John's eighteenth birthday, in April of 1856, Sarah's fiancé, David Galloway, returned from a visit to Scotland bringing his mother and seven sisters, along with their husbands and children. Shocked by Sarah's haggard appearance, Galloway immediately set about lightening her work load by a series of transactions that gave him control of the entire Fountain Lake property and increased Mr. Muir's Hickory Hill holdings to 400 acres.

While Sarah worked on her trousseau in preparation for her imminent wedding, the rest of the family prepared to move to the new home on Hickory

Hill. John's main share of the preparation was to dig a well through fine-grained sandstone, for there was no spring near the house. Morning after morning his father lowered him in a bucket to the slowly descending bottom, hauled up the bucket which John had filled with flakes of stone and left him chipping away with mason's chisels until dinner time. John spent each afternoon in the same way.

The Muirs had never heard that deep holes acquire a deadly concentration of carbonic acid gas (which miners call "choke damp") until one morning when the well was eighty feet down, John began to feel faint even before he reached the bottom. By the time he had climbed out of the bucket, unconsciousness had so far overtaken him that he did not hear his father's anxious calls. As he slumped against the sandstone wall, he instinctively looked up and saw a branch waving above the well-mouth. It was enough to orient him, though dimly, to his situation, and he called to his father to pull him up. but when Mr. Muir began cranking the windlass, there was no weight on the line. "Get in the bucket!" he yelled. "Get in the bucket and hang on!"

John did not remember climbing in, nor anything else, until his father laid him out on the turf, sick and gasping for pure air.

Two days passed before he was strong enough to go back into the hole and chip the last ten feet to reach a plentiful flow of water. But this brush with death brought an unlooked-for and important reward. News of his narrow escape traveled swiftly, and a neighbor named William Duncan hurried over. He had been a miner and stone mason in Scotland, and he thought very well of John. When he heard the full story he said gravely:

"Many a companion of mine have I seen dead of choke damp, but none that I ever saw or heard of was so near death as you were, John, and escaped without help to stand!"

Duncan taught the Muirs to test for choke damp with a candle and clear the air in the well if any gas was found. And Duncan took to driving over in the evening behind his old red ox, to bring books and admire the gadgets and inventions which had flowed from John's brain and hands ever since the success of his first sawmill model.

Among these was a series of measuring instruments: barometers, hydrometers and some extraordinary thermometers. The most spectacular of the latter had a dial three feet in diameter which could be read by plowmen working in the fields below the house. The heat-sensitive member was a three-foot iron rod from a broken-down wagon, and its minute expansions and contractions were multiplied 3,200 times by a series of levers made of hoop iron. John established the zero point by packing the rod in snow. The instrument was so sensitive that the pointer registered the body heat of anyone who stepped close to it.

But it was in the invention of automated devices that John really let himself out. For these he needed motive power and a timing device. Therefore he built clocks. It is not very far out of the ordinary that he made the works from hardwood, carving the cogs "with many a whittling nibble" as he went to and fro on the farm or drove a wagon load of freight to Portage behind deliberate oxen. But he had never seen the inside of a clock. Starting with the laws of a pendulum's motions learned from a book, he reasoned out the entire sequence between the force of the descending boulders, which he used for weights, and the motion of the hands — escapement, gear ratios and all.

His first clock looked rather like a piece of farm machinery, but it kept time and struck the hours. Even Mr. Muir was impressed and allowed the contraption to be set up in the parlor. But when John proposed to put a town hall-size clock on the barn, his father balked. John therefore turned his attention to more refined time pieces, which he applied to such purposes as feeding the livestock a measured ration at an appointed hour, lighting fires with no one present and making a remarkable bed which he called an "early rising machine."

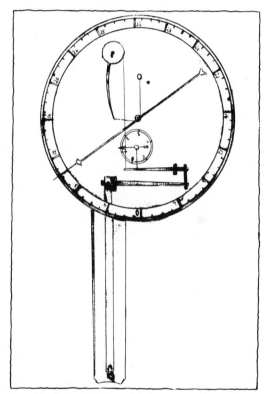

Barometer, drawn by John Muir circa 1860.

John's success with his machines did nothing to further Mr. Muir's efforts to keep him at home, which he attempted to do by breaking down his self-confidence, saying repeatedly that John was a "poor worm of the dust," and that if he left the farm he would find himself in a wicked and hard-hearted world with taskmasters so severe that his father would seem kind and humane in comparison. Nevertheless he seems to have realized that he must give John a few privileges, for he permitted him to attend a nearby one-room school for two months at age nineteen. John described this experience in a considerable poem, the gist of which is in the following lines:

> *"With grammar, too, old schoolhouse thou hast suffered*
> *While Plato, Milton, Shakespeare have been murdered*
> *Torn limb from limb in analytic puzzles*
> *And wondrous parsing passing comprehension,*
> *The poetry and meaning blown to atoms —*
> *Sad sacrifice in the glorious cause*
> *Of higher all-embracing education."*

John went on to write off the meetings held in the schoolhouse:

> *"Every ism and doxy hath been sounded*
> *On every key within thy patient walls*
> *Old schoolhouse; blasts of strong revival*
> *Enough to blow thy dovetailed logs asunder*
> *While souls were being saved and pulled and twisted*
> *All out of shape, till they no longer fitted*
> *The frightened bodies that to each belonged."*

School nevertheless introduced the older Muir boys to that important frontier social institution, the spelling bee. David fell in love with Katie Cairns — the only contestant to spell John down, and she only once. David mooned around the farm, slicked down his hair, became particular in his dress. But John, as his sisters said, was wild as a loon. When they tried to talk him into letting them cut his handsome mop of chestnut hair, he told them to get a pulpit for their sermons and disappeared. Away from home his behavior was not exactly meek. One chilly evening he and another youth arrived late for a spelling bee and found the schoolhouse locked, for it already had people wall-to-wall. John cut an oblong piece of sod and, with a little help from his friend, carried it onto the roof and laid it on the chimney. When the spellers came pouring out, gasping and rubbing their eyes, John and his partner solicitously helped them search for the cause of the sudden outpouring of smoke that continued to surge through the open door.

John had become, in fact, a subject of controversy in the neighborhood. Many called him queer, and his inventions freaks. On the other hand, he had many friends. Sarah's husband, David Galloway, only a few years older than himself, but much more mature and experienced, was a steadying influence and a link between the limited sphere in which John had grown up and the larger world beyond. David Galloway's mother, with more perspective than Mrs. Muir in regard to her son, predicted that John would go far. John's close companionship with his elder sister Margaret, begun in the harvest fields, had developed into an intimacy of mind and spirit that was a great help to them both in this period of lonely, late maturing — for John lingered on the farm until after his twenty-second birthday. William Duncan snapped the frayed tether which still held him.

One summer evening in 1860 this persistent friend came charging into John's workshop waving a newspaper. It described the Wisconsin State Agricultural Fair to be held at Madison in September. If John would exhibit his inventions there, Duncan insisted, he would have more job offers than he knew what to do with. John doubted that anyone would want to look at machines made of wood.

"Made of wood!" Duncan shouted. "Made of wood! What does it matter what they're made of? There's nothing like them in the world. Besides, they're mighty handsome things to come out of the backwoods."

When John told his father that he was about to leave and asked whether, if he happened to need money, he could depend on getting some from home, Mr. Muir said, "No! Depend entirely on yourself." He would not shake hands, nor walk with John to the wagon David had brought around to take him to the station.

The girls stood about weeping and taking what comfort they could from the look of John's hair, which he had at last permitted them to trim and comb. Mrs. Muir, hiding her pain behind composed features, reached into her black bag and handed her son a gold piece. Together with the sovereign his grandfather had given him eleven years before, and a little money he had made growing wheat on an unused patch of ground, John Muir had fifteen dollars for his adventure into the world.

Chapter 6
Passports to the World

T he diminishing crunch of wagon wheels can be a peculiarly lonesome sound. No one was in sight from the station platform at Pardeeville where David had left John with two of his clocks, the mechanism of his early rising machine and a thermometer made of metal from a worn-out washboard — all tied together in an awkward package that looked like one large machine. Entertainment was scarce in Pardeeville. By ones and twos, as bees gather, the townspeople clustered 'round the novelty. John stood outside the circle listening to their imaginative speculations, including a forcefully delivered statement that the machine was for taking bones out of fish.

John was more outgoing with the conductor of the train to Madison, and it earned him a ride on the engine, first in the cab, then on the footboard where he could watch the drivers and pistons and finally on the cowcatch with his hair and beard whipping in the wind.

The fair was held in a forty-acre enclosure overlooked by the university buildings on College Hill. The man at the ticket window took one look at John's machines and told him to take them to the Temple of Art. The university professor in charge of that building took two looks and assigned John not only a prominent exhibit space, but a carpenter to help him build the box-like bed and trestles of his early rising machine and a shelf on which to set the thermometer and his clocks. One of the latter was linked by gears and levers to the early rising machine. The other was a fanciful affair in the shape of Father Time's scythe, its pendulum a bundle of arrows to represent the flight of Time. It told the day of the month and week as well as the time of day (and continued to do so for more than fifty years). The weights of both clocks were boulders selected by John from the glacial drift that littered the fairgrounds. He had everything he needed except for a couple of enthusiastic assistants.

Two young boys had been hanging around, fascinated by his machines and his preparations. Would they be willing to demonstrate getting up early? The response was wriggles of delight and vigorous affirmative nods. These youngsters were the sons of two prominent professors at the university, but John was unaware of this at the time. It probably would have made no difference to him; he had a show to put on, and he loved to entertain.

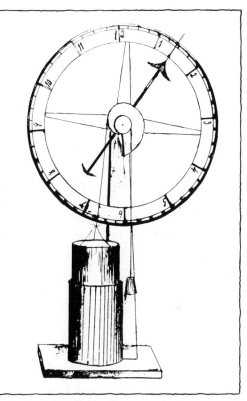

Clock, drawn by John Muir, circa 1860.

Twenty thousand people visited the fair on the first day, and the crowd seemed even thicker because of hoopskirts which enlarged the fashionable ladies and unusually tall because of the stovepipe hats on their gentleman companions. When John could see through the press beyond his booth, all he could glimpse was more people, as from a storm-tossed boat one sees only waves beyond waves. When he had time, he felt dazzled, bewildered, almost dazed. But he had too little leisure between demonstrations to be bothered much.

Sweeping the crowd with his remarkably compelling and expressive blue eyes — now seeming those of a boy savoring the prank he is about to play — he began with some remarks to the effect that they were about to see something unique in the history of getting up. The two boys then climbed into the bed and held their eyes tight shut while John covered them with a blanket. Setting his clock with a flourish, he promised that in two minutes — exactly two minutes — the audience would see the boys not only wake up, but get up immediately and with no argument.

He continued his spiel until the time was up, whereupon the bed, with many a clank and groan, began to tip up and kept on tipping until it reached an angle of forty-five degrees and the boys stood laughing on the footboard with the blanket around their feet.

The crowd loved it, and the washboard thermometer no less. An elaborate complex of levers connected the metal to a dial with a pointer which registered the body heat of anyone who stepped close — a wonderful source of conversation and fair-time kidding about who would prove hotter than whom.

Newspapers hailed John as a backwoods genius, to the great satisfaction of William Duncan and the delight of all his family except Mr. Muir, who wrote a long letter warning his son against the sin of vanity. The executives of the fair gave John a special prize of $15, and he received a number of job offers. He took the most glamorous and least profitable.

A man named Wiard had also been proclaimed a genius, for the steam-powered ice boat he had exhibited. The machinery was still under development, and John rode the freight train which carried this craft to Wiard's shops at Priairie du Chien, on the Mississippi, a hundred miles west of Madison. Wiard had promised an apprentice's training and lessons in mechanical drawing, but no wages. John therefore took a job doing chores in a small but popular hotel called the "Mondel House." The experience proved very educational.

The proprietor, Edward Pelton, lived in the hotel with his wife, two small children and his niece, Emily, who was near John's age. The school principal and several young teachers boarded there. They made a lively, bright nucleus for the social life of the more emancipated young people of the town. In spite of John's servant status, his home-spun, home-woven, home-dyed and home-made clothing, his backwoods manners and sometimes aggressive naiveté, they treated him as a friend and equal. Even when he discovered them playing kissing games and lectured them sternly on the sin of worldliness, they forgave him readily and forebore to laugh in his face. For John Muir had gilt-edged credentials for his introduction to the wide world.

To begin with he was very handsome — strong and virile as a python reaching its prime. His tenor voice was pleasant whether speaking or singing; his flow of words was articulately intelligent and bright with humorous twists of phrase and abrupt lapses into Scotch dialect. Moreover he needed to give and receive love, and knew how to accomplish both. In his arms the Pelton's baby daughter, who was chronically ill, hushed her fretful crying while he talked and sang to her as he had soothed his younger brothers and sisters. Mrs. Pelton most willingly became his friend and confidant. And the young Pelton niece responded to such an extent that in October, when John's brother-in-law, David Galloway, came up to explain that kissing games are a normal variety of fun and no sign of depravity, he concluded that Emily was John's girl.

In January Wiard's iceboat failed its third trial on the frozen Mississippi, and the inventor was denounced as a humbug. John had been given only one lesson in mechanical drawing, and the most important knowledge he had gained from work on the iceboat was that in engineering the state of the art does not permit everything one would like to do. He went back to Madison where he had wanted to be all along — wiser, but otherwise no better off than before.

He had no practical hope of entering the university. He just wanted to be near it — to walk the evening campus where glimpses of students going about their work in library and dormitory fed his dreams as a bakery window nourishes a deprived child. Meanwhile he sold a couple of early-rising machines activated by metal clocks which cost a dollar and doubled as clerk and coachman for a prosperous insurance man whose social-climbing family soured him on society-page society for most of his life.

One Sunday on the campus John fell into conversation with a student who had been impressed with his display at the fair.

"I assume," said the student, "that you can qualify for admission. Why don't you enter and join the Sorghum Club? We live on fifty cents a week."

John knew well enough that sorghum is a plant, one variety of which yields a sweet, somewhat nutritious syrup, cheaper than molasses. But a Sorghum Club? The student explained that the sorghum was poured on crackers and the mass washed down with milk, thus keeping the club members operative.

John felt certain that he could earn fifty cents a week and enough besides to pay the part of the $32 charge for tuition and fees he could not cover out of his meager savings. He therefore went to the acting chancellor, quaking inwardly, and outwardly armed with the brashness of ignorance.

The chancellor, John Sterling, who is still honored in Wisconsin for pulling the university through its most trying days, had no difficulty in appraising John Muir. All this applicant needed to do to meet the requirements was to spend a little time in the university's preparatory school. A few weeks of this sufficed.

Meantime John had moved into a dormitory, where his room became a lodestone to attract the curious and the interested. He slept in his early-rising machine, now activated by the sun's rays passing through a hand lens positioned in a windowsill in conformity with the sun's position and the moment John desired to rise. (The concentrated beam burned through a string, thus releasing the mechanism of the bed, which clearly must have been spring-loaded.) He devised a "loafer's chair" with an old pistol underneath which went off with a harmless blast and swirl of powder smoke when the seat felt the weight of the sitter. He also built a fantastic desk nine feet tall, which placed before him a textbook opened to the right page at the time he had scheduled for a particular study. When the allotted time was up, the desk took the book away and replaced it with another.

Many who came to gawk came back to listen to John talk. He was older than most of his classmates, in many ways more knowledgeable, but his chief difference from them was that, through seemingly-endless hours of farm work, he had thought about what he had seen and heard and read. Unpolluted by pretense or self-aggrandizement, his conversation, flowing from the artesian well of his interests, became celebrated among his college mates and long remembered by them.

Professors and their families also came to John's room, often bringing visitors to see his inventions. The place became more and more intriguing as he accumulated equipment and materials for experiments in electricity and chemistry. That first term he had thrown himself into chemistry with his usual headlong enthusiasm and earned the reputation of being the best student of that subject in his college generation.

One who came to John's room was Jeanne Carr, wife of his chemistry professor, Ezra Slocum Carr. They were already acquainted. One of her two sons had helped demonstrate the early rising machine, and the boys had persuaded their parents to have John babysit when they went out. Mrs. Carr was a pretty, intelligent, well-educated woman, then in her mid-thirties — a leader in university society and active in local affairs. At that time she was helping to plan the landscaping of the campus. But even better than gardening, she loved to roam the hills and lakeshores collecting wild plants to identify and add to her herbarium.

She came to John's room at the insistence of her sons, but she found more to interest her than the gadgets that intrigued the youngsters. On a sunny windowsill stood a pot with a green plant growing in it. From the stem protruded a needle with a girl's long hair threaded through its eye. To the other end of the hair was attached a pen which drew a continuous line on a finely ruled piece of paper slowly rotated by a turntable powered by one of John's clocks. The line was a graph of the plant's minute by minute growth.

As they talked, Jeanne Carr realized that the inventor of this instrument must be a more remarkable person than she had thought. In those days it was widely believed that a good woman could do a great deal for a man, especially in fostering and guiding his intellectual, spiritual and moral development. If

John Muir's fantastic desk performed many functions, including turning a book's pages for easy reading.

one enjoyed being with the man, it could be good duty. John Muir became Jeanne Carr's project.

The spring of 1861 was not an easy time for an isolated, almost sequestered backwoods youth to adapt to the ways and problems of the somewhat civilized world. With Lincoln's inauguration approaching, polarization into pro- and anti-slavery factions crystallized into intransigent antagonism which culminated on April 12 in the bombardment of Fort Sumter. President Lincoln immediately called for 75,000 volunteers, and there followed a period of perfervid enthusiasm. In Madison the State Legislature adjourned to welcome a national guard regiment in fancy, Turkish-style uniforms, and the university's upper classes were depleted by instant enlistments.

John had no share in these enthusiasms. The Civil War seemed to him as cruelly, tragically unnecessary as Scotland's fratricidal struggles, which left whole districts devastated and fellow countrymen embittered toward one another for generations. But there was no escape. The fairgrounds where he had exhibited his inventions was now Camp Randall, and through the window he kept open to hear the songs of the larks came intermittently the blare of bugles and the crash of musket fire.

Chapter 7
The Backlash of War

John spent the summer of 1861 working on the Hickory Hill Farm for seventy-five cents a day plus room and board. Some change had taken place in Mr. Muir; he now lapsed into brief periods when he acted like a human being instead of straw boss for the Almighty. At Mrs. Muir's urging he had sent his son a "store-boughten" suit and a trunk to keep it in when John was at Prairie du Chien. When a classmate wrote to the family that John had spent so much on books and scientific equipment that he was living on less than fifty cents a week and was ill from malnutrition, his father sent ninety dollars in installments. At the end of the summer, he agreed to subsidize David's first term at the university in the same amount that John had earned in the fields and woods.

This largess — amounting to less than $75 for each of the boys — got them through the fall term but no further. University students were then in considerable demand as teachers in the rural schools, and both Muir boys took such jobs in small communities near Madison. John arranged to keep up with his studies through correspondence and weekend visits to his professors.

The log schoolhouse where he taught was cold as Iceland until the schoolmaster had lighted the stove and it had done its work. John therefore linked one of his clocks to a vial containing two drops of sulfuric acid which, at the appropriate moment, was spilled inside the stove onto a mixture of sugar and chlorate of potash, with shavings, kindling and larger wood arranged in combustible sequence.

John's astonished landlord, when he saw smoke issuing mysteriously from the chimney of the locked schoolhouse, insisted that John was going to burn the place down. But the only results were a warm schoolroom and an extra half hour for John to study.

In a way, John was glad to be out of Madison for a while. The route from Camp Randall to the small city's business district was now lined with disreputable shops, gambling dives, saloons and dance halls associated with the brothels on the side streets — a soldier-trap to exploit the needs and frustrations of naive country boys suffering the deprivations and abnormalities of military camp life.

Some of these boys came from John's home neighborhood; he visited them at camp, and they came to see his room, bringing friends. He became an informal counselor to them, reaching out a friendly hand from the firmer ground of normal living. Yet many of these boys went off to war "on a half dance," as John wrote to Mrs. Pelton, "with a smile of their faces...and a loud laugh." To John their levity seemed both sad and indecent, considering how many would be rent by bayonets or mangled by projectiles and that their own weapons would do the same for the Secessionists who, if indeed they deserved to be killed, were not to be executed as a lark.

His log classroom was a relief, though after the first day he wrote to Sarah that he had felt as out of place "as a mud turtle upside down on a velvet sofa." In a very short time he had his pupils in the hollow of his hand, except for increasingly rare occasions when challenged by some youngster conditioned only to physical discipline. Then John felt constrained to lay on his birch switch, though it left him trembling to do so. Some parents complained that "he don't half whip," but there was little need. Because of John's own delight in both knowledge itself and in communicating it to others, school was pleasure for once. The pupils were especially intrigued by his "visual aids," ranging from simple scientific demonstrations to a clock-operated device that signalled each group to begin reciting by means of a rotation of shingles bearing such legends as "3rd Grade, Arithmetic."

Word of John's knowledge and his entertaining and effective ways of communicating it spread through the neighborhood, and he was frequently asked to lecture on science to audiences of isolated, knowledge-hungry people, many of whom tramped snowy miles to hear him. He presented an anti-image of the savant. His clothes were strictly backwoods, his beard wildly unkempt ("If I had a beard like yours," one of his classmates told him, "I'd burn it!"). His hair hung to his shoulders. It is probable that his audience liked him better that way; he had become a neighborhood celebrity by the time he returned to the university in March of 1862.

Slavery was not the only issue then setting people furiously against one another. Darwin's *Origin of Species* had been published in 1859 — only two years before John entered the university — but the ideas spread with the speed of an earth tremor, and the western world felt the after-shocks for a long time. To the many who had committed their faith to a literal interpretation of the Biblical story of earth's creation and man's fall, "Darwinism" was at best dangerous radicalism and, at worst, deadly sin.

John Muir, who had never accepted his father's fundamentalist beliefs, had no trouble in adopting the Darwinian conception of evolution. And he was wide open to an equally controversial theory concerning the history of earth itself, which was then outraging the orthodox, including many scientists who had spent their professional lives in trying to reconcile observed phenomena with a six-day creation and Noah's flood.

After extended field studies in the glacier-jeweled Alps, a Swiss scientist named Jean Louis Agassiz had come to believe that an enormous ice sheet once covered a large part of the globe to a depth of thousands of feet. In its deliberate advance it had carved out lake beds, sculptured canyons and fiords and left claw-like marks on unyielding stone. As the melting ice mantle retreated, it deposited ground-down boulders and gravel such as those strewn over many parts of Wisconsin. This creative interpretation of painstakingly gathered evidence was one of the truly great advances in man's understanding of his small planet, though subsequent research has considerably amended Agassiz' theory — and consequently Muir's — for John became a convinced "Agassiz man" through the influence of Dr. Ezra Carr, who taught him geology as well as chemistry.

Dr. Carr had adopted not only Agassiz' glacial theory, but the methods of teaching he brought with him when he joined the Harvard faculty in 1847. He took his classes out to learn directly from Nature herself, rather than spending most of the time on elaborate theories spun from the inadequate data then available in publications. He was the great pioneer of field trips, field stations and field laboratories which we take for granted today.

In Wisconsin the evidence left by ponderous mantles of ice is so plentiful and revealing that the state has given its name to two great epochs of glacial advance. Dr. Carr thus had a great outdoor classroom. He was a large, impressive and articulate man, well able to stimulate and enthuse his students — most especially John Muir, who felt that the world of nature was being opened to him as by a guide showing the way into his beloved homeland.

The Carrs lived in a large home built of cream-colored sandstone and set far back on a lane shaded by oak trees. To John the library was the "kernel" of the house. Dr. Carr's collection of scientific works was more complete and up-to-date than the university library could afford, and he made John free to use it whenever he chose. French grammar, which had been beaten into him in Dunbar, now surfaced to help him. Much of the geological literature of the period was in French, and with some effort John became able to read the language with enough facility to supplement the field studies he undertook, both with Dr. Carr and on his own.

He learned to recognize evidence of glaciation on land forms, rocks and gravel deposits, as well as the characteristics of glaciers and the techniques that had been developed to measure their movements.

The Carrs often invited John to dinner. In informal discussions at table and after, they introduced him to philosophical writers who had great influence upon the thought of the period. John found Thoreau particularly congenial, and Emerson, who was a personal friend of the Carrs, affected him greatly both in his university days and later, at a critical stage of his life.

Another home where John was very welcome was that of Dr. James Davie Butler, professor of Latin, Greek and rhetoric, and father of the second of the two boys who helped demonstrate the early rising machine at the fair. John was not much of a classical scholar, but his writing captivated Professor Butler. John tended to write the way he talked — in a style founded upon the rhythmic eloquence of the King James Bible, modulated by folk songs, hymns and other poems and "illuminated," as Dr. Butler put it, by backwoods images and idioms. Dr. Butler was a small man with a big, booming voice. He encouraged John by reading out passages from his papers and exhorting his pupils to follow John's example. "Do not," he told them "throw away Nature's sweet blush to buy rouge in Paris." Also he convinced John to keep a "commonplace book" as Emerson had done — that is, a journal in which to jot down experiences and reflections while they were fresh and uncontaminated by flawed memory or self-conscious cerebration. Few, if any, counsels proved more valuable to John Muir.

The terrible backlash of war made it impossible for John to throw himself into his work as fully as he wished. Camp Randall was a sink-hole where soldiers ate weevil-crawling hardtack and stinking pork; an army of rats throve, but men died at the rate of one a day throughout the winter and spring. Early in May 139 sick Confederate prisoners arrived, though there were not beds enough for them all, nor nurses and doctors to care for them. The burials, each celebrated by a volley of musket fire, rose to ten a day.

In the face of such suffering, John could not remain uninvolved. It seemed to him that the only way he could bring himself to participate in war was as a healer. John therefore went to Dr. Carr, who had practiced medicine in his younger days, and asked about his chances of entering medical school. All that he required, Dr. Carr said, was one more year of chemistry.

That summer John worked for his brother-in-law, David Galloway, on Fountain Lake Farm. But a new interest kept him on as short a ration of sleep as had his inventions in earlier days. Just before leaving the university in June, a fellow student named Griswold had demonstrated to him, by the taste, smell and structure of blossoms and leaves, that the locust tree under which they were standing was related to the garden pea vine. John Muir had a compelling delight in patterns to go with his lifelong love of growing things. Here, then, was a wonderful new combination — a way to increase his joy in the individual members of earth's plant mantle by understanding their familial relationships, a way to find wonderful order in the spectacle that had seemed a riot of form and color. Now he understood why Jeanne Carr spent so many hours roaming the hills and came home happy, though dirty as a playing child from the soil that clung to her specimens.

Griswold followed up by demonstrating how to analyze, classify and press specimens; John promptly bought a text and went botanizing with him. At Fountain Lake that summer he got up before dawn to collect specimens and sat up after midnight identifying them. When he went back to Madison in the fall of 1862, he botanized in all the time he could spare — on land and water — often swimming for hours along the shores of Lake Mendota. John did not need to earn his living during this school year. His father had moved the family — minus Sarah and Margaret, now Mrs. John Reid — into the town of Portage, so that the younger children could go to school. In this same period of amiability, he gave John eighty acres of Hickory Hill land, which John sold for $650, to be paid in small installments. He was thus able to join a private class in sketching and to enter more fully into university student life in which debating societies played a prominent part. He joined one, thus permitting his lifelong delight in argument to "go public." He also became president of the university Y.M.C.A.

These activities exposed him more fully to the winds of change. There was then forming in Madison a kind of nebula of democratic ideals which crystallized into the so-called "Wisconsin Idea" and influenced American political and economic programs for the better part of a century. The "Idea"* is most concretely defined as "a policy for improving democracy by enacting state laws on direct primary, initiative, industrial insurance" and other measures favoring the citizen as human.

Discussion of the Wisconsin Idea had far more influence on John than he had on the Idea. But it was part of his preparation, as was his acquaintance with Increase Lapham, an odd but effective little man who was one of the first to dedicate himself to the proposition that to destroy the forests is to destroy the productivity of our country.

War defers all other concerns. In May of 1863, President Lincoln signed the act creating the Civil War's first military draft. In the limbo inhabited by young men subject to call, John did what pleased him best when school was out during that summer of massive slaughter.

First he went to see Emily Pelton in Prairie du Chien. Her aunt and little cousin had recently died, which was a grief to John as well as the girl, for he had been fond of both. In long walks and long talks, John and Emily consoled one another. Apparently their intimacy annoyed her uncle, Mr. Pelton, for when John returned from a rugged botanizing trip down the gorges of the Wisconsin River, the man told him brusquely and falsely that Emily was not at home. When John called later, he received the same untrue answer.

Hurt and confused he went home to work on Fountain Lake Farm. While he had been on his trip, New York mobs had rioted against the draft and destroyed more than fifty buildings. A thousand people had been killed, including many negroes who were lynched out of blind rage. The draft was suspended until August. Even when the drawing took place, John's number was not called. But normal services, such as mail, were breaking down throughout the embattled nation, helping to thwart positive desire such as John's plan to enter medical school. The letter telling him that the University of Wisconsin had awarded him a fellowship never arrived. The man who had bought his land failed to keep up the payments.

In all this state of uncertainty, John lingered on the farm until winter, botanizing, keeping up his journal and corresponding with Emily Pelton — waiting — and all the while badgered by his family to go into business, to invent — to commit his life to any of society's conventional ways of "making something of himself." And, in any case, to marry.

The tide of war had turned at Gettysburg, and it was generally believed that there would not be another draft. John decided that when the first spring anemone appeared, he would leave for the wilds of Canada.

* Closely associated with Robert M. LaFollette, senator from Wisconsin from 1906-1925.

The signal bud poked up from the wintry ground on February 28, 1864. He left three days later.

Part II

WANDERER

"Father, you asked me to come home for a visit. I thought I was welcome. You may be sure it will be a long time before I come again."

Chapter 8
Hider of the North

John Muir sometimes claimed that bog juices ran in his veins, because he was a Scotchman and the Scots are romantic about their bogs, where the mosses, dying generation after generation, form peat that kept the cottagers warm through a history of stern winters. Back from the Ontario shore of Lake Huron he found wilder bogs than he had ever imagined to exist north of the Amazon. Around them the white cedars grew so thick that it often took all John's strength to fight his way through their interlaced branches. In the bogs themselves, tamaracks had fallen like jackstraws in great disorderly heaps, rising from the shallow water, brown from decaying vegetation and numbingly cold.

Where sunlight found its way in, these swamps were beautiful. A kind of moss called *sphagnum* — the principal constituent of peat — lay on the water in purple patches. Ferns adorned the banks along rising ground; the somber trees were dignified by light. In those pioneering days of botany there was unusual excitement in collecting for a personal herbarium of pressed, dried and mounted plants. One always had a reasonable chance of discovering a specimen never before identified. Even a collection that contained nothing new might add considerably to knowledge of a particular area. Also one might find a plant very rare and beautiful. One of John Muir's hopes — and he entertained such hopes with passion — was to find "The Hider of the North" — *Calypso borealis* — an orchid which had retreated deeper and deeper into the wilderness as man advanced. In months of exploring John had been unable to find a single specimen.

One late spring day he entered a swamp like a witches' camp ground. The sun penetrated scarcely anywhere. Fallen trees thrust up their withered branches in patterns imagination readily turned into clawed, clutching arms. Great jackstraw heaps of logs, so tremulous it was dangerous to climb upon them, barred his path. Often there was no way around, and he had to crawl beneath, crouching in the icy brown water among spiky roots and downthrust branches.

He was steering by compass toward a maple-crowned ridge seen earlier but invisible now that he was in the heart of the swamp. By mid-afternoon he had grown so weary that he began to doubt he could make the ridge before sundown. The shadows were already deepening, and this was no place to be travelling through the dark.

He stopped on the bank of a small, clear stream cutting through the swamp and looked around for some tree, standing or newly fallen, where he could rest for the night. "Like a monkey in its nest," he thought. But then his searching eyes were halted and their gaze fixed by a single, pure white flower standing up from a bed of yellow moss. Fording the stream John sat down beside "The Hider of the North," lost in one of the great experiences of his life.

"The Hider of the North," *Calypso borealis.*

In that dark, sinister place the flower, delicate as starlight and luminous as new-fallen snow, seemed a spirit come to bless him.

All weariness dropped from him. But it was a long time before he gathered the flower tenderly, roots and all, and started on across the bog. The difficulties that had seemed insurmountable now seemed trivial. He felt renewed and uplifted. At sunset he reached the ridge where maples grew, and he saw, rising above them, a plume of smoke against the evening sky.

An old Scotch woman came out of the cabin and approached slowly, staring John up and down. He became aware that he was wet, muddy from head to foot, clothes torn, face and hands deeply scratched and blood-stained.

"Where did you come from?" the woman asked, and when he told her she wrung her hands and said: "The swamp! That awful swamp. Many a poor body's been lost there and never heard of more. You're lucky to come out alive. Why did you go there?"

John tried to explain, but she had never heard of botany and could not understand. Nevertheless she gave him a good supper and a place to sleep.

The privations of John's childhood proved very useful during his months of wandering through Ontario's wildest areas. His body required very little food to maintain its strength and endurance. He could therefore travel very light and also inexpensively. His staples were tea and big loaves of bread he bought from farm wives. When he ran out of bread he toasted oatmeal on hot rocks. As a boy he had sampled every wild plant he found in the vicinity of Fountain Lake, unless they were obviously too tough or reputed to be poisonous. Now he ate seeds and flowers, berries and roots and even chewed up leaves. These wild foods, along with an occasional square meal at a farmhouse, balanced his diet sufficiently for health. He slept in a bed or a hayloft when he found hospitality, but often camped where night overtook him. Wolves occasionally made him nervous, but the only one who came close ran off when John made his fire blaze up and threw a stick at him. When he ran low — not *out* of money, for as he said "a Scotchman never likes to spend his last dollar" — he worked at whatever job came to hand in the woods or the harvest fields.

He ranged from the west of Ontario, where pioneers were chopping, burning and root-grubbing farms from the dense virgin forests, eastward through the settled countrysides of brick farm houses on productive lands cleared by previous generations and, in early September, 1864, camped in a cedar grove above the unceasing roar and upflung smother of Niagara Falls. His youngest brother, Dan, who had come to Canada to earn some money for college, joined him. Perhaps their mother's letter reached them here; perhaps Dan brought it. In any case Mrs. Muir, confident in the authority which custom then gave to parents over their minor children, ordered Dan to stay in Canada, for another military draft had been announced. She urgently requested John to stay with him. To get through the winter they would need steady jobs, and Dan recommended a wood-working mill where he had been employed earlier, on the Big Head river which runs into Lake Huron at Owen Sound. It was only 150 miles west of Niagara — less than a week's walk.

Chapter 9
Escape From Success

The Muir brothers pushed on through the evening of the last day of their trip and arrived with weary legs and empty bellies at the ample log home of the mill folk: William Trout, the head of the small firm: Charles Jay, his partner: Peter Trout, William's brother, and his sister Mary. She was the housekeeper, and had a hot supper ready for the Muirs by the time they had washed up.

These people had liked Dan for his fresh face, his frankness and his love of fun. The partners were glad to take him back as a sawyer. It turned out that John was just the mechanic they needed to help run the factory and also help to enlarge it. He took the job, at $10 a month plus good food and time off to go botanizing.

John was even more pleased to have found this situation when he saw it in morning light. Evergreens and deciduous trees shared the steep sides of "Trout Hollow" like a green and gold wall, with narrow openings where the Big Head River entered and departed. The mill straddled the river, whose swift current turned the big iron wheel that provided the power. John was vulnerable to the sheer physical excitement of the wood-working mill; he liked the shudder and snarl of the saws ripping a log into planks and the whir and grumble of the lathes turning these into broom and rake handles. He liked the smell of new-cut wood. It did not then occur to him that this mill, and others larger, could literally eat up the forest he found so beautiful.

Through the winter and spring John felt more nearly content than in a long while. The mill folk and their frequent visitors were near his own age — hardworking, hearty, boisterous, unsophisticated and rural, intelligent and upright. He had grown up among such people, and their backwoods, self-dependent social life was the one he knew the best.

At meals and free times a lot of teasing and verbal horseplay went on, much of it pretty silly. They played practical jokes and wound themselves up in long arguments about nothing more significant than whether a Muir (moor) is better than a Trout or a Jay because it contains them both.

Harriet, another Trout sister, taught school in a nearby town and often came home for the weekend, bringing young fellow teachers. On winter evenings they would gather in front of the logs blazing in the wide stone fireplace while John, with his plant collection to provide illustrations, yarned about his adventures in securing the specimens and in the process taught them a good deal about the characteristics and habitats of these plants which meant so much to him. By the time the ice broke up in the river, several of the group had started herbariums of their own.

The deeper feelings and convictions in which John Muir's enthusiasm for nature had its roots were too intimate and unconventional for this young and rural audience. He told them, rather, to Jeanne Carr, who wrote him late in the summer of 1865 suggesting that they "exchange thoughts." Lonely because Dan had left to hunt a better-paying job and seriously in need of companionship with reflective and cultivated minds, he accepted eagerly, though diffidently, for he sincerely believed her far above him.

He confessed to her that he took more intense delight in reading the power and goodness of God from the tangible forms of nature, than from reading the Bible. "Are not all plants beautiful? Would not the world be poorer for the banishment of a single weed?"

He described to her his frustration when, looking ahead, he realized that he could not possibly live long enough to specialize in all the endeavors that attracted him like an array of magnets: botany and astronomy, geology, chemistry and medicine. He liked to invent, but did not want to spend his life among machines. And he earnestly desired to be "a second Humboldt" and explore South America. The prospect of restricting himself by specialization was intolerable because he wanted the whole world of knowledge which, to him, was identical with the world of nature.

A more immediate reason for John Muir's resistance to specialization was realization that he might easily be entrapped by his tendency to commit himself, body, soul and breeches, to any project he undertook. At the time he began his correspondence with Jeanne Carr, he was inventing literally twenty-four hours a day. When he put his drawings away toward midnight, his subconscious took over, and when his new-model early rising machine dumped him out at five in the morning, he had at least some of his problems solved.

If the mill folk heard a double thump they knew he had been sleeping slantwise and the contraption had dumped him out on the floor. Then they gave him a hard time while he snatched a bite of breakfast before running down through the dark to chip the ice away from the mill wheel with a chisel on a pole by lantern light and put in two or three hours on models and prototypes.

William Trout, who was a master mechanic and millwright with several patents to his credit, had taught John all he knew by the summer of 1865. Realizing that John's ability to apply this knowledge creatively promised quick prosperity, he contracted with him to make thirty thousand broom handles and twelve thousand wooden rakes. John had *carte blanche* to improve the machinery, and was to receive half the resulting profits.

John did two days' work every day he did not do three, far less because of the

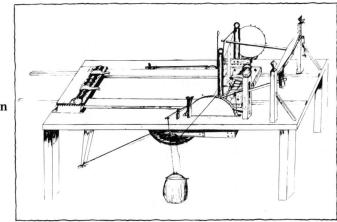

Table saw, drawn by John Muir circa 1860.

promise of money than because he was hypnotized by the ideas that seemed to pull one another out of the depths of his mind.

These were the early days of automation, and the mill was equipped with a self-feeding lathe that William Trout thought an almost perfect machine. By making it more fully automatic, John doubled its capacity — to eight broom or rake handles a minute. It kept him jumping to feed it. He also designed and built machines for automatically making the teeth of wooden rakes, for shaping the heads (called "bows") for drilling holes and still another for driving the teeth into the bows.

Absorbed as he was, John never neglected, when the mill folk were away, to put in a window a candle-lit star he had made, or to keep up a warm fire for them to come home to. These kindnesses were among the many things about John Muir the mill folk remembered all their lives.

By the first of March, 1866, he had produced thirty thousand broom handles and six thousand rakes. They were stored all over the mill, to season the wood before shipment.

That night a cold, furious storm blew up and an ususually big fire blazed in the fireplace of the log dwelling. Sparks blew over onto the mill roof, and it was burning furiously before anyone became aware.

Nothing could be saved; the partners were wiped out. Jay and Trout gave John a note for three hundred dollars, which he insisted on reducing to two hundred, and scraped up enough cash to pay his way to Indianapolis. He chose this growing industrial city because it was then surrounded by one of the most beautiful deciduous forests in the United States.

John found himself up to his neck in creative engineering before he could get really settled in Indianapolis. He had found a job almost at once running a circular saw in a prosperous factory that made wagon wheels, wages ten dollars per week. Within a few days he was put in charge of all the saws, and his pay raised to $18 a week. A short time later he designed a device by which the firm's patented wheel could be made automatically, except for putting on the iron rim. His salary became $25 a week, and he was given a free hand to make improvements as well as to supervise the installation of new machinery.

He became so absorbed in his work that he felt he might be an industrial engineer the rest of his life. "I feel something within," he wrote to his sister Sarah, "some restless fires that urge me on in a way very different from my *real* wishes, and I suppose that I am doomed to live in some of these noisy commercial centers." The letter is a little disconsolate in spite of John's job success. He felt lonely and homeless, did not even unpack his trunk, but for a month moved from one desolate rooming house to another.

Meanwhile he was making good friends at the factory, and one of the sawyers took John into his home as a boarder. In May he felt confident enough to present a letter of introduction from Dr. James Davie Butler to a prominent family named Merrill.

Their impressive house stood on a street that bore the family name; John was well aware that they were people of prominence in the city, and that Miss Catherine Merrill held the chair of Engish literature at Butler University — the second woman in the United States to have a professorship. It all made him feel so shy and uncouth that he walked up and down several times in front of the house, gathering courage to use the big brass knocker.

The door was opened by a ten-year-old boy who stared big-eyed at John. This was Merrill Moores, son of Miss Catherine's sister who shared the home with her. It was obvious to young Merrill that John was a working man, but he was also the handsomest man the lad had ever met.

He took the letter in to his aunt and John was immediately brought into the parlor, where the sisters greeted him expectantly because of Dr. Butler's enthusiastic recommendation. John did not disappoint them. He had the novelist's gift for talking about things he had seen and done, thought and felt, without intruding his ego — as if he were the narrator in a tale of adventure and discovery.

When he told them about the machines he had invented, Miss Catherine interruped to ask whether he had taken out patents on the devices. "No," John said. "I believe all improvements and inventions should be the property of the human race. No inventor has the right to profit by an invention for which he deserves no credit. The idea of it was really inspired by the Almighty."

It would have saved him a great deal of toil and trouble if he had taken out patents; during the rest of John Muir's lifetime most of the wooden wheels produced in the United States were made by machines based on his semi-automated device, and the royalties would have made him comfortably well off, at the least.

From the first encounter with the Merrill family a deep and lasting friendship developed. Even John Muir's temperamental moments were readily forgiven. As women liked to do in those days, Miss Catherine invited a group of friends one Sunday so that they could learn how wonderful he was. But John Muir could not be comfortable in any company where he was unable to establish a give-and-take, warm-blooded relationship. As soon as he found

-48-

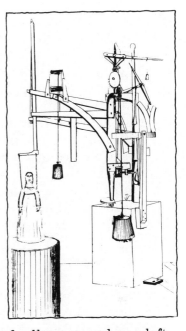

Drawing by John Muir, circa 1860, of one of his many inventions which he never patented.

that he was on exhibit, he became silent to the point of sullenness and soon left.

Out of doors he was happy with the Merrill's friends and relatives, young and old, and they with him. On rambles through the then-beautiful Indianapolis woods, it was as if a door had been opened into a secret garden within a house where they had dwelt for long. An attractive girl named Eliza Hendricks became his special admirer. His calls upon her — and "calling upon" was an inhibited Victorian version of present day "dating" — included her grandmother, whom he found delightful, for his pleasure in the creations of nature included human females of all ages. Eliza became one of the many women who corresponded with him for many years after he had left.

John also taught a Sunday class which Miss Catherine sponsored for boys of workers' families. In good weather their classroom was the woods; in foul they came to his room, where he taught them elementary chemistry and mechanics by means of simple experiments and his clock-controlled devices.

At the factory, John became a leader of the workmen without losing the confidence of the owners. The latter commissioned him to make an efficiency study of the plant and was startled when, among more purely technical and thus acceptable recommendations, he suggested reducing the work day from ten hours to eight. He had observed, as studies by others later corroborated, that production fell off sharply during the last two hours, and accidents increased alarmingly. At that time, even a ten-hour day was considered a great concession — many thought it "pampering the workers."

John Muir would have been well advised to act personally on his eight-hour-day recommendation. In the factories of that day, power was transferred to production machines from steam engines or water wheels by means of belts, there being no electricity available.

The plant where John worked had belts running every which way, all gliding swiftly 'round and 'round the many driving wheels and spindles, with slapping sounds like muffled drum beats underlying the snarling saws and chattering lathes. John was fond of these purposeful noises, but plagued by the inefficiency of the belts which tended to stretch, with a consequent loss of power. One late afternoon when all the workmen but one had gone home and the light was poor, he took off the belt of a new lathe to shorten it. He was using the nail-like point of a file to pry out the laces.

The file slipped, and the point pierced his right eye. Cupping his hand over the eye he walked to a window. When he took his hand away, he found in it a glob of slippery-feeling material — the aqueous humor which protects and lubricates the working parts of the eye. The one remaining workman, who was his friend, had followed him and heard John Muir murmur quietly but despairingly, "My right eye is gone. Closed forever on all God's beauty!"

He was able to walk to the house where he roomed. But soon the shock of the accident sent him trembling to bed, and his left eye also went blind in sympathy with the other so that he found himself in total darkness.

John Muir's next few days were terrible beyond even his great powers of description. The nights were even worse, for he was haunted by dreams from which he started awake, exhausted and terrified. The local physician who was called in told him that he would never see again.

The local man's diagnosis did not satisfy John's friend, Catherine Merrill. She sent for an ophthalmologist who had studied in Europe where, at that time, medicine was more advanced than in the United States. After a careful examination, this specialist concluded that, if John Muir would lie quiet in a darkened room for several weeks, he would be able to see from both eyes almost as well as before.

Many visitors lightened his days in darkness. Boys from his Sunday School came in relays to read to him. Merrill Moores and other youngsters searched the woods for early wild flowers to bring him as soon as his left eye, the first to recover, regained sight. And John Muir repaid them by telling stories of his wanderings and adventures — stories coming out of the dark, which they remembered all their lives.

And as the aqueous humor became gradually restored, the owners of the wheel factory came to offer him a partnership. John Muir put off the decision until the day he was able to take his first walk in the woods. He went by himself, on a day when filtered light descended in shafts from gaps between soft clouds.

When he returned, the course of his life at last was fixed. The wracking, death-like feeling that he had lost contact with nature in her wildness had taught him where his destiny lay. He must leave mechanical invention and devote the rest of his life to studying "the inventions of God."

His first move would be a walk of a thousand miles to the Gulf of Mexico with the intention of going on to South America, which had fascinated him ever since he discovered Humboldt. But first he went home, taking young Merrill Moores with him, to botanize and say goodbye.

Chapter 10

A Walk to the Hot Lands

Life was good for John Muir and the boy in the hospitable home of Sarah and David Galloway on their new farm north of Portage. They used it as headquarters from which they made several long trips and many short ones, including some family picnics with Sarah's children. On one of these outings, John discovered a dark, quiet pool with edges fringed by cattails and blackberry vines; the sides of the bowl in which it lay were grown with ferns that seemed to be looking down like people in a theater. John could not bear the thought of this enchanted place being trampled into mire, and he got his brother-in-law's promise to guard it so long as he should own the land. For the same reason he tried to buy Fountain Lake and forty acres surrounding it. But the price was too high. He felt that he must keep a reserve in case his father sold Hickory Hill, gave most of his money to the church and went off to Canada to be a missionary among the industrial-city poor, as he talked of doing. The burden of Mrs. Muir's support and the education of the younger girls would then fall upon the eldest son.

The idea of preserving some of the nation's superb wilderness as natural parks was then no part of the public consciousness. But here and there in minds akin to John Muir's, it had begun to occur as a spontaneous product of their wonder and love.

With his brother David — now a rising young merchant in Portage — John was less comfortable. He was well aware of what he had done in abandoning his career in Indianapolis. "I could have become a millionaire," he said when reminiscing about this period, "and I chose to become a tramp!" He rejected the society he had abandoned, conventions and all. He and Merrill arrived at Portage on a raft they had built thirty miles up the Wisconsin. During the voyage John's shoes had been washed overboard, and he scandalized his pillar-of-society brother by arriving barefoot at the store in which David was a partner. "Feet were made before shoes!" John said and compounded David's embarrassment by going barefoot to his home in search of a pair of shoes big enough for his unusually large feet. Nor was John at all conciliatory. When a fundamentalist minister, whom David had invited to meet his successful brother, attempted to put down organic evolution by proclaiming that he had never seen a chair develop into a chairman, John turned his back upon the man and remained silent the rest of the evening.

Most — perhaps all — creative critics of society are in some way dropouts. To achieve the perspective necessary to perceive what is wrong with one's society — and what must be done about it — requires standing aside, refusing to become entangled in the customary patterns and rejecting at least some respected values. The critic may find himself in an adversary position which leads him into exaggerations and forensic oversimplifications which, under some circumstances, are effective and, under others, handicap appreciation of his truths.

One then-popular philosophy Muir rejected was *laissez faire*, which holds that unrestricted competition is the natural and most beneficial way of getting and spending. He had seen too many pioneers defrauded by land speculators and railroad promoters to believe that such a system was good for mankind and came to call it "the gobble-gobble school of economics." And he rejected the "survival-of-the-fittest" interpretation of organic evolution, which was often summoned to support the laissez faire doctrine. He had found more mutual benefit occurring among species and varieties growing together in pure wildness than to believe that competition is the primary, overriding law. He saw in nature more harmony than lethal strife — except for the destructive intervention of man. Muir therefore turned against the society of men as he knew it, not only because of what it did to other, non-human citizens of the globe, but also because of what it did to humanity itself. "Civilization has not much to brag about," he wrote in one of his journals. "It drives its victims in flocks, repressing the growth of individuality."

John Muir had been wrestling with these ideas, so greatly against the grain of society surrounding him. It was a relief and a happiness to spend a farewell week in Madison with the Carrs and Butlers, who were at least sympathetic to most of his ideas and tolerant of those they could not agree with. It was very different during the few days he and Merrill spent at Hickory Hill, where his parents and younger sisters were once more living.

His father never missed an opportunity to condemn John for abandoning the ways of righteousness, as he conceived them, for the wicked paths of geology and botany. The assault was more or less continuous, except when John escaped into the warm-hearted company of old friends and neighbors.

At the moment of parting, Mr. Muir interrupted John's affectionate goodbye to his mother by asking, "My son, haven't you forgotten something?" "What have I forgotten, Father?" "Haven't you forgotten to pay for your board and lodging?" John did not speak until he had taken a gold piece from his wallet and put it in his parent's hand. Then he said quietly, "Father, you asked me to come home for a visit. I thought I was welcome. You may be sure it will be a long time before I come again."

On September 2, 1867, John Muir, age 29, steered by compass across Louisville, Kentucky, speaking to no one, and started walking toward the Gulf of Mexico. The distance is approximately a thousand miles — not really very far for legs, heart and lungs trained by following an ox-drawn plow through twelve-hour days that seemed without end. But this project had several unusual features. A plant press and a small personal bag were his only burdens: he carried no blankets, let alone a tent. And he would traverse from top to bottom a war-ravaged South, much of it on the verge of anarchy and all of it hostile to strangers from the victorious North.

Once, well out of Louisville, he sat under an oak, got out his maps and plotted a course of opportunity through the "wildest, leafiest and least trodden way" he could find; "not," he wrote, "as a mere sport or plaything excursion, but to find the Law that governs the relations subsisting between human beings and nature." In the course of that lonely journey his ideas developed, fragment by fragment, toward the conceptions that were to rule his life and influence generations of his fellow Americans.

For the most part, the journal he kept up faithfully is a lively narrative of travel through wilderness beautiful in its virginity and thinly inhabited by people brutally scarred by war. His scientific accomplishment is largely in the plant specimens he searched for every mile of the way.

A short day's walk was ten miles, the longest forty. He avoided most towns, not only because they usually depressed him by their run-down poverty, but because be disliked the musty, ill-ventilated inns. One night he slept on the "softest looking bench" in a log schoolhouse. Usually, he could talk some isolated family — white or negro — out of their fears and prejudices and get lodging and meals, more often than not corn bread and bacon or corn bread and beans. But many nights he lay down in the driest, most sheltered spot he could find. Some of these camps under the sky proved the most beautiful and interesting.

On September 10, having crossed into Tennessee, John Muir began the long climb up the Cumberland mountains on a zig-zag road roofed by arching oak branches that made it a green leafy tunnel. He had not gone far when a young man on horseback caught up with him and insisted on carrying John's small bag. John finally gave in, and the man immediately rode ahead. By fast walking and some running, John managed to come close enough to see him rifling the bag. He watched with some amusement as the fellow pulled out a comb and brush, towel and soap, a change of underwear and copies of Burns' poems, Milton's "Paradise Lost" and a small New Testament. The would-be robber replaced all the things in the bag and, riding back to John, handed it to him and departed, saying that he had forgotten something.

It took John seven hours to climb to the Cumberland plateau, which astonished him for he had never been in mountains before. Toward sundown he came to the last house for a stretch of forty miles, except for empty ones whose owners had been killed or driven away. He stayed here overnight with a hospitable blacksmith and his pretty wife. They warned him seriously not to go on across the Cumberland plateau because marauding remnants of guerilla bands — organized during the war to harrass the Union forces — were now robbing and plundering everyone too weak or alone to defend himself.

The blacksmith and his wife had reason. It was only a few months after John Muir passed that seven counties of Tennessee were placed under martial law to save them from anarchy in which the Ku Klux Klan played a lethal part. But John started on the next day.

Late in the afternoon he found his way blocked by ten unkempt, savage-looking and formidably-armed men sitting on their scrawny horses side by side. The roadsides were open here, and there was nothing for it but to try a bluff. Striding up to the phalanx as if he meant to go straight through, John swerved at the last moment around the horsemen, gave them a big grin and a "Howdy!" and kept on walking. He reasoned that his press, with plant specimens sticking out from it saved him by suggesting to the band that he was a wandering herb doctor whose throat there was no profit in slitting.

These were the last dangers John encountered for a while; the feuding Tennesseeans of the higher mountains proved more friendly to him than to one another; the forest-clothed vistas and swift, clear streams gave him almost hourly pleasures, the more delightful because they were new to him. Crossing a small corner of North Carolina, he was entertained by a sheriff in the first clean, tastefully-appointed, flower-surrounded home he had encountered in three weeks of foot travel.

Following the Chattahoochee River down to the low-lying valley of the Savannah which forms the boundary between South Carolina and Georgia, he came to the last outposts of northern plants that had migrated along the highlands. From here on the plants were strange to him — magnolias and cypress and the long-leaved southern pines; huge water oaks draped with silver-grey moss; scuppernong grapes that dropped into the streams, where they collected in eddies.

John went fishing for them with a young man named Prater, just now home on a vacation from the Indianapolis wheel factory where they had worked together. Prater warned him to watch out for rattlesnakes, for they were on the move.

John found them plentiful in the cypress swamps along the Savannah River. Fighting his way through thorny networks of vines and splashing through black, silent water, said to be the haunt of alligators and ghosts still more dangerous, exhausted him and tried his nerves. All plants and most birds and animals were strangers to him; the wind passing through the extravagant growth made him feel vaguely threatened — a stranger in a hostile land. He was in fact threatened, but by unseen enemies he had not taken into account when he planned this trip into the hot, wet lands. Disease organisms had invaded his body, and he already felt feverish.

Though he spent some comfortable nights at river bank plantations, worked by former slaves who still called the owner "massa," John Muir arrived in Savannah exhausted, ill and depressed. He had carried the least possible cash through the dangerous mountains of Tennessee and had only a couple of dollars left. He had asked his brother to send some of the money he had left in

David's charge, to the express office in Savannah. When he called at the office, they told him nothing had arrived for him. Friendless and ill he wandered out of town past weed-grown fields more desolate than himself until he came to the ruined estate of a long-dead rich man, with a little cemetery in its moss-draped heart. It was so beautiful that he thought he would be happy to live there among the peaceful dead rather than cope with the hostilities and confusions of post-war adjustment — North and South. This was no idle thought. General Sherman's devastating march from Atlanta had reached the sea at Savannah, and, when he left, many of the small city's displaced, demoralized people had turned to armed robbery in order to live. But few, if any, were desperate enough to go robbing in a graveyard.

John Muir reduced his funds to a dollar and a half by spending the night in a low-down flop house, and, when his money had not come by the next afternoon, he bought a supply of crackers and went back to the cemetery, which he reached at dark. He slept with his head on a grave — well enough, he reported in his journal — but not so well as the citizen beneath.

Next day he selected his hide-out in a stand of tall bushes called sparkleberry, four of which he used for posts to support a roof of rushes laid across small branches tied on for rafters. His bed was a thick mattress of Spanish moss spread upon the ground.

Day after day he trudged into Savannah and returned, a little poorer, to wash his crackers down with coffee-colored ditch water, listen to the wind sigh through six-foot banners of moss and wake to the chorus of warblers in the bushes, the screams of roosting eagles and the gutteral talk of wading birds in the nearby swamps.

He had been sketching ever since his university days, and by now his drawings had become almost as eloquent a part of his journal as the words; not works of art — though sometimes handsome, as were those he made in St. Buenaventure cemetery — but precise notes on what he saw from where he happened to be; memory aids more useful than photographs, for it was his own eyes rather than a lens that did the looking.

Unwell, undernourished and alone in the last home of people whose bodies had long since merged in the rich soil with flowers and trees, mice and the snakes that ate them, John Muir inevitably thought of death. But instead of becoming morbid, he threw off whatever fears remained from the terrifying ideas of death and the hereafter his father had tried by blows and sermons to instill in him. He saw that in all nature life springs from death and is supported by it. The cycles of birth, growth, decay and rebirth are the beautiful and permanent realities, transcending the tiny cell of time and place each individual occupies. Death therefore seemed to him beautiful; to be accepted equally with life as a part of the wonder of being.

He grew angry that children were still taught that death is the arch enemy of life — punishment for the original sin.

By the fifth day he had begun to stagger on his walks to town; the ground seemed to be rising in front of him, and the ditches looked as if they were

37

The vertical plane at right angles parallel with the face to the exclusion of all others

The Fig below gives a front view of a thin ridge near

Cathedral peak showing a dome section at A appearing like the section of an onion by the exposure of the edges of the layers

Also the union of vertical & dome ely is ... shown. This ridge was ground thin by the action of two ice tributaries of the great Lyell trunk wh flowed to Yosemite

His sketches became "precise notes on what he saw."

running uphill. He could not remember whether it was on that day or the next that his money came, but he recalled very well that even his brother's letter failed to identify him in that suspicious town. He finally got the money by convincing the agent that he was a botanist.

Outside the office he encountered a huge black woman with a tray of gingerbread on her head. He bought and ate it all, topped off the snack with a meal in a restaurant and took passage on a boat to the town of Fernandina on the north coast of Florida, thus by-passing an all but impossible stretch of the coast.

The trip across northern Florida was nightmarish though interspersed, as bad dreams usually are, by pleasant, though fantastic, interludes. He mainly walked the tracks of a tin-pot railway, but descended into the bordering swamps every time he saw a blossom or a strange leaf to add to his collection. Palmettos fascinated him, and he very nearly lost his life crossing a swamp in which he lost his way after visiting a small forest of those prickly palms. Murder — priced at $5 in Tennessee — was here said to be $1, and he felt fortunate to bluff a huge black who intended to rob him. A family of blacks, encamped as if they were in the swamps of Africa, gave him water and food when he was on the point of collapse.

On October 23 — eight days from his start across Florida — he arrived at a small Gulf Coast port called Cedar Keys, where he agreed to work in a sawmill while he waited for a ship to take him southward. Within three days he collapsed into a coma brought on by a raging fever. It took nearly three months to recover. The kindness of the mill owner and his family John Muir remembered gratefully all the rest of his life. They cared for him in their own home through the crisis and throughout his long convalescence, which he spent in casual botanizing and sailing in a small boat among the off-shore islands.

He had plenty of time for quiet brooding over the problem of man and nature, but Muir's unquiet spirit could never be at rest, no matter how relaxed his body. He became increasingly irritated by the generally-held notion that man is the supreme creation and that all other things exist only for his good: whales as store-houses for oil; hemp for ships' rigging, tying packages and hanging the wicked; iron for hammers and plows; lead for bullets; all intended for man.

The notion that everything that cannot in some way be made useful to civilized man should be destroyed or at the least, condemned, he attributed to belief in an artificial God. "He is regarded as a civilized, law abiding gentleman in favor of either a republican form of government or a limited monarchy...is a warm supporter of...Sunday Schools and missionary societies; and is as purely a manufactured article as any puppet in a halfpenny theatre."*

Out of these musings he developed the larger conception which became so important in his life and work — a conception which he progressively developed and refined. In the "Cedar Keys" section of his journal he wrote: "Nature's object in making plants and animals might possibly be first of all the happiness of each one of them, not the creation of all for the happiness of one. Why should man value himself as more than a small part of the one great unit of creation? And what creature of all that the Lord has taken pains to make is not essential to the completeness of that unit — the cosmos? The universe would be incomplete without man, but it would also be incomplete without the smallest transmicroscopic creature that dwells beyond our conceitful eyes of knowledge.

"From the dust of the earth, from the common elementary fund, the Creator has made *Homo sapiens*. From the same material he has made every other creature, however noxious and insignificant to us. They are earth born companions and our fellow mortals."

In early January, 1868, a small schooner came to Cedar Keys to take on a cargo of pine lumber for Havana, and Muir took passage in her. The crossing was rough, swift and exciting, and he enjoyed every minute of it. His spirits recovered their usual buoyancy, and he felt sure of accomplishing his dream of exploring first the mountains of Cuba, and then the great rivers of South

* William F. Badè, *The Life and Letters of John Muir*, Vol. I, p. 166.

America.

In this he overestimated his enfeebled strength and underestimated the outrageous fecundity of tropical vegetation. He lived on the schooner, anchored in Havana harbor, and went ashore to botanize almost every day during the entire month. But he lacked the stamina to go more than a dozen miles from the city. In the countryside he came upon stretches where the individuality of the vines was lost "in trackless, interlacing, twisting, overheaping union." Some individual plants of one variety he studied covered patches of several hundred square yards and bore as much leaf surface as a Kentucky oak. Florida had been almost too much to tackle alone. What he had seen in Cuba convinced him that the trip to South America, as he had planned it, was out of the question at least for the present.

He consoled himself by planning a trip to his second choice — the Yosemite Valley in California. Shipping in the Caribbean was so erratic that the swiftest passage meant a voyage from Havana to New York, thence to Panama, across the Isthmus, up the coast to San Francisco and a hundred mile walk into the high mountains. A brochure he had read — no doubt the work of J. M. Hutchings, Yosemite's first publicist — promised to make the journey worth the trouble.

Chapter 11
The Enchanted Sheepherder

In early April of 1868, Muir and a wandering Cockney named Chilwell, whom he had met on the boat from Panama, were holed up in a cabin near Yosemite, some six thousand feet above sea level. The snow outside lay eight feet deep, and Muir felt wonderful. The dry, aromatic air of original California spring had abolished the remains of his illness. Crossing the golden river of flowers growing petal to petal on the floor of the San Joaquin Valley had recharged his enthusiasm; from below, the towering Sierra Nevada had seemed his Promised Land, and he had not been disappointed once he got into it. But Chilwell was fed up with the diet of flapjacks and tea, which was all they could make from the meager supplies they had been able to afford. He persuaded Muir to teach him how to use the old army musket they had bought, at Chilwell's insistence, to shoot small game — and bears, if any should come very close.

Thinking to discover whether the sights were set too high, Muir stepped off thirty paces through the snow and took aim at a piece of paper fastened to the wall of the cabin.

"Fire away!" shouted the Cockney, now out of sight, and Muir pulled the trigger.

The result was a wild yell and Chilwell came charging out of the cabin shouting, "You shot me, Scotty! You shot *me!*"

The buckshot had gone through the pine-shake wall, against which Chilwell had incredibly placed his back, penetrated the three coats and three shirts he was wearing, and lodged in his hide. Muir picked the shot out with the point of his knife.

This was the last time Muir owned even a half share in a gun.

Floundering through the drifts the two men reached the rim of Yosemite Valley at a point where they had a clear view of a silvery strand of water falling from a dark cliff.

"I'd like to camp at the foot of it to see the ferns and lilies that may be there," Muir said. "It looks from here only about fifteen or twenty feet high, but it may be sixty or seventy." They were looking at Bridal Veil Fall, which is 620 feet high.

Yosemite is not called "The Incredible Valley" for nothing. In the ten days they spent there, Muir's perceptions, conditioned to flatlands, were unable to cope with what he saw. "The magnitudes are so great," he wrote to Mrs. Carr, "that unless seen and submitted to a good long time they are not seen at all." The giant redwoods in the Merced Grove, where they camped on the way out, were also awe-inspiring, but difficult for Muir to comprehend on first acquaintance.

His desire was to replenish supplies and go back up into the mountains at once, but the knowledge that his brothers and sisters might need his help impounded the money he had in reserve. To remain near the mountains, he worked in the harvest fields, sheared sheep, broke mustangs from the herds that still roamed wild in the San Joaquin and, in late December of 1868, he took charge of a band of 1,800 sheep.

His abode was a crazily-built shack on Dry Creek, between the Merced and Tuolumne Rivers where they emerge from the foothills. The previous sheepherder had left the shanty filthy, and the outside was worse — strewn with worn-out shoes, dried remains of dead sheep and other debris, among which wild hogs rooted aggressively. Muir went to sleep star-gazing through the cracks in the roof. His first attempt to make sourdough bread resulted in a black disk so hard he had to gnaw on it like a squirrel. The sheep were restless, scattering in every direction in search of a nourishing mouthful, for the only plants visible were dry, brown stems crumbling to add their dust to the tawny, sun-baked ground.

So began the happiest period John Muir had known since his first wild summer in Wisconsin.

He had no sooner gotten the roof fixed than the first of the winter rains came pouring out of the clouds and fell for ten hours. Dry Creek became a small

Head of 1st Merced Yo Val.

Head of the Merced River, Yosemite Valley.

river, and within days all the rounded hills, level stretches and little valleys were clothed in soft fuzzy green. These early comers were water-loving plants: mosses and their relatives, the liverworts, mushrooms and cresses.

On February 4 Muir found a yellow violet, and from then on through the next months the brightly colored blossoms appeared, species by species, as spring moved toward its April climax — when the whole valley was awash in yellow, set off by other colors in patches like enameled free-form designs.

Within John Muir analogous growth took place in those months of alternating rain and energizing sun. And, like the vegetation around him, he grew — not some specialized intellectual crop, as properly educated people are trained to do — but in natural diversity, as capabilities that had lain within him waiting to be fully realized flowered all together.

He became a much more scientific observer, to the extent of using his hand-lens to count the lichens on one square quarter inch of the rock upon which he was sitting. (There were 550.) Lying on the ground to look for sprouting seeds, he discovered a species of moss entirely new to him. The journal he kept during this period is a full and detailed record of unaltered California spring.

He freed his ability to establish those associations which distinguish scientific interpretation from mere observation. By examining the exposed roots of plants growing in the loose soil, he discovered that the nearby hills lost about a quarter of an inch during the high, rain-bearing winds of winter. The plants, he realized, saved themselves by pushing their roots deeper and deeper, riding the rise and fall of the land as sea-weeds ride the swells of ocean,

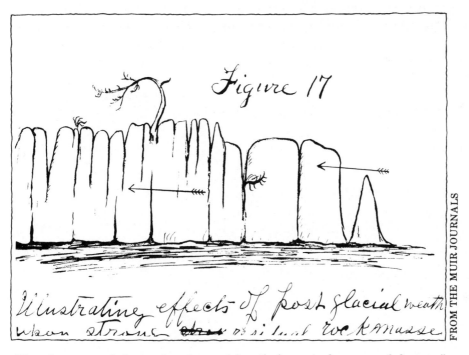

"The plants saved themselves by pushing their roots deeper and deeper."

though on a different time-scale.

His imagination blossomed into the metaphors that are so extraordinary a characteristic of his writing — "cloud shadows drifting heavily over the brown plains like islands of solid darkness in a sea of light" — and into speculation on aspects of nature unknown and unknowable. Considering the tiny amount of air churned in a meadowlark's throat to produce some of nature's loveliest sounds, he reasoned that wind flowing over a grain of sand must also make some kind of music, inaudible to human ears, and an even subtler sound when moving air caressed the delicate curves and ridges of flower petals.

Some of these musings originated in Muir's overmastering, and almost fatal, desire to experience all that nature does. If he could do whatever he wished, he wrote in his journal, he would not choose to go to the moon (as Jules Verne was dreaming of doing in the 1860s). He would rather voyage along the magnetic fields surrounding the earth; lie in the heart of a plant as it developed from stem to bud and from bud to flower; plunge down from the top of Yosemite Falls with the web-like strands of spray and comet-shaped masses of water.

In the torn-up period after he had left the university, John Muir had been tormented by undefinable desires he called *soul hunger*: "I began to doubt whether I was fully born . . . I was on the world. But was I in it?"

Close to the sheep camp he came upon one of nature's creations which seemed more perfect than any he had yet seen: twenty beautifully-modeled hills ranged in a circle around a flower-embroidered hollow. Beyond, but seeming to rise from the hollow's edge, stood the Sierra Nevada in bands of color — rose purple at the bottom, forest green next, then blue and white at the top where snow made lacework of the skyline peaks ninety miles away, and twelve to fifteen thousand feet above the valley floor. The mountains seemed not so much in the sky as part of it, not so much lighted by the sun as made of light. "Presently you lose consciousness of your own existence," he wrote to Jeanne Carr, "You blend with the landscape and become part and parcel of nature."

Part III

GEOLOGIST

"John the Baptist was not more eager to get all his fellow sinners into the Jordan than I to baptize all of mine in the beauty of God's mountains."

Chapter 12

Into the Range of Light

Shortly after John Muir's thirty-first birthday, April 2, 1869, the glory departed more suddenly than it had come. By May nothing of the flowers and grass was left except their tawny stems and their beautiful seed pods. The weather grew oven-hot. John turned the sheep over to their owner and went to visit the only man in the neighborhood capable of understanding why and how much he wanted to get into those mountains.

He was a tall, ascetic-looking Irishman named Pat Delaney — whom John Muir, who had worked for him previously, called Don Quixote. He had been educated for the priesthood, made a stake during the Gold Rush and was now getting rich as a wool grower. He offered Muir a job of overseeing a band of 2,050 sheep being taken into the mountains for the summer. An experienced sheepherder would do most of the work, and Muir would have plenty of time for botanizing and sketching.

Muir demurred on the grounds that he knew little about sheep and nothing about these mountains. But he was easily persuaded because he needed to send money home. A few weeks earlier, his father had exploded in an outburst of fanaticism against John's sister Mary. Under John's urging she had developed her talent for painting by secretly practicing with water color and crayon. One day Mr. Muir came home unexpectedly and found a box of her sketches on the living room table. In a fury he took them outside, threw them into a mudpuddle and stamped on them, shouting that he was doing this to save Mary's soul.

Mary took refuge with Sarah, who reported the episode to John. He immediately sent $220, with instructions that Mary was to enter the University of Wisconsin and study art, music and botany. He informed David that he had a reserve of $500 for any of his brothers or sisters who might need it. There was not enough money left for him to go long without a job.

On June 3 the expedition started in a cloud of dust which obscured the "Range of Light," as John Muir preferred to call that uplift of granite formally known as the Sierra Nevada — which can be literally translated "snowy saw teeth." It is an unbroken, wave-shaped wall five hundred miles from north to south, though less than a hundred miles east to west, and said by geologists to be the longest, highest, and grandest single range in the United States. It is divided by rivers rushing westward into the San Joaquin Valley and thence to the sea. The sheep band would be driven up between the Tuolumne and the Merced — the river which runs through Yosemite Valley.

The party was a mix typical of its time, place and mission:"Don Quixote," leading packhorses loaded with camp gear and Muir's plant presses; Billy the sheepherder, considerably degraded by too long a pursuit of that thankless occupation; a Chinese and an Indian to help on the long first drive; a mongrel sheepdog named Jack, now misshapen as the result of a rattlesnake bite, but competent in sheep work; Carlo, a superb St. Bernard, whom a professional hunter had entrusted to Muir to save the warm-furred dog from the ferocious heat of the Valley; John Muir, with a notebook tied to his belt. Ahead of them rambled the sheep, which Muir sincerely felt man had degenerated into neurotic wool-producing mechanisms. "A sheep scarcely possesses a separate existence — the whole flock is required to make an indivdual. The body of the flock contracts and expands like the body of a worm...."

Panting in the heat, and wishing they wouldn't because of the dust, men and animals moved slowly upward through the Sierra's lower zone. It had looked rose purple from the Valley below. Close up the sun-cracked ground was monotonous brown, scarred here and there with abandoned workings of once-profitable placer mines. Occasional outcrops of slate stood like black tombstones.

In the afternoon the trail petered out and Muir had his first experience of chaparral, the tangled brush that still covers great reaches of California's slopes. In Spanish the word means "place of the short ones"; some Californians call it the "Elfin Forest," because many of the bushes are dwarfs of oaks and other species which elsewhere grow into trees. The branches are tough, springy and hostile. If it were not for bays and little lanes, the chaparral in many places would be impassable.

The Indian found a way through in time to gather the sheep on a barren hill and camp for the night. Next day there was little else to see but barren hills, with jackrabbits skimming their curves like shadows of swift-moving clouds. But this purgatorial part of the trip was mercifully brief.

On June 6 they reached the true Sierra, at an altitude of 2,500 feet. John Muir felt as if he had reached Paradise without bothering to die. "Our flesh-and-bone tabernacle seems transparent as glass to the beauty about us...thrilling with the air and trees, streams and rocks, in the waves of the sun — a part of all nature, neither old nor young, sick or well — but immortal."

Their upward way now led through open, sunlit forests of pines and cedars so huge Muir would have had trouble believing if he had not already seen the giant sequoias. Within these woods grew patches of wildflowers — some old friends he had known in the Valley and many new to him. The sheep left them devastated: they even ate the poison oak, to which Muir was mercifully immune.

On the North Fork of the Merced, above the gorge through which the young river runs after leaving Yosemite Valley, Delaney selected their first base camp. To Muir it proved an enchanted small world.

The clear, musical stream was arched over by alders and willows, and dogwoods just now covering themselves with lucent white blossoms. Muir found wide-spreading oaks with trunks six feet in diameter and on the crests of the surrounding hills the giant pines, towering two hundred fifty feet and more, stood beautifully moving against the clouds that built into sky-mountains each afternoon, only to dissolve in refreshing rains.

Along the stream bank were gardens of lilies, many six feet tall and bearing up to sixty blossoms, some "as big as baby bonnets." On the rocks below grew ferns that dipped their fronds to make ever-changing designs of white water. Behind the lilies, on the bank, were massed a half dozen varieties of plants all now in bloom. It was as if some gardener had labored here lovingly, to make all beautiful. To John Muir this gardener was God, expressing his love through the processes of nature. To make one's self a part of pure, natural wildness was to share His love. In the first weeks at this camp, Muir became a love-intoxicated man.

"Snowy-saw teeth"—peak formations of the Sierra Nevada.

There were a couple of unloving things on the scene. One was a variety of small black ant more ferocious than the snakes, bears, mountain lions and wolves that inhabited this region. They were about a quarter inch long, mostly head and jaws like ice tongs, which they sank into any unprotected patch of human flesh and hung on even after they were pulled apart. Muir could see no sense in their desperate aggressiveness.

The second inimical element was Man, who had degenerated sheep into "hoofed locusts" and, for a profit, herded them into the mountains by ravenous thousands. Within eight days they had eaten out every edible plant within easy reach, and would certainly have destroyed the gardens near camp if Muir had not persuaded Delaney to order the sheepherder to guard them.

Delaney left for the Valley on June 9, taking the Indian and Chinese with him and promising to return soon with supplies. Muir and Billy made a simple division of labor. Billy cooked the meals and herded the sheep as long as they stayed on their usual range. When any of them strayed, Muir searched them out with the help of the St. Bernard, Carlo, and brought them back to camp. He also washed the pots and made the sourdough bread. He had plenty of time for observing and exploring — and for purely delighting himself.

On the sandy flats, which in some places edged the stream, grew a common fern, *Petris aquilina*, but here it grew so huge it seemed a new species. The plants grew close together on stems seven feet and more in height; their broad, undivided fronds overlapped to make a continuous roof. One day Muir saw a considerable part of the sheep band disappear into one of these fern beds and reappear a hundred yards away. He found that he could walk erect under this roof and, after strolling for a while, sat down on a log to savor the experience of a miniature jungle. Small animals moved about here freely and contentedly as citizens in their homes. The light streamed through the living ceiling with its pattern of leaf-veins as if through green and yellow glass. Muir was incensed that Billy saw nothing in this marvel except some "damn big ferns."

To Muir, at this time, precise observation became the fine grain of beauty and the foundation of wonder. He measured, counted and analyzed. And he began seriously to inquire how this environment had come into being and what would be its future.

He had spent some happy nights bedded down on the moss-covered top of a huge, rectangular boulder below a waterfall, and it set him wondering how such stones had arrived at their situations. It was clear enough that smaller — though still large — boulders were moved down by the yearly freshets when the river raged. But the huge rocks would require more power and would, moreover, remain in place a long time. From the age of trees growing among cyclopean boulders at the stream's edge, he deduced that the most recent torrent capable of moving such masses had occurred a hundred years earlier.

Speculation and delight were halted by running out of all supplies except sugar and tea. Their only food was fat mutton, and, though Muir berated himself for not being able to live on a meat diet as Indians and mountain men had done, he could not talk his cereal-trained digestion out of nausea. Billy, conditioned to beans, suffered equally.

At last, in early July, Pat Delaney arrived with coffee, flour and beans and a couple of extra hands to help drive the sheep. They set out immediately for the high pastures above Yosemite Valley. Rain had not fallen for some while. Over the flock hung a brown pall of dust raised by eight thousand sharp hooves. Their trail was bordered by wild gardens as lovely as those they had left. The sheep destroyed them. It was on this drive that Muir wrote into his journal one of his most prophetic passages.

"In this mighty wilderness they seem but a feeble band; a thousand gardens will escape their blighting touch. They cannot hurt the trees, though some of the seedlings suffer, and should the wooly locusts be greatly multiplied, as on account of their dollar value they are likely to be, then the forests too may be destroyed. Only the sky will then be safe, though hid from view by dust and smoke — incense of a bad sacrifice."

On July 10 they camped beside the ice-cold, delicious waters of Tamarack Creek, on the high plateau between Yosemite and the canyon of the Tuolumne. They were less than five miles from Yosemite, but could not see it. The upland on the southern side of the Valley has the same elevation as the one they were on, and Yosemite's walls are so sheer that the two rugged plateaus seem undivided unless one is very near the rim.

As soon as camp was made, Muir set out, as usual, to explore the neighborhood, and came presently upon a stretch of bare, gray granite so smooth that it threw back the sunlight with a strange glare. Here and there this polished pavement was scored by deep, straight scratches rigidly parallel to one another.

On this bare rock were scattered great boulders, some twenty to thirty feet in diameter. Very few small rocks or any gravelly debris lay round about them, which showed that the boulders had not been exposed by the weathering away of softer material in which they once had lain buried. They stood in their curiously raw, wiped-looking setting like strangers in a strange land.

When Muir examined them closely he found that they were indeed different from the pavement on which they rested — made of a sort of granite unlike any in this neighborhood. The boulders, then, had been brought here. But how?

As he stared about him, Muir recalled his studies of Wisconsin Ice Age remnants under Professor Carr during his university days. As chemicals combine to make a new product on the instant, what he now saw and what he remembered came together to create an answer. These boulders had been

FROM THE MUIR JOURNALS

Sketch of glacial movement causing deep scratches in a Yosemite plateau's granite surface.

brought here by a glacier which had quarried them from some mountain higher in the range. Creeping slowly down the mountains, the ice river had finally melted here, leaving the boulders behind. Gravel and sand on the glacier's underbelly had polished the granite pavement; extra-hard stones embedded in the ice had made the parallel scratches.

John Muir looked about him amazed and bemused, for — if there had been ice enough to bring the boulders — this whole upland, seven to eight thousand feet above the sea, must have been overswept to a great depth.

"A grand discovery this!" Muir wrote in his journal. Weak words, but the revelation was too sudden and too great to be grasped at once, let alone to foresee how it would affect his future. He needed a quiet time for assimilation and reflection. Instead the next few days were loaded with new experiences — some trivial, some overwhelming.

Pat Delaney, who had gone ahead to select a place to camp until the snow melted from the high mountain meadows, returned with a decision which pleased Muir greatly. They would camp near the head of Yosemite Valley. It took almost a full day of shouting, cursing, wading and sheepdog barking to get the band across Yosemite Creek. For, though sheep can swim well enough, they resist water more stubbornly than grubby children.

They set up the base camp next morning, and in the afternoon Muir took off for the high, western rim of Indian Canyon, which pitches steeply down to Yosemite Valley. Arriving at the top he was confronted with a view which seemed the noblest of his life. The fantastic canyons, through which high mountain streams leap and foam to merge on the Valley floor and form the mainstream of the Merced River, were laid out like a relief map — modeled and colored by God himself. Above and beyond the white water rose successive bands of forest and bare rock, to culminate in snow-mantled summit peaks against a sky as blue as a mountain flower.

Like the cowboy who, reining in his horse at the brink of the Grand Canyon, pulled off his hat and whooped, "Hooray for God!" Muir was unable to contain himself. He shouted and made wild gestures until Carlo came up with a serious, concerned, what's-the-matter look that made Muir laugh. No sooner had man and dog started on than a brown bear who had been watching from the brush took off in such a frightened rush that he tumbled over the gnarled, tough bushes in his path.

Arriving at the rim of Yosemite itself, Muir began searching for a place where he could look straight down. When he found one, the view took his breath. Some three thousand feet below his own the Valley stretched for seven miles — like a garden enclosed between towering, sculptured walls. Through it the Merced, the River of Mercy, wound its way calmly. And across from him the indescribable mass of granite — which the Indians and John Muir called "Tissiac," and we call "Half Dome" — rose nearly a mile from Mirror Lake at its feet to the top of its helmet-shaped head.

Still inexperienced with heights, Muir could not help but imagine himself falling through the clear, sunlit air to the boulders below, but his desire to see

Lower end of Yosemite Valley from the top of the south wall.

more was over-mastering. Most of the cliff edge was rounded, but as he worked his way westward toward Yosemite Falls he found, here and there, narrow ledges to which he gingerly lowered himself for an exhilarating straight-down look. Each of these ventures made him uneasy because he observed that the rock contained horizontal fracture lines. It was all too easy to imagine what would happen if the piece on which he stood broke off. Each time he climbed back up to security, he ordered himself not to go to the verge again. Yet his body seemed to have a commanding will of its own, and he went out on every view ledge he found.

Coming after a mile or so to Yosemite Creek — flowing in graceful curves down the smooth bed it has worn in the shining granite — he followed it down to the pool where the water seems to rest before taking its final leap over the cliff. From the pool Yosemite Creek descends a smooth, steep, chute-like slope to the brink of the cliff.

John Muir had dreamed of joining the whirling spray and comet-like masses of the fall as a disembodied spirit. Next best would be to watch the water start its magnificent plunge. He took off his shoes and socks and worked his way down the polished rock beside the rushing stream. But when he reached the lip he found there was a narrow brow below which hid the actual fall.

The water here was all around: above, beside and below him, and drenching him with spray. The roar of the stream as it went over, mingled with the booming from 1,600 feet below, where the fall struck — a strange, confusing, tension-making place to be. Nevertheless he looked for a way to see the water begin its plunge. The fall-concealing ledge was too far down for him to lower himself, and there appeared to be no foothold in any case. But presently he made out a shelf at the very verge. It was barely wide enough to rest his heels on. The rock face beside the fall was too smooth and steep to climb upon, but some distance to the right he saw a rough, steeply-sloping edge where a slab of granite had peeled off. It might provide finger holds. "No," he told himself. "The rock beside that edge is too smooth and steep. I won't try it." His body seemed then to over-rule his reason. Without willing to do so he plucked some bitter leaves growing beside him and chewed them to steady himself. Inch by inch, with such caution as he had never practiced before, he crept to the rough edge, made his way down to the little ledge below and, setting his heels upon this, shuffled twenty or thirty feet along it until he stood a few feet from the fall.

Here at the start of its descent, the stream breaks up into solid comet-like masses of water, feathering out into tails of intricately woven threads and fine spray. They seemed to chant together as they descended in a close-packed company. Occasional loners outbounded to fall, so that Muir could follow them for a thousand feet or more. He was so overwhelmed with wonder and excitement that he had no sense of where he was or how long he stood there. His body under guidance of his subconscious mind took care to preserve itself, leaving his consciousness to commune with the world's highest free-leaping waterfall. He did not even remember climbing up to the streamside where he had left his shoes.

The mood of exaltation lasted until he had gone to bed, back in camp. Usually his sleep was the deep and peaceful slumber of a hard-worked body housing a full-fed mind. But that night, and for two nights after, he started awake from real-seeming dreams of falling among broken rock ledges and water comets. Once he found himself on his feet exclaiming, "Where could a mountaineer find a more glorious death!"

He resolved never to take such a risk again. But this was his conscious mind talking to itself. His unconscious mind, having no voice, kept its peace and bided its time.

Chapter 13
The Incredible Valley

Perched on the helmet-shaped, 3,500-foot mass of granite called North Dome, which stands above Yosemite Valley near its upper end, John Muir felt the size of a fly. Before him the sheer, 2,200-foot cliff that makes Half Dome look as if it had been split with a cyclopean axe rose almost 1,300 feet higher than his perch. Eastward, beyond this overpowering monolith, domes, pinnacles and forest-draped slopes mounted steeply to the summit peaks, gleaming white against a sky like a huge bell-flower. In the tangle of wild canyons at Half Dome's foot, thundering waterfalls looked as evanescent as streamers of white smoke.

Muir was looking at one of earth's most varied, most unusual and most

Sketch of dome formation showing glacial movement with lateral moraines.

physically magnificent displays of natural rock formations. He was overpowered by it — humbled, and unable to do much more than respond with his whole being.

He wanted to sketch everything, but only put down "marks like words readable only to myself." For relief he drew the antic flight of a grasshopper who seemed to be mocking the grandeur of the scene with abandoned merriment. He spent most of a day studying a silver fir whose broken main trunk had developed a branch into a tree one hundred feet high, "as if a man whose back was broken . . . should find a branch backbone sprouting straight up from below the break...." By counting the annual rings in the new wood that had overlapped the broken stump, he determined the date of a snowstorm that had bent this fir grove down and covered it as if the trees were grass.

Entranced, uplifted and yet unsatisfied because he could not arrive at the understanding which is the firm and permanent basis of delight, Muir kept trying to put his experiences together in meaningful patterns. On July 20 he wrote: "What pains are taken to keep this wilderness in health — showers of snow, showers of rain, showers of dew, floods of light, floods of invisible vapor, clouds, winds, all sorts of weather, interaction of plant on plant, animal on animal, etc., beyond thought!"

But Muir was not going to get much farther toward understanding this wilderness until he stopped trying to embrace it all at once, only to find his arms full of nothing. He had to focus on some particular aspect of the huge and complex scene. For a person of Muir's omnivorous mind, to do so required that he encounter some overpowering attraction. That he had already found one in the ice-transported boulder resting on polished granite, he did not yet recognize. He therefore went on sampling every experience within reach at least once, with a tenderfoot's disregard of common sense.

Carlo, the St. Bernard, had been trained to hunt bears, and when the dog came up one morning with an expression that plainly said, "I've found something interesting!" Muir followed him through a stand of firs. When the light showed that they were near the edge, Carlo dropped behind as the hunter had taught him to do. Disregarding the fact that he was unarmed, Muir advanced to the outer trees bordering a flowering meadow and peered cautiously around the largest trunk he could find. No farther away than one can easily toss a stone, stood a brown bear — a large one that would weigh, Muir estimated, a good five hundred pounds. His forefeet rested on a log, so that he stood almost erect, his hindquarters buried in grass and flowers which Muir, being himself, identified as geraniums, larkspurs, columbines and daisies. The bear had not seen the man, but sensing some foreign presence stood swinging his shaggy head back and forth, ears erect and nose snuffling the breeze. Tall lilies swung their bells over his broad back.

An elegant tableau. But presently Muir decided that he would like to see some action. He had been told that this variety of bear always ran from his "bad brother man," so he dashed forward, swinging his hat and shouting.

The bear did not know the rules. Instead of running, he lowered his head, thrust it forward and stared at Muir with a fierce, level look. It was now Muir's turn to run, but it seemed unwise to move, so he stood looking fixedly at the bear and hoping that the power of the human eye over wild beasts would prove as potent as it was supposed to be. They were less than forty feet apart.

How long this "awfully strenuous" confrontation continued, Muir could not say. But at last the bear pulled his huge paws down from the log and with dignified deliberation ambled off, stopping now and then to look back, as if he did not trust the man any more than he feared him.

During that first summer in the Sierra, Muir wrote often to his family and friends. He insisted that he was not lonely because he could conjure them up so completely in imagination that they became once more his companions. Comforting as this evidently was, it could not suppress completely his desperate need for the real presence of people who had given him understanding and affection.

One of Muir's many sketches showing dome formation.

FROM THE MUIR JOURNALS

Late in the afternoon of August 2, as he sat sketching on North Dome, he had a sudden premonition that Professor James Davie Butler was in the valley below. The impression could not have been stronger if his old friend had touched him on the shoulder. Muir had descended through heavy brush far down into trail-less Indian Canyon before he realized that he could not reach the hotel before dark and that his appearance would be anything but reassuring. He returned to camp, and the next morning combed his hair and beard, put on clean overalls, a cashmere shirt and what he described as "a sort of jacket," and made his way down to the Valley, noting in passing that the same species of oak that grew only dwarf-size at the top was a great tree at the bottom.

Isolation had made him so desperately shy that it was an ordeal to endure the stares of tourists readying their fishing gear in front of the gloomy hotel and to inquire within for his friend. Dr. Butler was indeed in the Valley, but had gone up to the falls at its head. Just outside the spray of Vernal Fall, Muir inquired once more. The dignified gentleman whom he addressed stared at him suspiciously and asked with military sharpness, "Who wants him?"

"I want him!" Muir answered with equal sharpness.

"Why? Do *you* know him?"

"Yes. Do *you* know him?"

At this, the gentleman's curiosity overcame suspicion and he introduced himself as General Alford. He and Butler had come directly to Yosemite from the East, without getting in touch with any of their friends, and thought themselves undiscoverable.

Above the fall Muir found Dr. Butler wandering through the brush and looking lost and weary. He waited until Muir came up to ask him the way to the ladders leading down to the Valley floor. Muir told him; then, standing directly in front of his friend, he asked, "Professor Butler, don't you know me?"

"I think not," Butler began, but then he encountered Muir's memorable blue eyes and jumped up exclaiming, "John Muir! John Muir! Where have you come from?"

All the way back to the hotel the two kept up old-friends talk, Butler riding a cow pony and Muir striding along beside his stirrup. At the long table where dinner was served to all at once, the tourists stared at Muir with a different curiosity. Spiritualism was then much in vogue, and General Alford made a big deal of Muir's "call" from the wilderness on the very day his friend arrived. Muir was impressed by the experience himself, but attributed it to some natural characteristics of mind which would some day be explained.

If, indeed, he possessed some extra-sensory powers, they did not operate consistently. His dear friend Jeanne Carr was also in Yosemite that summer. Her husband had joined the faculty of the small but vigorous University of California, and she made the pilgrimage at the first opportunity. But the letter telling the time of her arrival in the Valley never reached Muir.

As happened to many of the old-time sheepherders, isolation and confinement to the society of muttons had made Billy an experience in himself. Muir could not persuade him to go near Yosemite Valley, which he called "nothing but a damn big hole, and dangerous for falling into." Each morning he hung a heavy revolver on one hip, and on the other a chunk of mutton fresh from the frying pan. The coarse cloth in which the meat was tied acted as a filter from which the fat dripped down to form gooey stalactites. Bill distributed each day's fat by rubbing his hands on his clothing, crossing his legs when seated on a log and rolling over during siestas. Since he never took off his overalls, they grew thicker and thicker, instead of thinner, and so sticky that Billy became a sort of walking museum. Embedded in the waterproof coating were butterfly wings, pieces of bark, seeds, flower petals, mica, feldspar crystals, etc., amounting to a representative sample of the environment.

They had used fallen timber to make the corral where the sheep were kept at night. One of the bottom logs was decaying and in the process covered the ground with fine, red powder. In this dust slept Billy, to be near the sheep, he said, in case the bears attacked them. But after the fifth of August, when bears stampeded the sheep just before dawn, carrying off two and causing six more to be crushed against the corral fence before it broke, Billy moved his blankets to the other side of camp, as far from the sheep as he could get.

Muir managed to round up the scattered flock with Carlo's help. But though he sat up all night with Delaney's heavy rifle and kept a ring of fires blazing, two bears got into the corral and made off with a sheep apiece. Muir judged by their tracks that they had leaped the fence carrying their prey as a mother cat carries a kitten.

Delaney came back next day, and they set off at once for the high pastures to the east. Their first camp was at Lake Tenaya, which feeds into Yosemite Valley through the perilous canyon of the same name. To Muir it seemed plain that a great glacier had been at work here. The lake's northern end was bordered by stretches of polished, glittering pavement where the pack animals slipped and even Carlo seemed puzzled. Rocks rising two thousand feet above the shore had clearly been overswept by ice. Beneath the clear water, as far out from the shore as he could see, the bottom also was polished and scored where hard stones on the glacier's bottom must have cut into the granite.

The sheep band ate its slow way upward to the big Tuolumne meadows. At an elevation near 9,000 feet, where they established a base camp, the winters must surely be most hostile to life. But here was a twelve-mile strip of fine, soft grass spangled lavishly with flowers. Nature was irrepressible. The great peaks that surrounded this garden spot seemed barren desolations of rock. But Muir knew this impression to be an illusion. On the bare-looking summit of 11,000-foot Mt. Hoffman, the highest he had yet climbed, he had found

"Flies, bugs, weeds and trees were liquid burning white..." seen through the light of the rising sun.

stretches of the crumbling granite covered with a multitude of tiny flowers whose colors combined with the reflection from crystals of tourmaline, hornblende, feldspar and mica to make the face of the mountain glow. And near the summit he discovered a variety of hemlock new to him, which seemed the most graceful of all conifers. These trees were in bloom, and when he climbed among their blossoms he found them lovely as the tree itself; the seed-bearing flowers rich purple, the pollen-bearing ones sky blue.

On Mt. Hoffman also, Muir first discovered the curious little pika which is named for him. This cousin of the rabbit lives at high altitudes, nips off lupines and other plants at the stem and leaves them in small heaps to dry in the sun. To Muir this miniature haying brought a curiously human and industrious touch to the seemingly-unfriendly rock.

While they were camped at Tuolumne Meadows, Delaney suggested that Muir follow the gold miners' trail through Bloody Canyon to Mono Lake, on the eastern slope of the Sierra. He had never been through this pass himself, but had heard it was one of the wildest places in these mountains. He believed it was named in memory of the horses, mules and driven cattle whose legs had been cut to ribbons on the rocks during a brief gold rush to the Mono Lake region. Others thought the name derived from the color of the rocks.

As far as Muir was concerned, either might have been true. He came through Mono Pass in the late afternoon and found the forbidding depths of Bloody Canyon already in shadow. On both sides 2,000-foot rock walls seemed to close in on him, mysterious and threatening. In places the polish wrought by the glacier that had dug this formidable chute made the walls glow with a strange, red glare. In other places beetling cliffs seemed about to fall on him. And there were many places where avalanches had dug great furrows in the walls and deluged the canyon with tons of rock in many shapes and sizes, but all sharp. Among these rocks the trail descended 1,000 feet to the mile.

Presently Muir saw below him a file of furry creatures walking half erect. They resolved themselves into a band of Mono Indians clothed in rabbit skins, on their way to feast on trout and trade for acorns in Yosemite. They gathered in a ring around Muir begging tobacco and whiskey, or anything else he had to spare. But all the provisions he had brought were tea and a little bread. Their blackened faces, where the expression-wrinkles looked like lines on a map, seemed unbeautiful, and he was glad to see them go, though half-ashamed of himself for preferring the company of squirrels, birds, deer and even bears.

On a bed of pine boughs part way down the canyon, Muir spent one of the strangest nights of his life — up to that point. Gusts of wind howling and roaring down the defile drowned the waterfall opposite his camp and turned his fire of resinous roots into a nest of vivid snakes writhing along the rocky ground. Before he slept, the moon, looking larger and closer than he had ever seen it, peered down into the slot of Bloody Canyon like a solemn face staring at no one in the world except John Muir.

Morning was more cheerful. The stream tumbling down the steep canyon

Red Lake in Bloody Canyon — formed by glacial action in the Mono Lake region.

paused here and there to produce lovely water-side gardens. The trees, which at the top had been ground-hugging dwarfs, became tall and stately, and when he reached the bottom he found himself in a climate warm enough for palms. There were no palms — only a desolate sagebrush flat stretching to Mono Lake. But in the canyon's mouth he found the most telling signs of ancient glaciers he had yet encountered. Along each side of the canyon stretched a wall-like pile of boulders — what geologists call a "lateral moraine" — made up of the rock debris a glacier carries on its flanks. These walls were joined at length by a curving band of rock — a "terminal moraine" — deposited where the glacier had come to rest and melted. The lowest of the small lakes in the canyon was formed by a terminal moraine serving as a dam. And from the end of the canyon two lateral moraines stretched far out onto the plain, which led Muir to believe that Mono Lake had once been much larger than he found it.

Between these ultimate moraines grew a stand of wild rye, its eight-to-ten-foot stalks bearing heads of grain. Indian women moved through this natural harvest field laughing and chattering as they bent down the tall stalks and beat out the grain, which Muir found sweet and likely to make good bread.

It was very dry hereabouts — a grey, lean country bearing sparse desert growth and decorated with volcanic buttes that looked interesting but inhospitable. Muir was glad to get back to the green western side, where the Sierra milks the moisture from the clouds rolling in from the Pacific and all living things prosper.

They remained at Tuolumne Meadows all through August, and Muir improved the time by climbing the great peaks which cluster about this garden spot. He was very probably the first to climb thirteen thousand-foot Mt. Dana, though he did not leave his name on that summit — nor on any other mountain, for he climbed for other purposes than competition. From the summit of Dana he had a view which finally and fatally welded him to the Sierra; peak after peak stepping ever higher southward down the axis of the range promised wonders and discoveries of which the experiences of this summer were a foretaste.

"The best gains of this trip," he wrote in his journal on the first of September, 1869, "were the lessons of unity and interrelation of all features of the landscape....Every natural feature...seems to call and invite us to come and learn something of its history and relationship.

"If I had a few sacks of flour, an axe and some matches I could build a cabin of pine logs, pile up plenty of firewood about it, and stay all winter....But now I'll have to go, for there is nothing to spare in the way of provisions. I'll surely be back, however. I'll surely be back."

He already understood that to comprehend the relationships he so devoutly wished to understand, he would have to begin with ice.

Chapter 14
First Winter in Yosemite

When Muir returned to Yosemite in November of 1869, he clearly did not expect to become involved with society. But it is far more difficult to remain detached in an isolated community than in an urban environment; one becomes some kind of member automatically, even though a rejected one, which Muir emphatically was not.

Within a few days after his arrival he went with Harry Randall, his "partner," to use the old Western term for companion and trusted friend, to work for John Mason Hutchings, Yosemite's leading citizen, up to then the most sophisticated member of its minute society. Hutchings, a tall and rather distinguished-looking Britisher, had prospered during the Gold Rush, not by panning gold dust, but by publishing a broadside called "The Miner's Ten Commandments." It began, "Thou shalt have no other claim except one..." and was decorated with lively illustrations by one of the better Gold Rush artists. It sold over a hundred thousand copies the first year. In 1855 he founded one of San Francisco's first monthlies, *Hutchings' Illustrated California Magazine*, dedicated to making the new state's wonders and beauties widely known. In 1855 Hutchings himself led the first party of sightseers into Yosemite Valley, which since its discovery in 1851 had been seen only by Indian fighters and wandering prospectors. From then on Hutchings promoted the Valley as a "don't miss" tourist attraction, in spite of the fact that the trip by stage coach and horseback was terribly rugged and the descent into Yosemite harrowing for any except experienced mountaineers.

In 1864 Hutchings, having sold his magazine, bought a small, primitive hotel on the shadowed south side of the valley, opposite Yosemite Falls. The builders had made do with what could be brought in on the backs of mules and lumber crudely whipsawed by hand from fallen logs. Some of the rooms had muslin partitions and carpets of cedar boughs in lieu of floors; cracks were plentiful. The hotel was no place to spend the winter — it received, on the average, only two hours of sunlight per day.

When Muir arrived Hutchings was living in a snug log cabin on the sunny north side, with his library of eight hundred books, his wife and three children and Florantha Sproat, his mother-in-law, who was a notable cook.

The only other Anglo woman in the Valley that winter was Bell Leidig, a do-everything pioneer woman who had ridden into Yosemite with two tiny children strapped in front of her on the side-saddle. With her husband she operated a barn-like hotel near the foot of Glacier Point, which towers vertically 3,200 feet to the curious shelf-like rock projecting from its top.

The rest of the Anglo population consisted of horse-wranglers, packers and mule-train drivers, wood-choppers, trail-builders and handymen, along with the prospectors, trappers and hunters who chose to winter in Yosemite, whose floor is only 4,000 feet above the sea and warm enough to grow apples (Hutchings had an orchard on part of the 160 acres he claimed as a homestead). The total population was increasingly augmented by the half-breed children of compliant squaws. The crushed remnant of the Yosemite tribe, only a few years beyond the proud time when it had lived up to its name, which means "grizzly bear," had been permitted to return after final defeat and exile, on the promise of "good behavior." They lived in the deep, twisting caves of Yosemite's walls and in expendable teepee-like shelters of bark or rails from trees splintered by lightning. The braves hunted and fished, and some of the women continued to make handsome baskets and laboriously process acorns into edible meal. The Hutchings children traded cornbread to the Indian children for *nupatty* — little cakes made of acorn flour which they thought delicious. The Indians' chief means for making life tolerable were whiskey and brilliant clothing discarded by tourists when they returned to the inhibited environments from which they had briefly escaped.

Muir's first task was to rebuild a small sawmill which would provide lumber for everything from feed-boxes and hen houses to cottages for tourists. It was powered by a millrace diverted from Yosemite Creek a short distance below the falls. Nearby Muir and Randall built a cabin out of shakes split from sugar pine logs. Its floor was paved with slabs set far enough apart for small plants to show green, and ferns framed the window looking out upon Yosemite Falls. In front of this window they built a small writing desk where Harry Randall often sat of evenings, struggling with the arithmetic Muir was trying to teach him, while Muir himself sat before the stone fireplace in a home-made chair padded with a sheepskin and read scientific literature — Humboldt then, as always, being his first choice. When Muir climbed into his bunk, which was suspended from the rafters, and lay down on the fresh boughs of incense cedar he used for a mattress, frogs in a little stream that murmured across one corner of the cabin sang him to sleep.

From the start Muir and Randall saw a great deal of the Hutchings family, for they had their meals with them. But it was the children who first admitted Muir to their affection. The eldest — five-year-old Florence, called "Floy" — became a frequent visitor at the cabin beside Yosemite Falls. It was a new scene to her, a change from the corrals and stables where the men egged her on to ride wilder and still wilder horses and presently taught her to roll her own cigarettes. A strange child, black-eyed and black-browed, she furiously resented the fate that had made her a girl and did everything she could to play a boy's role in that essentially rough and masculine community. She fascinated people, less because she was the first Anglo child born in Yosemite than for her own nature, which those who knew her had a hard time to describe. "Wild," "uncontrollable," "witch," and "gypsy" were words Muir applied to Floy.

He considerably preferred her little sister called "Cosie," an amiable, affectionate little creature who tagged Floy to the stables, where she got an early start toward the side-saddle horsewomanship for which she became noted. Cosie Hutchings' outstanding memory of Muir was of his gently talking to her baby brother as the child sat in a big dishpan filled with warm water. But Muir encouraged Randall to take Floy with him when he went to the barn and squirt a cup of milk for the child who was kept perpetually hungry by her mother's diet fads.

Elvira Hutchings was twenty-two years younger than her husband, and some three years younger than Muir — a fragile, dreamy woman whom contemporaries described as having a "madonna-like" look. She was much more interested in botany, literature and art than in hotel keeping. On her mother's side she was related to several professional painters; her own water colors were creditable. She had heard of Muir from Jeanne Carr, and her friendship with him had already begun to develop before James Hutchings left for Washington, D.C.

This trip in the winter of 1869-70 was one of many that Hutchings took to litigate and lobby in support of his claim. The federal law of 1864 which donated Yosemite Valley to the State of California to be kept in perpetuity as a state park had made no provision for the rights of the local homesteaders, Hutchings being one, and John Lamon, Yosemite's pioneer settler, the other.

To the scandal of gossips in the community, Muir and Elvira Hutchings walked out together on Sundays and late afternoons to observe and collect ferns and flowering plants which flourished on the sunny south wall of Yosemite even after the snows began. There was no evidence of a love-affair, but that this man and woman were unchaperoned was enough, in those times, to cause censorious and perhaps envious interpretations.

Muir's outings with Elvira Hutchings were in the nature of strolls. When he had a few free hours he ranged far and high by himself. He had already realized that in order to understand Yosemite he must learn its cliffs and abysses, domes and pinnacles, its weather and its leaping waterfalls that supported such a lovely array of living things. To do so he must climb as he had never imagined climbing. This, too, took some learning.

He celebrated New Year's Day, 1870, by climbing to the crown of El Capitan, the enormous and beautifully sculptured rock that dominates the lower end of Yosemite Valley. He did not, of course, go up the sheer, valley-facing front — a climb of 3,200 feet that was first accomplished some eighty years later by teams of men using highly sophisticated equipment which enabled them to spend several nights hanging like spiders on the face of the rock. Muir's route permitted him to enjoy the bright day, the young ferns unrolling on sunlit ledges and new, small waterfalls created by the recently-melted snow. From El Capitan's crest he could see half way across California; the Sierra slope descending like a succession of waves to the San Joaquin Valley and across that tawny plain to the Coast Range, blue on the horizon. Muir was pleased that he did not get dizzy when he stood on the cliff's edge and looked straight down into Yosemite half a mile below. But he was not yet a complete mountaineer.

Attempting to descend by a new route he encountered a six-hundred-foot cliff. "Had to march back to the very summit," he wrote in his journal, "and find my old route. I had two hours scrambling in the dark, but by running, jumping, sliding, besides other modes of locomotion both terrestrial and aquatic too numerous to mention, I accomplished my craggy task in half time and escaped a long fast and a cold night on the mountain." This was the first, and the clumsiest, of the night descents that helped to make Muir a mountaineering legend in his own time.

Muir had the sawmill operating by the middle of March and was busy from sunup to sundown sawing pine trees uprooted in a furious storm two years earlier. A million board-feet of lumber had blown down in that storm, and Muir had agreed to operate the mill on Hutchings' firm agreement that no living tree would be cut in Yosemite Valley. Hutchings was happy to make such an agreement. He had wished to expand his hotel, but finding a cedar tree 175 feet high and 24 feet in girth in the way, he built around it. This room became the hotel kitchen, where Florantha Sproat cooked meals for dozens in a fireplace equipped with cranes and grills. Her pots and pans hung on a wire strung around the tree trunk. This "tree room," or "cedar room," became a warm and friendly social center when meal preparation was at less than crisis stage.

Muir did some of the finish work on the tree room. And at times, when the sawmill had produced enough lumber to last the builders a few days, he doubled as a carpenter.

The first trains began to cross the continent in 1869, and, though the trip was harrowing, tourists had been riding them. Eleven hundred visited Yosemite in 1869, and 1870 was bound to be a bigger year. Hutchings wanted to be ready, and the burden fell on Muir. As it turned out Muir was far more ready than Hutchings, and in a way that led to results neither of them even dimly imagined.

Chapter 15
The World, the Flesh and the Countess of Avenmore

Hutchings had not returned from Washington when the tourists began to arrive in April of 1870. Muir was pressed into service as a guide, in addition to running the sawmill. He was unpleased because these duties interfered with the explorations which had become a necessity to him. It had dawned on Muir — not all at once, but through an accumulation of observations — that to understand this mysteriously wonderful scene, he must learn to read a cryptogram written on the rocks and by the rocks in characters tens to thousands of feet high, in capital letters which he had not at first been able to perceive.

Muir therefore devoted every free hour of daylight to seeking vantage points from which he could read the story of Yosemite's making. His concentration did not blind him to the plants, from daisies to huge trees, nor to the birds and animals which made him so happy he felt that they must be happy also, least of all to the spiritual experiences which the environment so plentifully provided him. "I have not been in church a single time since leaving home," he wrote in March to his brother David. "Yet this glorious valley might well be called a church, for every lover of the Creator who comes within the broad overwhelming influence of the place fails not to worship as he never did before."

But these responses were, so to speak, fringe benefits. For the time Muir was dedicated to the problem of how, and by what means, God had created so extraordinary a place.

It became evident to him that God — whom he conceived to be a creative and harmonizing force, the force of love perpetually operating to shape and reshape the universe — had here used ice as his instrument. The evidence lay all about, once he had the vision to see it. "Erratic" boulders of kinds and colors found farther up the course of the Merced River could only have been quarried and brought by the slow, inexorable power of a glacier to their resting place above Glacier Point. Moraines left by melting ice lay like gigantic wreaths around many of the domes clustered about the valley's head. The bare granite mountains, which seem to wall off the upper end of the valley and box it in, he saw to have the characteristic sheep-backed form (*roche moutonnée*) of great rock monoliths overswept by glaciers. Glacier-polished walls and pavements, some in rug-sized patches, some in thousand-foot reaches, were scattered all down the valley.

Muir not only felt frustrated by having to guide the tourists; they frustrated him additionally by their behavior. "They climb sprawling to the saddles," he wrote Jeanne Carr, "like frogs pulling themselves up a stream bank among the bent rushes, ride up the valley with about as much emotion as the horses they ride upon — are comfortable when they have 'done it all' and long for the safety and flatness of their own homes." To the girls in the tourist parties, expensively and inappropriately dressed, and educated by finishing schools in the Victorian arts of husband hunting, Muir was an attractive enigma — a workman in stained pants who wore a wildflower in a buttonhole of a buttonless shirt and quoted poetry; a wild-looking fellow who ran the slanting heaps of rocks thrown down by earthquakes with the supple grace of a ballet dancer and the controlled strength of a mountain ram; who seemed never to have combed his beard, but thought one's prettiest clothes silly and thin-soled shoes outrageous. If a girl called a waterfall that seemed to leap from the sky "pretty" or "darling," his blue eyes would blaze at her, and not with affection. It did no good to go into a faint when a snake glided away over the rocks; he would just let you lie there.

FROM THE MUIR JOURNALS

Tourists camping in Yosemite Valley.

Muir grumbled so much about the girls that Harry Randall thought he must be a woman-hater. But it scarcely seems possible that a young man who could thrill to the touch of a sky blue flower blooming high in a hemlock tree would be unresponsive to an encounter with a soft hand pressed against his own. It may very well be that Muir's grumbling was an effort to protect himself against intrusions of the flesh upon his dedication to the rocks of Yosemite. In any case at least one of the girls wrote to him persistently, long after she left the valley, and another — the daughter of a wealthy and prominent Boston family — would have liked to marry him.

In spite of his annoyance, Muir gave the tourists his best. He could not do otherwise, for he had all the needs, urges and capabilities that go to make up a confirmed and effective communicator: the entertainer's desire for immediate response; an enthusiastic urge to share his experiences; the ability to present thought and feeling by expression and gesture as well as in words; and the quality called by such inadequate terms as "charisma" and "magnetism."

There were, of course, among the tourists some intelligent and responsive people who received Muir's offerings appreciatively — people who were willing to ride and climb with him to the heights from which he could point out the features which told the story of Yosemite's past, beginning with how the valley had been filled from wall to wall with a glacier some 3,000 feet thick. Ice had lain heavy on the uplands beyond the rim and in some places had spilled over into the valley itself. But most of the ice, Muir told his listeners, had come in through the two canyons that form a broad Y at the valley's head. On the north, where Tenaya Creek now runs like a silver thread, the Tenaya Glacier had come down, carving the granite ever deeper to make its own pathway. On the south, the Merced Glacier had entered as a wild, frozen cataract, excavating the steps of the Giant Stairway from whose treads Vernal Falls and Nevada Falls plunge 317 feet and 594 feet respectively.

His listeners found it impossible to doubt Muir's sincerity; they were convinced by the story, illustrated with reality, which he told to them. But the more interested ones immediately realized that he was talking geological heresy. They had equipped themselves with a recently published volume called *The Sierra Guide Book*, by Josiah D. Whitney, professor at Harvard University and chief geologist of the State of California. In this book, and also in his six-volume *Geological Survey of California*, Whitney stated flatly that there had never been a glacier in Yosemite, nor anywhere else in the Sierra Nevada. He believed that the valley had been created when the bottom dropped out and sank to an unknown depth. Then the chasm was partially filled by rock falling in a "wreck of matter and a crash of worlds."

Muir had great respect for Whitney, who had persisted in making his geological survey a genuine scientific accomplishment, even though he was forced to support it with his own funds when state legislators, who cared only to find out where mines might be located, withheld appropriations. Moreover Whitney had played an important part in getting Yosemite established as a state park.

Muir simply believed that Whitney was wrong about glaciers and said so with eloquence and visual proofs. Naturally the tourists argued Muir vs. Whitney among themselves, thus embroiling Muir in a controversy that increased in scope and fury almost at once.

Hutchings came home to the valley in mid-May, and Hutchings was not pleased. Whether he heard talk of Muir's botanical walks with his wife is not known. But his jealousy of Muir's popularity with the tourists was immediately evident. He had been Yosemite's prime interpreter for years, the respected local authority to whom everyone turned. Muir had very nearly supplanted him. Worse still, Muir was contradicting Whitney, the establishment authority on whom Hutchings relied completely for explanations of Yosemite's formation.

Hutchings immediately took over the guiding; Muir was to confine himself to the sawmill except on Sundays, when he was free to continue his explorations. This arrangement suited Muir very well, though Jeanne Carr prevented it from working out completely.

She and her husband had a wide and increasing acquaintance among intellectual and influential people. When any one of these showed interest in visiting Yosemite, Jeanne recommended that he look up Muir. Her intentions were to do a favor to the person she introduced and, more especially, to further Muir's development. She persistently tried to get him to come down out of the mountains and be "polished." Failing to persuade him, she directed some very good minds to him.

Two, who came in early summer of 1870 and went with Muir on overnight trips, proved especially congenial and valuable. J. B. McChesney, superintendent of Oakland's schools, became his close and hospitable friend. With Gilbert Winslow Colby, a bay area judge, Muir established an association whose results neither envisioned at the time of their first meeting, they being mainly concerned with the beds of ancient ice rivers seen in a glistening dawn from a high, bare peak called Sentinel Dome.

Therese Yelverton, once and maybe Countess of Avenmore, proved a more dubious emissary from the world of culture. A tiny woman with a heart-shaped face, red-brown hair, hands said to be exquisite and a voice called magical, she had been almost as much talked about and written about as her contemporary Queen Victoria, though for quite different reasons. During the Crimean War she had been a nurse; previously she had been lady-in-waiting to the Empress Eugenie of France. At the close of the war, she had married a Captain Yelverton, son and heir of an impoverished Irish viscount. A few months after the wedding, he left her to marry a wealthier woman. To escape conviction for bigamy, he sued for annulment, claiming that Therese was an immoral woman.

Therese turned tiger and fought for her rights through court after court for nine years. The Irish civil courts decided that she was, indeed, Yelverton's wife. But Yelverton carried his appeal to the final tribunal, the House of Lords, and these nobles, feeling that they must stand by a fellow aristocrat, annulled the marriage and awarded her child to Yelverton.

By this time Therese had used up most of the money she had inherited and began writing travel books to support herself. In July of 1870, she arrived in Yosemite with some female companions and a note from Jeanne Carr to John Muir.

Therese had never encountered any man like him. At first glance he looked like an English folk-character called "Tom of Bedlam." But in certain moods and lights, he reminded her of an Italian painting of Jesus Christ among the mountains. Like most women she thought his long auburn hair beautiful. His erudite discourse, enlivened by frontier images and lapses into Scotch dialect, was novel and intriguing. It occurred to Therese that she might make a good thing of a Yosemite novel with Muir as hero and little Floy Hutchings, matured to womanhood, as the tragic heroine.

More reporter than novelist, her first move was to charm Hutchings into assigning Muir to be her personal guide so that she could make notes on his conversation and borrow his journals. Muir thus found himself penned in by the sawmill on the one hand and Therese on the other, his explorations increasingly frustrated until, in August, another of Jeanne Carr's emissaries invited him to go on an expedition to the backbone of the Sierra.

The man was Joseph LeConte, professor at the University of California and already well on his way to becoming one of the nation's distinguished scientists.

At their first meeting, LeConte was astonished to find so intelligent and personable a man running a sawmill — and not for himself, but for Hutchings. The explanation was revealed to him during the expedition. In his account of it LeConte wrote: "Muir gazes and gazes and cannot get his fill. He is the most passionate lover of nature....He seems to revel in this life. I think he would pine away in a city or in conventional life of any kind."

LeConte had nine students with him, under the leadership of a young West Pointer who had organized them into a sort of amateur cavalry squad with rifles and bandoleers slung from their shoulders and pistols at their belts. They loved to wake the echoes with gunfire and impetuously forged ahead until a mountain forced them to leave or lead their horses. Then the scientists took the lead without slackening their rapt conversation concerning the meaning of mountain and gorge, grove and stream and cold blue lake. LeConte, convinced that Muir was essentially correct in identifying glaciers as the sculptors of this mountain landscape, returned to Berkeley talking enthusiastically about "Muir's discovery."

Muir returned to the sawmill and Therese, who had become increasingly infatuated and dependent. Therese was no amateur in the art of attracting men. But she did not at all realize Muir's sublimated love for Jeanne Carr. After one of his Sunday escapes into the higher country, he wrote to Jeanne: "I am rich — rich beyond measure, not in rectangular blocks of sifted knowledge or in thin sheets of beauty, hung picture-like about the halls of memory, but in unselected atmospheres of terrestrial glory diffused evenly throughout my whole substance...Would that you could share my mountain enjoyments! In all my wanderings through nature's beauty, whether it be among the ferns at my cabin door, or among the high meadows and peaks, or amid the spray and music of waterfalls, you are the first to meet me, and I speak to you as verily present in the flesh....I thank you for sending me so many friends, but I am waiting for you."

Muir grew increasingly restive in Therese's company, and especially so when they were trailed by hangers on who expected to gain some social advantage from association with a countess. When Therese invited him to go to China with her, Muir began looking for an excuse to be gone.

He did not find one until late fall, when Harry Randall decided that he had had enough of Yosemite. The two of them made their way down the gorge of the Merced, which is so narrow and rugged below Yosemite that no one before them had attempted its passage. Now, at the edge of winter, the canyon was dark, cold and inhospitable. Plentiful signs showed that this was grizzly bear country. Muir became unusually depressed and did not come out of it until they reached a grove of giant redwoods. There he wrote, in the purple sap of a Sequoia, an exuberant and boyish letter in which he compared the courtly bow Therese had made him at their parting unfavorably with the gestures of the "king of trees."

Once down in the San Joaquin Valley, Muir went to work for his friend Delaney. Therese wrote him several times, begging him to guide her down from Yosemite, for the snows were already deep on the uplands. He refused — to his subsequent remorse. Therese became separated from the party with which she started out and spent a night of snowstorm in a hollow tree. In the dim light of dawn, she discovered that her horse had disappeared. Wandering half-dazed in search of the trail, Therese fell into a twenty-foot declivity and lay unconscious until Leidig, a Yosemite hotel man, chanced to pass that way and followed the prints of her little feet.

Therese was as durable as she was unfortunate. Bruised, but not damaged, she was soon able to make her way to the San Francisco Bay area, where she finished her novel and in January sailed for the Orient aboard a small schooner. In her letters to Muir, she grieved because he was not with her and complained because critics were unkind toward the composite of reporting and wild melodrama she called a novel.

Chapter 16
The Hang-Nest

Geologists are among the more violent scientists and inclined to defend their opinions most vigorously. It is reported that a modern authority literally frothed at the mouth when shown a paper supporting a theory in which he disbelieved — one which has become a foundation stone of contemporary explanations of the dramatic relationships between the ocean floor and the continents. Josiah Whitney was no exception. When he learned that Muir was insisting that Yosemite had been carved by glaciers, the great man dismissed him with one contemptuous sentence, "What does that sheepherder know about it?"

Clarence Starr King, who was then making some literary success with dramatic accounts of his mountaineering feats in the Sierra as a member of Whitney's survey team, exploited every opportunity to pour scorn on Muir and support his former chief's cataclysmic theory of Yosemite's formation.

John Muir was no man to back off from a challenge. When Hutchings asked him to come back and run the sawmill, he accepted in order to tend to his unfinished business in the Sierra, which included searching for the still-active glaciers he had come to believe were still shaping the mountain landscape.

Quite possibly the decision saved his life. He was angry with Hutchings and had been tempted to go to Brazil with the Carr's eldest son — a venture which the boy did not survive.

An infected hand may also have preserved Muir by sapping his strength and thus forcing him to give up a plan to reach Yosemite through the Tuolumne Canyon, then unexplored and supposed to be impassable. It seems improbable that he could have gotten through it in winter.

The trip by way of the upland between Yosemite and the Tuolumne proved trying enough. The last couple of days were a wearying wallow through soft snow five feet deep on the level. Muir felt compensated by the extraordinary beauty of the dew crystals that formed on the new-fallen snow which now became the bottom of the atmosphere. He was reminded of the little plants that grow upon the leaves that sink to the bottom of a lake to form its nourishing floor.

Hutchings had broken his promise to keep Muir's cabin for him, and Muir's first chore was therefore to build himself a shelter. He extended the roof of the mill at one end to cover a snug room hanging out like an enclosed balcony. To reach it one had to climb a "chicken ladder" of sloping planks with slats nailed across them. This difficult passage had the advantage that people he disliked were afraid to come up to Muir's abode, which he called "a hangbird's hangnest." A more considerable benefit was the view: the single window looked down the valley with its pattern of groves framed by soaring walls of sculptured granite. In the roof were two hatchways. From one he could poke out his head to look at Half Dome, which mysteriously dominates the valley as

Muir's "hang-bird's hang-nest" at one end of the mill.

if it were a living presence; from the other hatch he could watch the drama of Yosemite Falls, changing in its descent with every shift of wind and light and weather. Muir had still another hole in the mill roof for undistracted star watching.

The snows fell heavily that winter, and when the melt began in late March the voice of Yosemite Falls rose to a sonorous climax that seemed to Muir "the grandest anthem of the year." The evening of April 3 was clear, and there would be a full moon. Muir grabbed up some chunks of bread and a blanket and climbed to a fern-grown ledge on the cliff's face. From here he could look down 500 feet into the fountain of upflung water where the upper fall strikes after its 1,400-foot plunge. When the moon came out, its light laid a double rainbow at the fall's foot. The fall itself was silver, cloudlike gauze at the edges and, within, dark with water masses and even blacker spaces like caverns. It seemed to him that every fountain of spray and every thunderbolt of sound and energy felt the hand of God.

As he watched, Muir was overtaken with desire to see what the fall looked like with the moon shining through it instead of upon it. The wind had swayed the descending water a little outward, away from a continuation of the ledge where he lay which ran back of the fall itself. It was very narrow in some places, but he managed to get out far enough to see the moonbeams sifting through the translucent edge of the fall. His look proved very brief. Heavy splashes striking the wall above his head gave him an instant of warning; then all became dark and water began to beat on him like gravel mixed with a choking spray.

The attack was savage and, to keep from being knocked off, Muir clung to some rock knobs protruding from the wall behind until the pounding slackened. Then he flung himself behind a big block of ice, partially frozen to the wall, and crouched there until the return of moonlight showed him that the fall had shifted outward. Then he made his way to the safety of Fern Ledge, built a fire to dry at least his socks and, as soon as he was calm enough to manage a pencil, wrote to Jeanne Carr describing the experience. "Oh, Mrs. Carr, that you could be here to mingle in this night-noon glory! . . . from the first baptism hours ago, you have been so present that I must fix you a written thought...."

Muir said nothing to Jeanne Carr about having feared for his life when the fall first struck, but admitted as much two days later in a letter to his sister Sarah — a letter decorated with a sketch of the hang-nest and enclosing a violet picked for her from the bank of the millrace when he went to shut the diversion gate that let in part of Yosemite Creek.

At the end of the month, he had a letter from Mrs. Carr saying that her friend Ralph Waldo Emerson was coming to Yosemite and expected to see something of Muir. Few Americans have been so much revered in their own time as Emerson. Thousands who had never heard him lecture or read his essays, let alone his poems, knew of him and had been at least a little affected by his ideas. It was almost as if he had been canonized by popular acclaim, though Emerson himself made no pretension of saintliness.

Whenever Emerson stepped out of Leidig's Yosemite Hotel, people clustered around his tall, slender figure to shake his hand if they could get close enough and simply to stare if they couldn't. For three days Muir hesitated to press in upon this beleaguered, frail-looking man whose thoughts had meant so much to him. Then, realizing that he might miss contact with Emerson altogether, he wrote a letter of respect and admiration and gave it for delivery to a young disciple named Thayer who had appointed himself protector, aide and gatherer of phrases that fell from the famous man's lips, whether jewels of wisdom or not.

The next day Emerson, with the inevitable Thayer, came to the mill and introduced himself. Emerson was sixty-eight — a more advanced age in those days than it seems now — but he scrambled up the chicken ladder to the hang-nest and spent a long time poring over Muir's maps, notes and sketches and, as Muir himself reported, "pumping unconscionably." Muir fascinated

Emerson. He came about as close as anyone the poet-philosopher had ever met to making an all-out individual effort to achieve the moral excellence which Emerson believed necessary if the promise of America's democratic society were to be realized. Muir's methods of striving for excellence were those Emerson favored: he relied on himself, trusting to the impulses that came to him in his best moments; he fostered these impulses by studying nature, the finest of men and the finest in Man.

During Emerson's remaining days in Yosemite, they were together a great deal, talking in the hang-nest, riding up and down the Valley while Muir unfolded the Yosemite story written on the cliffs and domes and by the waterfalls.

When Emerson left, Muir rode with him as far as the Mariposa grove of giant redwoods and was bitterly disappointed when members of his entourage prevented Emerson from sleeping out beside a blazing campfire among the huge, ruddy columns which have been breathing and reproducing for more years than we call A.D. When Emerson reached Oakland, he drove in a horse-cab through blinding fog to thank Jeanne Carr for the opportunity to know John Muir.

On the face of it, the almost instant friendship between America's most renowned intellectual and an ex-sheepherder, now a mill hand, seems extraordinary. But the two of them were much alike. After he reached home, Emerson added Muir to "My Men," a short list of acquaintances such as Carlyle, Wordsworth and Coleridge whom he had found most "excellent." Muir wrote of Emerson, "His smile was as sweet and calm as morning light on the mountains....He was sincere as the trees, his eyes sincere as the sun."

Chapter 17
Mountain Weariness, Mountain Hunger

Emerson's friendship and approval strengthened Muir's spirit as a cup of nourishing broth revives a half-starved body. The long struggle against the pressures from without and from within himself to become a conventional, settled, "respectable" member of society, sank to sleep in the depths of his subconsciousness. He felt, as he wrote in an intimate notebook, "born again . . . I'll interpret the rocks, learn the language of flood, storm and the avalanche . . . and get as close to the heart of the world as I can.

"Hunger and cold, getting a living, hard work, poverty, loneliness, need of remuneration, giving up all thought of being known, getting married, etc...." no longer made any difference.

Muir had now become a formidable mountaineer capable, according to Hutchings, who was scarcely his admirer, of accomplishing two or three days climbing between a Saturday evening and Monday morning. He now began a systematic examination of what he called the "alphabet canyons," the ice-marked pathways that would enable him to trace the Yosemite glaciers back to their birthplaces among the towering peaks of the Sierra's climax and the subsidiary ranges that form an intricate pattern upon the broad back of this enormous granite wave. Every time he could get away from the sawmill, he took off for the high regions with only a sack of bread and tea-leaves to sustain him during days, and sometimes nights, of climbing.

Though concentrating upon geology, Muir continued to observe the whole scene. He not only added to his own botanical collection, which he had considerable trouble in keeping track of because of his many moves, he also collected for others. One of these was Harry Edwards, a San Francisco actor whose collection of butterflies and beetles was then considered one of the finest in the world. When Edwards reported in a scientific journal on some Sierra specimens Muir had sent him, he wrote concerning one hitherto unknown butterfly, "I have named this exquisite little specimen for my friend John Muir, so well known for his researches into the geology of the Sierra Nevada, who has frequently added new and interesting species to my collection."

Although, as Muir had written, his work required him to neglect some of the ordinary needs and desires of men, it nevertheless brought him remarkably deep and full-bodied rewards. To use the resources of science to find out how

God had worked, and was working still, in these mountains was a religious enterprise — a mission that fed the spirit as well as the progressive solution of a real world mystery that enticed him at every stage with promise of a new adventure of the mind.

Books were not much help. He had to learn by the methods he enjoyed most — by climbing to heights from which he could read the big pictures and lying on the rocks to discover their makeup and the lines of cleavage along which some had broken and others might break. The pursuit left him no peace; rock forms and ancient ice haunted his dreams and filled his daytime mind.

One morning in early summer, some observations and interpretations that had been arranging themselves deep down, with only their tops showing above the level of consciousness, came together to form one of those enlightened hunches that have resulted in so many scientific advances, great and small. It was Sunday, and Muir was free to go. Climbing swiftly up through the rainbowed spray beside Yosemite Falls, he reached a canyon-mouth where his inspiration told him a small glacier had once lain, at first shedding ice, then slowly melting into Yosemite Valley. Up the canyon he came to a narrow gorge with walls polished and deeply grooved — the signature of a glacier wedging through under great pressure. All along the canyonsides were long banks of rock debris, the lateral moraines glaciers leave on their flanks when they melt. Before the day was out, he came to a shadowed hollow in the side of 11,000-foot Mt. Hoffman. Here the glacier must have been born and received the cold nourishment for its growth.

Muir was tremendously excited, for this ancient pathway was his first conclusive evidence that tributary glaciers had flowed into Yosemite Valley along the sides. Before dark he had measured and roughly mapped the twelve-mile length and five-mile breadth of the shallow bed. He then went to Yosemite for supplies, intending to return at once and measure the distance from the highest moraines to the bottom, which would give the depth. But another of Jeanne Carr's emissaries was waiting for him, this time Clinton L. Merriam, of the Smithsonian Institution.

The evidence Muir showed him convinced this influential scientist that the lonely rock-runner of the Sierras was near to adding a significant paragraph to the earth's dramatic story. He urged Muir to write up his findings as soon as his data were in shape to do so.

Muir was too engrossed in tracing the "big writing" that spelled out the formation of the Yosemite region to pause for any reporting except his field notes and plentiful sketches. He was ready even to commit his livelihood to his research. On July 10 he settled accounts with Hutchings, left his job at the sawmill and started on a trip among the jagged peaks of the Sierra's summit. He did not come back for several weeks, when hunger drove him down for a new supply of bread and tea.

He found John Daniel Runkle, president of the Massachusetts Institute of Technology, waiting for him. They left at once for a five-day trip to the summit peaks, tracing the canyons through which glaciers had flowed to Yosemite.

Runkle, like Merriam, was completely won over — not by Muir's accomplishments, but by Muir himself. He offered this tattered, wild-haired mountaineer a position on the faculty of any department of M.I.T. which he cared to join. When Muir refused, saying that his work and his very life were in these mountains, Runkle urged him at least to write up the glacial system of Yosemite for the Boston Society of Natural History.

Except for visits of the two scientists and King, an artist who had carried the box of butterflies down to Harry Edwards, Muir was painfully alone during that period. He had been dazed with disappointment that Jeanne Carr, whom he had expected to come that summer, had once more found reasons for not doing so. Nevertheless he turned down her invitation to visit the Carrs' home, saying that the power of the mountains was too great to resist. But he snatched at every opportunity to correspond with old friends with whom he could exchange thoughts and feelings. Some of the latter were violent.

To Professor Catherine Merrill, who had been primarily responsible for saving his eyesight after the accident in the Indianapolis wheel factory, he wrote to congratulate her on escaping (evidently by retirement from Butler University) from a "Christian college . . . I glanced through the regulations, order, etc., in the catalog . . . and the grizzly, thorny ranks of cold, enslaving 'musts' made me shudder as I fancy I should had I looked into a dungeon . . . full of rings and thumbscrews and iron chains . . . I suppose you were moved to go among those flint Christians by the same motives of philanthropy which urged you amongst other forms of human depravity....

"Come to Yosemite! Change the subject!"

And he immediately launched into an account of finding the path of the small glacier that had come inching down through Yosemite Creek Basin. This discovery dominated his thoughts during the summer months of 1871. He wrote a fuller account to Jeanne Carr, also telling her that the artist King's report on him was nonsense, that he was neither melancholy nor in need of polish, nor a home, nor a career as inventor. All he truly needed was freedom to search, without regard to time, for the true meaning and interpretation of God's mountains.

He had about five hundred dollars — enough to last him considerably more than a year. The Canadian brothers whose factory had burned still owed him money for his broom handles and rakes and would send it if he asked. Emerson, Merriam, Runkle and Jeanne herself had all been urging him to write. Perhaps he would do so; it would probably be easier than guiding tourists. But still he hung back, doubting that people would really be interested in what he had to offer, fearing that writing would interfere with his research.

One September day Muir climbed the western rim of Yosemite Creek Basin, coming out on top of the divide between the Merced and Tuolumne watersheds. Before him lay a large, shallow bowl and within it ten small, blue lakes like robins' eggs in a nest. Gaps in the wall of trees beyond the lakes seemed to sink suddenly, which suggested that he might be near the unexplored gorge of the Tuolumne. Skirting the bowl and pushing through the hemlocks, he came out on the brink of a tremendous cliff from which he looked straight down upon the bright, loud-talking river winding between groves some four thousand feet below.

Muir located a possible way down, but did not try it until the next morning. It proved impossible. He had to climb back up five hundred feet of granite smoothed by snow avalanches and so steep that he had to come down on his rump, wetting his hands with his tongue and pressing them against the rock to keep from sliding out of control.

His only hope of reaching the bottom, still 2,500 feet below, was, as he wrote, to climb up to the wall of the gorge itself and pick his way down its face, clinging to the bushes in the seams. "I knew from my observations of the previous day that this portion of the canyon wall was crossed by well-developed planes of cleavage that prevented the formation of smooth vertical precipices of more than a few hundred feet in height and the same in breadth. These can usually be passed without much difficulty."

It took two hours of what Muir euphemistically called "hard scrambling" to reach the floor of the canyon, here less than half a mile wide, in contrast to the walls, which in some places met the sky a full mile above him. An awesome place, but to Muir a scene of beautiful wonder. As he made his way down the river, shouting to warn the bears (for he had noted flowers freshly pressed down by their wallowing in the wild gardens he traversed), he saw no sign of man. If Indians had been here, they had left no trace, and Muir was the first of his own race to enter this lively solitude which belonged entirely to the humming insects and busy birds, the unseen animals, the river and the brooding wall where mile-deep ice had written its history. Every rock seemed to him "as elaborately carved and finished as a crystal or a shell."

He reached his camp among hemlock trees as the last light was fading and mechanically made his customary camp meal of dry bread and tea. He had walked some fifteen miles that day — a short stroll, except that two of the miles were almost vertical. He was just about done in and as he lay on his bed of boughs, he had a curious and memorable experience, born, as he said, of "mountain weariness and mountain hunger."

Sometimes when grave danger interposed between where he was and where he wanted to go — as when he descended to the brink of Yosemite Falls — his body seemed to take charge, shouldering his mind out of the way and, with some primitive understanding of its own, taking him safely through actions which his reason told him it was death to attempt. Now his mind seemed to go off on its own, wandering in realms of imagination and altered awareness. And when his spirit tried to return to his exhausted body, so that they could find rest together, he had some trouble in finding his own physical being.

Chapter 18
Birthplace of a Landscape

Returning to Yosemite Muir rested a while in a hotel owned by an amiable couple named Black, where he intended to hole up for the winter. It was during those late September days that he sidled into writing like a boy asking for his first date. He summarized his conclusions concerning glaciation in the Yosemite region with supporting data in two detailed letters, one to Merriam at the Smithsonian and the other to Runkle at M.I.T. And he combined and revised parts of these letters into an article on his discovery of the bed of the small glacier which had lived and died in Yosemite Creek Basin. This he sent off to the *New York Tribune*. Muir then resumed what he considered, at the time, to be his real work — tracing the "alphabet canyons" through which glaciers had come to Yosemite Valley, this time exploring the tributaries to the south.

If... he thought... if the Merced and its tributaries were stood upright, they would look like a gigantic elm tree. The lower trunk would be Yosemite Valley, the tributaries the branches dividing and subdividing into twig-like brooks, some down-curving, some rising upward to the sky, scratching peaks the Sierra crest. And each branch would be hung with adornments: bright, flowery meadows on the lower reaches of the streams; small, glistening blue-green lakes on the branchlets and twigs. But to Muir the design was more beautiful in its real, sloping position than his imaginary tree, however lovely this might be, shining in sunlight and starlight. And it gave him greater satisfaction to use his imagination to recreate the way the design actually developed.

Steeply inclined glaciers had ground out smooth basins in the massive granite of which the Sierras are mainly made. When these glaciers melted, lakes were formed behind the terminal moraines — the curving piles of rock the glaciers had carried and dropped when they stopped growing and began to melt. But the moraines were not entirely made of boulders. Much rock had also been crushed into grains — some as fine as stone-ground flour. Weathering had crumbled the surface of most of the boulders to add still more fine material. Especially in spring, when the streams ran violently, some of this detachable stuff washed out and was carried to the lakes downstream as extremely nourishing soil. Gradually the lower lakes were filled, except for a stream running through a meadow. Flowering plants and trees grew where first the shining ice, then the sparkling water, had been.

Early in October, John Muir made his way up the basin of the Illilouette — one of the largest and lowest branches of the Merced "tree" — passing from older meadows where the growth was lush, to boggy newer ones where he often had to wade, then along a chain of partly filled lakes with flowers and trees growing on new soil that had washed down and settled around their margins.

It was Indian Summer and spectacularly beautiful. The glacier-scrubbed granite of the canyon walls glowed silver. Clumps and bands of flame-yellow aspens and willows adorned the lower flanks; on the canyon floor goldenrod made gold on gold with crimson and purple of fall-turned leaves to set it off.

But Muir was heading for some formidable peaks in the Merced Range, which juts out irregularly toward Yosemite Valley from the Sierra crest. As he mounted higher, the lakes became more and more naked. And he presently found himself between huge lateral moraines — rock walls two hundred feet high. Beyond them loomed two dark, jagged peaks — one red, one black — which still bore on their crests the slate that had overlain the granite when the Sierra was young. Except for pines growing high above on sunlit benches, the vegetation was dwarfed, and presently even these strugglers disappeared. The canyon had a strange, raw, unfinished look — a primordial look, as if the landscape were just being born. Icicles bordered the stream Muir was following. This was not a safe place; as the sun warmed the rocks above, small avalanches came rattling down from cliffs and pinnacles.

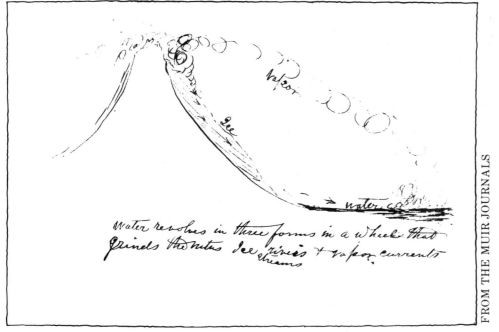

A melting glacier contributes to the water cycle.

The canyon widened into an amphitheater sloping toward a wildly fractured ridge between the red mountain and the black. Just inside the entrance, Muir made camp, scrounged enough branches for a bed and scribbled the day's notes before the night sky came down over the canyon like a lid.

The sun shone bright, but not warm, when he woke. Neither the birds nor the high mountain animals were out. The primitive fears that had haunted him in this strange place the night before subsided and a growing excitement took its place. He pressed on over a series of terminal moraines laid out in beautiful arcs across the ampitheater, each marking the place where a glacier had held its own for a while during its melting period. The stream now curved off toward a gloomy hollow in the black mountain, which today is called Mount Merced. The stream now ran among naked rocks between borders of ice and bare earth. Nothing grew here. Muir had never been in such a place.

Nor had he seen such a stream, its waters grey as if with a peculiar sediment. He dipped his hands and drew them out covered with stuff that reminded him of the gritty paste that comes off a water-lubricated stone grinding wheel when one sharpens an axe. "Glacier mud!" he said to himself, "Mountain meal!" — knowing this material to be stone pulverized by a glacier to create soil.

Looking up he saw that the stream gurgled out from beneath a loosely piled, muddy and unsettled-looking wall of boulders, sixty feet high at the lowest and a hundred where highest. He climbed with great care, for the huge stones were scarcely more firmly positioned than the rubble pushed before the blade of a bulldozer.

On top he found himself standing on a rock-strewn surface of granular ice crystals, more like hail than snow. It stretched away into a hollow in the black mountain. Nearby the ice was banded with lines of dirt and rock which had exactly the same shape as the wall he had climbed — the same shape as the moraines he had clambered over in the ampitheater below. Where he stood the bands were crowded closely together, as if their motion had been slowed by the massive wall in front of them which, he now saw, could be nothing but a terminal moraine being pushed slowly forward. In that moment John Muir realized that he was standing on a glacier, not stationary, not melting, but alive and inching downward.

It was too much for his mind to accept at once. "What?" he said to himself. "What?" like a child wakened to look at a harvest moon or his first Christmas tree. When scientific discipline brought him out of his trance-like state, he made his way upward to the place where the ice joined the mountain wall. All across the head was a deep crack twelve to fourteen feet wide, the typical upper crevasse of a glacier — the *bergschrund*. Creeping cautiously along the edge, Muir found places where the beautifully layered structure of the glacier was revealed: pure individual crystals matted together just under the surface; next, porous ice of different shades of pale color; and at thirty feet, where the pressure from above was great, blue ice in bands, some pale as the horizon, some dark as the sea on a windy day.

Still bemused Muir zig-zagged down into the crevasse. He entered chambered recesses where icicles hung like crystal chandeliers through which the subdued light pulsed indescribably. Water dripped and tinkled above, and from below came strange, solemn murmurs from water finding its way through fissures and veins.

He was in shirtsleeves and soon grew cold. But it was hard to leave this wonderland, and when he finally climbed out he was still transported, not only by the beauty of the scene, but by so suddenly having the experience which is one of the scientist's great rewards — to predict that something exists and then to find it in reality.

As he threaded his way down the glacier among the little rills making music in their shining channels, the practical side of Muir's mind began to grapple with the problem of what he must do to fully convince himself of what he had found and, beyond this, to convince others. No one else believed that there were living glaciers in the Sierra.

Chapter 19
Storm, Ice and Earthquake

hen Muir wrote Jeanne Carr that he had been shouting among the peaks like a preacher in revival time, he was not exaggerating much. On his lonely "raids," as he called his expeditions into the high country, he yelled to keep himself company and to let out his enthusiasms; since he had been brought up to do so, it was natural to praise God, intending no offense to the spirit of scientific inquiry. He also sang, whistled, recited poetry; he talked to flowers, animals, birds and even moonlit drops of water falling from ferns.

But in the days following his discovery of ice that seemed to be an active glacier, he found virtually nothing to talk to. He pushed upward to the bare and freezing flank of 13,000-foot Mt. Lyell and discovered, both there and on neighboring Mt. McClure, ice and stone structures that had the same characteristics as the one on Merced Peak, though they were considerably larger. At first sight they looked like snowfields — which Whitney insisted they actually were. Proof that these were glaciers was a first requirement, and Muir therefore cut chunks of ice at different depths and started back to Yosemite lugging them.

Eight miles from the valley, he realized that a snowstorm was coming and holed up, literally, at Lake Washburn (which Muir called "Shadow Lake" and sometimes "Lake Nevada"). On the south side the granite plunges a sheer 1,500 feet into deep water, and the entire bowl where the lake lies is so cliff-bound that no one except occasional Indians had walked on the shores until Muir came. The bowl had been excavated, he believed, by the southernmost glacier descending from Mt. Lyell. A fine place to weather out a storm, which is a far better and safer thing to do than trying to fight through.

Muir selected a sheltered spot under the overhanging lip of a huge, weathered boulder, cut boughs for his bed, then dragged as much firewood as possible within easy reach. The notes he scribbled while the storm expended its passionate energy above him indicate that he had learned well the lesson his father's penury taught him during bitter Wisconsin winters: *as long as you have a fire, you won't be too cold.* The notes also reflect Muir's method of contenting himself under conditions so severe that most people would think them hostile. He concentrated upon the wonder of the scene, let it have its way with him and wished that he could share his experiences. "The whole living lake with its seamless basin is a pure mountain cup, perfect and pure, as if, like one unbroken snow crystal it had come softly down from the sky.... John the Baptist was not more eager to get all his fellow sinners into the Jordan than I to baptize all (of) mine in the beauty of God's Mountains."*

The storm blew itself out in three days, leaving a still, white mountain world. Muir made snowshoes of bark and came swiftly down to the relative comfort of Black's Hotel, now empty except for himself and a carpenter. He was out of provisions and, as he passed through the village to its single store, his appearance frightened little Cosie Hutchings, who ordinarily adored him. His clothes were in tatters. His blue eyes, surrounded by the black of charcoal smeared on to protect his skin from the glare of sun on snow, had a strange, unearthly look, for he was still under the spell of his experiences and the greater wonders his vision made from them.

The cleanest, best appointed accommodations in the Sierra were those of the bath house behind the Cosmopolitan Saloon in Yosemite Village. It seems inevitable that Muir enjoyed a long, hot soak — inexpressible luxury for one who has been cold and dirty for over two weeks — even before he packed his ice samples in moss, ready to be sent by the next pack train to Professor Joseph LeConte in Berkeley.

The Cosmopolitan Saloon gave him material for the second of the several pieces he wrote that winter for the *New York Tribune*. The first, on ancient Yosemite glaciers, was published on December 5, 1871, and paid for. Muir was happily astonished, for he did not realize how experienced a writer he had already become through journal-keeping and letters to family and friends, nor did he understand that remembering and loving and living with the words of great writers may be better preparation than formal scholarship. The "seven whiskey soirées a week" at the Cosmopolitan must have been lively, considering the 150-proof whiskey brought up in kegs by pack train, and Muir was no doubt welcome whenever he cared to attend. Like the celebrants, he was a "working man" and a mountain man, a spell-binding yarn spinner who knew all the words and could sing and dance if the occasion arose.

Nevertheless that winter he was longing for people with whom he could go beyond joking and discussing the purely physical facts of life. He reached out more than ever through correspondence with old friends and new: with Merriam and Runkle and LeConte; with Emily Pelton, who was coming to California; and with Professor Catherine Merrill, who wanted to send out her nephew, Merrill Moores, for a Sierra summer with John Muir. And, as always, he wrote to Jeanne Carr.

He had a great deal to tell her, for he spent most of his days and many nights roaming the winter-bound valley — to get, as he had said, "close to the heart of the world" by sharing with living nature the experiences which nature's elemental forces provide. In Yosemite these forces create spectacles as dramatic as the cliffs and domes among which they move.

On the sixteenth day of December, a strange, crimson cloud thrust across

* Linnie Marsh Wolfe, *John of the Mountains*, p. 85.

the sky to herald a storm that dropped ten inches of snow on the valley floor in one night and so much more on the uplands that the streams were choked, hushing the voices of the falls. Heavy snows alternated with torrential rains creating, at first, snow avalanches booming down from all around the valley's rim. These changed to water avalanches while Muir was dressing on the morning of the nineteenth and, when he stepped outside, the entire rim and upper walls were spurting with fountains. Falls that were normally mere silver threads had grown to the size of Yosemite Falls, and there were dozens of newcomers. The whole valley throbbed as if in response to some gigantic organ. Amid the clamor Yosemite Falls was strangely hushed until mid-afternoon, when the smothering snow was finally washed out and ten times its usual maximum of water came down with an earth-shaking crash like that of a rock avalanche.

The furious wind, meanwhile, made a chaos of clouds and rain in which Yosemite's domes and pinnacles seemed to change form and position as their watery drapery shifted to conceal and reveal.

This "jubilee of waters" lasted for three days, in which no living thing — not man nor insect, beast or bird — moved abroad, except for John Muir. Dr. Carr took Muir's description of the event to Benjamin Avery, who had succeeded Bret Harte as editor of the *Overland Monthly*, the best of the lively magazines published in San Francisco during the early years when that city was relatively independent of the eastern literary establishment. Avery gladly accepted the piece as an article, thus establishing for Muir a hospitable and relatively remunerative market close at hand.

In January Muir climbed an incense cedar to cut fragrant boughs adorned with golden staminate flowers. He sent these to special friends, among them Ralph Waldo Emerson, who thanked him in a remarkably graceful and warm letter. "I have everywhere testified to my friends, who should also be yours, my happiness at finding you — the right man in the right place — in your mountain tabernacle."* But Emerson was convinced that Muir had been in the Sierra long enough and that he should rejoin civilized society. "There are drawbacks to solitude, who is a sublime mistress but an intolerable wife," he wrote. "Here in Cambridge, Gray** is at home, and Agassiz will doubtless be after a month or two returned from Tierra del Fuego . . . you must find your way to this village and when you are tired of our dwarf surroundings, I will show you better people.... I send two volumes of (my) *Collected Essays* by book post."

Muir was pleased and complimented, but he was in no respect ready to leave the Sierra. The idea of going to that "heathen town," as he called Boston, with its "high-heated educational furnaces," frightened and repelled him. And he had a great deal of detailed exploration to accomplish before the scientific community would believe that he had discovered living glaciers. Joseph LeConte had been unable to make up his mind as to whether Muir's

* William F. Badè, *The Life and Letters of John Muir*, Vol. I, pp. 259-60.
** Dr. Asa Gray, the foremost American botanist of that time.

samples were actually glacier ice. He reserved judgment pending further proofs, which could not be gathered until warmer weather brought the High Sierra out from under its deep mantle of snow.

Meanwhile the ice cone was building on the shelf where Upper Yosemite Falls strikes at the end of its 1,430-foot plunge. Throughout most of each winter, echoes are waked unpredictably by the crashing strike of huge sheets of ice loosened by the sun from the cliff behind the fall. Each night the fragments are cemented by frozen spray into a symmetrical structure which, in some years, grows to a height of more than 300 feet. At its climax, this cone sits more than 1,000 feet above the valley floor, shining like an improbable pearl.

Muir had been fascinated by the phenomenon since his first visit to the Valley. He had tried repeatedly to climb the cone, for he wanted to look into its mouth — the cone being hollow, receiving the descending waters like a reverse volcano and ejecting them through arch-like openings in its base. But the water is so violently churned within that icy spray spouts up around the entering column and blows down the slope in a smother that, together with the falling ice masses, drove Muir back each time he attempted the ascent.

One exceptionally calm day in March he succeeded in backing far enough up the slope so that the choking blast passed over him. Turning about he mounted slowly but steadily by cutting steps with his axe. He had almost reached the top and was wondering how far he could see through the chaos within that made the entire cone throb like a gigantic drum, when a huge sheet of ice, detached from high above, struck near him with a stunning crash. Great fragments whizzed around him like shrapnel. Thanking his guardian angel, Muir got out of there before the next ice-mass fell.*

Another striking feature of the Valley fascinated Muir as much as the ice cone and puzzled him still more. All along the base of the walls, rock debris had accumulated to depths ranging from fifty to two thousand feet. In some places piles of boulders ("taluses") extended so far out onto the valley floor that it is natural to suppose that they are the remains of towers and pinnacles thrown down by earthquakes. Yet no earthquake had been reported from this region during the hundred years since the Spaniards discovered the Sierra Nevada. The Yosemite Indians had no earthquake legend, as far as Muir could discover. It must have been a long time between quakes — if indeed earth tremors were the cause of the strangely-placed rock piles.

Muir had been building a new cabin, with what he called a "Carr corner" (actually a gallery bedroom under the rafters), in anticipation of a visit from his dearest friends. It stood near the river; behind it Sentinel Rock towered three thousand feet into the immaculate sky. By late March of 1872, the cabin was nearly enough completed for him to sleep there.

* On another day, when the wind moved the fall aside so that the cone stood clear in the sunlight, Muir was able to look into the mouth from Fern Ledge, two hundred feet above the cone's crest. The lips were black with debris, and he estimated the opening to be one hundred feet north and south, by two hundred feet east and west — about the normal early-spring dimensions of the fall itself.

Rock debris at the base of Yosemite Valley wall.

Deep in the night of March 26, he was thrown almost out of his bunk by a tremendous blow from beneath, as if a pile-driver had struck upward. In the next instant the cabin was shaken as a terrier shakes a rat. Though Muir had never before been through an earthquake, he had no doubt that he was doing so now. Frightened, but at the same time tremendously exhilarated, he pulled on trousers and shoes and ran out into the moonlight. The shocks became more violent, and a twisting motion was added, making it as difficult to walk the solid ground as the deck of a storm-tossed ship. Looking up he realized that if, as it seemed, Nature was wrecking Yosemite, Sentinel Rock would come down on his cabin. He took shelter behind a big pine tree, hoping that the massive trunk would deflect at least the smaller fragments.

The pathetic inadequacy of his shelter he found out shortly. The valley seemed to be holding its breath while strange, muffled, bubbling, rumbling sounds from underground mingled with the frightened whispering of the pines in a prelude that ended in a tremendous roar.

Eagle Rock, a lonely spire half a mile up the Valley, was falling in a fifteen hundred-foot arc of green fire created by the friction between the great blocks into which the tower had broken. The mass descended as gently and perfectly as a rainbow and struck with a crash louder than the combined thunder of all storms Muir had heard in his lifetime.

Muir was off and running before the echoes died, all fear wiped out by his compelling urge to join this new-born earthquake talus in its first moments of existence. The rocks were still warm when he climbed up on them, and groaning and grating as they settled into their places. But he could see no further motion except small stones pattering down from the cliff where Eagle Rock had stood. A dust cloud hung overhead like a ceiling. The air was pungent with the odor from a grove of Douglas fir trees that had been mashed like weeds — ironic reminder of Muir's feeble attempt to shelter himself behind a pine.

A second severe shock came about half past three, and all the rest of the night the ground trembled gently to the accompaniment of hollow, rumbling sounds. But no other part of the valley's walls came down; the earthquake's most lasting effect was upon the human inhabitants. The Indians moved to the center of the valley and bathed in the cold river to prepare themselves for life in the next world. The white inhabitants gathered in front of Hutchings' Hotel to discuss the quickest way to get out before the bottom sank and left the trails ending thousands of feet above the floor. Muir tried to joke them out of their panic by telling them that Mother Nature was simply bouncing them on her knee. But at that moment an after-shock set the domes to trembling like jelly and the heavy-tasseled boughs of the pines jerking like jumping-jacks. The men muttered that Muir was as crazy as they had thought and departed — the storekeeper illogically handing his keys to Muir for safe keeping.*

The earth continued to tremble, off and on, for over two months. Muir estimated the strength of the diminishing tremors by the ripples set up in a bucket of water he kept in the cabin. Carlo, the St. Bernard, who was once again with Muir, also proved an effective indicator. Every time his footing shook, the big dog looked around to find what was shaking it.

---

* This *trembler* is known as the Inyo Earthquake because its epicenter was in Inyo County, southeast of Yosemite. It was at least as powerful (8.5 on the Richter scale) as the earthquake that devastated San Francisco in 1906. The Inyo quake destroyed the mountain town of Lone Pine and killed many of its inhabitants.

Chapter 20
The Speed of Ice

Muir's refusal to leave the Sierra by no means deprived him of the intellectual companionship his friends prescribed. Four distinguished scientists visited him that summer of 1872.

First to arrive was Joseph LeConte, who spent several days with Muir exploring his new discoveries. The evidence that these were actually glaciers now seemed to him overwhelming, and he returned to the University of California an enthusiastic and articulate supporter of Muir's interpretation of ice action in the Sierra.

A few weeks later came John Tyndall, director of the British Royal Institution, and one of the great leaders — whose number included Darwin, Huxley, Faraday and Agassiz — of the scientific revolution in the mid-nineteenth century. Among Tyndall's several research interests was the motion of glaciers. He had already made important contributions to the understanding of this curious and complex phenomenon. And, at fifty-two, he still loved to climb mountains. Though neither man left an account of his exploration of the newly-found glaciers, it is virtually certain that Muir took Tyndall to see them, and that Tyndall endorsed Muir's conclusions.*

In mid-July Merrill Moores arrived. He had been first to greet Muir at the home of the Indianapolis family that saved his sight after his accident in the wheel factory. Now an able lad of sixteen, Merrill made himself useful almost at once. He had scarcely gotten settled in Muir's cabin when Asa Gray, the Harvard botanist, arrived. He and Muir were already acquainted through correspondence, and they set off immediately for a week of botanizing within, above and beyond Yosemite Valley. With Merrill to take care of the horses when they reached a promising location, the two scientists rambled and scrambled on foot through days that delighted them both. Gray was then

* When Tyndall left, he gave Muir his aneroid barometer, a readily-carried instrument which registers atmospheric pressure and, hence, the height of mountains, since pressure decreases with altitude. It was a precious gift because Muir, lacking such an instrument, had been forced to estimate altitudes. Some months later a box containing an inclinometer and other specialized instruments arrived from Tyndall — evidence, not only of his regard for Muir, but of his generous concern for the advancement of science. He donated all of the fees (amounting to several thousand pounds) from his highly successful lecture tour of the United States in 1872-73, for the education of young American scientists.

sixty-two, but his long legs, heart and lungs were still muscled for walking, and he proved to be one of the few men who could keep up with Muir in rough country. He was as kindly and companionable as he was intellectually powerful, and his friendship with Muir ripened rapidly.

Before he left Gray urged Muir to join the Harvard faculty, promising that respected and influential friends would further his career. Muir declined. But Gray was not willing to give up so good a botanist to geology if he could help it. As soon as he reached Cambridge, he sent Muir a set of his own works (several of which were standard texts and reference works) to get him studying botany again. He also left Muir money to defray the costs of shipping plants he particularly wanted for the arboretum at Harvard, of which Gray was director, and any other specimens Muir found curious and interesting.*

Late in the summer John Torrey, Gray's most influential teacher and later his collaborator, also visited Muir. "Never shall I forget," Muir wrote, "the charming evenings I spent with Torrey in Yosemite, and with Gray, after the day's rambles were over...and they told stories of their lives, Torrey telling fondly all about Gray, Gray about Torrey..."**

In August Agassiz arrived in Berkeley on his way home from Tierra del Fuego. Muir wrote to him, outlining his discoveries of glaciers vanished and present and urging Agassiz to come and see them for himself. But Agassiz was then sixty-five, and his trip to the extremity of South America had all but finished him. On his part Muir was too impatient to get on with the study of his Sierra glaciers to descend to the lowlands. He received, nevertheless, Agassiz' wholehearted endorsement. In a letter to Muir, Mrs. Agassiz reported that when her husband read Muir's account of his discoveries he said, "Here is the first man who has any adequate conception of glacial action!" And when LeConte remarked that Muir probably knew more about what had been done by glaciers to transform the Sierras, Agassiz banged his fist on the table and exclaimed, "He knows all about it!"

Pleased and gratified as he was, Muir recognized that this was the kind of enthusiastic overstatement a scientist permits himself only in private. A great deal more cold and rugged work had to be done before the scientific community would accept his new truths as true. He therefore gently and affectionately turned aside Jeanne Carr's suggestion that he stay in their home and make trips to study the mountains of the Coast Range. She was right, he told her, in saying that his best companions were those who shared his devotion to nature and responded to it as he did. But spiritual contact was the most real contact of all, he said. He was learning to live with his true friends without ever seeing them, and no distance — however measured —

* A mid-Sierra specimen, which Gray described in a letter to Muir as "that little mouse-tailed Ivesia," proved new to science. Gray named it *Ivesia muiri* and told his friend to find some new plant higher up so he could call it *Muiri glacialis*.

** Torrey's discovery of an unusual, picturesque variety of pine on the cliffs at the northern edge of San Diego has kept his name green in tawny Southern California. Botany has the "Torrey pine"; society has the Torrey Pines State Park and the golf course which it embraces.

could separate them.

So saying, he took off with Merrill Moores for the glacier-jeweled flanks of Mt. Lyell and Mt. McClure, which stand close together near the southeast corner of Yosemite National Park. On the east bank of the McClure Glacier, Muir built a framework of sticks and hung from it a horsehair weighted with a stone. Sighting past this plumb line, Muir directed Merrill with hand signals in driving four stakes in a straight line. The fourth was approximately half way across the glacier. Merrill planted a fifth stake midway between the fourth and fifth, but considerably above, approximately in the center of the glacier's top-to-bottom dimension.*

When Muir returned on October 6, forty-five days later, the stake nearest the east bank had moved downward eleven inches, the one half-way across, forty-six inches and the stake above, forty-five inches. The center of the ice stream was thus flowing at the rate of approximately an inch a day, the sides about one-fourth as rapidly. The McClure Glacier thus had the characteristic motion observed in all glaciers that had been measured; there could no longer be any doubt that it was "alive" — that is, neither stationary nor receding.

Muir at this time was under considerable pressure to make his work public before others appropriated it. Professor Samuel Kneeland, Secretary of the Massachusetts Institute of Technology, had gathered some letters from Muir to M.I.T.'s president and together with "Death of a Glacier," published in the *New York Evening Tribune*, "hashed them into a compost called a paper for the Boston Society of Natural History, gave me credit for all the smaller sayings and doings, and stole the broadest truth to himself. I have the proof sheets...."

In September Joseph LeConte had made the first announcement of Muir's discovery of living glaciers in the Sierra in a lecture. LeConte gave full credit to Muir, but Jeanne Carr feared that less scrupulous persons might preempt his discoveries.

In the same letter in which he wrote off Kneeland, Muir outlined his glacial discoveries thus far and also, with Victorian delicacy, admitted that he was pooped. "I got down last eve, and boo! was I not weary? Besides pushing through the rough upper half of the great Tuolumne Canyon** I have climbed more than twenty-four thousand feet in these ten days!...three times to the top of the glacieret on Mount Hoffman and once to Mounts Lyell and McClure."

Muir's purpose in climbing the mountains mentioned was, of course, to read the evidence of glacier flow provided by the stakes he had planted. He had also planted stakes on Red Mountain.***

---

* This technique had been developed by Agassiz, Tyndall and a glaciologist named Forbes.

** "Rough" is an extreme understatement. All of this part of Tuolumne's narrow slot is extremely difficult, and Muir Gorge is so narrow that he and Galen Clark (who seems to have been with him on this trip) had to take to the furiously rushing stream and vault from boulder to boulder with poles.

*** These were the first of a sequence of glacier measurements in the Sierra which is still continuing. Muir discovered sixty-five glaciers during the ten years in which he studied the range intensively. There are about the same number today. Some, such as the first one he discovered on Merced Mountain, have vanished. Others have been born. We are in what geologists call the "Little Ice Age," which began about four thousand years ago after a long period in which there were no glaciers at all in the Sierra. The advance, retreat, wastage and growth of glaciers provide extremely sensitive and important information concerning changes in climate, both local and world wide.

Chapter 21

The Ultimate Scootcher

<hr>

Muir's body had responded to a quarter century of hard labor and physically demanding adventure by developing not only extraordinary endurance, but equal capacity for recovery. Exhilaration nourished by discovery among scenes that fed his almost insatiable appetite for beauty and, also, by the athlete's joy in pitting himself against tremendous odds, now gave him an additional range of capability. On October 7, the day after his weary return, he wrote a very long letter to Jeanne Carr outlining his discoveries of the past two years and the theories derived from them. Next morning he set out again for a ten-day trip to the crest of the Sierra.

In this region so many high peaks crowd the great sweeps of landscape that views tend to be inspiring rather than picturesque, in the sense that they seldom compose themselves into natural pictures. But Muir, returning along a tributary of the upper Tuolumne, encountered an extraordinary view.

Turning about where the stream entered a canyon at the foot of an ample meadow he stood transfixed, for the canyon walls framed Mts. Lyell and McClure, towering into a blue heaven, and below them were ridges and domes of granite draped with dark forests, descending to the meadow which was aflame with small trees and bushes wearing the colors of autumn. He regretted his inability to paint this scene enough to record his frustration in his journal.

Muir had no more than gotten a fire going when little Floy Hutchings emerged from the bushes and vines which enveloped his Yosemite cabin. She was leading three men. The evident leader — a broad-shouldered, bearded person with a mop of intractable wavy hair — announced in a deep voice with a Scotch burr in it that he was William Keith and handed Muir a letter of introduction from Jeanne Carr. He and his companions were painters looking for pictures. Did Muir know of any Sierra views they might like to paint? Muir said he knew exactly the one: he had seen it on his way home to Yosemite and would take them to it tomorrow. Meantime how about a cup of tea?

In the course of the afternoon and evening they spent together, it came out that Keith had been born in Scotland in the same year as Muir and that, like Muir, he had Highlanders for ancestors. And it also became clear that their natures responded to one another in a way that predicted a friendship in which deep affection and admiration were expressed through a kind of verbal boxing, counter-jibe answering jibe, counter-insult responding to insult.

When, next day, they reached the mouth of the canyon which framed the magnificent view, Muir reined his horse aside so the artists could discover for themselves. They dismounted in silence and stood in wonder, until Keith — unable to contain his ebullient spirits — dropped the reins and dashed forward, shouting and waving his arms.

The next morning Muir left the artists busily sketching and making color notes and took off by himself for Mount Ritter, the bastion peak that stands between the Merced and San Joaquin River watersheds. The weather was golden, but Muir had been caught in enough winter snow storms to warn the artists that, though he expected to be back in three days, he might be gone as long as ten.

Mt. Ritter was in sight when he made camp above eleven thousand feet, beside a cold lake in a tangle of evergreens so dwarfed and matted by the winter snows that the interior was like a many-chambered cave. Small birds hopped in to keep him company, for they had not learned to fear men. He kept a fire going at a safe distance from the tangle and went out to it several times during the night to warm himself, for he had no blankets. A small waterfall pouring into the lake made a lonesome music.

It was a beautiful morning when he set off along the crest of the range — the high peaks bathed in light and the Mono Desert stretching away eastward in a warm glow. But as he worked his intricate way southward, by-passing the most difficult obstacles, he found himself hemmed in by rugged mountain spurs, ancient glacier moraines and huge projecting buttresses of fractured rock. For a while he even lost sight of Mt. Ritter.

It reappeared spectacularly. Muir had mounted a ridge separating two gorges and thus gained a commanding view. Completely blocking out all else stood Ritter's dark, seemingly vertical wall, its crest 13,156 feet above the sea and 4,000 feet above the chasm between itself and Muir. From where he stood Muir could not see this gorge, and the glacier sweeping down the mountain's flank appeared to come almost to his feet before curving off westward to drop bergs into a dark blue lake: one mountain, one glacier, one lake — all enveloped in one huge blue shadow.

He crossed the chasm and began to work his way up the glacier. He saw no flower or blade of grass, no living creature; he heard no sound except gurgling of little streams in the glacier's blue veins and the rattle and echo of falling stones. As he went Muir lectured himself. Ritter had never been climbed; Whitney's survey team had reported it completely inaccessible. And so seemed the great dark wall, fractured into a labyrinth of towers, battlements and crumbling buttresses gashed with avalanche chutes and steep gulches. Besides he might get caught by a sudden storm among these bleak crags where there was no shelter and nothing to burn. He would not climb this mountain now, he told himself. He would only investigate its skirts and come back next season.

Yet when he reached an avalanche chute, partly filled with angular blocks that aided climbing, he went up, hammering the ice off the rocks as he advanced. It was as if Ritter had challenged him, as he had been challenged in boyhood by the steep slate roof of his father's high house and the other scootchers in which he had risked his young life.

Dangerous places became more frequent, and Muir felt increasingly uneasy because his reason told him not to go on. Anxiety grew exponentially when he realized that he no longer had the option to descend, that it would be more dangerous now to try to go down than to continue to the top.

The somber, mottled rocks of Ritter are some millions of years old — remnants of the ancient crust that once covered the Sierra and were lifted to their present height by molten rock welling from deep in the earth and finally hardening into granite. The old rock tends to fracture into sheer walls, knife-like ridges and angles that can slice one's hand. Knobs and crannies tend to be fragile and thus insecure supports for the climber. When Muir, having reached a height of 12,800 feet, according to his barometer, came to the foot of a fifty-foot cliff, he was brought to an unhappy halt. Nowhere on this rock face could he see sufficient hand and foot holds. He tried the walls on either side of the cliff and found them unclimbable. Returning to the cliff, he scanned its face again and again, then began to climb it, face tilted upward to choose the safest-looking fissures and projections. About half way up he came without warning to a place where there seemed to be no way to go farther.

He was suddenly brought to a dead stop with arms outspread, clinging close to the face of the cliff, unable to move hand or foot, either up or down. His doom appeared to him certain. He must fall. There would be a moment of bewilderment and then a lifeless rumble down the one general precipice to the glacier below.*

When this danger flashed upon him, he became nerveshaken for the first time since setting foot on the mountains, and his mind seemed to fill with a stifling smoke. But this terrible eclipse lasted only a moment. Life seemed to blaze forth again with preternatural clearness. He seemed suddenly to become possessed of a new sense, his trembling muscles became firm again, every rift and flaw in the rock was seen as through a microscope and his limbs moved with a positiveness and precision with which he seemed to have nothing to do. He felt as if his deliverance could not have been more complete if he had been borne on wings.**

* John Muir, *The Mountains of California*, pp. 51-52.

** Many outstanding athletes report the same type of experience on days of extraordinary performance. In almost every reported case, the athlete recalls going into a sort of psycho-physical overdrive in which his sensory perceptions and muscle control reach a new range of effectiveness. Yet none reports knowing how he reached this state, or any conscious control over his actions. The experience seems to be quite similar to evidence from carefully controlled bio-feedback experiments in which people who are in no way unusual are able to control such internal functions as heart rate and circulation without being able to say how they do it.

Muir's new-found capabilities stayed with him while he readily climbed the remaining four hundred feet, though the way led through a maze of chasms with sharp ridges between and loose piles of rock ready to rumble down at a touch. When he reached the summit, he emerged suddenly from the great blue shadow through which he had been climbing and came into clear afternoon sunlight that seemed a benediction and a symbol of his deliverance.

Directly below him the clump of strange rock towers called the Minarets sprang 1,000 feet or more into the sky from the glaciers at their feet. Beyond them peak beyond peak mounted successively higher until the range reached its climax at Mt. Whitney, 14,495 feet above the Pacific. To the east Mono Lake and the desert glowed softly in warm light. To the north the fountain peaks of the Merced and Tuolumne marched to the horizon. To the west the Sierra rolled downward in gigantic waves of granite striped with forests, set with gleaming lakes and scored by great canyons that seemed fathomless from where Muir stood in the whistling wind.

He had not encumbered himself with so much as a coat; the summit of Ritter was no place to be caught by darkness. He made his way down to a glacier on the east side of the mountain, crossed its gentler slopes by running and sliding warily for fear of crevasses, descended an ice-cascade by digging holes with the heels of his hobnailed boots and reached the lower slopes as night closed in.

His life-force died with the light, and the miles back to his camp through the dark were a test of endurance and mountaineering skill. Guiding himself by the trend of the canyons and the procession of peaks against the stars, he came at last within sound of the waterfall tumbling into the lake beside his camp, found the nest in the dwarf pines and lay there a while in that strange disembodied state that mountain weariness and reaction from a tremendous experience often brought him. Then he washed his face in the glacial lake, made himself a cup of tea, ate a crust of bread and slept until morning, in spite of the cold.

The artists had despaired of seeing Muir again, though he had been gone only three days. When he drew near, wearing the marks of his exaltation and exhaustion on face and body, he seemed to them like Christ himself come down from the mountains, or at least a prophet. Keith often called him "Jeremiah," but whether he did so in respect to Muir's otherworldly appearance or his opinions of the suicidal greediness of mankind, the record does not show.

Chapter 22

The Naked Rock of Tenaya

During the two weeks the artists spent in the Yosemite region, a deep friendship sprang up between Muir and Keith. Encouraged by the security he felt in this man's company, Muir came down with him to Oakland. His sojourn there proved devastating, and its aftermath nearly cost him his life.

Oakland had only some eleven thousand people, San Francisco about one hundred fifty thousand, but they seemed monstrous cities to Muir. The Carrs, McChesneys (with whom he stayed), LeContes, Keiths and other friends all wanted to entertain him and introduce him to their circles. He had been in the Sierra almost continuously for three years, most of the time alone or among people who made few demands upon him, either intellectual or social. Responding to so many new acquaintances, hurrying back and forth across San Francisco Bay by ferry and through the noisy streets in horse-cars and carriages, dressing in the uncomfortable habiliments of respectability, walking flat, artificial surfaces instead of the unmodified earth, became multiple pressures that dazed and confused him and, at times, made him surly. A photograph taken during this visit has the eyes of a forest creature that has blundered onto a city street.

He endured for two weeks, then fled to the mountains. One good thing had been accomplished: the *Overland Monthly* asked to publish everything Muir wrote. His "Living Glaciers of the Sierra" came out in the *Overland* for December, 1872, and was reprinted the next month by the nation's most influential scientific periodical — the *Journal of Science and Arts*, published at Yale University. During Muir's time it was known as "Silliman's Journal" because of the great influence of its editor, Benjamin Silliman, who founded this publication in 1819. It is the nation's oldest scientific journal which has enjoyed continuous publication. In 1879 the word "*Arts*" was dropped from the title.

When he reached Yosemite, Muir's hunger for physical contact with wild nature made him overeager. He had been back a short time when an early December storm laid several feet of wet, heavy snow on the valley floor and deeper deposits in the gulches and avalanche chutes. Stepping out into the sunlit morning after the storm, Muir realized that as the day wore on purple-white avalanches would be foaming and thundering all through the Sierras.

He wanted to see the landscape before the sun changed the snow pattern and, therefore, began to climb out of the valley through a narrow gulch which was very steep but had no cliffs. The wallow through snow, usually waist deep and often up to his chin, proved more difficult than he had anticipated, and it was very late in the afternoon when he arrived within a few hundred feet of the top. He had just reconciled himself to seeing no more than sunset on the mountains' white mantle when the snow around him gave way.

In the instant of realization that he had started an avalanche, Muir threw himself backward and flung out his arms, hoping that this spread-eagle position would keep him from sinking. Jostled from side to side, bounced up and down, sometimes with his face covered, sometimes riding clear on the surface of the white flood, but never striking the bottom or sides of the chute, Muir went down so fast that he had no time for any feeling except breathless exhilaration. When his motion stopped, he found himslf lying on a delta of snow at the mouth of the gulch. In less than a minute, he had ridden down the half mile it took him all day to climb.

Not only Muir's judgment had been put somewhat awry by his sojourn in the bay cities. The sensitivity to the natural environment which preserved his life during lone-hand feats of mountaineering comes clear in a passage he wrote into one of his High Sierra journals. "Compare walking on dead planks (most of the sidewalks of Oakland and San Francisco were then made of planks) with walking on living rock where a distinct electric flash seems to attend each step. Then there's the soothing softness of mossy bogs and brushing past lily stalks and columbines in ravines.... There is no danger in night walking."

Thus when Muir, a short time after his ride on the avalanche, set out to make a detailed exploration of Tenaya Canyon, he was slightly out of condition, as any highly skilled athlete will find himself after a lay-off.

Section of the Channels of the Tenaya Fork of the Great Tuolumne Glacier

Section of the channel of the Tenaya Canyon fork of the great Tuolumne Glacier.

Tenaya Canyon forks off to the northeast from the head of Yosemite Valley. It is very deep, flanked by towering masses of bare granite, and so dangerous that no one had yet been through it. Tenaya challenged Muir and fascinated him because he realized it had been the channel of one of the two great ice-streams that merged to form Yosemite Glacier. Some geologists believe Tenaya to have been the main tributary, rather than the Merced Glacier, which entered from the southeast, sculpturing the "Little Yosemite" Valley as it came.

On the morning Muir started up Tenaya, he lingered a while at Mirror Lake, impounded just inside the canyon's mouth by the fragments of rock spire thrown down in an earthquake. On the tranquil surface, Half Dome's 4,770 feet of majesty lay reflected in perfect miniature. Muir could scarcely ever pass Half Dome without pausing to commune with it. Nor was he ever able to put its effect upon him into words. Neither has anyone else. Half Dome seems to speak directly to the spirit, out of another world and in an unknown tongue. That morning the stupendous cliff and vaulted crown glowed softly purple in the early light.

Through the lower part of Tenaya, Muir had easy going. But when he reached the vicinity of Snow Creek, which cascades twenty-five hundred feet down the canyonside, he had literally to burrow his way through a tangle of dwarfed oaks and other plants of the chaparral which proved extraordinarily tough, though from a distance this "elfin forest" looked like green plush.

He left the tangle by climbing the steep side of Mount Watkins, a huge mass of glacier-swept granite that flanks Tenaya Canyon on the northwest side. Part of Muir's objective was to measure the slope of the canyon walls, and he carried his inclinometer and barometer securely slung from his shoulder, pausing now and again to read them.

He was working along a bare slope where it curved around a bulge in the rock face when, for the first time since he came into the Sierras, he made a misstep and fell completely out of control. He was conscious during the first somersault of his wild tumble, but struck his head during the second. The blow knocked him unconscious. When he came to, he found himself lying against some stiff bushes that had stopped his descent only a yard from a precipice.

Muir reacted as he had when, as a boy, he panicked and almost drowned in Fountain Lake. As soon as his trembling stopped and he realized he was not seriously hurt, he became furious with himself. Climbing shakily to the feet that had betrayed him, he lectured them for having indulged in "intercourse with stupid town stairs and dead pavements." The nerve-muscle system on which his mountain life depended must be disciplined, and Tenaya Canyon was an ideal place to do so. He spent the rest of the day on the bare face of Mount Watkins and slept that night on rocks at the foot of a dark, narrow gorge.

He felt steady when he woke, ready for one of the most dangerous and difficult passages in the Sierra. The Tenaya Glacier, unable to do more than smooth Mount Watkins and Clouds' Rest, which flank the canyon on the opposite side, sliced downward like a plowshare four thousand feet deep. The ability of glaciers to remove great blocks of granite depends largely upon the nature and pattern of "joints" — cracks that open up when molten rock is hardening and also during the periods when portions of earth are being bowed up to stand at higher elevations.

Approximately sixty million years ago, during the early Cenozoic era of geologic time, the Sierra Nevada was a warm, wet lowland. During the following fifty-seven million years, the terrain was upwarped to approximately its present height, which is great enough for glaciers to form and maintain themselves except during warm periods of "climatic optimum." The walls of Tenaya Canyon, like El Capitan in Yosemite Valley, are made of extremely tough granite, with joints spaced as much as one thousand feet apart. Even the Tenaya Glacier could do no more than grind off the surface. But at the bottom of the canyon the glacier found rock fractured into closely-spaced joints and sliced through it like a ditch-digging machine, carrying away the debris in its underbelly.

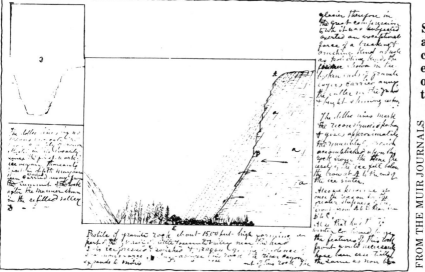

Sketch showing a valley wall carved by the enormous force of glacial action.

Full daylight had come when Muir started up the gorge, but he immediately found himself in gloom. At no place was this glacier-furrow more than sixty feet wide, in many stretches no more than twenty. Down its channel Tenaya creek came brawling, its banks littered with ragged rocks fallen from walls so fractured by earthquake, frost and water that parts of them were ready to come down at a touch, or even at a change in temperature.

The walls were rarely less than perpendicular; in many places they overhung. Yet Muir was compelled to scale them at intervals, sometimes because there was no way up the constricted, rockstrewn bottom where the stream roared and foamed, more often to take measurements on the precipitate granite faces above. He was so engaged in late afternoon when thirst and hunger drove him down to the stream near the head of the gorge.

He camped in the shelter of a twelve-foot square boulder which an earthquake had sent down from Clouds' Rest. In the light of his fire of resinous roots this slab gleamed, and he knew it to have been polished by ice. This word, out of the book of the earth, both calmed and revived him. The moon rose early. Up-canyon, a sweetly-talking cascade gleamed white; down-canyon, one of the Yosemite domes rose like a spirit. A few graceful plants nodded in the firelight. Muir opened a notebook on his knee, fished out a stub of pencil and wrote a letter to Jeanne Carr.

Neither his feet nor the canyon — not even the 600-foot cliff at its head down which Tenaya Creek pours in a beautiful ribbon fall — gave Muir any further trouble. He went on to Lake Tenaya, which lies at 8,400 feet, and found it frozen firmly enough to walk upon, but with ice so clear that it seemed fragile, and he stamped at every step to test it.

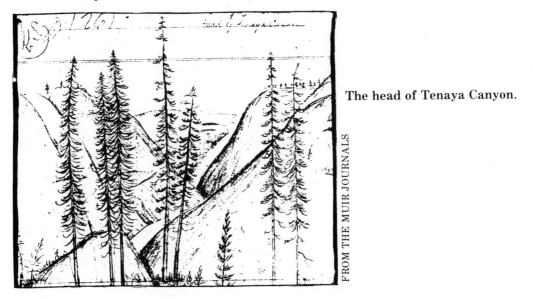

The head of Tenaya Canyon.

FROM THE MUIR JOURNALS

Muir returned to Yosemite to warm himself and fill his empty stomach, but within two days he was on the upper slopes of Clouds' Rest, making measurements and collecting primroses for Asa Gray. To preserve the roots he dug out large sods, pausing often to watch the wonder being wrought by the late light on the high mountains.

Next day he wrote a letter which Asa Gray kept, in spite of his own restrained, unemotional, scientific nature which Muir described as "angular factiness":

"Not one of the assembled mountains seemed remote — all had ceased their labor of beauty and had gathered round their parent sun to receive the evening blessing, and waiting angels could not be so solemnly hushed. The sun himself seemed to have reached a higher life as if he had died and only his soul were glowing with rayless, bodiless *Light*, and as Christ to his disciples, so this departing sun soul said to every precious beast, to every pine and weed, to every stream and mountain, 'my peace I give to you.'

"I ran home in the moonlight with your sack of roses slung on my shoulder by a buckskin string — down through the junipers, down through the firs, now in black shadow, now in white light...through the groves of Illilouette and spiry pines of the open valley, star crystals sparkling above, frost crystals beneath...."

Part IV

ECOLOGIST

"*Brought into right relationships with the wilderness, man would see that his appropriation of Earth's resources beyond his personal needs would only bring imbalance and beget ultimate loss and poverty for all.*"

Chapter 23
From Sunnyside Bench

During the often-sunlit winter of 1872-73, Muir opened himself to all nature more fully than at any time since his first summer in the Sierra. He had not abandoned his intention to devote himself to science, but articles for the *Overland Monthly* and the *New York Evening Tribune* were now providing most of his living. Geological studies could furnish only part of the material needed, and he exploited the opportunity to indulge himself in freedom.

He observed every kind of thing, from tiny, iridescent drops strung on spider webs by vapor from sun-warmed ground, to miles-long clouds of pulverized snow, streaming like banners from the tops of the summit peaks. All that he saw, heard, felt, smelled, tasted, he responded to and set down in his intimate journals like strings of radiant beads.

He felt a little guilty and defended himself to himself. "Instead of narrowing my attention to book-making out of material I have already eaten and drunken, I would rather stand in what the world would call an idle manner, literally gaping with all the mouths of soul and body...hoping and enjoying enormously.... But in the midst of these methodless rovings, I seek to spell out by close inspection things not well understood."*

Muir was far better equipped to observe and interpret than he had been during his first summer of overwhelmed delight in the Sierra. Emerson, Tyndall, Torrey, Gray and other able scientists and thinkers of lesser renown had been to him an on-site graduate faculty and had continued their instruction after departure through correspondence and the books they sent to him.

The central "thing" Muir wanted to elucidate was what he called "the mystery of harmony." He now knew the Sierras well enough to understand that it was not the chaos of forms, animate and inanimate, which it had at first appeared to be. Each manifestation of Nature stood where it stood, grew as it grew, lived as it lived, for reasons having to do with other phenomena, past and present. He saw these relationships as harmonies, in part because it was to him inconceivable that God would express His love by creating a disharmonious world — however much it might be temporarily dislocated by

* Linnie Marsh Wolfe, *John of the Mountains*, pp. 102-103.

floods and earthquakes, or locally disturbed by hungry predators. "Nature does some heavy pruning in her Yosemite groves and sometimes weeds her gardens roughly," he wrote on observing a live oak with a three-foot trunk snapped off by a single stone coming down with an avalanche.

Also Muir saw harmony wherever he saw beauty; the one was indispensable to the other. Scientific insights often came to him from trying to find out why some segment of wild nature seemed so beautiful, and science often deepened his perception of the beautiful.

Gray and Torrey had revived his interest in botany just at the time when he was coming to understand the geology of the region. Without pausing to theorize about his method, he now began to use these sciences together to discover and interpret the harmonies around him. His observations became increasingly ecological.

The term "ecology" was coined (as "oekologie") in 1869 by Haeckel, the German scientist who is known as "the father of mechanism." He considered its field to include the general economy of the household of nature. The American Ecological Society defines ecology as "the study of organisms in relation to environment." There is no evidence that Muir was familiar with Haeckel's formulation; the term does not appear in any of his writings. But Humboldt, the scientist who influenced Muir most profoundly, helped to lay the foundations of the synthesis of knowlege from many fields which we know today as "ecology."

During that winter and spring, Muir spent days at a time in a rough camp he made for himself on a broad shelf five hundred feet above the Valley floor between Yosemite Falls and Indian Canyon. He called it "Sunnyside Bench" because, being on the north wall, it receives sunlight all year and is the winter home of resident birds — snow melts quickly even after a heavy fall, flowers bloom and butterflies flit when the drifts lie deep on the uplands above.

Muir became fascinated with the contrast to the dark, rugged, icy south

Illustrating Geological Effects of Shadows on Mt. Farm

Sketch illustrating the geological effects of shadows on a mountain's form.

wall which the sun touches only in summer. Yet some of Yosemite's most beautiful groves grew along the base of the north wall. It presently came to Muir that these trees were growing on moraines left by tributary glaciers which had lingered in the shadowy, twisting canyons long after the main Yosemite glacier had melted. In effect the shadows had created the groves by preserving the glaciers long enough to grind plentiful quantities of granite into soil.

From Sunnyside Bench Muir went on to identify groves growing upon avalanche taluses, and still others upon soil outwashed from canyons during floods. The entire pattern of the Valley's trees — so beautiful in its present state — became for Muir more beautiful still as he grew to understand its creation.

In April the *Overland Monthly* brought out a long letter Muir had written to Jeanne Carr describing his exploration of Tenaya Canyon. With what seems deadpan irony the editor entitled that feat of mountaineering "A Geologist's Winter Walk." Muir had several other articles in preparation. But writing for the public became very hard. He had always to struggle against an underlying sense of futility. "Books...are but piles of stones set up to show coming travelers where other minds have been," he wrote in his journal, "or at best smoke signals to call attention....No amount of word-making will ever make a single soul *know* these mountains. As well seek to warm the naked and frostbitten by lectures on caloric and pictures of flame. See how willingly Nature poses herself upon the photographer's plates. No earthly chemicals are so sensitive as those of the human soul. All that is required is exposure and purity of material."

He was convinced that he did not know how to write and struggled to burnish every sentence. The effort to put his responses to nature into language often frustrated him. Most words, he felt, were "muddy" because they had been developed for commonplace, material purposes. Those that were supposed to convey spiritual and esthetic experiences were as vague as the ragged edge of a disintegrating cloud.

In June Jeanne Carr — after putting him off time after time — finally came for a visit in Yosemite. It was not the meeting of his dreams. She arrived, as it seemed to Muir, "like a comet tailed by the whole misty town." In fact there were only eight or ten people, including Albert Kellogg, the botanist, William Keith, the painter, and Muir's first and almost love, Emily Pelton. They camped together in a grove near the mouth of Tenaya Canyon and had, it appears, a jolly Victorian time which left no chance for the soul-to-soul sharing of experiences which Muir longed for.

Even when the rest left, leaving only Jeanne Carr and Albert Kellogg with Muir, the relationship remained more companionable than intimate. The three of them went through the "grand canyon" of the Tuolumne — an adventure, before trails were built, to tax the hardihood of any mountaineer, let alone a Victorian woman in her mid-forties.*

* It was shortly after this adventure that Muir's first article on Hetch Hetchy Valley appeared

Muir had lost none of his affection for Jeanne Carr. But it seems to have been clear to him that she could no longer serve as his soul-mate, even *in absentia*. He left her to botanize with Kellogg on the big Tuolumne Meadows, and went off alone on a several-weeks trip to the Minarets — a promised land of savage rock spires, glaciers, berg-dotted lakes and new-born rivers which he had seen from Mount Ritter.

---

in the *Overland Monthly*. Muir was in love with this Yosemite-like basin, created by a confluence of glaciers which carved and polished its sides. In some ways it seemed to him lovelier than Yosemite Valley itself. His account together with that of Jeanne Carr — a mere woman — incensed Josiah Whitney, who had declared Tuolumne Canyon impassable. He immediately organized an expedition to traverse it and published a report which nit-picked Muir's description as to heights and similarities to Yosemite.

Chapter 24
Ice and Black Rock

On September 12, 1873, Muir crossed the divide between the headwaters of the Merced and San Joaquin Rivers and camped on a rocky isthmus between cold, blue lakes at an elevation above eleven thousand feet. On this isthmus were two dwarf pines — a dead one whose still-resiny wood made a quick and welcome fire and a living one which Muir knew to be at least three hundred years old, though it stood less than five feet tall. Everywhere that he had climbed to the limit of tree growth in the Sierra he had found this curious little pine, crumpled and matted by the great weights of snow that buried the trees each winter, but surviving and reproducing splendidly.

On many steep slopes the dwarf pines looked, from a distance, like moss on a roof. These thickets were impenetrable, but Muir found no difficulty in walking across the tops of them, for their tufted, spreading branches are exceedingly tough and springy. When he cut into the trunk of a typical dwarf pine under four feet tall and used a magnifying glass to count the growth rings, he was astonished to find the trees 426 years of age. A branch one inch in diameter was 75 years old and so supple he could have tied a knot in it. Such branches made arched roofs with soft accumulations of needles beneath them — high mountain bedrooms for birds, rodents, deer, mountain sheep, and lonely, far-wandering men.

Beneath the lone pine on the rock isthmus, Muir sank gratefully into his bed, for he had burdened himself with blankets to keep out the chill of nights at glacial altitudes and food enough for several weeks. He slept deeply without hearing the woodrats that stole his snow goggles,* his teapot lid and his precious barometer. Fortunately the woodrats had dropped the barometer on the rock outside Muir's bedroom tree, but they had taken the goggles and lid.

Thereafter Muir slept with his sack of provisions for a pillow and his barometer, as he said, "in my bosom." Yet a couple of nights later, when he was camped under a mountain juniper that had survived a snow avalanche by resting its weight on one large limb, like a man leaning on his elbow, he was wakened by a metallic scraping sound. In the gloom he could not at first discover the cause, but at length made out a large woodrat dragging his

* It is probable that these were the type of eye-protectors the American Indians and frontiersmen made by cutting slits in discs of wood or leather.

hatchet by the leather thong attached to the handle. Muir grabbed the hatchet and banged on the tree trunk to frighten the animal away, but it returned again and again, chattering its teeth with a sound like a rattlesnake's warning.

At the time Muir felt annoyed. But the bushy-tailed woodrat of the Sierra was one of his favorites among the animals that kept him company on his lonely journeys. Twice the size of common rats, with white bellies and brown backs, eyes bright, full and liquid, they seemed to him handsome creatures. Their homes are rough conical piles of sticks up to six feet high, sometimes built near together so that Muir, coming among them suddenly, sometimes had the illusion of being in an Indian village. Again, they may be perched in trees thirty feet above the ground. Muir found that within these stick-castles the woodrats built nests lined with down from birds and seeds. And here were born and nursed the delicate young, who made Muir think of flowers protected by an armament of thorns.

Now, in mid-September of 1873, Muir was in one of the most fascinating canyons he had yet explored. As always, on encountering new and wonderful country, he scarcely knew where to fix his attention: on the white violets and ferns around his feet, the great dark cliffs that literally leaned over him, the

Can S. F San Joaquin

"Groves of graceful hemlocks and firs..." along **"...the bright young branch of the San Joaquin."**

groves of graceful hemlocks and firs, or the bright young branch of the San Joaquin, here thirty feet wide by only two feet deep.

He solved the problem of distraction in the ecologist's way — by relating phenomena to one another. At 8,400 feet he found the first anemone he had seen in California, growing among rough volcanic boulders brought down by an avalanche. It was clear that ice had carved and polished the black walls of this valley, and that the wide portion where there was room for groves and meadows was a "yosemite" formed by the confluence of several glaciers. Here grew the most remarkable mixture of alpine and lowland plants he had ever encountered. Muir theorized that the seed of the high-mountain species had been brought down by the several streams that plunged into the valley to join the growing river. These observations of living things in relation to altitude and other conditions were the first systematic observations of life zones in the Sierra Nevada and among the earliest made anywhere in the world.

Driven into the shelter of a grove by a sudden storm, Muir watched a rain-loosened boulder fall a thousand feet down a mountainside — a dramatic reminder of the mountaineer's greatest peril. Beyond and above him the Minarets loomed through the storm in ominous grandeur. They are, in fact, extremely dangerous terrain for climbers.*

The Minarets are a narrow ridge of the Ritter Range, lying west of the main crest of the Sierra and considerably higher. They are composed of "sedimentary and volcanic rocks, baked and metamorphosed out of semblance to their former state.**

According to Matthes these rocks were once the crust of a low-lying, worn-down range and have been raised by the upwelling, molten granite which formed the present Sierra block. The streams rising in the Ritter Range, as do those in some other parts of the Sierra Nevada, follow the valley cut in the ancestral mountains and, therefore, run either northwest or southeast for considerable distances before turning westward down the tilt of the range, by which time they have merged into large streams. Muir was thus forced to spend five days in crossing canyons before he reached the foot of the Minarets.

Except for four lakes that lay like wide-open blue eyes at the foot of steeply-sloping fields of *nevé*, Muir found himself in an overpowering magnificence of black and white. He had never seen rock towers so narrow for their height or so elaborately carved as the darkly-soaring Minarets, nor unblemished nevé so compacted that pieces broke off to float in the lakes like icebergs, leaving behind them caverns filled with mysterious blue light.

At first he considered climbing the highest spire, whose summit is 12,281

---

* In 1933 the Minarets took the life of Walter A. Starr, Jr., known to all climbers of his generation as "Pete." Between 1929 and the summer of his death, at age thirty, Starr climbed, during vacations from his law practice, forty-two main peaks between Yosemite Park and Sequoia Park and backpacked over two thousand miles of trails. From the splendidly organized data he collected on distances, altitudes and other information necessary to travel in the Sierra Nevada by foot or horseback was assembled his classic Starr's *Guide to the John Muir Trail and the High Sierra Region.*
** François E. Matthes, *The Incomparable Valley,* p. 59.

feet above the sea. It is now called "Clyde Minaret" in honor of the man who first climbed it in 1928. Clyde ascended on the east side; as Muir thought, this Minaret is inaccessible on the west. Having made this judgment, Muir set out to explore a curious avalanche talus which appeared to divide a steeply sloping glacier in two. He found that the big, rough fragments of black rock were loosely piled on top of the ice; they had evidently come down during the earthquake of 1872, which Muir himself had experienced.

Insecure as this talus proved to be, Muir went up it, the glacier being so steep that it could only be mounted by cutting steps and so hard that chopping proved intolerably laborious and slow.

Above the glacier Muir had his second experience with the peculiar rocks of the Ritter Range, the first having been the time he almost fell when climbing Mount Ritter itself. These rocks are extremely durable, but when they do give way they tend to peel off in such a manner as to leave faces that are vertical, or nearly so, and have knife-like edges. The Sierra Club warns that, though hand and foot holds are plentiful in the Minarets, they are treacherous and the climber should test each one before trusting his weight to it.

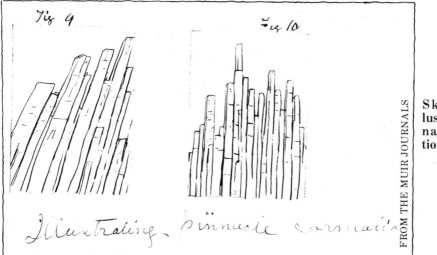

FROM THE MUIR JOURNALS

Sketches illustrating pinnacle formation.

The higher Muir climbed the more determined to frustrate him the rock face seemed to be. When he reached a place where he had to hang on with one hand while, with his hatchet, he cleared away loose gravel that covered the only possible handholds above him, he paused to consider his situation.

Muir always hated to give up; in fact he occasionally boasted that he never turned back from an objective. But in truth he was not irrationally determined. The sky had turned black. From his precarious perch he could see rain falling on nearby mountains. When wet and windlashed, the cliff he was on would be fatal.

Muir descended even more cautiously than he had come up and safely reached the moraine at the glacier's foot. But his intention to go straight to his protected camp was foiled by a narrow pass between two of the Minarets which seduced him by a glimpse of fascinating ice and rock beyond.

Throughout the day Muir had kept up his life-zone observations — primroses all along his way, up to 11,000 feet; yellow-bellied marmots, fat and happy at 10,700 feet; and at the summit of the Minaret pass, two wind-whipped currant bushes of a species new to him, and upon them half-benumbed bumble bees and a fly or two. The altitude was 11,600 feet.

Beyond, Muir glimpsed through a second pass the volcanic cones of Mono, dreaming in the warm desert light. He cut steps down the glacier leading to the second pass, wedged his way between the ice and rock and paused, as he wrote that evening in his journal, "to look back at the wild, wild cliffs with the wild, wild clouds rushing over them. A weird unhuman pathway, and as I now look back from my campfire it seems strange I should have dared its perils."*

Nevertheless Muir spent the next week exploring the dangerously crevassed glaciers, rugged passes and sheer precipices where the many sources of the San Joaquin are fed by perennial ice and snow of the Minaret-Mount Ritter area. For one of the few times in his life he admitted that he had gone where no one should venture alone. As usual Muir was interested in everything he encountered in this wild environment. At the head of the main San Joaquin canyon, at an altitude of 9,800 feet, he counted thirty-three large gentian blossoms in a patch no bigger than his hand. On the twentieth of August he came across the whitened skull and big, curving horns of a mountain sheep. When several blows of his hatchet failed to break the skull, he wondered whether hunters' stories of mountain sheep leaping off precipices onto their heads without coming to harm might after all be true. This notion, which was widely believed, had nagged him for some time and continued to do so, for though he saw mountain sheep leaping up precipices in the Sierra, he did not find any leaping off them.

On the way back to Yosemite Muir climbed, in one day, a twelve thousand-foot mountain and an adjoining summit over thirteen thousand feet. According to Linnie Marsh Wolfe the latter was probably Rogers Peak, the first recorded ascent of which was not made until 1897. Muir's account of this climb is very circumstantial, and there is no reason to doubt him. He was the first man up many high mountains without receiving credit for his primacy. As a climber he was the purest of amateurs, ascending peaks for the several private satisfactions which his complex nature craved: to pit his strength and skill against formidable obstacles; for excitement; for the joy of discovery; to search the landscape for phenomena that interested him; to discover feasible routes of travel; and for the uplift of magnificent views.

He left no record on any mountain — not even on 14,496-foot Mount Whitney, which he climbed a month after his adventures among the Minarets.

The summit of Mount Whitney was reached for the first time by three fishermen from the Owens Valley on August 18, 1873. On September 6 of the same year, Carl Rabe left the following on Whitney's summit in a yeast-powder can: "Notice. Gentlemen, the loky finder of this half dollar is welcome

* Linnie Marsh Wolfe, *John of the Mountains*, p. 151.

to it." On September 19 Clarence King and Frank Knowles left their record in the same can. Muir's seems to have been the fourth ascent and was unquestionably the first up the difficult "Mountaineer's Route" on the northeast side.

Chapter 25
Death Exhalations of Towns

Jeanne Carr and other friends had finally persuaded Muir that he had to publish what he had learned of the Sierra's geologic history before someone else took the credit without doing the work. Beside Silliman's *Journal of Science and the Arts*, there were precious few scientific periodicals at that time. Muir, nevertheless, could have won more reputation among scientists if he had published in the "proceedings" of one of these societies, or in one of the prestigious periodicals of the East such as *The Atlantic Monthly* or *Harper's Magazine*. Instead he made an arrangement with San Francisco's *Overland Monthly*, which offered advantages more attractive to a free-lance writer than to an established scientist sustained by a grant or salary: assured publication, a sympathetic editor and good prices for his work. John H. Carmody, who claimed to have lost thirty thousand dollars in an effort to make the periodical a success, said: "....Never have such prices been paid for poems, stories and articles as I paid to the writers of the old *Overland*."

Muir needed direct contact with the editor; also with scientific and literary minds. And he needed reference works quite unobtainable in the mountains where he would have preferred to remain. When the first snowflakes began to dance between Yosemite's walls, Muir came down to Oakland expecting to stay with the Carrs.

He found them in deep mourning for their eldest son, who had recently died of a tropical infection acquired on the Amazon. Muir therefore accepted the invitation of his friend, J.B. McChesney, to live and work in his hospitable home.

It was not at all a bad work situation — besides Mr. and Mrs. McChesney, his very good friends, Muir had the companionship of their little daughter, Alice. This meant a great deal to him, for he had a deep and permanent need to be with children. But Muir, for the first long stretch of time, was up against the complete loneliness and lack of outside stimulation which are among a writer's most formidable handicaps. He described his life at this time as being like a movement of a glacier — one endless grind.

The *Overland* did not require him to write conventional scientific articles, but in order to present his findings convincingly, Muir had nevertheless to wrench the factual material on glaciers and their accomplishments out of the total experience he had enjoyed; to separate them from the matrix which included all the other natural phenomena he had observed in the Sierra. He had also to leave out the high rewards of emotional and spiritual exaltation and the deep gratification of intellectual curiosity. The totality of experience — "the grand design" — meant so much to him that it was painful to separate out any part and present it singly.

The town environment was not helpful. At this time Oakland had about twenty-five thousand people, many of them housed in dingy shacks and even less sightly boarding houses along the really tough waterfront where, a few years later, a teenager called Jack London earned his reputation as one of the toughest and hardest-drinking among the oyster pirates. The fast-growing city was sightly only in spots, as was San Francisco across the bay on a much larger scale — for both better and worse. In the 1870s the people living around San Francisco Bay were quite literally money-mad. The enormous wealth in gold and silver being brought up from the bowels of Nevada's earth was multiplied many times over through stock speculations and other financier's devices. While all types, from bankers to barbers, were making quick fortunes — and losing their shirts — three groups of monopolists were rapidly consolidating a major share of California's wealth and power. These were the railroad magnates, the large landholders — including speculators, stockmen and lumbermen — and the manipulators of the money which financed all these types of enterprise. Sometimes they collaborated, sometimes they cut one another's throats. But, made or lost, money dominated life and thought around San Francisco Bay to an extraordinary degree.

Muir felt frustrated and degraded by having to write about God's wonderful Sierras for the "money-clinking crowds." The materialism of most of the people with whom he came in contact affronted and angered him. He said they "hooted morbidness at him." It was the numbers of these "practical" people which seemed to overwhelm him. Muir was well able to hold his own in face-to-face argument. One of his old friends remarked to W. F Badè that "No one who did not know Muir in those days can have any conception of Muir's brilliance as a conversational antagonist in an argument."* What riled and disappointed him most was the idea, enshrined in both religious dogma and tradition, that the earth and everything upon, within, or above it was made primarily for man's use. According to this theory, man was free to do anything he liked with nature — except enjoy it in brotherhood with other living creatures and in harmony with its elemental forces. Enjoyment was not useful. But it was useful, people said, to breed sheep into witless wool-producing machines and turn them loose to overgraze and trample the loveliest of mountain meadows and turn them into dust.

Muir's spiritual ecstasy was still at its greatest pitch of sustained intensity. He felt, he said, that God's love as manifest in all of constantly changing creation shone through him as the sun's rays pass through a flake of glass, which transforms them simply because its nature is to do so. His experiences

* William F. Badè. *The Life and Letters of John Muir*, Vol. II, p. 9.

showed on him. William Keith, the painter, who passed a good deal of the time he spent with Muir in bantering matches as rough as the game they had played in the schoolyards of Scotland (a contest in which two boys switched one another on the bare legs until one wept or cried "Enough!"), said, remembering how he had felt on seeing his friend come down from the high mountains, "We almost thought he was Jesus Christ. We fairly worshipped him!"

Muir also reminded Keith of a well-known mural of the prophet Jeremiah. He was, in fact, much closer to St. Francis of Assisi, who preached to birds and felt the wind, the moon, fire, water and all of nature's elemental forces were his brothers and sisters. Lynn White, Jr., the historian, has suggested that St. Francis should be the patron saint of modern ecology.* If so Muir must be considered his spiritual brother. Though it appears he knew little of St. Francis, he derived from direct experience the same kinship with nature that Il Poverello of Assisi achieved from pure inspiration.

Under the circumstances Muir's like-minded and compatible friends meant a great deal to him. He passed many evenings discussing scientific problems with professors John and Joseph LeConte of the University of California faculty. In the Oakland library he spent less time reading than in talking with Ina Coolbrith, the librarian, who is better remembered as friend and encourager of Bret Harte and other writers than for the poetry she contributed to the *Overland Monthly* when she was a member of its first editorial staff.

The most important of Muir's new friends was John Swett, the bantam-weight battler for excellence in education. He had been California State Superintendent of Education for five years, but had been put out because he insisted on such radical reforms as adequate buildings, state textbooks and state certification of teachers. In 1873-74 when Muir was working on his *Studies in the Sierra*, Swett was principal of an elementary school in San Francisco. He was a published writer himself and had the master teacher's gift for helping others to develop their thoughts and their talents. He was a friend of William Keith, and throughout Muir's ten-month ordeal of writing up his geological observations the two of them crossed the bay almost weekly, Keith in an effort to get Muir to make his illustrations less stiff, Swett to counsel him to write less self-consciously and more in the conversational style that charmed everyone.

Nor were all the readers of the *Overland* so insensitive and material-minded as Muir assumed. When Louisiana Strentzel, wife of a well-to-do physician who was spending his retirement years in experimental horticulture, read the first of the *Studies in the Sierra* in May, 1874, she wrote in her diary: "How I should love to become acquainted with a person who writes as he does. What is wealth compared to a mind like his! And yet I shall probably never see him."**

The Strentzels had been aware of Muir for a couple of years. Their only

* Lynn White, Jr., "The Historical Roots of Our Ecologic Crisis."
** Linnie Marsh Wolfe, *Son of the Wilderness: The Life of John Muir*, p. 175.

child, Louie Wanda, was personable enough to have attracted many suitors. She was very well educated for a young woman of her time, and played the piano so well she had been encouraged to attempt the concert stage. But the girl, twenty-seven at the time her mother read the first of Muir's geological series, seemed determined to become a career daughter. She kept the complicated books in which were noted the progress of each individual among the hundreds of varieties of fruit trees and vines her father nurtured on their considerable ranch situated on the valley side of the Berkeley hills. She seldom left the ranch and appeared content with the love between herself and her parents and the society of their many interesting friends. One of the latter was the confident Jeanne Carr, who never hesitated to arrange Muir's life for him when she could.

As early as 1872, Mrs. Carr had written to Louie Wanda: "I want you to know my John Muir. I wish I could give him to some noble young woman 'for keeps' and so take him out of the wilderness into the society of his peers."

Muir was seldom averse to girls, but he strongly resisted meetings prearranged by others who might have matrimony in mind. Jeanne Carr outflanked him by a simple strategem: she arranged with the Strentzels to call one summer day at a certain hour and then gave Muir an urgent invitation to be at her home a short time earlier.

Dr. Strentzel, a refugee, was an especially charming representative of the Polish aristocracy and, being a scientist in both medicine and horticulture, had much in common with Muir. Mrs. Strentzel, who had been named Louisiana because she was born there, had the hospitable grace of an antebellum plantation mistress. Both of them urged Muir to come and visit at their ranch behind the Berkeley hills, in a valley leading down to Carquinez Strait where the Sacramento and the San Joaquin merge and pour into San Francisco Bay. Muir promised to come "some day." Whether words or glances passed between Muir and Louie Wanda on that afternoon is not recorded.

Muir finished the seventh and last of his *Studies in the Sierra* in September, 1874 — ten months after he had begun the long grind, during which he had also written a couple of incidental articles and a paper on mountain formation in the Sierra Nevada for the American Association for the Advancement of Science. The late François E. Matthes, the most respected modern authority on the geology of the Sierra, has said "The great Naturalist John Muir...became more intimately acquainted with the facts (concerning the evolution of Yosemite and other Sierra features) than any professional geologist of his time." He also said that Muir was the first to recognize the elaborate carving of the Sierra rocks as works of ice. Other geologists have paid similar tributes. There is thus good reason to consider *Studies in the Sierra* an important contribution to scientific knowledge.* Yet the publication failed to establish Muir's reputation as a scientist, probably

---

* From François E. Matthes, *The Incomparable Valley* (p. 60 et seq.):

Geology, and the tools with which it conducts research, have made great advances during the hundred years since Muir published this series. Several major discoveries make

because of a combination of factors: Muir's disregard for academic conventions, the resistance of the geologist establishment, in which Josiah Whitney's influence was powerful, and the fact that the *Overland Monthly* was a popular, general publication and a provincial one at that.

Shortly after he had delivered the last part of his *Studies in the Sierra*, Muir came upon a goldenrod blooming among weeds beside an unfrequented plank sidewalk. It seemed a symbol of himself, at the end of summer, on alien ground. He was off to the Sierra before night fell.

He went by train as far as Turlock, where he slept, and next day set off in baking heat across the San Joaquin plain where every withered stalk and crumbling leaf expressed the valley's longing for the winter rains. Muir was out of condition and wearied quickly in the heat. But freedom regained was a stimulant, and he dawdled happily along the sandy road, indulging in his greatest delight — to find puzzles in nature, try to solve them and let his imagination play as it would with the entire experience. Today his fancy was caught by delicate ribbons embroidered by unknown feet upon the sand. The first turned out to be those of a small lizard — *walking*, not running; the second was the track of a walking grasshopper. Then a hawk caught a little fieldmouse and dropped him on the road where, being somewhat out of breath, he also showed Muir the tracery of his walking gait. Muir had been long

---

certain amendments necessary to bring his statements into line with the facts as currently conceived. There were at least three and possibly four principal advances of ice with periods of retreat between them, rather than the prolonged and continuous Ice Age which Agassiz envisioned. At no time did the ice lie upon the upper portion of North America in an unbroken sheet; many areas were not glaciated at all. (Curiously, Muir clung to the "universal ice sheet" conception in spite of finding areas in both the Sierra and the state of Nevada where there was no evidence of glaciation. It seems probable that he could not bring himself to dispute Agassiz, who was genuinely revered.)

The earth before the Ice Ages (which began about one million years ago) was a tantalizing mystery to Muir. Modern geologists have been able to trace the pre-glacial development of the Yosemite and other valleys and to show that the glaciers ground their slow way down these preformed pathways, deepening and shaping them, adding to the beauty of gigantic rock and leaping waterfall, but having less influence than Muir supposed upon the pattern of the Sierra's water courses. Nor did glaciers shape the strangely round-headed granite monoliths such as Half Dome. *Roches moutonnées* — huge sheep-backed rocks — were shaped by over-riding ice, but not the domes which in effect have formed themselves by means of internal stresses in combination with climatic forces which cause the granite to peel off in concentric shells analogous to the rings of an onion.

Though the Sierra bore only an independent and isolated center of glaciation which did not cover the entire range, it must have been as spectacular as the mind can conceive. Between Lake Tahoe and Yosemite, for eight miles along the crest of the range, an ice field averaging forty miles wide swelled into a true domed ice cap. From this field glaciers plunged in frozen cataracts to drop their bergs into Mono Lake and Lake Tahoe. On the western slope, glaciers winding down the canyons receded much farther: the Tuolumne glacier, the longest, reached a maximum of sixty miles; the Yosemite glacier, maximum thirty-seven miles, was the shortest. Southeast of Yosemite another sea of ice, fifteen hundred square miles in extent, sent long glaciers down the many-branched canyons of the San Joaquin and Kings Rivers. This pattern repeated itself, with variations, all the way down to the Kern River at the southern end of the range.

convinced that falling boulders, air, water and snow, as well as grasses and trees, all make music. Now he decided that the little creatures of the sand wrote music as they went, and he jotted down their footsteps as if it were musical notation.

In the afternoon Muir heard a different kind of music even before he saw the heavy grain wagon it came from: a mule driver cursing his animals with the rhythmic, high-colored, imaginative flow of language which, to those who remember, makes today's "shit-sayers" sound like little boys trying to learn to spit through the gaps in their teeth.

Muir was greeted with more of the same from Delaney when he reached his friend's ranch at dark. It made him feel at home; there existed between himself and these ranchers and mountaineers bonds of empathy far stronger and more secure than any urban population could furnish.

On "Brownie," the small, tough mule he had left at Delaney's to graze the months away, Muir rode up the Sierra's steepening flank to Coulterville where he met his friend, A.G. Black, owner of the Yosemite hotel of which Muir had been winter caretaker. Together they rode on through white moonlight, higher and higher toward Black's ranch on the upland between the Merced and the Tuolumne. The great pines stretched their branches above as if blessing the wayfarers; smaller trees brushed their cheeks with redolent needles; the voice of the high mountains was in the dashing stream that ran far below their trail. Muir knew that lily gardens were nearby, for they were riding close to the track he had taken with Delaney's sheep in 1869. He felt that he was *in* the mountains, rather than *on* them.

Though it was pleasant to relax in the firelight that glinted on Mrs. Black's knitting needles and the guns ranged on a rack of antlers above the fireplace, weary John Muir went to his room early. But before he slept he wrote in his intimate journal a passage celebrating his escape.

"Tell me what you will of the benefactions of civilization...as part of the natural upgrowth of man toward the high destiny we hear so much of. I know that our bodies were made to thrive only in pure air, and the scenes in which pure air is found. If the death exhalations that brood the broad towns in which we so fondly compact ourselves were made visible, we should flee as from a plague.... Go now and then for fresh life — if all humanity must go through this town stage of development — just as divers hold their breath and come ever and anon to the surface to breathe...go up and away for life! I know some will heed this warning. Most will not, so full of pagan slavery is the boasted freedom of the town, and those who need rest and clean snow and sky the most will be the last to move.

"Once I was let down into a deep well into which choke-damp had settled, and nearly lost my life. The deeper I was immersed in the invisible poison the less capable I became of willing measures to escape from it. And in just this condition are those who toil or dawdle or dissipate in crowded towns, in the sinks of commerce and pleasure."*

* Linnie Marsh Wolfe, *John of the Mountains*, pp. 191-192.

Chapter 26
Wild Mountain, Wild Wool

On October 6 Muir told Jeanne Carr in a brief letter, "My feet have recovered their cunning," which meant that he felt able to go anywhere in the mountains, day or night, without danger. He said also that he had decided to start on a ramble of some four hundred miles to Mount Shasta, by way of Mono and Tahoe Lakes.

He was plodding along the dusty stage road leading to Oregon when Mount Shasta appeared fifty miles ahead. He had read Clarence King's dramatic accounts of this lone mountain, but nothing had prepared him for the incredible white cone rising some 8,000 feet above the drapery of forest extending from Shasta's waist to the brown, braided hills that concealed its foot. (The total height of Shasta is 14,162 feet above sea level.) Muir wrote Jeanne Carr that when he saw the mountain from afar, his blood turned to wine and he had not been weary since.

He made his headquarters at a hunters' lodge run by an old-timer named Sisson on the mountain's flank. Everybody told him he could not possibly go to the top of Shasta in November, but Sisson outfitted him with venison, bread and blankets, an experienced guide named Jerome Fay and horses to take them as far as the beasts could make it through the snow.

About sunset, when they were near the timber line, the horses broke through into a tangle of volcanic rocks where they were in danger of breaking their legs. When the men had extricated them, they made camp, broiled venison steaks and rested until two-thirty in the morning. Under the glittering stars, Fay pointed out the best route to the summit and with the horses on lead headed back to Sisson's. With a chunk of venison tied to his belt, Muir made his difficult way upward, wallowing through deep drifts, scrambling and clawing up steep slopes of ragged volcanic rock made perilous by ice. In places he had to go on all fours. But by mid-morning he stood on the bare summit watching a panorama one hundred miles in diameter reveal itself as he slowly turned.

North, east and west the view was a wilderness of great peaks, for Shasta stands in an area where the coast ranges, the Sierra Nevada and the Cascades merge to form the northern rim of California's great central valley. Many of the mountains were clearly of volcanic origin, and Muir knew that Shasta itself was still hot inside, though its upper slopes bore three glaciers, and elsewhere the sides had been deeply scored by ice. How recent volcanic action had been hereabouts Muir saw by the fact that the sides of a subsidiary cone down on Shasta's northwestern flank bore no marks of ice. Obviously an explosion had occurred here after the last great ice age ended ten thousand years ago.

In the afternoon the wind began to rise steadily, and the feeling of snow was in the small clouds that came bumping against the summit where Muir stood. He descended much more quickly than he had come up, running down the rock slopes, sliding through the snow where he could. When he reached his cache of supplies, he found himself looking out upon a cloud landscape of sun-silvered domes and peaks and crags with violet shadows in between, all as evanescent as a dream — giving no obvious sign of the fury within.

In the still-rising wind, he made camp under the overhang of a low cliff of red lava, close by dead trees whose resinous roots would provide a hot, durable fire. He pegged down his blankets to keep the wind from getting under them and crawled into his shelter like a badger into its burrow. The first flakes were already in the air, and before Muir slept the storm had increased to a swirling, blinding smother.

For three days Muir lay there "snug-bug-rug," as he wrote to little Alice McChesney. When his fire was blown into writhing snakes of flame and Muir could see no more than three feet through the storm, he worked on one of the projects for which he had come up here. With his hand-lens he carefully counted samples of snowflakes, to determine the proportion of whole ones to those that had been broken. And he carefully observed — for the snow fell intermittently — how each fresh accumulation compacted the layer beneath. These phenomena were important to him because glaciers are formed by the layering of heavy snows compacting more and more solidly as time goes by. The layers are often composed of broken flakes, blown into the place where the glacier forms, rather than falling there.

Muir was not entirely alone. During brief intervals when the sun broke through, he found that his animal friends were keeping him company as usual. A Douglas squirrel dug down to a cache of seeds so unerringly he seemed to see through the snow; a band of mountain sheep lay under a nearby clump of pines calmly weathering the storm, while a small flock of grouse with feathers to their feet like pantalets sat upon the branches above, talking about the weather.

On the fourth day after the storm Sisson arrived with horses to take Muir to the lodge, where wild flowers were still in bloom. Everyone who knew that Muir was alone on the mountain had given him up for dead and blamed Sisson for allowing him to go up Shasta so late in the year. Muir descended, grumbling at the interruption of an experience he enjoyed. He had not yet realized how treacherous Mount Shasta could be.

During the next few weeks, Muir spent his energy even more prodigally than usual, for the great mountain fascinated and delighted him. In what he called "one Shasta day" (actually two-and-a-half days without food and virtually no rest), he made the hundred-mile circuit around the base. He ranged in many places up and down the steep sides, discovering in the course of exploring deep fissures in the lava that there had been successive eruptions which built the mountain up to a considerably greater height than it now was. As rain and snow-melt washed down the crumbling rock of the barren summit, this debris became fertile soil supporting two beautiful bands of vegetation: an upper one of evergreen trees in which wild flower gardens lay concealed, and a lower one of deciduous trees and chaparral where belated bees still hummed.

He was especially intrigued by the streams of Shasta, which formed in fissures in the porous rock and proceeded underground until they found tunnel-like passages leading to the light. One day among the deciduous trees on the mountain's southern flank, he came upon a sizeable swift-flowing stream whose waters were an unusual dark blue. Mountain rivers tugged at Muir as a well-written mystery story pulls its reader onward — with the difference that Muir generally wanted to reach the beginning rather than the end. He had become a connoisseur of water music, and part way up the steep-sided, green-bowered canyon he began to hurry, for his ears had caught sounds no river had ever brought to them before.

Rounding a sharp bend he came face to face with a cave fifty yards across, at the base of a red lava cliff, and from this cavern the river leaped full-born. It was the McCloud, one of the chief tributaries of the Sacramento.

On September 8 Muir set out with two wealthy sportsmen, one from England, the other from Scotland, to hunt sheep north of Mount Shasta. Muir was very glad to go; he admired the big horn sheep greatly, for they were better mountaineers than he — to his way of thinking, supreme examples of nature's ability to create organisms able to live good lives in environments that seemed superficially hostile to all creatures of flesh and blood. Moreover, Muir was still trying to check out the story that mountain sheep dove off cliffs onto their horns. The evidence of the local residents with whom Muir talked was contradictory. One rancher pointed out a cliff 150 feet high on a lonely butte called Sheep Rock and said he had cut off the retreat of a band of sheep at the top, but the animals had gone over the virtually perpendicular precipice like water over a fall. At the foot he had found the tracks they had made when they galloped away after landing. Another man said that he had been chopping wood at the base of an even higher cliff when a band of sheep came down it. They proceeded in perfect order, making short, controlled leaps until they were near the bottom, then sailing off to land on their forefeet with hindfeet closely bunched behind.

Sisson had come with the party as guide and chief hunter, and Jerome Fay drove a wagon to haul camp gear and supplies and bring back their game. They shot antelope, foxes, geese, deer and sage hens, but the sheep were exceedingly elusive and the visiting sportsmen did not get a good shot at any until they had pushed on to Bremer Mountain, seventy miles from Shasta and close to the Modoc Lava Beds.* Here, on the next to the last day of the hunt, Muir was riding with a rancher and the two sportsmen when they caught a band of fifty or more sheep in the open between the mountain and the lava beds. At first the animals seemed bewildered, indecisive as to whether to run for the lava beds or the mountain. The rancher and one of the sportsmen stalked the bank on foot, and the latter creased the skull of a ram who presently got up and dashed after the flock. He also wounded a ewe which all four men pursued. Muir's feelings during the chase startled him.

"I, who have never killed any mountain life," he wrote in his journal, "felt like a wolf chasing the flying flock....We went up to the ewe...she was breathing still, but helpless and with so gentle an eye she inspired pity as if she were human.... A moment before, unarmed as I was, I could have worried her like a wolf.... Bremen (the rancher) drew a big knife and coolly shed her blood, which formed a crimson pool in the hollow of the gray lava."

Scientist John Muir quickly took over from the primitive man within. He examined the ewe with meticulous care and was happy to find the solution to the mysterious myth that these animals dove from cliffs. Instead of being horny and rigid, as are the hooves of most grazing animals, mountain sheep grow pads which give the ends of their toes some flexibility, conform precisely to every protuberance and hollow in the rock and even provide a little suction. Thus these animals have some of an insect's ability to cling to walls, and this, combined with a magnificent set of muscles with the nerves to control them, enables the bighorns to go almost anywhere among the rugged crags that are their habitat.

* The Modoc Lava Beds are a bleak, black and white area of 46,000 acres where a flood of molten rock hardened into fantastic and labyrinthine forms. Very little grows there except occasional tufts of sagebrush. It is a favorite refuge for wild sheep and other animals. In many of its large, airy caves Indians have made pictographs, and Muir found a number of campfire remains with animal bones strewn about them. In 1873 a small band of Modoc Indians holed up in the Lava Beds stood off a strong force of U.S. cavalry from January until June, when the Modocs retreated voluntarily. During the siege it was almost certain death for a trooper to enter the Lava Beds, for some of the natural tunnels run for miles and an Indian might at any moment rise literally out of the ground to shoot him. In the cemetery at the edge of the lava flow, Muir counted thirty soldiers' graves. The Lava Beds National Monument was set aside in 1925.

Chapter 27
The Volcanic Breath of Shasta

Muir had promised to visit Emily Pelton, and in late December of 1874 he made his way from Shasta to the small town on the divide between the Yuba and Feather Rivers where she was living with relatives. Muir and Miss Pelton were both in their late thirties by this time, and the vitality was gone from the magnetism which had once attracted them to one another. This visit turned out to be a farewell. Muir reported in a letter to Jeanne Carr that he had enjoyed a fine social time — and said no more about Emily.

He was much more enthusiastic about the weather. The day after he arrived, he pushed out into a furious wind storm blowing through a bright, sparkling day. Muir was always exhilarated by storms, and this wind proved one to remember. Branches and tufts of pine needles sped through the air like pursued birds. Every few minutes he heard the falling crash of some tree weakened by fire, or one whose roots had not taken a firm grip on the earth. Nature — whom Muir often likened to a patient, skillful gardener — was pruning her forest.

Leaning against a big pine, Muir felt it strain clear to the roots as the gusts whipped the feathery branches into berserk windmills. It occurred to him that he would like to see and feel what a treetop went through in such a wind. To find one that was in no danger of breaking or being uprooted, yet not so big around as to be difficult to climb, took some looking. He finally selected a Douglas fir a hundred feet tall which was growing with others in a clump on a ridge, climbed into its top and anchored himself among the branches.

The motion was wild. In gusts the treetop swung through an arc he estimated at 30 degrees, with fantastic dips and swoops. But Muir felt safe as a bobolink on a reed. His tree would not be uprooted unless the whole clump went down, which was unlikely, and he had seen Douglas firs bend almost double without breaking.

The wind became visible in surges of light. Up on the higher slopes ranks of yellow pines — "silver pines" as Muir preferred to call them — flung back the sun in a deluge of silvery particles reflected from their needles which were vibrating, he judged from estimates made during previous storms, at least 250 times per minute. As the silver moved down the slope it was merged with other qualities of light reflected from other pines and firs in the mixed forest.

In the canyon bottom the luminous gray of oaks and the gleaming red trunks of madronyas added to the display. And when the whole massive wave reached the opposite slope it seemed to break into a foam of light, as sea waves fill the air with spray when they break upon a cliff.

The sounds of the storm did not strike Muir's ears as one undifferentiated roar, but as a chorus in which he could identify the chanting of each different kind of tree.

The weather continued favorable to Muir, though not to anyone else in the neighborhood. The wind storm was followed by a rain storm equally violent and even more destructive. It melted and washed down the snow clear to the eight thousand-foot level. Every canyon became a booming torrent. As Muir worked his way along Dry Creek — a tributary of the Yuba, now surging up beyond its most ancient high-water marks — he heard great boulders grind together as they were moved downstream from century-long resting places. Banks were caving, streamside trees undermined. But in spite of these casualties the storm was beneficent. Every tree had its own water system of rain running down the trunk and branches in little streams, dripping from leaves and tufted needles, to trickle among grasses and forest debris and sink into the tangle of roots where much of it would be held to nourish this wilderness in the dry weather to come.

It was down below where the riverbeds were choked with rock and gravel torn from steep canyonsides by hydraulic mining that people cursed the flood as they helplessly watched barns and bridges, trestles and flumes, hencoops and houses swept away by the swirling brown water.

Crossing the stream on a foot bridge now almost awash, Muir climbed a one thousand-foot hill. From this vantage point he saw rain as he had never been able to see it before. On a plain or in a valley, the currents of a storm are a confused welter: one cannot read the pattern. Looking down upon the canyons and lower slopes he saw the flow of the almost-opaque atmosphere as clearly as a river system seen in the sunshine from a mountaintop. Cascades of rain descended converging slopes to form massive currents that dashed and foamed against the steep sides containing them and eddied wildly at the confluence of canyons.

Also, Muir was looking through the rain. He saw that drops were fragmented by striking against one another as they fell, beaten as fine as mist where the current smashed against the canyon walls which reflected the main mass and sent it whirling and jostling until it found the easiest way to go.

When he arrived, waterlogged and dripping, Emily Pelton and her relatives bustled about to stir up the fire and make hot tea, all the while offering sympathy for poor John Muir who had felt compelled to be out in such frightful weather. He told them he had enjoyed a much better day than they and that they should get out from under their roof sometimes to be with nature in her beautiful wild moods.

Returning to Oakland in mid-January, 1875, Muir sorted through his many intense experiences on the Shasta trip in order to select and organize some of them for articles. He always found this process difficult, and this time it was complicated by his disturbing memories of the sheep-hunt beside the Modoc Lava Beds. Ever since he left the university Muir had deeply believed that nature is a universal harmony in which forces great and small collaborate to create beauty and the beneficent interplay between all living things and their surroundings, providing each kind the opportunity to prosper for its allotted time on earth. At the lava beds he had been brought face to face with his own innate savagery.

In the process of assimilating and understanding this experience he found that he must face the fact that many species feed upon one another and that all, to a greater or lesser extent, compete with one another for life's necessities and favors. Taking the wide view in both time and space, beyond individual lives and deaths, he found that he could reconcile his fundamental belief in harmony with the more brutal facts of nature. In so doing he evolved what might be called a law of co-existence.

We are governed more than we know, he concluded, and ruled most of all when we are the "wildest"; that is, attuned to nature and thus directly subject to natural laws and recipients of both the opportunities and disciplines of natural conditions. Plants and animals prey on one another, and it is right that they should do so to the limit of their healthy abilities and desires, for harmony results as long as killing and being killed, eating and being eaten are kept within the necessary limits and proportions. In our own time such ideas seem modern when expressed by scientists and others who are deeply and knowledgeably concerned with the future of man in relation to his environment. It is as if we had to re-think thoughts Muir gave to his fellow-citizens a hundred years ago in the relative obscurity of the *Overland Monthly*.*

In these essays Muir also went more deeply into his long-held and quite unpopular belief that nature does not exist solely for man's benefit. Though every atom is in some way connected with every other, nature differentiates sharply between her creatures and gives them distinct individuality. Otherwise the universe would be felted together like the wool of a wet sheep. The "improvements" made by turning wild cattle into helpless milk producers and wild apple trees into bearers of commercial fruit are no doubt good for man, but no better for the tree or animal than the "improvement" a hawk makes in a finch when he plucks out the songster's feathers before eating him.

Proceeding further along this line, Muir wondered whether, since defects continually appear in domestic species, it might not be helpful to go back to the wild forms and make a fresh start. This is also a conclusion some modern scientists have reached through their own researches.

Muir also advised his readers not to be afraid of nature in her most violent

* "A Flood Storm in the Sierra," published in June, 1875, and "Wild Wool," September, 1875. The latter was re-published in *Steep Trails*, a collection of Muir's articles selected and edited by W.F. Badè.

manifestations. Storms, he said, were not only beautiful and interesting, they also reminded humans that however much man might control the elemental forces he was still a minute, frail creature who existed by the sufferance of the universe.

On April 30, 1875, Muir with Jerome Fay went to the summit of Mount Shasta to locate the site for a geodetic monument (a conspicuous marker for line-of-sight measurements required in accurate mapping). Around the lower skirts of the mountain the "bee pastures" were in bloom and buzzing. The summit stood in a blue vault, perfectly clear except for a few clouds boiling around the foot of still-hot Mt. Lassen, to the east. There was no hint of bad weather until early afternoon when clouds that had been gathering around Mt. Shasta merged with those drifting over from Lassen. In a remarkably short time the summit where the men stood was an island in a billowing sea rising inexorably to engulf them.

Jerome Fay, long experienced in Shasta's peculiarly moody weather, abruptly declared that they would either have to go down now or spend the night on the summit. They were completely unprepared for such exposure. Muir had even left his coat in their base camp at Timberline. Inwardly he recognized that Fay was right, but his stubborn, driving urge to complete any project he started trampled this judgment back into his subconscious. He persuaded Fay that a couple of experienced mountain men like themselves could get down through any storm.

Wisps and tendrils of cloud were curling around their feet as Muir and Fay packed up the instruments after the last measurements taken at three in the afternoon. The sky darkened rapidly, and before they were fairly started the storm broke in a burst of hail driven by a furious wind. Each hailstone, Muir noted, was an elegant six-sided pyramid with a rounded base, and it occurred to him that Nature was throwing away some of her loveliest creations on the desolate crags.

As they forced their way down the ridge leading from the summit and over a muddy area where steam and evil-smelling gas were escaping from the mountain's smouldering heart through narrow openings called *fumaroles*, the air temperature dropped 22 degrees. Darkness came on and the storm grew inconceivably violent. Lightning strokes followed in such rapid succession that the thunders became one continuous crashing roar, louder and more terrifying than any thunder Muir had heard. It was as if this ancient volcano had waked to life, and Shasta was being rent to its foundations.

Muir and Fay could have gotten down no matter how wild the storm became, except that they had to traverse a mile and a half of narrow ridge between a precipice and the steeply inclined head of the Whitney Glacier. Muir, as was his custom, had fixed every rod of this passage in his memory and had reviewed it as they descended. He was sure they could make it.

Just above the dangerous passage he waited for Fay in the lee of a lava rock. But when Fay came up he positively refused to go any farther. Their only chance, he insisted, was to go back to the fumaroles and spend the night there.

He started up, wavering and staggering against the storm blast. Muir felt that he could not leave his partner, and went after him.

The bed of hissing, sputtering fumaroles covered about a fourth of an acre with jets of hot, gas-laden steam which pushed up only about an eighth of an inch before they were sheared off by the wind. Lying in the stinking mud, Muir and Fay were all but scalded by the jets. To get to their feet meant death, for they would have frozen where they stood. All they could do when the heat became agony was to inch along a little way to a new spot and turn so that different parts of their bodies were exposed to the heat and cold that sandwiched them. Otherwise there was nothing to do but lie there, lie there and lie there while two feet of snow fell and covered them.

At first they were glad of this, thinking the snow would form a protective blanket. But it soon froze into an icy crust. Muir strictly warned Fay against falling asleep — not because of the cold but in fear that they would be overcome by the volcanic fumes. They called out to one another weakly and plaintively as the hours passed like half-forgotten years.

Some time after midnight the wind died and the snow ceased to fall. But it was too cold and dark to resume their descent. They lay there in alternating periods of stupor when only their eyes, gazing upon the wheeling stars, seemed to live and dreamed of bright campfires and roasting venison. Even when dawn came it seemed to take forever for the light to reach them.

When they finally tapped their last reserves of strength and stood up, their frozen trousers almost refused to bend at the knee. But they traversed the dangerous ridge and descended the long snow slope, not minding their many falls because sliding on their faces was faster than staggering. They reached their base camp at timberline about 10 a.m. Half an hour later they heard Sisson calling and led him to them by feeble answers. But they could not start down until they had kept their frozen feet packed in wet snow for some hours to try to prevent permanent frostbite damage. Muir was so crippled that he had to be dragged on a tarpaulin down to the place where Sisson had left the horses.

Once down in the chaparral belt, flowers and small animals appeared like old friends suddenly re-discovered. Next morning at the lodge Muir and Fay felt as if they had risen from the dead. Sisson's children covered Muir's bed with wildflowers, and out the window the cone of Shasta rose calm and white and beautiful into a clear sky. Their desperate night seemed a bad dream. Yet when Muir reached the shores of San Francisco Bay he felt, he said, like a log buffeted, bruised and scarred in a spring flood; he was permanently lamed.

Chapter 28

From Human Depths
to Highest Peak

I n the 1870s California was a maelstrom of change created in part by the newly completed transcontinental railroad, which ended both the isolation and independence of the West Coast, and partly by conflicting currents of greed and idealism, prophetic vision and reaction. Most of Muir's closest friends were deeply involved. The Carrs had been very active in the organization of the California State Grange* in 1873. Now, in 1875, Dr. Carr got himself elected State Superintendent of Education. During his incumbency Jeanne Carr served as his deputy, handling most of the routine work in the Sacramento office besides lecturing to teacher institutes and Granger groups throughout the state on women's rights and other topics.

When Jeanne Carr wrote Muir about the activities of her husband and herself, he was confused and indifferent. She seemed, as he told her in a letter, "buried under musty Granger hay." Isolated in the mountains and completely absorbed in the doing of nature — his head literally in the clouds — he could not regard these lowland strivings as worthy of serious consideration. But when, on returning from his near-fatal adventure on Mt. Shasta, Muir moved into John Swett's comfortable home in San Francisco, his education began abruptly and in earnest.

John Swett was helping Henry George, the pugnacious printer who had dropped out of school in the seventh grade, to develop *Progress and Poverty*, the book that shook establishment economics to its foundations. George had become so enraged that technological progress brought increasing misery to the many at the same time it multiplied the wealth of a few that he committed his life to an effort to find the causes and the remedies. He had already

---

* The National Grange of the Patrons of Husbandry had become powerful as a means by which farmers could protest against the monopolists who were exploiting them. In San Francisco the men who controlled the shores of the Bay, as well as land and water transportation to and from it, presumed to examine the accounts of every customer and charge freight rates which permitted him to make only as much profit as the magnates thought fit. Farmers, as a matter of course, were charged rates which kept them on the verge of bankruptcy. In Wisconsin and some other mid-western states the Grangers managed to elect majorities of state legislators and pass laws establishing commissions empowered to set freight rates. When, in 1876, the Supreme Court declared these laws constitutional, the political clout of farmers was greatly increased. But the Granger movement was not nearly so successful in California as elsewhere.

published several widely-read pamphlets and articles, in one of which he predicted that the transcontinental railway, completed in 1869, would create poverty rather than the prosperity its enthusiasts had promised.

In this Henry George had proved entirely correct. San Francisco wages had fallen from their Gold Rush high of sixteen dollars a day to two dollars a day. Naturally there was a great deal of discussion of George's ideas in the Swett household which was a social center for thinkers, activists and artists, among whom was William Keith, who lived nearby. Neither John Swett nor John Muir adopted Henry George's belief that a single tax on all land — even that held in idleness for speculation — according to its value if used, would prevent most economic ills.*

But the evidence of hardship caused by strangling monopolies of land, water and transportation was incontrovertible. Having had this evidence brought forcibly to his attention, it was inevitable that Muir would become concerned with what was happening to the forests under political and economic conditions which provided no check upon exploitation of resources regardless of consequences.

During that spring Muir opened up two new markets for his writing. At the urging of William Keith he revised his newspaper piece on living glaciers in the Sierra and sent it to *Harper's Magazine*. The editors were delighted to publish it, thus establishing for Muir the beginnings of a national audience. The *Overland Monthly* was about to fold; Muir replaced it, as a way of providing a steady income, by making a connection with the *San Francisco Daily Evening Bulletin*, which agreed to publish almost anything he would send.

When school was out in June, and Swett's youngest daughter Helen was seen safely into the world, Muir, Keith, McChesney and Swett took off into the High Sierra on a holiday. Muir remained in Yosemite when the others went back to the city, and in early June started on an expedition to Mt. Whitney as guide for a San Franciscan named Bayley, who seems to have been wealthy as well as adventurous. A college student and "Buckskin Bill," whom Muir calls a "mule master," made up the rest of the party. They were very well mounted.

Muir planned to take the route he had followed in 1873 which led through a "yosemite" — a valley sculptured by several glaciers at their confluence — on the South Fork of the Kings River.

By going down into the hot foothills, in sight of the San Joaquin Valley, they were able to find an easy crossing of the Kings after its three main branches — each of which runs in a tremendously deep canyon — have joined to become one river. From the ford they rode upward and eastward into a superb forest

---

* In fact no important legislature adopted Henry George's solution or his further idea that government land should be granted or sold only in parcels of 80 acres or less to each recipient. But two million people bought *Progress and Poverty*, and its effect upon economic thinking was profound. Up until that time, economics had been largely an arm-chair exercise. Henry George looked at, analyzed and drew conclusions from the real-world evidence around him — which is the method of modern economics.

of giant redwoods. And as they made their way through the colonnaded aisles that seemed to have been in place since the dawn of time, the sound of busy axes led them to a most curious sight.

Lumberjacks had felled a Big Tree twenty-five feet in diameter, cut off a sixteen-foot section from the butt end, and split it into eight immense staves which they were now hewing down to a thickness of eight inches inside the bark, which was nearly two feet thick. Careful counts of rings of annual growth showed this tree to have been nearly twenty-two hundred years old. The staves would be shipped to Philadelphia and re-assembled as an exhibit at the Centennial Exposition of 1876.

"Many a poor, defrauded town dweller," Muir wrote in a short article for the *Bulletin*, "will pay his dollar and gain some dead arithmetical notion of the bigness of our Big Trees, but a true and living knowledge of these tree gods is not to be had at so cheap a rate. As well try to send a section of the storms on which they feed."

From the exhibit makers, the party pushed on through the Big Tree forest, into the alpine pine trees above and at long last caught sight of a granite chasm which told Muir they had found the "yosemite" they were looking for. Three thousand five hundred feet below the canyon's rim, the South Fork of the Kings River ran like a silver cord. This canyon was part of a regular route by which Indians crossed the Sierra; Muir's party descended by their trail, which Muir described as "carelessly crinkled and seemingly endless." Bayley was an impulsive, uninhibited character who expressed his enthusiasm by war whoops and, on the way down, set the echoes reverberating from wall to wall of the narrow gorge.*

Muir felt that this "yosemite," carved by glaciers that once filled the big Kings River canyon and its tributaries, was very nearly the rival of the "old" Yosemite of the Merced, not in the size and grandeur of its rock formations, but in the sheer beauty of its south wall and the groves and gardens of its floor. He also felt that the cascades by which tributaries entered the Kings were as lovely, though not so spectacular, as the leaping falls of Yosemite proper. The whole ten-mile length of this beauty seemed just the way Nature had made it — except for a sign nailed to a conspicuous tree announcing that three men claimed this valley for the purpose of raising livestock.

They camped that night at the foot of a high, ice-sculptured monument of granite, in a wild garden of head-high lilies and ferns which contrasted wonderfully with the bare rock. In spite of Muir's willingness to undergo long periods of severe privation — a genuine "mortification of the flesh" — and wander entirely alone for weeks at a time, he was more sybarite than anchorite. When the opportunity came he did not hesitate to indulge either his whims or his tastes. He had become a connoisseur of water, savoring the

* The paved road which now descends this canyonside also seems crinkled and endless — and breath taking — to the modern traveler accustomed to freeways from which every curve, vertical and horizontal, has been eliminated if possible. The road leads to the well known Cedar Grove campgrounds in Kings Canyon National Park.

different taste-blends derived from both mineral and vegetable inputs contributed by the environment of each particular spring and stream. He enjoyed, as deeply as he breathed it, the mixed fragrance of the mountain air containing everything from cedar and pollen and the fragrance of violets to fine rock dust and the lingering aroma of mountain ram. Like mountain water the atmosphere was to him a marvelous example of Nature's ability to achieve balance. That night Muir cut from the wild garden — so opulent that his takings had no effect — ferns for his bed, shooting stars for his pillow and enough mint spikes to provide a subtly pungent ambiance to sleep in.

Following the Indian trail, the party climbed out of the canyon at its head and crossed the Sierra crest among the stupendous rocks of Kearsarge Pass, nearly twelve thousand feet above the sea. Continuing down the Owens Valley they ascended Mt. Whitney by the quite difficult route taken by Muir in 1873 when he climbed this peak which was, before the admission of Alaska to the Union, the highest mountain in the United States.

To avoid an almost impossible tangle of alders and willows in a narrow gorge, Muir led the group up an even narrower gulch, a mere slot in which there was no chance to turn aside. Washburn, the student, was an inexperienced climber, and the other three reached the top considerably ahead of him. Bayley thoughtlessly loosened a big boulder that went bounding wildly down the slot, picking up speed and energy with every yard. It seemed that Washburn must inevitably be killed. The others shouted a warning and held their breaths until his answering shout came up to them faintly. Washburn himself presently appeared, breathless and considerably shaken, to report that he had crouched in a small hollow while the boulder, having struck some projection, leaped mercifully over him.

They camped at 11,500 feet in a meadow spangled with buttercups and daisies. By ten the next morning they were resting on the summit, and would have been there earlier except for Muir's caution. On his first ascent he had taken a more direct route which necessitated climbing where the only hand and footholds were stones more or less securely frozen into the ice covering the steep slopes. He had sworn never to lead anyone up such a dangerous way.

Chapter 29
The Beautiful Riddles of
the Redwoods

As Muir said many times, there is really no way to describe the *Sequoia gigantea*, California's Big Tree.* The latter name has been approved when written with the initial letters capitalized. When fully mature, this vegetable titan is simply *too* tall, at nearly three hundred feet; *too* big in girth, at a circumference of one hundred feet or more; *too* old, at thirty centuries; *too* other-worldly, unlike any other tree — even its nearest relatives, the *Sequoia sempervirens*, the Coast Redwood of California and Oregon and the Dawn Redwood of China. It is not to be comprehended, even by direct contact, in a fleeting, tourist sort of visit. One cannot even see a Big Tree all at once from close by, and from a distance one loses the sense of size as well as many lovely and interesting details.

Though Anglo-Americans had seen some of the Big Trees as early as 1833, only the smaller groves near Yosemite had been frequently visited up to Muir's time; it is probable that in 1875 no one had seen more of the Sequoias than himself. He had not seen enough to suit him, for both aesthetic and scientific reasons. Even among botanists firm evidence was scanty and guesswork plentiful. Therefore Muir set out southward from Yosemite in late August with a wild, tough mule named — as all Muir's mules seemed to have been named — "Brownie." He did not know how long he would be gone or how far he would have to go to answer the questions he wished to "put to the forest" concerning the ecology of the Big Trees. But his previous explorations had shown him that all but one of the Sierra rivers came down the western slope, and that in going south he would have to cross a succession of canyons, some quite unexplored and several among the deepest and steepest in North America.

Muir was well aware that new lumber mills were being built each year, adding their insatiable appetite for trees to the forces already at work to destroy the Sierra as he knew it. By one of his earliest campfires he wrote into his journal a further question — one which turned out to be the most important

* The name "Sequoia" was given to the "red" trees to commemorate a "red" man, the Cherokee Indian, "Sequoyah," who was the first and only American Indian to create an alphabet for the language of his people. The Cherokee alphabet reached its final form in 1821: a newspaper was published in Sequoyah Cherokee in 1828. Congress awarded Sequoyah five hundred dollars for his work.

and most modern of the ecological queries he was trying to answer.

"Will all this (wild) garden be made into beef and mutton pastures, and delved by the hog-herd and the ditcher's spade? I often wonder what man will do with the mountains — that is, with their utilizable, destructible garments. Will he cut down all the trees to make ships and houses? If so, what will be the final and far upshot? Will human destructions, like those of nature — fire and flood and avalanche — work out a higher good, a finer beauty? Will a better civilization come in accord with obvious nature, and all this wild beauty be set to human poetry and song? Another universal outpouring of lava, or the coming of a glacial period could scarce wipe out the flowers and shrubs more effectively than do the sheep. And what then is coming? What is the human part of the mountains' destiny?"*

If anyone before Muir had given man his real and perhaps fatal place in the ecological dynamics of an environment, he had not done so as directly or so cogently. Nor had anyone before him expended so much of himself or risked more to substantiate and elucidate his fears for man and his relation to his world.

From the start, Muir's observations on this trip were (at least to the layman) astonishingly detailed. In one late August afternoon on the headwaters of the North Fork of the San Joaquin he noted thirty-five plants, exclusive of trees, many of them in flower; to most of the names he added a few words of description. Next morning, lying in a fir grove (Muir considered a spot where three or four tall trees interlaced their branches high above him to be the ideal place for a camp bed), he noted five birds he recognized and two he did not know. He was very fond of birds, but for the most part as forest and stream companions rather than objects of intensive study.

Near this camp a high, bare, rounded rock rose surprisingly from the forest. The Indians called it "Wah-Mello"; it is now known as "Frasier Dome." Muir could never resist a challenge to climb, and from the summit of Wah-Mello he was delighted to see exactly what he was seeking — the rounded tops of giant Sequoias apparently motionless above waving miles of yellow pine and fir, among which many individuals would be counted gigantic in other forests.

Hurriedly packing Brownie, Muir reached the Big Trees before evening. Wandering about next morning anxious to see every tree in the grove, which turned out to be only four square miles in extent, he was astonished to come upon a handsome log cabin so new it was still redolent of balsam. Beside the door sat a gray-haired man reading a book. He looked up at Muir with weary, speculative eyes and seemed a little annoyed to have his hermitage discovered. But when Muir told him he was studying the Big Trees he immediately became friendly and insisted that Muir stay with him. His name was John Nelder, and he proved to be, as Muir put it, "one of the interesting wrecks that lie stranded in nooks of the gold region." Since he came to California in the days of '49, Nelder had been a wandering prospector, "sinking hole after hole like a sailor taking soundings." He had made and lost

* Linnie Marsh Wolfe, *John of the Mountains*, pp. 215-217.

several small fortunes and worn himself out in the process. Alone in his retirement home he was content among the birds and squirrels that came at his call to be fed and the red-barked Sequoias, all the way from the giant behind his cabin — bigger in diameter than the dwelling itself — to snow-crippled seedlings whose tops he gently touched and hoped out loud that they would recover and grow tall and straight.

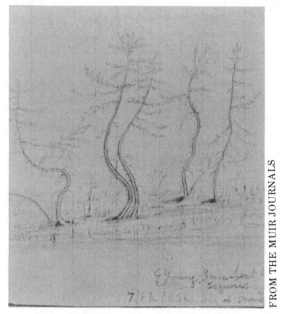

Young, snow-bent Sequoias, seven feet high, one to three inches in diameter at ground level, 1875.

FROM THE MUIR JOURNALS

Nelder gave considerable help to Muir by leading him to places which provided preliminary answers to several of his ecological questions. In one place the bank of a stream had caved in, trees and all, to a depth of fifty feet, and the earth had slipped into a ravine. The original pines, cedars and Sequoias were still growing upon it as though nothing had happened. The landslip had occurred about seven years before, and on the freshly-exposed soil along the broken front, companies of Sequoia saplings were growing confidently, competing well with the pines and cedars which had the same start in life. Farther down stream Muir counted 536 promising young Sequoias growing on two acres of rough, bouldery soil. These vigorous young trees gave quite definite answers to two of Muir's questions. Apparently the prevalent idea that *Sequoia gigantea* was a dying species was a delusion created by the small and scattered, but well-known, northern groves where the giants were almost childless. It now appeared that the Sequoias were able to hold their own against other trees competing for light, water and nourishment.

In another area Nelder showed Muir some ancient fallen trunks that enabled him to trace the Sequoia back toward the end of the Ice Ages. One huge tree when it fell had made a ditch two hundred feet long and five to six feet deep. The middle of this log had been burned away by successive fires and in the gap grew a silver fir four feet in diameter. Muir cut into the fir to make a count of the growth rings and found it to be 380 years of age. Because in Big Tree groves fires occur naturally only at long intervals and the ditches the trees make in falling may remain unplanted for centuries after they are cleared, it appeared that more than a thousand years had elapsed since this particular tree fell. To this period Muir felt two thousand or more years must be added for the Sequoia's own life before it fell. From a remaining section of this trunk he cut a specimen block so sound and firm that it could not be distinguished from a sample of a living tree. Yet Muir feared for the continued existence of this beautiful grove: a sawmill was being built near its edge.*

Muir spent a week in Nelder Grove; but it took him twice as long to cross the three enormously deep, steep canyons of the San Joaquin. It was in these canyons that Brownie became a real nuisance. Sometimes he rolled like a barrel. Sometimes Muir had to untangle him from trap-like rocks and sometimes from stiff, springy chaparral where the little mule became entangled like a fly in a spiderweb. One night when descending one of the steeper San Joaquin canyonsides Muir made camp on a meadow growing above an underground stream which ran so close to the surface that he could hear the water music every time he woke during an unrestful night. His bed was on a thirty degree slope, for the meadow had formed over boulders which anciently had slid into the streambed during a landslip. As he usually did when sleeping on steep slopes, Muir built a wall of rock to keep from rolling downhill.

He found no Big Trees at all in the two weeks he spent in crossing the San Joaquin watershed. It was then Muir began to realize that where the river-like glaciers had lain longest and deepest the *Sequoia gigantea* did not grow. Their place was on the higher ground where little or no ice had been, though the Big Trees grew luxuriantly on crumbled granite outwashed from glacial moraines.

Finally in the latter part of September a chance-met sheepherder led Muir to a small grove of well-developed Sequoias on Dinkey Creek, one of the northernmost tributaries of the Kings River. He found it especially beautiful because of a crystalline stream of water filtered through the gigantic root-mat of the grove. The brook came musically down a fall into a still pool bordered by ferns and flowers. It seemed to Muir that the Greeks would have consecrated this place to some lovely naiad. He was especially interested by some Big Trees growing on a bare granite ledge, gripping the rocks as pines do, with roots spread wide to penetrate every crack where water might be reached.

Like those of the San Joaquin, the glacier-carved canyons of the Kings proved to lack Sequoias. But when Muir had "led, dragged and shoved" Brownie across the great chasm of the South Fork, he found a scattering of Big Trees near Mill Flat; striking northeast he came upon a Sequoia forest two miles wide and six miles long, with outlying groves still farther

* Muir was quite justified in this apprehension; the grove, formerly called the "Fresno" but now known as the "Nelder," was logged over in 1888-1890. But he was also justified in his optimism, for the Sequoias here have been reproducing abundantly since the last logging.

east. This area contained the famous Converse Basin where, at that time, grew one of the most magnificent stands of Big Trees. Here Muir spent nearly a week delighted, as he wrote, "to learn from countless trees young and old how comfortably they were settled down in concordance with climate, soil and their noble neighbors." In a sort of bay burned into a stand of dense chaparral he counted eighty-six young Sequoias from one to fifty feet high — clear evidence that fire is one of the agents which prepares ground for germination of the tiny seeds the Big Trees produce by millions. From the picturesque wet meadows of Converse Basin, Muir also received a strong suggestion of the true relationship between the Big Trees and water — though he did not develop his conclusions fully and firmly until he reached the Giant Forest.

On his way there Muir encountered, in the small but magnificent General Grant Grove, a considerable number of shake-makers happily destroying a stand of sugar pines which — except among the Sequoia neighbors — would seem huge. These were itinerant workmen of the breed who established the long-cherished American belief that any man willing to work could earn a living. This was more or less true as long as free land, free water, free timber and plenty of wild game were readily available.*

With no greater investment than a cheap mule or mustang, a pair of blankets, a sack of flour, a cross-cut saw, an axe and a splitting tool called a "frow," the shake-maker headed for the mountains as soon as the harvest was over down below. Chopping deep into as many six- to eight-foot trees as necessary to find a trunk with straight grain and no knots, the maker felled the selected tree and cut off four-foot sections from the first thirty feet of the butt end. These were split into "shakes" four feet long, four inches wide and one-quarter inch thick.

The first section of a single log provided enough shakes to build a cabin, the second enough to trade at a mill or store for the season's grub. The remaining six sections were clear profit, for the shakes found a ready market among ranchers and others who used the shingle-like boards for barns, sheds and roofs. The rest of the tree, which often totalled over two thousand feet in length, was left with its branches to rot or feed a forest fire. The maker meanwhile went on killing more trees in "prospecting" for straight grain and felling the choicest for more shakes. No individual shakemaker destroyed very much, but the cumulative effect of even small battalions of them created havoc.

Following a scattering of Big Trees southward Muir came to a ridge where the giants stood in long ranks one above the other, their lacy yellow-green tops looking curiously like cumulus clouds rising from the mountain toward the

* Even in pioneer times some had doubts about the complete efficacy of the work ethic. Folk songs frequently express such misgivings, as in the following stanza:

"Hooray for Lane County, the land of the free!
Home of the rattlesnake, bedbug and flea.
I'll fight for her always, uphold her fair name
While I starve like a man on my government claim!"

sky. The boom of dynamite told him that a sawmill was busy near this forest.

A tree trunk that contains enough wood to load 280 freight cars and build a village of 150 five-room houses is bound to make lumbermen very eager. Because a log big enough to supply so much can scarcely be managed, Muir found that the men feeding this mill were cutting young trees eight to twelve feet in diameter. If all the wood in such a tree could be utilized it would build thirty-five or forty houses.* But the wood of *Sequoia gigantea* is very "brash" —to use Muir's term — that is, brittle. When the Big Trees came crashing down they tended to splinter into pieces, some so huge they were unmanageable. The lumberjacks simply left these in the forest. Long strings of oxen dragged the transportable pieces to a great chute which skidded them to the vicinity of the mill, where they were dynamited in the hope of obtaining some fragments the saws could handle. Thus only about one-fourth of a felled Sequoia became lumber. Worse still, the "slash" — unusable pieces, tops and branches — was left to dry out and feed running fires.**

The mill — that "sad center of destruction" — depressed Muir and, after replenishing his bread sack, he and Brownie pushed on southward into forests scarcely known to anyone.

* Figures are from *Big Trees*, by Walter Fry and John R. White, p. 51.
** The branches of an eight-foot Sequoia contain about 30,000 pounds of wood. The branches of the General Sherman Tree, an exceptionally large Sequoia, contain 4,325 cubic feet of wood weighing 219,494 pounds.

Chapter 30
The Giant Forest

$\boxed{\text{M}}$uir described his course southward as "wavering," for one of his important objectives was to locate as many Big Trees as possible and discover all he could about climate, soil and other conditions under which they grew. He ranged from the four thousand five hundred-foot hills overlooking the valley of the San Joaquin to alpine groves at eight thousand feet, just below the fountains of perpetual ice and snow. Inevitably this meant crossing many deep and steep ravines where small, swift streams ran, as well as all five branches of the Kaweah River, each of which runs in a chasm. Their uncharted course was terribly difficult for the mule and laborious for the man; in many places he had to make a trail for Brownie, or extricate him from situations with which two feet and a pair of hands could cope more readily than four hooves.

Muir was happy because at least some Big Trees were nearly always in sight. When he had struggled across the Middle Fork of the Kaweah and reached the divide that separates it from the Marble Fork, he found himself in a Sequoia forest beyond any he had dreamed. Trees twenty-five feet in diameter were common here, and those of thirty feet or more were not rare.

On the morning after his arrival he stood at the edge of a meadow three-quarters of a mile long, the brown and purple of the vegetation on its floor threaded with green along a network of little streams. The fall tints of the bushes and vines that made the border were vivid enough to have been painted — and more beautiful. Behind this frame the great trees rose nearly three hundred feet, a colonnade of fluted pillars so thick and strong they seemed to be holding the sky on their green heads. When not gazing as if transfixed, Muir moved to new vantage points or made small forays to discover which plants were responsible for particular blocks or patches of color. Thinking himself entirely alone he expressed his joy in wild shouts and murmurs of endearment to the "plant people."

The rhythmic thudding of a rapidly ridden horse startled him abruptly out of his communion with primal nature. Glad to encounter another human after so long a time alone, Muir hailed the rider and stepped forward to meet him. The man reined in his mustang, but said nothing until Muir had pleasantly told him how glad he was to have some company. Instead of answering, the rider continued to stare down grimly and harshly asked: "What are you doing?

How did you get here?"

When Muir explained that he had crossed the canyons from Yosemite and that he was only looking at trees, the rider's manner changed entirely. "Oh, then I know!" he said — "You must be John Muir." The rider gave his own name as Hale Tharp. And when Muir mentioned that he had only a handful of crumbs left in his breadsack and asked if Tharp could spare him a little flour, the answer was "Of course! You're welcome to anything I've got. Just take my track and it will lead you to my camp in a big hollow log two or three miles from here. Make yourself at home! I've got to ride after some strayed horses, but I'll be back before night."

Muir saddled Brownie and by mid-afternoon had located Tharp's "cabin" — which turned out to be a 56-foot section of a fallen Sequoia. It had been estimated that this tree stood 311 feet tall at the time of its fall. Fire had hollowed the inside so that Tharp had a one-log home 8 feet in diameter at the front and 4 feet at the rear.* Muir found the inside sweet and clean and not at all sooty, though shiny black. He also found some bread and sat in the opening gazing out across Crescent Meadow as he sat munching.

Tharp galloped up before long, driving the runaway horses before him. While he cooked supper he told Muir how and why he came to be here in the Giant Forest and the reason for his initial unfriendliness. He had homesteaded his ranch in 1856, toward the end of the Gold Rush, near the site of Three Rivers, an old town at the point where the Kaweah's branches finally merge to form one river. At that time there were some two thousand Indians of the Potwisha tribe living on the Kaweah watershed. Tharp liked these Indians, for whom he sometimes shot deer and bear; the Indians trusted Tharp and told him a good deal about their part of the Sierra. In 1858 when two Potwisha offered to take him to the Giant Forest he accepted — partly from curiosity and partly to look for a suitable summer range where he could take his stock when the valley became as hot and barren as an empty oven with the heat left on.

The Giant Forest seemed ideal for his purposes, and, in 1861 when white settlers were beginning to increase in the Three Rivers area, Hale Tharp realized that he must establish his claim to it by continued use. He and his stepson drove a band of horses up to the meadow beside his hollow log and kept them there until fall. Each summer thereafter he brought up stock to graze in the shadow of the Big Trees. He continued to get on well with the Indians, but any white stranger immediately came under suspicion. The good grazing in this open, sunlit forest was tempting to any stockman, and the trees

* At that time there were a good many large, fire-hollowed Big Tree logs lying in the Sierra groves. Some were big enough to ride through on horseback. Muir believed that only the very large logs are bored out by fire inasmuch as the flames, which for a time burn fiercely in the crack between the sections into which a tree had broken when it falls, eventually widening the gap so much that the fire is no longer sustained by the proximity of the two ends, but burns on in the center of each section. The heat is then intensified by reflection from the sides of the hole and the log burns on until its inside is completely consumed, leaving a stout shell of wood around the bore.

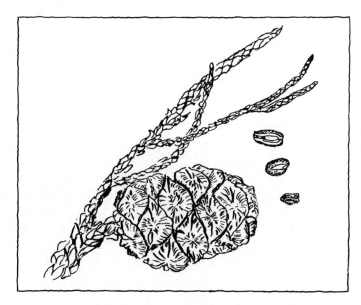

Sequoia sempervirens—cone with seeds.

themselves were almost more than a timber cruiser or mill operator could bear to leave standing. He had explored the neighborhood extensively and was of considerable help to Muir, who spent over a week with him.

Each morning Muir started his day's ramble to birdsong, for all of the conifers of the Giant Forest shed flights of nestlings as deciduous trees shed leaves; from some Sequoias the feathered crops had spread abroad summer after summer for over three thousand years. Throughout the day the forest stillness was broken by the bumping, pattering fall of Sequoia cones cut from the branches by squirrels and the whisper, as faint as dry snow blowing, of tiny brown seeds drifting by millions down the wind. Muir estimated that the seeds produced by a single Big Tree grove in a fruitful year would be enough to plant all the mountain ranges of the world.*

By the time he explored the Giant Forest Muir had already learned that, in order to germinate and take root, Big Tree seeds require freshly exposed and pulverized soil — "pure" in the sense of being free of forest debris and contaminants such as inimical fungi. Like most of the Sierra conifers, Sequoia seedlings seemed to prefer soil made up largely of glacier-ground granite; yet

* Muir did not mean this statement literally but used it to suggest the characteristics of Big Tree propagation, which are as extraordinary as the size and age of the giant itself. The seeds are only one-quarter inch long. The kernel is enclosed in a stiff shell equipped with a pair of wings and has the diameter of a fine needle. Fry and White state that from the time a Big Tree matures, between the ages of 125 and 175 years, it produces "untold millions" of seeds each year. Three thousand seeds weigh one ounce. Some idea of the fecundity of the tree and the industry of the Douglas squirrel is given by Judge Fry, who says that when he was collecting for experimental purposes he took from under a big log, where a single squirrel had stored them in about twelve days, enough cones (5,353) to furnish 1,248,000 seeds (twenty-six pounds of seeds). However only one seed in a million germinates; of the thousands that germinate only a small fraction take root, and of these only a few reach their first birthdays. Once a Sequoia seedling survives the perils of its first year it is likely to live on for thousands of years, unless attacked by fire, which is naturally beneficent to the species, or by man, who is not.

he found them prospering in places too dry for other trees which compete with them elsewhere. This observation was partial disproof of the prevalent idea that the Big Trees were doomed because the Sierra Nevada was gradually drying out. Muir's careful counts of the annual growth rings of huge old stumps, one of which had a diameter of thirty-five feet inside the bark and seemed to have been over four thousand years old at its death, assured him that the Sierra climate had not changed appreciably during the past fifty centuries. In view of the Big Trees' adaptability to areas where the roots had to go far in search of water, it was paradoxical that the species grew most luxuriantly in damp areas where one was likely to find well-watered meadows and bogs as well as streams — places such as the Giant Forest, where meadows and bogs rise one above the other like terraces on some hillsides.

Examining some of the wetter areas, Muir was surprised to find that many large Sequoias had fallen into them, each log a dam twenty feet or more in height and as much as two hundred feet long; each place where a great tree's roots had been torn from the earth was now a bowl as much as two hundred feet across and filled with water. Thinking back over what must have happened here, Muir realized that many of these prostrate trees had been felled by water impounded by giants that had come crashing down before them. More and more water was thus stored behind the log dams and in the root bowls. Gazing at the huge expanse of roots fanning out from the bases of newly fallen trees, Muir realized that in a grove or forest of Big Trees the roots — which form an underground circle having the same diameter as the height of the individual tree they support — interlace to form water-retaining networks larger and more effective than those found in any other forest of the world. Moreover the Big Trees grow along the elevation-band of the Sierras where snow falls most heavily, which gives them plenty of water to store when summer comes.*

The inescapable conclusion Muir reached was that the Big Trees, rather than seeking wet areas, actually created such areas by restraining water that would otherwise come roaring down in destructive floods. *Sequoia gigantea* was thus an incalculably important factor in the water system of the Sierra Nevada and of the fertile and eminently farmable San Joaquin Valley at its foot. Even Sequoia foliage helps preserve water during dry spells for, as Muir wrote in a paper for the American Association for the Advancement of Science, "...the air is entangled in masses and broad sheets, while thirsty winds are not allowed to go sponging and licking along the ground."

* In the Giant Forest on February 25, 1905, the snow on the level lay a record twenty-nine feet deep. There were still twelve feet on the level the following June.

Chapter 31
Camped in a Burning Grove

[H]ale Tharp told Muir that the Big Trees extended far to the south, but just how far he did not know; in early October Muir left to find out for himself. His course was even more rugged than he had anticipated — especially for Brownie. Each of the Kaweah's main branch canyons bears the marks of a wildly turbulent glacier, spectacular with frozen cascades where the ice stream inched its way down rough, steep formations of unyielding rock.

As he crossed the divide between the Middle and East Forks of the Kaweah, Muir met a fire coming up from the latter's canyon through dense chaparral.* It was coming as fast as a horse can run, with occasional pauses when the flames reared up as if looking for the way to go. Each time they chose the course which would take them into a handsome grove of Big Trees.

But the moment the wild blaze reached the grove it calmed down, for a time, like a mountain torrent entering a lake. The forest floor was covered by a two-foot mat with a foundation of humus and a topping of twigs, needles and seed cones. The fire crept forward, nibbling its way in search of food more readily consumable.

Muir had always loved fires for their beauty and excitement as well as their comfort. He had long understood the constructive role of natural fires in the ecological dynamics of the wilderness. As always he was impelled to come as close as he could to nature in action.

He led Brownie to a safe distance and tethered him on good grass beside a stream. Then he entered the forest, skirting the fire, and selected for his camp a tree directly in its path. The Sequoia was very large and, though a hollow big enough for him to stand and lie in had been burned at the base, he felt sure that it would not fall. Only a succession of fires burn through a mature Big Tree. Their trunks, protected by two feet of fire-resistant bark, scarcely burn at all except when a large pile of fallen branches has accumulated at the base of a tree standing on a slope. Muir's tree had no such pile; the last accumulation of branches had probably been consumed in a previous fire. Muir piled green, succulent ferns into the hollow, stored his breadsack and

* It is characteristic that in his journal Muir noted that this "Elfin Forest" was composed principally of wild cherry, manzanita and ceanothus.

water supply and settled down while the fire burned around him and passed on. Then he went out to observe.

Though the advancing fire was only a few inches high in most places, with little jets shooting up from the heaps of dry cones and twigs here and there, tall flame spires and sheets with ragged, flapping edges seemed to dance around the clumps of dried grass, bushes and seedling trees. Where fallen branches lay smashed together in piles containing as much as one hundred cords of wood, bonfires raged in storms of furious energy.

These branch fires accomplished the conflagration's most heart-breaking work. Young *Sequoia gigantea*s grow as shapely cones, like conventionalized Christmas trees, with branches drooping close to the ground. The fire ate these in one gulp. But the branches of youthful trees, one hundred and fifty years old or thereabouts, could not be readily reached by the ground flames. Those which had large piles of smashed branches about their feet stood quite calmly, like martyrs at the stake amid raging bonfires, until the heat had distilled a critical amount of gas from their foliage. Then the tree exploded in a spout of roaring fire two to three hundred feet high. These bursts lasted only a few seconds. When they subsided the tree trunk was a black spar with funereal decorations of burned and lifeless limbs.

High in some larger trees, two hundred fifty feet or more from the ground fires, huge dead limbs were blazing furiously. By day Muir could not imagine how these fires were ignited. But after dark when he left his hollowed trunk to watch the fireworks, he found the answer. Standing as close as he dared to a relatively small blaze licking the base of a large tree, he saw rivulets of pale blue flames run up the trunk like darting, whispering snakes. When these flame rivulets reached a dry, lightning-riven branch it immediately burst into flame. How the flames climbed the tree was immediately clear to Muir. He had observed earlier that the furrows in the bark which gave a Big Tree trunk its fluted look have along their sides whiskers of fibers, parted as the tree grows in girth. Obviously the flames fed on these whiskers as they ran upward.

Muir slept little, for the awful beauty of the burning forest called him out night after night. Fallen logs were burning like gargantuan bars of red-hot metal. High overhead stricken limbs burned on like beacon fires lighted on headlands. From these disembodied blazes, coals and embers sifted down unpredictably, and every now and then a branch weighing half a ton fell comet-like to continue burning on the ground. Muir moved about cautiously, his ear tuned to sounds from above amid the strange fire symphony of whispers, murmurs and roars surrounding him.

Weary and red-eyed from virtually sleepless days and nights in the burning forest, Muir retrieved Brownie and set off southward under brown clouds of Sequoia smoke. Their way across the canyons was so rough that trails had to be made for the mule in many places, and Muir was so weary that the work taxed him. They made only three miles on the first day.

The spot Muir found for a camp was a beauty, with good grass on the edge of a forest that had not known fire for many years. But a number of trees were marked from a height of eight feet downward with interlaced, pointed arches — hieroglyphics drawn by bears in cleaning their claws. Bear scent was evidently heavy in Brownie's nostrils; he refused to leave the vicinity of the camp fire when turned loose to graze — but was careful not to step on his master. Wild when they started, the mule had become more and more dependent on the man. And Muir had come to regard Brownie in something the way a man feels toward a willing, amiable boy who is not quite up to the journey they have undertaken together.

A couple of days later four deer breakfasted with Muir in a small, flowering meadow surrounded by dense chaparral. They came almost near enough to touch, backed off snorting, then returned to feed like Chinese gourmets at a banquet — a mouthful of wild cherry here, a few wild lilac leaves there and occasional spikes of mint for seasoning. When they had gone, Muir examined the wild garden minutely to test his long-held belief that deer do no damage with their sharp hooves. Not one crushed flower could he find, nor any grass stem that had been bent or broken.

The Big Tree forests he found along the North Fork of the Tule River seemed to Muir the finest and most luxuriant he had seen. Here they were the dominant species. "Where rival trees mix with them," he wrote, "they mostly grow up like slender grasses among stalks of Indian corn." From these circumstances Muir concluded that when *Sequoia gigantea* re-established itself after the Ice Age, it began in the south and worked northward to the limit of its range in Placer County, 270 miles from the Tule.

Hard times awaited man and mule in the basin of the Tule's South Fork. Successive bands of sheep had been driven through this section, each band hungrier than the last. They had eaten out everything they could chew — even the young evergreen trees which sheep never touch unless they are on the edge of starvation.

In this desolation Brownie was actually starving. One morning when Muir was kneeling over his breakfast fire making a cake from the last of the flour some Indian sheepherders had given him, the mule came up behind him and begged for help in a pitiful mixture of bray and neigh that wrung Muir's heart. He gave Brownie half of the cake and promised to take him straight to alfalfa and barley the next morning.

They had worked their way only half a mile through chaparral when they were led to a sawmill by its shrill whistle. Both had a good meal, and Muir could have gotten enough supplies to finish his exploration of the Tule region. But Brownie was "played out," and Muir felt that he must keep his promise to his dumb comrade.

Ten miles down the dusty road, they were hailed by a man no longer young, but pine straight, who come toward them from his commodious cabin.

"Where in the hell did you come from? I didn't see you go up!"

"From Yosemite, looking at trees."

"Then you must be John Muir! Come in and rest and I'll cook for you. Turn your mule into that corral yonder. It's full of hay and grain. How in hell did you get him across those canyons? Roll him or carry him?"

This talkative and hospitable cattleman furnished Muir a horse, and together they set off for the rugged region to the south — the rancher to hunt deer, Muir to explore the Sequoia belt to its southern limit, which he found to be on Deer Creek, a tributary of the Tule. On his way back to join the cattleman, Muir crossed a seven thousand-foot divide and discovered that the Big Trees had also come this way to establish themselves in the south-trending canyon of the Kern River.

Brownie had to be returned to Yosemite, and Muir made the trip north much more quickly than he had come down. He was determined (it cannot be said that Muir was ever eager to start writing) to get back to book-making. But before he left, he topped off the year's adventures with an experience like none he had known before, and one which he was destined never to repeat.

Up until that fall of 1876, Half Dome had never been climbed. On two sides it descends sixteen hundred feet almost vertically; a third approach to the summit presents a very steep curve of one thousand feet. Where the Dome's structure joins the granite mass of Clouds Rest, one can, with relative ease, ascend to a point called "The Saddle," about seven hundred feet from the crest. But the curve here, though gentler, is also too steep to climb without mechanical aids. In 1873 John Conway, the master trail-builder of Yosemite, and his two little barefoot boys, who could climb like lizards, had gone part way up this curve by driving eyebolts into cracks in the rock and stringing a rope through them. But when they reached an uncracked surface where drilling would be necessary, they gave up.

While Muir was exploring the Big Tree forests, a man named Anderson had started where the Conways left off and, by standing on the topmost eyebolt, managed to drill and hammer in the next. By repeating the process, he reached the crest in a few days.

Muir arrived on a day between Indian summer and winter when the clouds came down around Yosemite's walls as if looking for work. Snow might fall within an hour. But though Anderson and others urgently counselled him not to go up, Muir would hear no voice of caution; he had to surmount Half Dome — now.

At first the view from the summit was pure glory; a lustrous pale gray cloud arched across the Valley from wall to wall, spanning it from El Capitan to Cathedral Rocks. But soon a flock of smaller, pure white clouds came in through the canyons and, merging with the pearly arch, filled Yosemite with a cloud river on whose surface the sun glowed lustrously. As he gazed Muir was startled to see, for the first and last time of his life, a phenomenon the Scotch call the "Specter of the Brocken" — the shadow of himself, but magnified to enormous proportions. Never one to miss a chance to amuse himself, he raised his arm, and an arm bigger than a Sequoia signalled back to him. He danced a few steps of the highland fling, and the monster danced in response. He took off his hat. His shadow raised a hat thirty stories high.

It was, in a way, a farewell salute to the John Muir who for seven years had been the desperately lonely, supremely happy lover and student of the Sierra Nevada.*

* In Muir's account of the "Specter of the Brocken," he says that he ascended Half Dome on November 10, 1875, immediately after returning from a trip to Mount Sierra. This is evidently a slip of the pen or a misreading of his own notes for, on November 2, 1875, he wrote to his sister Sarah that he had returned the day before to Yosemite from an exploration of the redwoods. See his *The Yosemite*, pp. 125-128.

Part V

EXPLORER

"Don't pity me. Pity yourselves. You stay at home, dry and defrauded of all the glory I have seen. Your souls starve in the midst of abundance!"

Chapter 32
What Will Man Do With the Mountains?

uring the remaining weeks of 1875 while Muir was settling once more
into John Swett's commodious San Francisco home and, meanwhile,
striving to assimilate his overwhelming experiences of the past few months,
his mind became more and more dominated by the culminating ecological
question he had asked himself in sight of Wah-Mello Dome, at the start of his
Big Tree pilgrimage: "What is the human part of the mountains' destiny?"

The alternatives were now starkly clear to him. If current practices of
lumber companies and sheepmen were continued, the Sierra Nevada would
become a wasteland and the fertile San Joaquin Valley a desert ravaged by
uncontrollable floods that left no life-giving water behind in their furious rush
toward the sea, but only gravel and boulders outwashed from the mountains.
Man — at least California man — would thus commit not only spiritual suicide
by destroying the Sierra as a place to renew oneself by once more becoming a
member of Nature's great family, but would also commit literal, physical
suicide by destroying irreplaceable resources of land, water and forests upon
which his very life depends.* The alternative was to check destruction before
it had gone too far. The best time to do so — perhaps the only time left — was
then, when a very considerable part of the nation's wilderness was still public
domain, in spite of the enormous acreage already given away.

Muir put the urgency of saving the Sierra's forests cogently before the
American Association for the Advancement of Science in a paper read at its
twenty-fifth meeting (August, 1876) and published in its proceedings. Muir
was not then a member of that august body; his paper was delivered *in
absentia* at the urging of Asa Gray, the Harvard botanist. In it Muir presented
the conclusions he had reached concerning the Big Trees during his field
studies of the previous summer. The piece is too interesting, personal and

---

* The Converse Basin, just north of the long-protected General Grant Grove of Big Trees, lies as
a sad memorial to the correctness of Muir's vision. Once-flowering meadows embroidered with
living streams are now fields of brown dust surrounded by enormous stumps and the great logs
cut from them — logs the lumbermen did not even attempt to move to the chutes leading to the
mill. According to Fry and White, not more than one-fourth of the trees cut during the
destruction of this once-superb forest were ever sawed into lumber. One of the sourest ironies
of the continuing battle between exploiters and conservationists is that the attempt to harvest
the redwoods of Converse Basin bankrupted the company which undertook the exploit.

vivid for a conventional scientific paper. But neither Gray nor any of his colleagues found fault with either the research plan or the logic by which Muir derived his conclusions from his evidence.

In California as elsewhere in the United States, more or less serious study groups were popular in those days. They provided informal adult education to people largely cut off from the seats of learning and environments of cultural activity — people who, it should be remembered, had no electronic means of receiving culture in their homes. The Literary Institute of Sacramento invited Muir to give a lecture on January 25, 1876. Muir was literally frightened sick. Though he had lectured readily and successfully to farm audiences during the period when he taught grade school to earn a living and kept up his work at the University of Wisconsin by correspondence, the very thought of speaking to educated city folk made him feel nauseated. Possibly his lonely mountain and forest years had made him morbidly shy. It seems more likely that his father's brutally reiterated opinion, that John was less than the dust and "the world" would account him worthless, had seeped through some cracks in Muir's very strong ego to appear on the surface when he was faced with even the prospect of a cultivated audience. In any case he was persuaded to give the lecture only when William Keith lent him one of his High-Sierra landscapes saying, "You can look at that, Johnnie, and imagine you're in the mountains."

Muir had become very well known in California. The *Overland Monthly* issues containing his "Studies in the Sierra" had even been carried through Bloody Canyon down to the mining camps in the Mono region on the eastern Sierra slope. On the evening of his lecture, the Congregational Church in Sacramento was filled with a large, expectant audience, which frightened Muir more — as a friend put it — "than a wilderness of wild beasts." He began so haltingly and apologetically, deprecating himself so much, that the audience began to share his fear of failure.

In the midst of his misery Muir's good angel — and no one in the past ages of belief could have doubted that he had a special one — made him look at Keith's large picture, which had been set on an easel beside the lectern.

Next morning's *Sacramento Record-Union* gave an on-scene account of what happened: "He forgot himself and his audience, only remembering that he was to make clear some wondrous mysteries...his manner was so easy...his style so severely plain and so homely as often to provoke a smile, while the judgment gave hearty approval to the points. Indeed, Mr. Muir was at once the most unartistic and refreshing, the most unconventional and positive lecturer we have yet had in Sacramento."*

Muir's topic was "Sierra Glaciers," but he managed to get in a good deal about the forests and the critical need to preserve them. The lecture also gave him a splendid opportunity to further his unrelenting and increasingly successful campaign to make both the critics and the public more appreciative of Keith's paintings.

A week later the *Record-Union* published a communication (actually a short

* Quoted by Linnie Marsh Wolfe in *Son of the Wilderness: The Life of John Muir*, p. 190.

essay) in which Muir stated the case for government action to save the forests even more eloquently and urgently than before. The copy desk of the paper produced a headline-writer's masterpiece which combines both the spiritual and material aspects of the case Muir presented:

"GOD'S FIRST TEMPLES"
HOW SHALL WE PRESERVE OUR FORESTS?
The Question Considered by John Muir, the California
Geologist — The Views of a Practical Man and a Scientific
Observer — A Profoundly Interesting Article.

Muir's article created considerable stir among the legislators in Sacramento — a stir about as effective as leaves moving in a breeze. It takes more than a few lectures and an eloquent newspaper article to get a movement started.

The Swett household was a happy place to be (except for the children's piano practicing, which nearly drove Muir — as he would have put it — daft). He was especially fond of baby Helen, for whose arrival into this world Muir and Keith, as well as her father, had delayed their trip into the High Sierra during the previous summer. Mary Swett was a lively, high-spirited, independent young woman — daughter of a prominent judge who had strenuously objected to her marrying an impoverished school teacher. When times were hard she took in "paying guests," of whom Muir was doubtless one. When an actor or poet or some such impractical boarder could not pay up, Mary Swett let him stay anyway and somehow managed to keep them all fed.

She was very fond of John Muir — in a genuinely companionable way — and happy to contest with him in the hair-splitting arguments which provided one of his few sources of entertainment when confined to the city.

In spite of his good and helpful friends Muir's writing went slowly and toilsomely, with many interruptions. He accepted lecture engagements because they were profitable, but the overhead to himself was high because of the terrors he continued to suffer beforehand. Moreover San Francisco was an uneasy, often depressing place to live just then.

Thousands of Chinese, imported to help build the western segment of the transcontinental railway, had already displaced caucasian workers in San Francisco, and many more small, tough men with pigtails were streaming back to the metropolis now that the first rail line to Los Angeles had been completed. Resentment on the part of caucasian workers was rising toward the dangerous pitch that produced the "Sand Lot Riots" of 1877, when even the wealthiest and most powerful were threatened. The latter included, among other well-remembered *nouveau riche*, Leland Stanford, Sr. and George Hearst, the most consistently successful mine-owner of his generation.* Their pseudo-chateaux and ersatz villas, built of redwood with the outside treated to

* It was George Hearst's custom to give his son William Randolph, the future publisher, a ten dollar gold piece each time he left the house in order that the lad might learn to handle money and also buy a kind of popularity.

look like stone, were rising rapidly on the top of Nob (for "nabob") Hill which had recently been made accessible by the first cable line on which cars ran with no visible means of propulsion. San Franciscans have never made up their minds whether to think of them as toys or vehicles.

The Swett's house was lower down on the slope of Nob Hill, and instead of looking toward the instant elegance above, Muir's windows looked down upon San Francisco Bay and the intervening slum called "Tar Flat," a suburb of the notorious "Barbary Coast," where a sailor was lucky to spend twenty-four hours ashore before being shanghaied aboard a ship that would not return through the Golden Gate for a year or more.

Tar Flat, where the clip-joint merchants and dive keepers of the Barbary Coast were inclined to keep their families (if they had any), was a breeding bed for the original "Hoodlums," San Francisco's unique contribution to the youth gangs of America. They wore fantastic costumes (exaggerated bell-bottoms were *de rigeur* for the young dandies) and fantastic hairdos. Their usual arms were clubs or "brass knuckles," which were sometimes pieces of corrugated iron strapped to the backs of the hands — weapons that could chop a face to pieces. The Hoodlums' behavior models were the Barbary Coast "Rangers," who lived by mayhem and the earnings of prostitutes who admired their physical prowess. The Hoodlums ran in packs and would attack any persons who appeared incapable of defending themselves. But their particular pleasure was to maltreat, terrorize and rob the Chinese, whose overcrowded, partly-underground, crime-ridden ghetto also bordered on the Barbary Coast.

On his days of escape Muir went to the superb forests of Coast Redwoods across the Golden Gate from San Francisco. The direct route to and from the ferry took him through Tar Flat. The wondering delight the children of that dismal community took in the wildflowers he brought home touched Muir deeply. Leaving their play in the muddy street they gathered 'round him, begging in small, uncertain voices: "Give me a flower, Mister! Please, Mister, give me a flower!" Muir always brought plenty of blossoms to hand out.

Not every adult in Tar Flat was a thug, a Hoodlum or a drunken slattern. Some decent people lived there because they could not afford to live anywhere else. One of these was a widower named Dumkroger who had several young boys and a daughter in her early 'teens. The girl had her hands full keeping house for all those males, but on the back porch, which was directly below Muir's window, she had a shelf of plants — geraniums, tulips, some roses and other green flowers — growing in cans and cracked pots.

At times — and there were many of them — when Muir's writing would not move, he liked to stand at his window and watch this girl tend her garden, or simply touch the plants lovingly as she hurried by on her housekeeping chores. It seemed to Muir that if so driven a youngster could manage to love natural beauty and keep it alive in Tar Flat, there must be some hope for humanity after all.

Girls seem to have been considerably on Muir's mind. The "circle of adoring ladies" an Indianapolis correspondent teased him about had already begun to form around him. To his sister Sarah he wrote, "Little did I think when I used to be, and am now, fonder of home and still domestic life than any one of the boys, that I should be a bachelor and doomed to roam always....But we are governed more than we know and driven with whips we know not where...."*

He was soon driven (enticed is probably a more accurate term, for he had the itch to go exploring as soon as spring began to color the hills behind Oakland) to the eastern side of the Sierra Nevada and the mountains to the south which are virtually a continuation of that range. He does not seem to have had a firm objective, but rather to have been looking for something — and perhaps someone — to commit himself to.

Late in the summer his wanderings took him to the green, refreshing ridge of the Cuyamaca Mountains that stand between the rolling littoral of San Diego County and the Imperial Valley, which at that time was an uninhabited wasteland of rock, dust and sand graced here and there by the ocotillo cactus. For several weeks Muir stayed near the small town of Julian with a family named Talley. The Talley's daughter was an outdoor girl named Mary Jane, then twenty years of age. On foot and on horseback Mary Jane and Muir explored the Cuyamacas together. Legend suggests that the senior Talleys came to disapprove of the association — though for what reason has never been stated. In any case Muir returned abruptly to San Francisco, and a month after his departure Mary Jane married a former suitor.**

By the end of 1876, Muir, besides lecturing, had produced only an unsatisfactory draft of a book about the Sierra Nevada and a couple of articles for *Harpers*, which had been paid for but not yet published. Still restless and relatively undirected, he took off in April,1877, for Utah. From there he sent several pieces to the *San Francisco Bulletin*, the most memorable of which was a tribute to the beauty of a young granddaughter of Brigham Young, a girl he called "The Mormon Lily of San Pitch."

From Salt Lake City he went to Los Angeles, which he described as "that handsome, conceited little town where one finds Yankee shingles and Spanish adobes overlapping in very curious antagonism." Nearly everyone he met

* William F. Badè, *The Life and Letters of John Muir*, Vol. II, p. 62.

** The evidence for Muir's stay with the Talleys rests solely on the visit of a Mrs. Marvin E. Shigley to the San Diego Historical Society in 1939. Mrs. Shigley, who was the wife of a U. S. Navy Captain, said that her mother, née Mary Jane Talley, had asked her to present the Society with two objects John Muir had given her sixty-two years before. One was a "scrap book herbarium" of pressed California and Arizona plants, which is now in the library of the University of California at San Diego; the other item — now in the possession of the Serra Museum of the San Diego Historical Society — is a curious and quite charming collage made of ferns and pine needles of a squirrel in a forest setting. Three circumstances help to lend credence to the authenticity of these items. First, it seems improbable that a rational woman would journey to San Diego to present frauds for which she asked neither money or acclaim. Second, the squirrel is in character; Muir had both the talent and the whimsey to produce such a work for a girl he liked. Third, Muir had been encouraging girls to keep herbariums as early as his stay in Canada during his early twenties.

tried to sell him bouldery land on which to plant an orange grove.

Muir was much better pleased with the "bee pastures" — foothills and mountain slopes where wild lily gardens lay concealed in the flowering chaparral. He wrote a good deal about bees, for man could get food from them, and even money, without doing wild nature anything but good.

Working his way northward via Santa Cruz, Muir conceived a project that could have genuinely absorbed him. He would study the Coast Redwood (*Sequoia sempervirens*) as he had studied the Big Trees. But in San Francisco he found waiting for him Asa Gray and Sir Joseph Hooker, the world's most distinguished botanists of that day. They wanted him to take them on a field trip to Mount Shasta. At the moment this trip seemed to Muir a mere detour. It turned out to lead in totally new directions.

Collage made of ferns and pine needles presented to Mary Jane Talley by Muir.

Chapter 33
Snagjumping Down Two Rivers

The three botanists, with Asa Gray's wife who had come west with him, took one of the small stern-wheelers that labored wheezing and clanking northward against the Sacramento's current. They debarked at Bidwell's landing where a carriage waited to take them to the big home — more manor house than ranch house — from which General Bidwell and his wife managed twenty-two thousand acres of Rancho del Arroyo Chico. In 1841 Bidwell had been co-leader of the first organized party to reach California by crossing the Sierra Nevada. He was still one of the state's most respected citizens.

Mrs. Bidwell and her sister, Sallie Kennedy, as well as the General himself, had decided to come along to Mt. Shasta. They set out in a considerable cavalcade, which included mounts for packers, a cook and camp helpers and baggage animals to carry tents, camp gear and supplies to make everyone comfortable.

It was not Muir's style of camping, but he enjoyed himself greatly. The field trips the three botanists took from their base camp near timberline on Mount Shasta were interesting and productive. Sir Joseph Hooker had been a collaborator of Darwin, Huxley and Tyndall and had botanized all over the world. His reminiscences by the campfire ranged all the way from the Himalayas through the deodars of India to the cedars of Lebanon and back to Kew Gardens, of which he was director. One evening in response to a pointblank question by Muir, Hooker stated that in his opinion no forest on the globe rivalled the coniferous forest of the Sierra Nevada in grandeur, variety and beauty.

At night Muir often lit huge campfires which turned the silver firs, as Mrs. Bidwell put it in her diary, "into enormous pagodas of silver filigree...Mr. Muir would wave his arms and shout, 'Look at the glory! Look at the glory!'" Hooker and Gray would sit there expressionless and unresponsive, as if they saw nothing unusual whatever. Mrs. Bidwell became increasingly piqued and finally confronted the scientists. "Why do you tease Mr. Muir?" she asked. "Don't you think it's beautiful?"

"Of course it is!" they answered. "But Muir is so eternally enthusiastic we like to tease him."*

* Linnie Marsh Wolfe, *Son of the Wilderness: The Life of John Muir*, p. 194.

After the Grays and Sir Joseph Hooker returned to San Francisco, Muir went with the Bidwells on a leisurely trip to Mount Lassen and the volcanic region around it. A long camping trip, especially one in which members of the same family participate, almost invariably produces legends and jokes that are remembered within the group as much more important, or thrilling, or funnier than they seem to others. On the Lassen trip the antics of the saddle mules when they chanced to step into a nest of yellow jacket wasps was a prime cause of merriment. Each animal put on a characteristic display, but it was the performance of Sallie Kennedy's mule "Lize" that sent Muir off into roars of laughter. She would rear and plunge and flail her tail around with a corkscrew motion that amused everyone so much they forgot to admire the horsemanship which prevented Miss Kennedy, who of course was riding side-saddle, from being thrown into volcanic rocks no friendlier than dragon's teeth.

In a letter to the Bidwells, written on October 10, Muir described the antics of the skiff carrying him down the Sacramento in terms of Miss Sallie's mule. The craft had been built by the Bidwell's carpenter and christened "Spoonbill." But Muir re-christened her "Snag Jumper" because of her ability to slide over algae-covered snags and skid past slanting logs with one end stuck in the bottom. There were many such obstructions, for the river was very low, but Muir did not mind. The strata of the banks stood revealed and he was able to learn a good deal about the formation of both the valley and the river. On a straight, glassy-smooth stretch where there appeared to be no danger, Muir became detached through trying in imagination to trace the Sacramento to its underground sources in Mount Shasta and the lava-encrusted surroundings. Suddenly, as he wrote the Bidwells, the Snag Jumper "reared like Lize-in-Jackets, swung around stern downstream, and remained on her beam end, erect like a coffin against a wall. She managed, however, to get out of even this scrape without damage either to herself or to me."

Other than some geologic history the trip was more notable for sensory delight than scientific observation. From the vine-grown banks with their overleaning trees, land birds came every morning by the thousands to bathe in the river. Water birds were moving south — waders in pairs and small groups, geese in flocks so great they sometimes formed a canopy over him. Paddling, rowing and drifting by turns from dawn to dark, Muir reached Sacramento in five days. He fully intended to go on through the delta where the rivers join and part way up the San Joaquin. But when he found and studied some good maps, he realized that the distance was over three hundred miles. Also he learned that the upper San Joaquin at this season was too shallow even for the Snag Jumper. He therefore left her in the care of a dubious character who had boats for rent, made a quick trip by steamer to San Francisco and set off for the Sierra. There was one gorge, said to be impassable, which he had glimpsed but never explored. This was the canyon of the Middle Fork of the King's River, which comes down from very high country where the snows might begin any day. He would have to hurry or leave this project for another year. He went on foot, since this would be no journey for any except a mountain animal or a mountain man with hands trained to help in climbing.

At Hyde's Mill, that "sore, sad center of destruction" at work among the redwoods between the Kings and Kaweah Rivers, Muir got some flour to add to the chunk of dried beef, sugar and tea left over from the bounteous supplies provided by the Bidwells. He also carried a quilt Mrs. Bidwell had given him.

From the mill Muir pushed on into Converse Basin, where he spent two days studying the still erect and awesome Sequoia giants. When he came near the great chasm of the Kings River South Fork, he turned eastward. Still

Head of the South Fork of the King's River.

following the course of the river, he crossed three tributary canyons ranging from fifteen hundred to two thousand feet deep. In the middle one he found Big Trees growing among other conifers in a forest several square miles in extent. Muir was very pleased, because the topography and the quality of glacier-ground soil had led him to expect *Sequoia gigantea* thereabouts.*

Down one of the side canyons in this vicinity, he descended four thousand feet to the floor of the South Fork Canyon, a couple of miles above the confluence of Boulder Creek. Taking his time about it, Muir came up the South Fork as far as the Yosemite-like widening of the gorge. Here he spent two more days

* This may have been the grove now called "Little Boulder," which has some two hundred Big Trees ten feet or more in diameter. Picturesque details of this trip are considerably lacking because Muir's notes, which he always carried tied to his belt, were wet several times when he fell into the river and are therefore largely illegible. Locations, altitudes, etc. are given here for those who may take pleasure in following Muir point to point during one of his most difficult feats of mountaineering.

making measurements of cliffs and cascades, then climbed out by way of Copper Canyon and headed northeast toward the Kings Middle Fork. At midnight he was trying to keep warm under the Bidwell quilt beside a glacial lake at 12,200 feet* when the wind that had been playing storm music in the crags above brought the first flurries of a snowstorm.

Muir was practically out of provisions at this point and did not care to take shelter under a rock ledge and wait out the storm. Instead he determined to get below it. In complete darkness, by memory of what he had seen at sunset and the feel of slope and ground beneath his feet, he found a tributary canyon that led to the bottom of the North Fork gorge. An hour after sunrise he was safe, nearly five thousand feet below his starting place.

The Kings Middle Fork was supposed to be absolutely impassable, especially the lower portion Muir now had to tackle. But by crossing and re-crossing the swift river several times to pass places where the current swept against unclimbable rock formations, he traversed its entire length, making measurements and sketches as he went.

Robert L. Smith, writing in the Sierra Club's *Climber's Guide to the High Sierra* (pp. 185 et seq.), says the spectacularly beautiful Tehipite Valley on the Kings Middle Fork was discovered in 1869 by a sheepman named Frank Dusy, who was following the track of a bear he had wounded. Smith also says that Dusy built a trail to get his sheep to Simpson Meadow, some distance above Tehipite. However if sheep had entered this canyon before Muir came through, he would have noted the evidence — with anger.

On the contrary he says, reminiscing about his trip of 1877 in "A Rival of the Yosemite" (published in *Century Magazine*, November, 1891): "The valley was purely wild. Not a trace could I see of man or his animals, but of nature's animals, many. I had been out of provisions for two days...but still I lingered, sketching and gazing enchanted....As I sauntered up to the foot of Tehipite Falls, a fat buck with wide branching antlers bounded past me...within a stone's throw....A mile below the falls, I met a grizzly bear eating acorns under one of the large Kellogg oaks. He stopped eating and came slowly lumbering toward me, stopping every few yards to listen. I was a little afraid and stole off...behind a large *Libcedros* (incense cedar) tree. He came on within a dozen yards of me — the first grizzly I had seen at home. Turning his head he chanced to catch sight of me; after a long, studious stare, he good-naturedly turned away and wallowed off into the chaparral."

Below the merger of the Middle and South Forks of the Kings River, Muir climbed out of the canyon, which meant five thousand feet of "very trying cliff work," as he wrote to his sister Sarah. Four days earlier he had eaten the last of his food. His final meal in the canyon was "one-tenth of a hummingbird's breakfast" sucked from scarlet *Zauschneria* flowers.**

* Frederic R. Gunsky in *South of Yosemite*, p. 94, says that if Muir was at so great an altitude he must have crossed either Cirque Crest or Windy Ridge.

** It is said that a young man named John Rigby persuaded Muir to take him on this trip, that Rigby gave out and that Muir had practically to carry him up the final ascent. The evidence is

Muir got a square meal at Hyde's Mill and by foot, rail and stage went to a tiny valley town called Hopeton. Here on the banks of the Merced he built a small skiff out of some gnarled, sun-twisted lumber from an abandoned fence and set off for the San Joaquin River and San Francisco Bay. He had bought some nails in Hopeton, but otherwise seems to have built the skiff with his jacknife, a rock and his capacity for improvisation — developed on a frontier farm and honed in pioneer factories and primitive wildernesses.

"Snag Jumper II" was cranky and leaky, and the San Joaquin proved very uncooperative. In some places Muir had to drag the skiff over riffles and sand bars. Down toward San Francisco Bay he was unable to penetrate to shore through the jungle of tough, tall water-reeds called *tules* and had to sleep cold and wet in the bottom of the boat. It took him two weeks to row and drift the 250 miles from Hopeton to Carquinez Strait, from which the San Joaquin and Sacramento, now combined, pour into the northern bulge of San Francisco Bay. The only real delight he enjoyed was his first glimpse of white pelicans, who sailed over him on their nine feet of wings with the silent majesty of a fleet of galleons.

At the small town of Martinez on the strait, Muir tied up Snag Jumper II and inquired the way to the Alhambra Valley. He had remembered that a charming elderly couple named Strentzel had invited him to their ranch in a place of that name. Walking through the now-leafless orchards and past vineyards gracefully ranged along the lower slopes of the enfolding hills, he remembered that the Strentzel's quiet daughter was agreeable to look at, especially if one met her remarkably clear, serene, gray eyes.

John Muir reached the Strentzel's white, rose-embowered ranch house looking like a walking scarecrow; gaunt, bearded so that his eyes looked like mountain lakes in a straggling forest, his faded green coat considerably out at wrists and elbows, his hair — which women insisted on calling beautiful — reaching almost to his shoulders.

The Strentzels welcomed him with instant enthusiasm and sustained warmth. They used all the resources of an old time California ranch — almost unbelievable opulence today — to fill the bottomless pit Muir had for an appetite after so long a starving time. He slept between soft sheets he remembered for their snowy whiteness (though he was proud to have brought Mrs. Bidwell's quilt this far "tolerably clean"). Dr. Strentzel responded to Muir's narrative with questions and comments that brought out the best in their guest, who had been as long without conversation as without adequate food. The women beamed upon him and vied with one another in offering comforts and pleasures of the palate.

---

inconclusive. Rigby left no known account and Muir, who rarely spoke of the shortcomings of companions, does not mention Rigby at all.

Chapter 34
Getting the Ear of the Nation

Before the horseless carriage made human legs obsolete, to "ride shanks mare" meant to walk, and that is how Muir got from the Strentzel's to San Francisco Bay, casually crossing 3,849-foot Mount Diablo on the way. Once settled into his third-floor room in the home of John and Mary Swett, and having quieted his appetite with a series of Thanksgiving dinners, he began to write very well.

Muir claimed that two and one-half year old Helen, whom he liked to have in his room when he wrote, was responsible for his success. But all of the Swetts seemed to have helped get some of the best of Muir to flow out of him through the sharpened eagle feather he used for a pen. The older children balked at going to bed until their "Uncle John" had told them a story. Their parents, equally delighted, persuaded Muir to tell his true stories on paper the way he gave them to the intimate audience by the fireside.

One of his true tales, told in a considerable setting of information and vivid description, is about a happening on one of the High Sierra tributaries of the San Joaquin. While Muir — alone as usual — was eating his early and frugal breakfast, he heard several heavy thuds, which he recognized as cones of a yellow pine striking the needle-strewn ground after a Douglas squirrel had cut them from a high branch. In any company except the redwoods, a yellow pine eight feet in diameter would be accounted a big tree. The cones are the size of pineapples. Muir well knew that the squirrel would be down presently to gather in his harvest. He therefore swallowed his tea at a gulp and moved a few yards in the direction from which the sounds came. He was in time to see the squirrel dart down from the tree and go to a wild lilac bush under which Muir could see, once the direction had been shown him, a number of fresh-looking cones that had evidently rolled there.

The squirrel was average size for a Douglas — about eight inches long not including his tail, with which he could cover his nose in cold weather. The pine cone was larger and obviously heavier than the animal, but after some maneuvering the Douglas got it into a position in which he could drag it by backing up and hanging on with his sickle teeth. He dragged the cone clear up to the base of the tree from which he had cut it, then began his breakfast by turning it bottom up and methodically biting off the scales as he turned it with his paws. At the base of each scale, Muir knew, he found two sweet nuts shaped like little hams and spotted with purple.

When the squirrel had demolished the cone Muir began to whistle a tune, to see what would happen. The squirrel darted up the tree, but then ran out on a dead limb and settled down to listen. As Muir went on to whistle and sing other tunes the squirrel made no sound, but his eyes brightened at every change and he turned his head this way and that as if trying to hear better.

Other squirrels gathered 'round and were joined by some chipmunks. Birds perched on the lower limbs of the trees, and one — a speckle-breasted thrush — poised for several seconds in the air, like an oversized hummingbird, within a few feet of Muir's face.

Muir sang and whistled for half an hour, his audience increasing all the while. He had begun with "Bonnie Doon " and other airs remembered from his boyhood. When he ran out of Scottish songs he shifted to hymns. These were well received too, so long as they were cheerful. But as soon as he launched into "Old Hundredth" — the "Doxology" — the first member of his audience screamed the Indian name for the Douglas squirrel — "Phillilloolet!" — and darted up the tree chattering and scolding. All the other animals vanished into the forest and the birds flew off, though more reluctantly.

Some time later Muir tried the same concert on ground squirrels. They too listened attentively until he tried the Doxology, which sent them into their holes.*

Muir's piece on his wild audience was published in the December, 1878, issue of *Scribner's Monthly* under the reasonable title, "The Douglas Squirrel of California." Another article (really a prose poem) on Muir's favorite bird was published in *Scribner's* in February of the same year. It has a title that seems outrageous, even though the editor adapted it from a sentence in Muir's text. The piece is called "The Hummingbird of the California Waterfalls, " but is about a robin-sized brown bird called the water ouzel, which flies with rapid, steady wing-beats like a quail's. The ouzel also flies through the whirling spray of waterfalls and disappears into eddies and rapids where it feeds on insects, being particulary fond of mosquito larvae found on stones along the bottom. Sometimes when feeding in the shallows and heading upstream, the water passes over the ouzel to form a crystalline shell — a bird in a bell jar

"Among all the mountain birds, none has cheered me so much in my lonely wanderings. None so unfailingly," Muir wrote, "for winter and summer he sings, independent alike of sunshine and love; requiring no other inspiration than the stream on which he dwells. While water sings, so must he; in heat or cold, calm or storm...."

* Some laymen have thought that Muir was putting his readers on in recounting this squirrel behavior, but Dr. Mark Rich, assistant curator of the San Diego Zoological Gardens, tells me that the episodes are well within the limits of probability. When animals and birds have not been subjected to the experience of man, curiosity overmasters caution and they often approach closely to look and listen. Moreover, many animals and birds are sensitive to tones, generally preferring the higher ones. Muir was a natural tenor, and it seems likely that the Doxology required a lower register than the one he had been using.

The articles on the redwoods, the most influential of which came out in *Harper's* during 1878, and other pieces — especially the one on the water ouzel — went far toward establishing a national reputation for Muir. They also made him some friends who profoundly influenced his career and furthered his efforts on behalf of the wilderness. David Starr Jordan, an icthyologist of considerable repute and president and chancellor of Stanford University from 1891 to 1913, was then a member of the faculty at Indiana University. He was totally enchanted with the ouzel piece, and read it to one of his classes in which Katherine Merrill Graydon happened to be a student. As a small girl she had been one of the children who came bringing wild flowers to Muir's room when he was recovering from his eye injury. With great and girlish humility she wrote to Muir hoping that he would remember her and that he might be willing to meet Professor Jordan, who admired him so much. Muir wrote back that of course he remembered and would be delighted to meet her professor.

The second influential friend the ouzel piece made for Muir was Robert Underwood Johnson, at that time on the editorial staff of *Scribner's Monthly*. Johnson became at once a committed devotee of Muir's writing and of his attitude toward nature. To Muir animals were not "dumb," rocks were not lifeless, water was no mere chemical compound; all of nature's individuals, including man, were living parts of the great, ever-changing, dynamic whole, which created even when it destroyed. The animal essays were, it appears, the easiest for his audience to grasp and, through them, to make contact with the fundamentals he wished people to understand. He never confused the animals and birds with humans, but they were all individual citizens of his world — his trusted companions — from the suspicious and indifferent bears and magnificently detached mountain sheep to the perennially scolding, comically aggressive and marvelously acrobatic Douglas squirrel.

There is little doubt that Louie Wanda Strentzel had a good deal to do with the liberation of Muir's talents during 1877 and 1878. They seem to have been attracted to one another from the time of Muir's first visit. But they approached one another with the cautious decorum for which the Victorian period is noted (whether the reputation is entirely justified or not). Muir and Louie Wanda went on walks together unchaperoned. But from the correspondence between Muir and the Strentzels during this period, one might think he was courting the parents rather than the girl herself.

Chapter 35
Heat, Thirst and Love

Muir had accepted the invitation of Captain A. F. Rogers to join himself and a man named Limbeck on a geodetic survey across Nevada. Their mission was to determine altitudes and establish line-of-sight survey monuments along a five-sided, geometric course that began at Genoa Peak, just east of Lake Tahoe, extended into Utah and returned to their starting place.

They made up their pack train at Genoa on July 6, 1878. They were well mounted and well equipped, and they needed to be. If Nevada's entire 1878 population of about sixty thousand had been spread evenly over the state, each man, woman and child would have had nearly two square miles to himself. Actually the people were concentrated in the limited areas where rich ore deposits lay and along the few streams that flowed consistently enough to make ranching possible. One could ride for days without seeing another human — white or Indian. Moreover the five thousand or so Pah Utes (Muir's spelling) in Nevada were sullenly hostile; some of them had gone to fight beside their neighbors, who were engaged in a bitter war against the whites in Idaho.

But Muir looked forward to the trip across the geologically young desert where the ranges lay "like stranded islands," as he wrote to Dr. Strentzel on July 11. This letter, postmarked "Poison Switch, Nevada," announced that he was sending a box of wild prunes which might, Muir thought, compare with peaches and oranges if made larger and softer through cultivation.

Dr. Strentzel thought very poorly of the prunes. In a letter Muir received three weeks later he pushed their running argument concerning the relative merits of wild vs. civilized products and offered to send some of his own Tokay and Alexandrine grapes.

"Try me, Doctor," Muir wrote back. "Just try me on tame, tame Tokays!"

No promise could have meant more than the vision of refreshing fruit to these three men who had just crossed the "Forty Mile Desert" between Carson Lake and Carson sink, where the trail was marked with the broken vehicles and whitening bones left by Gold Rush wagon trains inching their way to California. The flat alkali expanses of the ancient lake beds threw back the sun in a glare that intensified the heat and the dryness. Their already weather-beaten faces were cracked and peeling like puddles of adobe mud baking in the sun.

As usual Muir's observations kept him from dwelling upon himself and his condition. A species of nut-bearing pinyon fascinated him especially. It covered mountains appearing entirely bare from a distance, but which turned dark as one approached — as if they were heavily forested, as indeed they were. But once one entered these woods he found no shade, for the needles of the small trees were too fine and too sparse to block the sun. As if to compensate, the pinyons bore such quantities of nuts that the total was, at this time, greater than California's wheat crop.

In the fall groups of Indians dressed in gay calico prints and bright scarves rode into these curious forests on tough mustangs. The men knocked down the cones with long poles. The women and children gathered them, laid them out in thin piles and covered them lightly with brushwood, to which they set fire. When the cones were roasted it was easy to beat out the nuts, half an inch long by a quarter inch in diameter and delicious. When the crop was large the Indians brought in quantities for sale, and pinyon nuts were eaten around every Nevada fireside. Some people fed them to their horses in place of barley.

The survey's angular course now took them southward through the Big Smokey Valley to the vicinity of the present town of Tonopah. At this point Captain Rogers decided that they must climb 9,000-foot Lone Mountain, forty miles from any known water. Muir, who had been in Nevada in the summers of 1876 and 1877, advised strongly against this venture but was overruled.

They made the difficult, shadeless climb through furnace heat. The very rocks were too hot to touch. By the time they started down, every drop of water was gone and the descent was even more energy-consuming than the ascent. When they reached the mountain's foot, Muir's already thickening blood seemed to flow as sluggishly as molten metal. It seemed to him that he had never suffered so intensely as now. Yet he was the only one of the three with enough stamina left to go up a sandy canyon and find the horses.

When he returned with the animals his companions had disappeared. The desperate necessity of finding them made Muir forget his own exhaustion. One lay nearby, death-like on the hot sand, scarcely conscious, his voice only a frightful whisper. Muir half carried him to his horse and boosted him into the saddle. The second man he found wandering among the chaparral in a delirious stupor.

They reached water at daybreak of the second day, having had nothing to drink for forty-eight hours. The dryness of their mouths prevented eating; their fevered condition prevented sleep. But all recovered within a few days except Captain Rogers, who was still feverish when they set out for a town named Hamilton in the then-famous White Pine mining district in eastern Nevada.

It was typical of Muir that in the letter to the Strentzels telling of this adventure,* he did not report it until he had talked of several cloud-bursts seen

* Muir's letter to the Strentzels was written from a camp near Belmont, Nevada, August 28, 1878. See William F. Badè, *The Life and Letters of John Muir*, p. 106.

all at once from a gigantic table-land of black lava and of Nevada pines and traces of vanished glaciers. He did not mention their brush with death at all in the series of articles he wrote for the *San Francisco Evening Bulletin* during his trip, nor in any other published writing. This escape was among the many perilous events which he merely hinted at or ignored altogether. He had no wish to appear adventurous nor to attract attention to himself. He wrote in the first person because he could find no other way to communicate the total experience of nature which he believed to be the only entirely true one.

The more Muir and his companions became dessicated, the more they dreamed of those juicy grapes Dr. Strentzel had promised to send them. But frustrating events made the dream seem more and more impossible. Delays and changes of route required Muir to telegraph three times asking that the shipment be forwarded. A town called Belmont was their last chance. Beyond this point they would be crossing territory where there were scarcely any trails, let alone railroads.

Arriving weary at a knoll from which they could see the lights of Belmont, Captain Rogers decided to bed down in a corral. Muir feared any ground much used by men and their animals because it was sure to be trampled into dust well-mixed with dried manure and urine. But he hated to make a point of his distaste when darkness had fallen and spread his own bedroll near the others. The men had been asleep only a short while when a gale-force wind blew their camp gear and accouterments slamming, rattling and rustling into the corners of the corral. Their hair and beards were soon heavy with corral dust, and as the wind continued the fine grains sifted between their blankets and penetrated their clothing.

They rose at first light, red-eyed, itchy — and stinking. When they had packed up their gear they rode straight for the town's only hotel and spent some hours bathing and combing themselves and beating their clothing into some semblance of decency. Captain Rogers then went out on a forlorn hope expedition to the railroad station.

Muir had found on the Hot Creek mountains a species of pine (*Pinus aristata*) which he thought the most picturesque and ornamental he had ever seen. The Nevada miners called it "fox-tail pine" because its needles formed thick, graceful tassels.* Muir now emptied the sack in which he had stuffed his specimens and selected some for Dr. Strentzel. He was wondering where he could find a box to send them in when the door opened and Rogers came in with a good-sized box on his shoulder.

The grapes were in miraculously good condition. Plump, juice-full, darkly gleaming spheres disappeared as fast as the men could crunch and swallow them — all except for one perfect bunch, which they hung to the chandelier to feast their eyes upon.

In the once-famous White Pine mining district where, a few years earlier,

* This is the bristle-cone pine found in the mountains of California. It has been shown to be the world's oldest living tree.

twenty-eight thousand claims had been located in an area twelve miles long by six miles wide, only fifteen mines were working when Muir passed through. The towns were fading like the Cheshire cat's grin. In a piece he wrote for the *Evening Bulletin*, Muir said he found five dead towns for every one that was alive. In a stretch of empty desert he came upon a tall, beautifully-constructed stone chimney surrounded by shops with machinery installed and tools laid out ready to be used. The mines this facility was meant to serve had not played out; before production could start the men had rushed off to a new strike over the hill.

When Muir returned to San Francisco late in 1877, he found that his letters to the *Bulletin* had made him still better known and sought after as a lecturer. Nevada was still the imagination-stirring land of exotic treasure. In 1877 the Comstock Lode alone had produced $36,301,537 in gold and silver. But San Franciscans had been supplied with precious little reliable information about the state and conditions there, until Muir's reports.

Little Helen Swett had fallen critically ill. Muir therefore moved to the home of a bookseller on Valencia Street. He was comfortable there in body, but not in mind. In January he wrote to the Strentzels, with tongue somewhat in cheek: "The vast soul-stirring work of flitting is at length done and well done. Myself, wooden clock (the 'Father Time' clock he had made on the Wisconsin farm during his 'teens, using a jack knife and a saw filed from a discarded corset stay), and notebooks are once more planted for the winter out here on the outermost ragged edge of this howling metropolis of dwelling boxes." Nevertheless, he added, "Helen is well out of danger...and I can see her at least once a week."

His feeling for little Helen Swett seems to have been, in part, a sublimation of his increasing love for Louie Wanda Strentzel. Wanda herself made the move which broke through the inhibitions which were holding them apart. One April day Muir had sat down to write his first letter to her, but had not been able to get his pen past "My dear Miss Strentzel...."

At this point his agony of composition was relieved by the arrival of an expressman with a long box. Within were boughs of fruit trees in full flower. Muir had no more trouble with his letter. "Boo, aren't they beautiful!" he wrote. "An orchard in a bandbox...." Which would sound pretty silly except that "Boo!" was Muir's polite society euphemism for a much stronger and more pungent expression.

That spring Muir spent so much time at the Strentzel ranch his San Francisco friends complained that they could never find him. The Victorian courtship moved forward through romantic pacings in blossom-laden orchards and on hillsides where the new grasses and wildflowers brushed their knees. Muir presently reported to Wanda that he had found in his pocket "that slippery, fuzzy mesh you wear around your neck."

That summer of 1878 Muir intended to explore the forests of Oregon and Washington. But in June he was diverted by the administrators of a Sunday School convention, who offered him one hundred dollars to speak at a large gathering in Yosemite and lead a few gentle field trips to points of interest. During the public meeting Muir — looking with his plowman's stoop as farmerish as he usually did when seen in the middle distance — completely put down and converted a famous divine who had used Whitney's cataclysmic theory of the formation of Yosemite Valley as a text. The episode enhanced Muir's reputation in the Bay Area still further. More important to himself and Louie Wanda Strentzel were some conversations with a missionary who told him about the glaciers of Alaska.

There was no way Muir could prevent himself from going at once to see those ice rivers. But neither could he live much longer without Louie Wanda.

When Muir arrived for his first visit after the convention, Mrs. Strentzel's romantic eye told her that he had something on his mind besides Sunday schools and fruit trees. She and the doctor retired early, leaving nature to take its course. About midnight Louie Wanda slipped into her mother's room and knelt beside her to whisper, "All's well, Mother, and I'm so happy!"

Breakfast next morning was a love feast at which it was mutually decided not to announce the engagement until Muir's return from Alaska.

Only eleven years had passed since a United States secretary of state bought the Alaskan territory from the Czar of Russia for the scandalous price of $7,200,000. People were still calling it "Seward's Ice Box." Little was known about it except that it was very cold, very dangerous and the water, between ice floes where polar bears roamed, was full of whales.

If Louie Wanda was frightened by Muir's decision or disappointed by the postponement, she let no one know.

Chapter 36
The Adventure on Glenora

Muir left San Francisco in May of 1879, but spent some time cruising around in Puget Sound and did not leave Portland for Alaska until the dark morning hours of July 10. He was intensely interested all the way, both in the forests and the evidence of work done by long-vanished glaciers. But for him the trip really began just north of Vancouver, where the mail ship *California*, on which he had taken passage, entered the "macrame" border of islands that follows the shore to what is now called Glacier Bay,* where the Alaskan coast swings westward.

It was not long before Muir began to sight living glaciers on the mainland mountains. Even some of the larger islands bore peaks of five thousand feet or more, where canyons descended from rounded, shell-like basins — *cirques* — which Muir thought of as "glacier wombs."

The influence which affected Muir most profoundly was the Alaskan magic, which has enthralled and enchanted every sort of human from tough deck-hands and prospectors to wandering poets. "Never before this had I been embosomed in scenery so hopelessly beyond description," Muir wrote during the voyage. Nevertheless he tried to describe it and succeeded well enough to delight his contemporary audience.

Part of the magic, Muir realized, came from the never-quite-ending days. For three hours or so each night the sun disappeared, but the horizon was colored nevertheless, even when the gentle rain of Alaskan summer fell. At times the sunset-sunrise light, mingling with the saturated air, created a translucent atmosphere of hazy wine-purple in which the islands seemed floating half-dissolved.

The islands themselves, with the shining waterways between, provided a subtly changing kaleidoscope of view. Some seemed as large as continents, with their mountain tops dusted with snow and their timbered slopes scored by deep canyons. Tiny islands, forested to the rim, seemed like planters in which trees were set out for pure ornament; on some slightly larger islands, trees and rocks were so aesthetically balanced that it seemed impossible they

* This body of water, much smaller in Muir's day than now, has existed for only a short time — as earth phenomena go. Vancouver's charts, made ninety years earlier but still the best available for Muir's journey of 1879, do not show Glacier Bay at all. When Vancouver passed by, it was part of a gigantic ice-field which no one could imagine entering in boats.

had not been put there by design.

Three doctors of divinity — major powers in the Presbyterian Missionary establishment, which itself was then a power in many lands — were Muir's fellow voyagers on the *California*. The ship was not large enough for them to avoid one another completely — though they disapproved of one another heartily. When they landed at Fort Wrangell, in southeastern Alaska, it was with considerable stiffness that the divines introduced Muir to S. Hall Young, the local missionary. He was a young fellow, small in stature, but physically tough and of an adventurous, realistic spirit well adapted to understanding both Indians and miners. He took to Muir immediately, but there was nothing Young could do, without riling his superiors, to make Muir's introduction to Wrangell more agreeable.

The town was strung out two streets wide for a mile along the shore of a little cove from which small stern-wheel steamers came and went, carrying miners and supplies to the head of navigation, one hundred and fifty miles up the Stickeen River. From there the miners went on foot and the supplies by packtrain and canoe one hundred miles farther, to the recently discovered Cassiar gold mines.

Stickeen Indians lived at the two ends of the town; about fifty caucasians, most of whom were merchants, lived in the middle. Between the Indian and most of the Caucasian houses there was little difference; the Stickeens were excellent builders, and each structure had to conform to the peculiarities of rocks which underlay the boggy ground. The result was that no two houses faced in precisely the same direction or followed the same lines.

Walking the two miry streets, bypassing the hog wallows and stumps that had been left to grow moss and lichens (for Wrangell had never possessed any wheeled vehicles that required clear streets), Muir could find neither lodgings nor any good news. The interior of Alaska, people told him, was impassable; the Indians were unfriendly and treacherous. On first encounter the Indian men he met in the streets seemed to bear out this judgment. On the raised platforms in front of the stores, Indian women were selling berries — old crones with faces blackened except for a ring around their blankly-staring eyes, girls in the brightest calicos and ribbons Vancouver and Seattle could supply, children dressed down to the waist and no farther.

Difficulties, as usual, served to make Muir more determined. He decided to build a bark hut on a little hill which he could see back of the town through a gently falling rain and camp there until he could find a way to go exploring. He was still turning this project over in his mind when he met one of the visiting missionaries, who very kindly offered to let him sleep in the carpenter shop then being used in the work of enlarging the mission house.

Muir spent one night on the floor among the shavings, but on his second day was invited to stay with a Mr. Vanderbilt, a merchant who lived in the best house in Wrangell. It was one of the dozen buildings inside the rectangular fort, built shortly after the American occupation and sold to civilian interests in 1877. A drainage system put in by the military kept the fort and the ground around it relatively dry in contrast to the rest of the town.

Opportunities for exploring soon opened up. The visiting mission dignitaries chartered a small river steamer called the *Cassiar* and permitted Muir to share the expense and come along. The trip up the swift and treacherous Stickeen was a delight to Muir, for by the time they reached Telegraph Creek, the extreme limit of navigation at high water, he had seen more than one hundred glaciers adorning the walls of the great canyon or emerging from tributaries.

On the return the captain tied up shortly after noon at Hudson's Bay Station near the foot of Glenora Peak. He explained to his passengers at lunch that a gale blowing from the sea made the narrows below too dangerous. "Amuse yourselves," he said.

Friendship between Muir and Hall Young had developed very rapidly into intimate understanding. Muir now gave Young a look that plainly said, "Let's go climb a mountain!"

Young slipped away from the missionaries like a boy planning to play hooky and met Muir behind the pilot house. "Where is it?" he asked.

Muir pointed up to Glenora Peak, which showed as a clump of jagged summits in the sky above them. "It must surely be one of the most magnificent viewpoints in the world," he said.

"How far to the highest point?" Young asked.

"Eight or ten miles."

"How high?"

"Eight or ten thousand feet," said Muir and went on to warn Young that they would be making, in an afternoon and part of the night, a climb that an experienced mountaineer might hesitate to make in a full day of sun. He urged Young not to come with him, saying that he could not be responsible for anything that happened. Young told Muir not to worry, assuring him that he was a strong hiker and had done considerable mountaineering.

They were somewhat delayed in starting. To cover his absence, Young arranged to have a band of Indians who were catching salmon nearby come to a *hayu wawa* — a big talk. They would keep the dignitaries happy with the appearance of "simple faith and child-like docility" and high-flown compliments intended to gain material favors from church and government.

"Take off your coat," Muir said when Young re-joined him. And, handing over a couple of sea biscuits, "Here's your dinner."

By the time they had wallowed and clambered through an area where fallen trees lay concealed under thick brush and forced their passage among dwarf evergreens that seemed to Hall Young to be guarding the steep slope like angry gnomes, Muir was convinced that his companion could make the mountain top. He not only ceased to worry about Young, he all but forgot him. For, beyond the "gnomes," they came to an alpine meadow more luxuriant than any Hall Young had ever imagined. One could scarcely see the ground for the flowers. Every form of natural garden loveliness seemed represented —

from daisies and campanulas to Muir's favorite, the cassiope, with its little pink and white bells shaped like lilies of the valley, filling the nearby air with a perfume delicate as themselves.

Inhibitions dropped from Muir like discarded clothing. He ran from clump to clump, kneeling beside the flowers and talking to them in an outlandish mixture of endearments and scientific terms which Hall Young scarcely understood.

"Ah! My blue-eyed darlin', little did I think to see you here...and who might you be with your wonder look? Is it possible you can be (two Latin polysyllables)? You're lost, my dear; you belong in Tennessee." And he kept pulling up plants by the roots and stuffing them, dirt and all, first into his pockets, then inside his shirt and, finally, filling Hal Young's pockets until they both had roots and bulbs and blossoms sticking out all over them like mythical nature-men in medieval pictures.

Young tagged along after Muir asking naive questions and quarreling with himself for having neglected botany in favor of the "more important" studies of language and metaphysics. For he saw that beneath Muir's childlike enthusiasm lay a foundation of scientific knowledge and a disciplined urge to inquire so deeply into Nature's forms and processes that he felt united with Her in a deep and genuine love. It was thus that he achieved the spiritual exaltation that set him apart from all men Hall Young had ever known. Muir's baby talk to the flowers was no more than a man whistling as he went about the work he loved.

Young's hero-worship of Muir began that afternoon in the mountain meadow. It strengthened to a kind of idolatry as the day wore on. They were on the southwest slope of the mountain, with the sun looking on them from a cloudless sky when, passing around a spur of rock, they found themselves in shadow. Muir looked up, startled. "I was forgetting," he said. "We'll have to hurry now or we'll miss it."

"What?"

"The jewel of the day — the sunset!" and Muir took off up the mountain at a lope.

Muir loved sunsets as a connoisseur loves his collection. But his underlying motive was to see the panorama of mountains about the Stickeen and get an idea of where he wanted to go and how to get there. He now climbed with a speed and economy of motion Hall Young had never seen or imagined, attacking jagged cliffs with only a momentary pause to discover the easiest route and threading his way around and across fatal crevasses in the blue-ice glacier that lay in their path. Hall Young longed for rest, for his strength was taxed to the limit. But his pride forced him to keep up with Muir uncomplainingly.

At the head of the glacier they halted briefly while Muir studied a one thousand-foot cliff they would have to climb to reach the summit. The precipice was made of wildly-fractured slate, overhanging in some places, vertical in others and everywhere too steep for a footing. Young would have turned back in frustration. But Muir simply said, "We'll have to climb carefully here," and started up by the route his experienced eye told him was feasible.

Compared to any climber Hall Young had ever seen, Muir was as superior as a mountain sheep is to a domestic wooly. He climbed with no visible pause, arms, legs, thighs, knees and even his chin supplementing his feet and hands. His lean, supple body curved itself around outthrust rock bosses, flattened against sheer faces where he worked sidelong with fingers and toes digging into tiny niches and clinging to little knobs. He moved so steadily that sheer momentum helped to overcome gravity. To Hall Young he seemed weightless.

Young kept his eyes on Muir as much as he could, and he strove to keep up with him. He had complete confidence that where Muir went was the best way up and he must follow. It was certain that fragile knobs and shelves Muir tested before trusting his weight to them would bear his own 120 pounds, for Muir weighted 150. But Young had a handicap he had neglected to tell Muir about for fear of being left behind. As a teenager he had enjoyed breaking colts, which is a good way to get thrown and damaged. Both his shoulders had been dislocated; the left would not support his weight. As they neared the top of the cliff he now and again felt the arm bone move away slightly from the socket as he pulled himself up some precipitous stretch. His strength was ebbing; his breath now came in painful gasps and his muscles began to tremble. Yet he did not dare lose sight of Muir and pushed himself onward with reckless desperation, not clearly seeing the supports where he placed his feet and hands.

After climbing 950 feet of cliff, according to Muir's barometer, they came to a shelf about two feet wide that corkscrewed around the cliff. Here Muir paused for a brief rest, and Hall Young, gasping beside him, was treated to the most magnificent view of his life. They stood on the rounded neck of the mountain, looking southwest across a rolling upland blazing with acres of crimson fireweed set off by patches of dark blue lupine and darker evergreens; the Stickeen crossed this panorama as a silver line broken here and there by the variegated green of the trees along its banks.

The horizon, three-quarters of a full circle, was rimmed with helmet-shaped peaks, some snow-covered, all wearing white glaciers as collars. In between, thirty or forty lakes lay gleaming among long, rounded hills like sleeping human forms.

"The sunset!" Muir exclaimed suddenly, "We must have the whole horizon!" and began to lope along the narrow shelf. Young followed as fast as he could, but fell farther and farther behind. Muir was out of sight when Young came to a notch about five feet wide which descended for twelve feet or so to the cliff's edge above the glacier — filled to within four feet of the top with pieces of disintegrating shale.

Young could have easily jumped across had he not been exhausted. He heard Muir shout something, but could not understand.

191

Desperate to catch up, he leaped for a shell-shaped boulder sticking out of the shale. It disappeared into the delicately-poised mass as soon as his foot struck it.

Young whirled to fall face downward, with his head toward the top of the chute, and thrust out his arms to brace himself against the walls, for he knew that the shale would begin to slide. But when his hands struck, his arms were wrenched so violently that both jerked from their sockets and lay useless and agonizingly painful above his head.

Though Young dug in his toes and his chin, the slowly sliding shale carried him inch by inexorable inch until he felt empty air beneath his feet. Stones rattled past him and piled up against his head.

He had no hope of escape, but after the first wild moment of panic he felt no fear. Thoughts great and trivial whirled through his head: anguish for his wife, who would bear their first child within a few weeks; fury at the insurance companies that had refused him a policy; the fate of his Indian converts among the islands; memories; speculations as to how long he would be in the air before he struck the glacier below; a wish that Muir would come in time to take a message to his wife.

A voice spoke above his head. "My God!" Muir said, "Grab that rock, man! Just by your right hand."

Young was afraid to take a deep breath. He mumbled weakly, "My arms are out."

When Muir spoke again, his voice was cheerful, confident, unexcited. "I'm going to get you out of this. I'll have to come down to you from the other side. Keep cool!" and he went off whistling "The Blue Bells of Scotland."

His encouraging sounds — whistling, singing, calling out — diminished, but never ceased, while Young suppressed as well as he could the automatic twitching of his muscles and endured the sickening pain in his shoulders. Yet he was slipping, slipping, until it seemed that the weight of his own legs must drag him over the brink.

He heard Muir's voice close by and a little below him. "Hold steady. I'll have to swing you out over the cliff."

Young, with only gravel before his eyes, felt Muir's hand get a hold on the waistband of his pants and gather in his shirt and vest. Then he was suddenly slid over the edge and found himself face down, staring at the glacier one thousand feet below. Gradually he was tipped upward until his feet touched the cliff.

"Work downward with your feet," Muir said, and drew him close by crooking his arm. As Young's head came past, Muir caught his collar with his teeth. Young's feet found the little ledge on which Muir had a toe-hold. He turned his head to see that Muir's left hand held onto a spur of rock above his head but that his body bent sidewise to maintain his bite on Young's clothing. "I'll have to let go of you," Muir mumbled. "I need both hands here. Climb upward with your feet!"

The niches Young could find thus blindly were few. He never knew how

Muir managed to claw his way up twelve feet of sheer rock face with Young's weight, still held by his teeth, dragging him outward, sideward and downward, but when they reached the shelf along which they had come, Muir had enough strength left to support his companion when he sank down exhausted and trembling all over.

The sun had set, the air had turned icy, and they had no coats. Dusk was deepening on the cliff below them. After a few minutes Muir roused himself and went to work on Young's shoulders. The right had been dislocated in such a way that it snapped back into place fairly easily. But the head of the left humerus was buried deep in Young's armpit and could not be withdrawn. Muir made a sling from Young's suspenders and their handkerchiefs for this arm. Then he went off in the gloom to search for a route by which he might get Young down the cliff.

They had no sooner started than it became evident that Young's right arm (his "good" arm) was nearly useless. Its upper muscles refused to respond. Muir was forced to make a series of hair-raising maneuvers. In some places he descended to a safe foothold, braced himself and had Young reach down and grope until he had his arm in a position where Muir could grasp the wrist. Then Young would literally fall, but in such a way that his descent was checked by Muir's body. In other places Muir carried Young on his back, and in still others he lowered him by the wrist of the "good" arm. This right arm came out of the socket three times before they reached the glacier, about midnight.

Young was too weak to jump the crevasses, so they climbed up to the glacier's steeply sloping earth margin, which was covered with loose gravel. They sat down, Young with a leg on either side of Muir, and slid on their pants for half a mile. It was the easiest part of the trip — and the only time Muir ceased the stream of cheerful chatter which helped Young forget the agony in his shoulders and the faintness that required Muir to dash his face with icy water whenever they came to a stream or spring.

When they reached timberline, Muir offered to make a lasting fire to keep Young warm while he went down the mountain for help. But Young had something to prove and made the difficult descent through unfriendly trees and shrubs on his own feet.

It was 7:30 a.m. when they started up the wobbly gangplank of the *Cassiar*. Blocking their way stood the Reverend Dr. Kendall, a formidable divine some six feet tall, with bushy white eyebrows.

"See here, young man!" he began, "Give an account of yourself. Don't you know you've kept us waiting?"

At that moment the captain came lumbering up like an angry bull. "Hell's fire, etc.!" he roared, almost knocking Kendall overboard with an elbow to the stomach. "Don't you see the man's hurt?"

But Dr. Kendall returned to the attack when his wife — a tall, grim woman who had never smiled since the death of her children some years before — was sitting on the cabin floor, with Young's head in her lap, feeding him whiskey with a spoon.

"Suppose you had fallen down that precipice," said the divine, making severely with his eyebrows. "What would your poor wife have done? What would have become of your Indians and your new church?" Mrs. Kendall leveled her spoon at him like a dagger. "Henry Kendall, shut right up and leave this room! Have you no sense? Go instantly I say!" and the doctor of divinity left.

With two men holding and two pulling, Young's arm was set. But it slipped out again, into a worse position than before. This time they called the captain, who swore he would pull it into place or pull it off. Young fainted before the bones at last came together properly.

For the rest of his life, tears came to his eyes when Hall Young remembered what Muir had done for him on Glenora Mountain.

Chapter 37

"Icta Mamook?"
(What Gives?)

Before the mission dignitaries left, the Wrangell Indians got up a grand dinner and entertainment to celebrate their acceptance of Christianity. The food was "Boston," but the dancing was purely Stickeen Indian: stamping, clapping performances with the dancers dressed in spectacular costumes and the leader strewing white, downy feathers over the floor as a blessing. These were followed by individual performers dressed in skins of animals they represented. Muir was fascinated because the mimicry was so perfect that he felt he was actually watching bear, deer, seal and salmon indoors.

At the conclusion the Indians made long speeches saying that they had previously lived in darkness, but the missionaries had brought them the light. They would not dance in this way any more, but would give away their costumes though they valued them highly. They did in fact give away a number of beautiful fur robes and fantastic head-dresses that had been worn by shamans. Acceptance of Christianity thus turned into a *potlatch* — the traditional ceremony in which wealthy Northwest Indians procured status by giving away their treasures — as contemporary Americans endow foundations and institutions.

Muir received a shaman's head-dress. He was also adopted into the tribe and given the name "Ancouthan" which means "Adopted Chief." Muir thought this honor empty and childish until Hall Young and Mr. Vanderbilt explained that it might very well save his life. Travelers lacking an Indian name might be killed and robbed with impunity, so long as the deed was kept secret from the whites. But since Muir had been taken into the tribe, no Indian would dare to attack him, for the Stickeens would hold the murderer personally responsible.

The Stickeens, like most of the other coastal tribes, welcomed the missionaries of Alaska during that period for two basic reasons. First the white man's God, who provided him so many advantages, such as steel axes and firearms, might be induced to give the Indians equality. Second, the missionaries were then the only outsiders who brought education to the tribesmen. Moreover being agreeable to missionaries might induce the government in Washington to do Alaska some favors. These motives Hall

Young understood very well, but he was truly devoted to his calling and saw no reason for missing the chance to Christianize a few savages while doing them some material good.

He was therefore bitterly disappointed when failure of the *Cassiar's* engine aborted a trip to the Chilcats, the richest and fiercest tribe of the Alaskan coast. Muir was almost equally put out, for he had heard, though somewhat vaguely, that the Chilcat region was one of the iciest in the entire territory.

He partially contented himself by exploring the more accessible region nearby. Going by steamer up the Stickeen to the head of navigation, he pushed on by shank's mare a hundred miles farther to the placer mines scattered along the mountain streams. He had a fine time and on his way back climbed Glenora Peak, from which he had rescued Hall Young, and solved a couple of natural mysteries that had been bothering him. As Hall Young put it, "Any unanswered question about nature lay on his (Muir's) mind like a personal grievance until it was answered to his own understanding."

One of the Stickeen puzzles was the cause of sudden floods which made the river navigable at seasons when the riverboats (which, as Muir said, drew scarcely more water than a duck) were ordinarily tied up. After fighting his way through an almost impenetrable jungle of undergrowth made vicious by thorny devil's club (*Echinoponas horridum*), climbing a cliff and leaping crevasses on the back of the so-called "Dirt Glacier," Muir discovered that this ice river formed a dam that impounded the drainage from a tributary glacier which had melted back some three miles. Since the ice-dam was continually in motion, it occasionally liberated the waters of the natural reservoir thus created, causing sudden floods on the Stickeen all the way to its mouth.

A second mystery concerned the legendary attempt of an Indian to get rid of his wife. According to the folk tale, he had put her in a canoe which he set afloat down a swift stream that disappeared under the great wall of ice that formed the terminus of the "Big Stickeen" glacier and connected it with its flanking tributaries. By the time Muir arrived, the end of the glacier had melted, leaving the river to sweep around the graceful curve of its terminal moraine. But the moraines, the residual glaciers and other evidence showed Muir that the glacier's main drainage stream, which now entered the river directly, had once flowed through a tunnel under the vanished ice wall and entered the Stickeen through a deep gap in the terminal moraine. The wife needed only to duck in order to emerge unharmed, to the historic chagrin of her husband. This was the first time Muir recognized a fact now considerably depended upon by scientists, that legends and traditions out of man's past often provide important clues to actualities.

It cost Muir several of the wettest, most uncomfortable and exhausting days he had yet endured to explore the Big Stickeen Glacier. But he was well rewarded. He found an ice cataract which permitted him actually to crawl beneath the glacier and watch its ponderous motion pluck out great chunks of stone as it inched its way along. Muir himself, as well as other geologists of his time, had assumed from contemporary evidence that glaciers "quarry" out great blocks of stone, which they sometimes transport for many miles. But he had never before seen the action taking place; he may quite possibly have been the first to do so.

He was tremendously excited, and his appetite for glaciers was further whetted by some miners with whom he rode back to Wrangell in a canoe captained by an Indian woman. They had been to the Chilcat regions, and they told him: "All the high mountains up there seem to be made of ice, and if glaciers are what you are after, that's the place for you. All you have to do is hire a good canoe and Indians who know the way."

When Muir proposed a round trip of five hundred miles through the eleven hundred islands of the Alexander Archipelago, Hall Young agreed at once — though it was already fall, and the chill rains had settled down to their winter's work of keeping southern Alaska perpetually drenched. But Young's missionary zeal was not equal to leaving his wife until their first child, who would be born any time now, had safely entered this world, and he himself had made sure that mother and baby were doing well.

Muir put in the intervening time writing up his notes, botanizing and getting acquainted with the Indians. He had never before come into close and natural contact with Indians. He had encountered many, but they had all been to a greater or lesser extent made sullen and hostile toward the whites who had cheated, abused and degraded them.

So far most of the Tlingit* tribes had profited from the whites almost as much as they had suffered from them. They were still capable of being their genuine selves with these strangers — so sophisticated in some ways, so childishly naive in others. Ordinarily full of laughter and small talk, they were also devoted to their ideals, and capable of both great dignity and formidable anger — as one of the visiting missionaries discovered when he ordered a Cassiar deckhand to chop out a large, ancestral woman from a totem pole in a deserted village still held sacred by the Stickeens. The workmanship in this village, which had been built with stone tools, Muir considered superior to the products of United States pioneers, who used implements of steel. Muir came to admire totem poles greatly, though they violated all his previous conceptions of art outrageously.

One of the best times Muir had on Wrangell Island was an outing with some Indians and the collector of customs, who wanted to locate wild hay for his cow — the only one in that part of Alaska. They went, of course, by canoe, which was about the only way to go anywhere in Tlingit country. In the forests which came down close to the water almost everywhere, and on some shores overleaning it, trees grew thick as corn in a farmer's fertile field. In many sections the roots did not reach solid earth, but drew nourishment from a

---

* "Tlingit" is the general name for a language-group of tribes who lived along the northwest coast of North America, and also for the basic language of which each tribe spoke a variant. The "Chinook jargon" became a kind of *lingua franca* spoken in the American Northwest after Europeans began to trade in this territory. It is a compound of Tlingit (for the most part the Siwash dialect), English, Russian and a little Spanish.

fantastic layer of fallen timber, moss and decaying vegetable matter. It was so difficult to make one's way through these forests that even the Indians hunted deer from canoes, lying in wait at places where deer were most likely to take the water in flight from dogs they had sent to drive them from the woods.

The Indians on the outing, except for a couple of boys who had gone fishing with the collector, scattered among the huckleberry bushes that grew in great profusion beside a small stream. They returned humming and singing like nectar-laden bees to deposit basket after filled basket in the canoe. They would eat some fresh, sell some to the whites and mash some into inch-thick cakes to be dried over a slow fire and stored against the dark days of winter.

To Muir, the fecundity of this country was a continually unfolding miracle. Besides huckleberries, yellow salmon berries and blackberries, raspberries and delicious small strawberries grew in the woods and meadows; service berries in dry open spaces; and cranberries in the bogs—enough fruit to feast every bird, beast and human in Alaska, with thousands of tons to spare. He was almost as much impressed with the skill with which the Indians used what nature provided—from the salmon in the streams to the hair of the wild goats that ranged the high peaks.

The Indians liked Muir much better than they understood him.

"Why does this strange man go into the wet woods in stormy nights?" they asked Hall Young. "Why does he wander on bare peaks and dangerous ice-mountains? There is no gold up there, and he never takes a gun or a pick. *Icta mamook?* (What makes?)"

They were in fact a little afraid of Muir and considerably awed after one wild night at the beginning of October when Muir left the shelter of Young's home to see what the driving rainstorm was doing among the trees. No one else besides Young saw him go.

About 2 a.m. Hall Young was wakened by persistent knocking. When he opened the door, he found half a dozen frightened Indians dripping in the downpour. They told him all the Stickeens were scared, and they wanted him to "play (pray) plenty." Hovering above the mountain, a bad ghost, or something even more sinister, was dancing around, flapping its glowing red wings. It would surely bring a great evil down upon Wrangell unless the Christian God could make it go away.

Hall Young went out in the rain to a point where he could see this colorful apparition leaping on the place where the horizon must be. At first look, he broke into a roar of laughter, to the consternation of the Stickeens. The weird spectacle was only John Muir's fire, coloring the storm with its changeable light.*

---

* Muir loved campfires because of their warmth and the new beauties they revealed in the forests. He was proud of his ability to build them under any conditions, and considered this one a masterpiece. Anyone interested in this sort of woodsman's lore will find a detailed description of how he built a fire in Muir's *Travels in Alaska* (pp. 22-24).

Chapter 38
Witnessing the Birth of Glacier Bay

The explorers finally got off on their voyage in early October: four chiefs and two Indians — John Muir, the Ice Chief; Hall Young, the Sky Chief; Toyatte, a senior chief of the Stickeens and a younger chief named Kadachan; Stickeen John, the interpreter; and Sitka Charley, who had been seal hunting in the icy regions where none of the others had been, but where Muir and Young were determined to go.

Their craft was a thirty-six-foot canoe hollowed and carved from a single log of red cedar. High at prow and stern in the traditional Alaskan form, with lines "fine as a duck's breast," as Muir put it, she was about perfect for exploration among the islands of the Alexander Archipelago — except for one lack. The men were completely exposed to the rain, and at this season one could expect rain every day.

It was not a light-hearted departure. Chief Toyatte fully expected to die, either at the hands of his enemies to the north, or by some disaster that would sink the canoe in water below freezing temperature. Toyatte had a heart to match his big, powerful body; he ignored his forebodings with a quiet fatalism. Kadachan had more difficulty in ignoring his mother, who also expected disaster. Kadachan's father, a Chilcat sub-chief and related to Hard-to-Kill, the most powerful chief in Alaska, still lived among his own people. Blood feuds made Chilcat country perilous for his son.

Kadachan's young-looking mother came down to the dock in a last attempt to prevent his going. But when neither pleas nor scoldings nor tears would move him, she turned to Hall Young with an intense foreboding look in her dark eyes and said: "If anything happens to my son, I will take your baby in payment."

When they at last pushed off, the sun was shining — a rare event for that time of year. The six men, glad to be rid of clinging women, responded like boys at the start of a camping trip, laughing at and with each other, making and playing jokes, talking excitedly about excitements to come.

The Indians had brought their own staples, mainly dried salmon and seal grease. They would eat separately, but the white men invited Toyatte to share their first meal of the trip. One of the few luxuries they had brought along was butter, in two-pound rolls. Muir quietly put one of these down beside Toyatte.

With his eye the Chief sized up the amount of butter against the number to be fed, cut off one-third and divided his portion into bite-size pieces. As he began to eat, Hall Young opened his mouth to explain how butter should be eaten. Muir stopped him with a wink, and they watched Toyatte, with his usual dignified determination, swallow the butter piece by piece. *"Hyas klosh!"* ("Very good grease!") he said, rubbing his stomach.

The voyagers soon developed an easy, companionable relationship that enabled them to enjoy themselves in spite of being huddled together soggy wet, day after day, in a space the size of an average living room. Work and authority fell into natural assignments. Toyatte was steersman and indisputably captain, not only because the canoe belonged to him, but because his knowledge of wind and weather and the soundness of his judgment were acknowledged by all, and exercised by the venerable chief as simply a matter of common sense.

Technically Hall Young was leader of the expedition, because of his responsibility to learn all he could about the Indians and establish contacts favorable to missionary work. But he deferred to John Muir's wish to botanize along the way and his ambition to discover unknown realms of ice. In fact Muir very soon attained a spiritual and intellectual leadership which placed him above them all.

Muir had brought a volume of Thoreau's essays, Young a volume of Emerson's; Young had a second book — a Bible. Muir had the Bible in his head. They had read and memorized the same poets. Above and beyond these similarities of taste and background, Muir's unorthodox spiritual insights (which Young called "theism" for lack of a really appropriate category) became one of the most powerful influences in the young missionary's life. God was everywhere and continually at work to make His world harmonious and beautiful. If at the moment it seemed unbeautiful, wait; in a day, a year, ten thousand years, it would be beautiful beyond man's dreaming. Therefore accept all you saw and understand it, though natural fires and storms and ice laid forests waste and creature preyed on creature, for this too was part of the Almighty's love-work — a continuous creation. And if you saw — as you certainly would if you looked for them — scenes of great beauty and events of wonder, rejoice and give thanks, for these were gifts of God. Only, Muir believed, you would see much less and be illumined by it very little if you did not try to understand what God had done and was doing. To study nature scientifically was to know God better; to enter into the harmony of nature was to love God and receive his love. Hall Young's intellect, trained in Presbyterian doctrine, could not agree. But the intensity of Muir's informed, questioning wonder and his perceptive delight stirred the missionary's deepest responses. He felt that Muir was introducing him not only to the natural world which had lain unseen before his eyes, but to a new realm of spiritual experience.

The Indians were by no means impervious to Muir's influence. Their natural environment was all they had to depend on; they had observed much and along with their fellow tribesmen speculated a great deal about natural phenomena. Muir's explanations fascinated them. They even had some notions of their own about balance in nature, though they found very little love in storms or among animals. Kadachan told Muir that wolves were the masters of the woods; wicked, sly and very powerful because they hunted in packs. When Muir asked why the deer on the islands were not all killed by these super-enemies, Kadachan answered that the wolves knew better than to kill so many that their most important food supply was wiped out.

Muir, on his part, was very grateful to Young for enabling him to get to know the Alaskan Indians. Every party of hunters or fishermen or berry-pickers encountered was interviewed. When they came to a village, Hall Young first paid a call on the chief in his large fort-like house of hand-hewn cedar planks and carved pillars, gave him a *potlach* of rice, leaf tobacco and sugar, and asked him to call his most important people together. There would follow a series of speeches, sermons and counter speeches, for oratory to these Indians was a chief source of entertainment as well as a way of carrying on affairs. They were especially receptive to the belief that Christ laid down his own life to redeem sinful humanity. Among the Tlingit tribes many a fatal quarrel had been settled in just this way — by a chief whose life was thought to be worth ten or more ordinary lives allowing himself to be killed to settle a blood debt no pile of Hudson Bay blankets — the usual indemnity — could satisfy.

Toyatte and Kadachan were both orators of renown, but more than these men, who spoke in Tlingit — as did Hall Young — the Indians enjoyed listening to Muir, even though his words had to be translated. The intensity of his personality, radiating sincerity and good will, attracted the red men as it did the whites. And they deeply appreciated what Muir told them.

All men were brothers, he said. God loved the Indians equally with the whites; He had proved it by creating so beautiful a country — bountiful in food and other necessities — for them to live in. Some white Americans, he pointed out, were beginning to acknowledge their brotherhood and send people such as Hall Young. He hoped the Indians would listen to them and learn from such men and accept their help. At this point Muir's irrepressible humor broke out and he added that he hoped the tribesmen he was speaking to would not cook the missionaries in pots and eat them, as happened in some other parts of the world. The Indians appreciated this, also.

In breaks during the speechifying, Hall Young took the village census, family by family. When an Indian named a man, the missionary put down a large white bean; when a woman was named, a large brown bean. Small, white, Boston beans represented children.

The upshot of these sessions, which lasted up to three days, was usually the request by the chief that Hall Young send a teacher to the community.

Having visited the Kuprianoff Kakes, the voyagers came to the Hootzenoos, on the next island north. At the first village they visited they were welcomed and well treated. But at the tribe's main village they were met by a strange, complex mingling of howls and yells rising from a massive base of moans and groans. Muir, who had never before heard the "whiskey howl," wanted to backwater and get out of there at once. But though Hall Young knew all too well what the sound meant, he wished to land.

The most deadly instrument introduced into Alaska by civilized man was neither firearms nor money. A lonesome, bored and thirsty soldier taught the Hootzenoos how to make stills out of a couple of five-gallon tin cans, one of which was cut up and curled into a spiral worm. Into the intact can was put molasses, potatoes, any dried fruits available and such flavoring agents as pepper and ginger. After fermentation the can was heated and out of the worm dribbled the distilled essence. Few if any alcoholic beverages concocted by man have been so lethal.

Whiskey-making spread rapidly to other tribes, but the Hootzenoos were the first and most dedicated practitioners and the most inclined to attack anybody within reach when "under the influence." Their accomplishments were immortalized in the word "hootch," which used to be a popular side-word for strong drink of doubtful quality throughout the United States.

At first no Hootzenoo appeared. But presently a few old crones came tumbling out of the small dark opening of the chief's house, presently retreated, and were replaced by a number of men. One of these danced up and down in front of Toyatte, threatening to kill him. Toyatte contemptuously stared him down, without uttering a word. Kadachan had more trouble in escaping the embraces of a former friend, but by this time Hall Young had recognized the futility of their visit. They shoved off, set their square sail, and made for Hoonah ("Place of the North Wind"), on the northernmost large island of the archipelago.

The Hoonahs gave them a warm welcome, but also disturbing news. The Chilcats, they said, were fighting among themselves. Kadachan's father had been shot. It was obviously unprofitable to visit the Chilcats and especially dangerous for Toyatte, since hootch would certainly revive the vengeful feelings smoldering in some of these tribesmen.

Since Young, the "Sky Chief," was frustrated, the "Ice Chief" would now have his inning. Sitka Charley, the young boatman, hunter and camp helper, said he had been seal hunting in a great bay northwest of Hoonah. Many great glaciers came down to the water and filled the air with a continuous thunder made by falling bergs.

The Hoonahs said there was indeed such a bay very near. But it was foolish to go there, especially now, at the edge of winter, when skim ice was beginning to form and might any day weld the bergs into compact masses from which there was no escape. There was no gold on those great ice mountains. The Hoonahs advised their friends from the south to give up this bad trip. If they insisted on going, they must take aboard a supply of wood at an island at the mouth of the mysterious bay.

The voyagers hoisted sail early on October 24 and reached the wooded island (today called "Pleasant Island") about 1 p.m. No one except Sitka Charley actually believed that they would find no wood whatsoever on the shores or islands of the bay beyond. None of the rest had ever seen a shore where there was no wood. Nevertheless they took on a supply, made coffee and pushed on northwest through a cold, driving rain. Considerably after dark they made camp on a desolate beach on the shore of an inlet (now called Berg Bay) on the west side of Glacier Bay, near its mouth. The rain had turned to sleet. It was here that Muir gave Hall Young his first lesson in the art of draping one's body around a boulder, which made a better bed than wet sand strewn with cobble stones.

Searching the surroundings in the gray dawn to find some clue as to where they might be and what course they should steer, Muir saw nothing, at first, except rain and the low-hanging clouds from which it fell. Charley, their guide, admitted that he was confused and lost. Everything seemed different from what he remembered. Vancouver's chart, which had proved so helpful thus far, showed no bay here at all. The exploring party he had sent out in longboats in 1794 saw only shallow indentations filled with bergs moving restlessly in the wind and rimmed by mountains of solid ice — actually the meeting place with the sea of a trunk glacier more than a thousand feet thick and fifteen miles across.

The great glacier had already started to diminish when Vancouver's men saw it. By the time of Sitka Charley's boyhood it had gone back about thirty miles, leaving behind an island-dotted bay. Along the sides, finger-like fiords grew as the tributary glaciers retreated.

Since Charley's first visit the ice mass had divided and divided again as melting proceeded, exposing new land forms. The whole landscape had changed so much that it was strange to him

As the voyagers prepared to shove off, the gray rain was stained by smoke rising from the other side of the inlet. They paddled hopefully across, but were stopped near shore by a shot fired over their heads by an Indian with a blackened face. When they had identified themselves, men, women and children poured out of a small bark hut on the shore and welcomed them enthusiastically. Sitting with these nineteen Indians around a smoky fire in the small shelter, redolent of seal meat and fish in various stages of preservation, turned out to be one of the most curious episodes of the trip. These Hoonahs had heard of Young's missionary work. But what was he going to do up in Ice Bay among the glaciers and rocks? Preach to the seals and sea gulls? The interpreter's explanation that Muir was only interested in Ice Mountains soothed them. Nevertheless it took some time to persuade one of the seal hunters to go with the expedition as a guide, though Muir offered to pay him well.

Though the Hoonahs hunted to the fronts of the remotest glaciers, they were afraid of these ice-cliffs and the bergs — some the size of a building — that fell with a rumbling, reverberating crash, or rose solemnly without warning from a glacier's underwater foot to leap into the air and fall back with a wave-making splash big enough to swamp a canoe. Melting bergs would suddenly turn over, raking the nearby water with projections like fantastic antlers. Swept by great winds and the thirty-foot tides, the bergs charged up and down the bay and through the mill-race channels and the tortuous fiords.

The Hoonahs, embroidering these real dangers, said that an enormous killer whale lurked in these swift waters waiting for canoes which he devoured, crew and all, at one bite. In quieter waters lived a devil-fish with arms as long as tree-trunks with which he seized canoes and dragged them to the bottom, where he broke them up with his beak. Most frightening of all was the Land Otter Man, who could seize you dead or alive. He was whimsical, and might compel you to live among his people forever, or deposit you on a mountain ridge or in the top of a tall tree.

At last the seal-hunter's wife finished assembling her husband's cedar bark sleeping mat, his blanket and his sausages of lean seal meat braided around a core of fat.

"This is my husband you are taking," she said, giving Muir a winning smile. "See that you bring him back."

The voyagers left Berg Bay about 10 a.m. Just after noon they passed the towering front of the first glacier they met in Glacier Bay proper. (Muir later named it the "Geike," after the famous Scotch geologist.) Its blue cliffs, glimpsed fitfully through storm clouds from which the cold rain fell unremittingly, and the roar of falling bergs gave an impression of tremendous power. Nevertheless, Muir was in a fever to push on to other, bigger, ice mountains. But the seal-hunter guide insisted that they make camp in mid-afternoon, saying that the big glaciers at the head of the bay were too dangerous to approach except in full daylight and this inhospitable beach was the only reasonable campsite within reach.

They therefore carried the canoe up the rocky beach beyond reach of the bergs. Muir spent the rest of the afternoon studying the area. Rock surfaces down below high tide line, and the deep scratches they bore, showed clearly that ice had covered this beach very recently. All the earth here seemed newly created and raw. He found scarcely any living things except a few mosses.

As he explored Muir looked about him with rising excitement, realizing that here in this strange bay a landscape was being born, as Yosemite had once emerged from its carving, polishing, slow river of ice.

Most curious of all, stumps of good sized trees stood upright here and there from the wastes of sand and gravel. Muir thought them fossil stumps, but their Hoonah guide insisted that they would burn.*

The next day came up Sunday, and Hall Young adamantly refused to travel on the day the Lord had set aside. Muir, uninhibited by theology, set off in the rain to climb a fifteen-hundred foot ridge beside the camp. It proved very hard going — snowdrifts up to his armpits, brown glacial torrents carrying boulders that ground and gnashed together. And it was disappointing when

---

* Modern scientists call these remnants "interstadial stumps." They are the remains of forests overwhelmed during advances and retreats of the ice. See *Glacier Bay*, by Dave Bohn, Sierra Club, Ballantine Books, 1967.

he reached the crest to find storm clouds obscuring all.

He took some satisfaction in the fact that his limbs, after weeks of being cramped in the canoe, poulticed in damp clothing, were still capable of mountaineering, and as he sat resting on the ridge, the clouds lifted enough for him to glimpse what was for him a promised land. At his feet lay a great glacier, and at a distance four more. Though at first this newborn wilderness seemed dreary and mysterious, Muir made his jumping, sliding, wallowing way back to camp full of hope and enthusiasm — feelings which were immediately dampened. Hall Young told him that the Indians were discouraged and ready to turn back. Even Toyatte, the most steadfast and courageous of the lot, had told Hall Young that Muir must be a witch to seek knowledge in such a place, with winter coming on. This was more sinister than mere rhetoric, for all the Tlingit tribes considered witches to be authors of fatal misfortunes, and therefore killed them.

The crew had become increasingly doleful as they took turns telling sad old stories of crushed canoes, drowned Indians and hunters frozen in snowstorms. Toyatte said that he feared they were entering a jail of ice from which there was no return.

That night, beside a smoky fire of "fossil" wood, Muir made one of the most effective speeches of his life. He told them that for ten years he had wandered alone among high mountains and through savage storms, and good luck had always been with him. The sun would soon shine to show them the way to journey safely among the icebergs, for God cared for them and would guide them so long as they were trustful and brave. Simple as his words were, Muir managed to convey to these legitimately frightened Indians his own unquenchable optimism and faith that if one were wise and strong and trusted completely in Nature, she would not only let him live, but would reward him.

The Indians reacted as if Muir had somehow distilled his own supreme confidence and injected them with it. Kadachan said he always liked to travel with good-luck people; Toyatte declared that his heart was now strong and that he would go with Muir as far as he liked. Even if the canoe was broken, he added, it would not matter, for he would have a good companion on his journey to the next world.

Chapter 39
An Island Emerging

Next morning it was still intermittently snowing and raining. Wind and tide drove the herd of bergs up the bay and the canoe after them. In an hour they reached the fiord leading to a glacier Muir named for Hugh Miller, another Scotch geologist, examined the jagged pinnacles and battlements of the glacier's berg-dropping front and continued up the northwest trending arm of the bay.

Twenty-three years earlier this arm had been one huge ice river that joined with the Muir glacier to form a thundering front fifteen miles wide and two hundred and fifty feet high that completely blocked the bay. As Muir and his companions paddled up the arm that afternoon of October 27, 1879, they passed inlet after inlet leading to retreating glaciers. In late afternoon they came to the final inlet, at the head of which their guide told them were the best sealing grounds.

Pausing to take on a store of dry wood left at the mouth of this fiord, they set sail and drove swiftly up its five-mile length before a furious wind. At its end they found themselves looking up at an ice wall two miles broad. Against its foot the storm-driven bergs lay huddled as if the glacier (now called the Grand Pacific) had summoned its ice children home.

They landed near the foot of this glacier, carried the canoe up the rocky beach out of reach of bergs and berg-waves, and while the Indians made camp, Muir climbed a nearby mountain, hoping to get some kind of comprehensive view in spite of the weather. He had climbed scarcely one thousand feet when the clouds began to lift and sunshine streamed from their lower edges to set the bergs and the glacier front sparkling like crystal against the background of green water. Climbing still higher he found himself spellbound as he looked off over a prairie of ice, dotted here and there with peaks more than half submerged in snow and ice, to the white ramparts of the ten to fifteen thousand-foot Fairweather Range — the womb of glaciers.

Muir thought no other view could be more sublimely beautiful. But early the next morning, when they were setting out to explore the glacier front, Muir suddenly exclaimed, "Glory be to God!" Mt. Fairweather, the highest peak, had begun to burn with a crimson glow, as if it had been dipped into the very sun itself.

Peak after peak caught the indescribable color until the whole range stood

One mouth of the Fairweather ice-sheet (now called the Grand Pacific) north of Cross Sound in Glacier Bay.

incandescent. Then the light descended as though God were walking down the mountain, robed in celestial fire. Or so Muir and Young felt. The Indians also were in the grip of an experience beyond the ordinary life of man. They stopped paddling and sat like statues until the light turned creamy and left the cliffs and frozen torrents of the glaciers shining like crystal against the unblemished white of perennial snow.

Then they paddled out to a smooth, polished rock that thrust its thousand-foot front from the ice which covered two-thirds of it. In this morning's calm, the tide had swept the bergs down the fiord, leaving the green water dotted only by the whiskered faces of seals. The voyagers were able to land, and Muir climbed the glacier's front by cutting steps between the ice and rock. He surmised that a glacier-carved-and-polished island was being born here. Once on top, he saw that the forepart of the glacier rose gently in steps, as if the sea were undermining it progressively. On this evidence he predicted that a considerable fiord would take the place of this portion of ice. Both these predictions have proved correct: the great rock is now Russell Island, and behind it Tarr Inlet stretches for over ten miles before it reaches the Grand Pacific Glacier's front.

They coasted slowly down toward the main part of the bay, poking into every inlet they came to, but seldom reaching the glaciers at their heads. Ice had begun to form between the bergs — in some places they had to break a lane for the canoe with the tent poles. Each day the danger of being locked in grew greater. The Indians were greatly relieved when Muir gave up climbing every mountain he could reach, and they headed out of this icy jail.

Just beyond the point where the northwest fork begins, there loomed through the misty air an ice front a mile and a half across and in places seven hundred feet high. This was the first recorded sighting of the glacier that was to bear Muir's name. Huge masses of ice were falling from it continuously, creating waves that made a close approach impossible.*

* Muir himself says that they saw this glacier in passing. But Hall Young says that they landed a mile and a half from its front, that Muir spent a day and part of the night on this ice river, got lost in the darkness among bewildering crevasses and was guided out by torches the Indians made from tree stumps buried hundreds of years before and recently uncovered by the glacier's retreat. In any case no thorough exploration was made at this time.

Chapter 40
Chilcats and Apple Blossoms

T he voyagers returned their Hoonah guide to his village and set out immediately for the country of the Chilcats. The Hoonahs had told them that earlier reports of the fighting had been greatly exaggerated, and peace now reigned among Chilcat villages strung out along the narrow waterway called the Lynn Canal and the rivers at its head.

The Chilcats were rich, powerful and ruthless — not unlike the robber barons of medieval Europe. They made slave raids as far south as the Columbia River, and they controlled the passes into the frigid interior, passes over which a motley procession of starry-eyed Americans was to scramble and struggle during the Yukon gold fever of the 1890s. The Chilcats traded furs to the whites for guns, ammunition, knives, cookware, tobacco and other delights of civilization. These goods they traded to the northern Indians at old-fashioned Hudson Bay Company rates. The price of a ten-dollar musket, for example, was a pile of pelts as high as the gun stood on its butt.

At the first large village up the Lynn Canal, the voyagers were greeted by a shower of bullets that fell all around them. Muir and Young, who had been helping to force the canoe upstream, instinctively stopped paddling, but Toyatte peremptorily ordered them to keep digging. When Stickeen John had identified Muir and Young as a "great sky chief" and a "great ice chief," they were informed that the village head, "Old Silver Eye," would entertain them, and, as the canoe grounded in the shallows, forty braves rushed into the water, picked it up with the voyagers still aboard and carried it to the door of the Chief's large house.

Silver Eye had on the large, silver-rimmed spectacles which had earned him his nickname. He could see through them only a little but felt that they lent him dignity. After fifteen minutes of being left alone, a courtesy all the Tlingit tribes accorded to guests to enable them to get over any feelings of embarrassment and review what they wanted to say, the Chief told the voyagers that he would feast them first — a great honor.

They were seated on a low platform facing the bright fire in the center of the Room. Before Young and Muir, slaves placed large washbowls of Hudson Bay blue enamelware. The first course was a washbowl full of dried salmon (which the Tlingit tribes ate as we eat bread) with a dressing of seal grease. Hall Young and Muir could not eat it all, nor were they expected to. All that they left was dumped, according to custom, into a receptacle placed in their canoe. Slaves guarded this present from the dogs while the bowls were cleaned and filled with the fat back of deer, also served with seal grease dressing. The third course was small Russian potatoes cooked in seal grease. For dessert they had the long, fleshy apple of the wild rose, with seal-grease dressing.

Later that day Hard-to-Kill, the notorious chief of all the Chilcats, paid them a visit, and, for two days following, Silver Eye's house was jammed with audiences eager to hear the Sky Chief preach and the Ice Chief speak. There were even Indians on the roof peering down through the smoke hole.

Hall Young took time off to select the sites for a mission and a fort. He considered the visit a great success, though they did not go up river to visit the great chief's town. They were warned that Toyatte's enemies would certainly kill him if they did. Before they left Silver Eye requested a piece of writing stating that he had not killed the voyagers; this for protection in case some other Indians killed the Muir-Young party and brought down the vengeance of the U.S. Navy, which then ruled Alaska with one sailing vessel.

They had no trouble with Indians on the way back to Wrangell. But this part of the trip was the most hazardous because of the November weather and Muir's compulsions. He insisted on hunting glaciers up every fiord they came to, even though skim ice was beginning to form and the runoff from the constant rains caused glacier fronts to weaken and discharge ominous quantities of bergs.

At Sum Dum Bay — a long, twisting two-pronged fiord where the bergs charged up and down like cavalry battalions — Toyatte called a formal council and told Muir that he could risk his own life if he liked but the life of Hall Young should not be sacrificed. The crew would go no farther. Muir accepted the ultimatum with reasonable grace, though he was frustrated almost beyond endurance. They were all fast friends by now and Muir realized that these Indians had put up with a good deal. When they tried to shoot ducks he would rock the canoe, and refused to eat the meat of deer they killed. They called him the duck's friend and the lover of the deer, and joshed him about the big Sum Dum glacier hiding its face from him. All this Muir took in good part and bided his time.

Toyatte himself was capable of taking chances that frightened even Muir. One night when they had been fighting adverse wind and tide for strength-sapping hours, the aging Indian took them across a reef formed by the drowned terminal moraine of a vanished glacier. There were no more than two feet of clearance between the canoe and the boulders on each side, and probably less water beneath the bottom. When they were safely over and headed for a sheltered beach, Toyatte told Muir that he had been wrecked twice attempting to make such passages and had swum to shore each time — with a gun in his teeth. In this case, he said, if they had hit a rock Muir and the younger Indians might have saved themselves, but he and Hall Young would have drowned.

They arrived at Wrangell on a day in late November, surrounded by canoes full of welcomers. Among Muir's accumulated mail was a sad, sweet letter from Louie Wanda Strentzel saying how dearly she wished that he could be home for Thanksgiving. It was too late. The November mail boat had already gone, and he must cool his impatient heels until December.

Even when he got back to the States, Muir could not quickly come to his love. He was, as he wrote, "kuffed" into lecturing — first in Portland and then in San Francisco. Mr. Vanderbilt, the Wrangell Island merchant who had been so helpful, was in a financial bind, and Muir had promised him half of the one thousand dollars in his own bank account. Five hundred dollars was not enough, said Muir's pride, for him to take into marriage with an heiress. A series of articles he had sent from Alaska to the *San Francisco Bulletin* had increased his fame by a leap, and lecture fees were ready for plucking like apples in an orchard.*

Muir finally got to Martinez to see his fiancée in February. The next few weeks were largely spent in planning the wedding, set for April 14, 1880, when the Strentzel orchards were awash with flowers. On the wedding day the walls of the ranch house living room were almost concealed by blossoming boughs of red astrakhan apples.

It was a lovely old house with deep verandas curtained with climbing roses. The Strentzels had given it to their son-in-law and daughter, along with twenty acres of orchard. For themselves the elder Strentzels were building a sixteen-room manse on rising ground a little farther down the valley.

With the probable exception of certain girls who would like to have stood in Louie Wanda's shoes, Muir's marriage was a great satisfaction to his friends — to some a fulfillment of their hopes and dreams. Letters of congratulation flooded in from all parts. Self-important men wrote somewhat presumptuously that they now "expected even greater things" from Muir; close friends were simply happy in his evident happiness. Muir's own relatives were greatly relieved that the family's inexplicable, far-wandering member had "settled down" at long last. His Petticoat Brigade of female admirers sighed between the lines with pleasure and satisfaction. To them it had been almost unendurable that this attractive, entertaining, affectionate, virile,

---

* Muir believed himself to be the discoverer of Glacier Bay, and is so regarded today, though other white men had been there before him. According to Hoonah tradition, Russian traders had visited some of their villages, and two years before Muir's canoe voyage the fantastical Charles Erskine Scott Wood — soldier, poet, painter, lawyer and adventurer — had penetrated through and over floating ice to the limit, at that time, of canoe navigation. Dave Bohn, in *Glacier Bay, The Land and the Silence*, estimates that the temporary camp where Wood stayed with a party of goat and seal hunters was on a rock shelf at the mouth of Queen Inlet. This would be a little over forty miles from the Gulf of Alaska. Wood, however, was much more interested in the Indians than in either glaciers or topography. Moreover his account is vague respecting where he actually was and what he saw. He did not publish any account of his expedition until 1882, long after Muir's rich, and surprisingly accurate, report of his much more complete exploration. Wood, in fact, did not wish to be known as the discoverer of Glacier Bay. See correspondence between Wood and E.R. Scidmore referred to in "Report on Population and Residents of Alaska at 11th Census, 1890," cited by Dave Bohn in *Glacier Bay, The Land and the Silence*, p. 43.

sensitive and successful friend should not enter matrimony, the duty and reward of man. Jeanne Carr wrote to Louie Wanda saying that more than the acknowledgment of his genius, she had desired for Muir "the completeness which can only come in living for others — in perfected home relations." She believed this marriage "fore-ordained." Only Mary Swett, that loving realist, took the occasion to warn Louie Wanda that Muir, with his propensity for hair-splitting argument and quick temper was not the easiest person to live with, and that if he became truly angry with someone, he was not likely to forgive him.

None of these well-wishers had a notion of the results Muir's overwhelming sense of obligation and his compulsiveness were to have, though they might have taken some warning from the fact that he went to work in the orchards the morning after the wedding.

Chapter 41
The Hidden Glacier
of Sum Dum Bay

Muir kept hard at the farming until the early harvest had been gathered and sold. Then, at the end of July, he sailed for Alaska. August and September were ripening time, and he and his bride had agreed that he should spend this interval doing his chosen work in the wildernesses that were his true home. Louie Wanda, who had been a career daughter, keeping books and helping more and more to run the ranch as her father's fragility increased, was now a career wife, which inevitably meant being torn within, as she had already found out. Before he returned the year before, she had written — Thanksgiving and Christmas having come and gone with no word from him — "you are more precious to me than any work, and it hurts me to feel so utterly powerless in aiding you and shielding you from pain...though my weak fears so often dim all else...sometimes I think I comprehend the delight and precious value of your work to your own soul. I dare not call to lead you away from that you feel best, wherever it may guide."*

As if to make up for silences past and silences to come, Muir wrote to his wife several times a week until mid-August, when he and Hall Young left Wrangell by canoe for Glacier Bay and the ice-choked fiords along the way. The letters were affectionate and nostalgic and filled with sidelights his all-gathering eyes observed — including the pollution that civilization dragged behind it as it crept northward. At Victoria, British Columbia, the water was cleaner than in most harbors, he wrote, "but not without the ordinary drift of old bottles, straw, and defunct domestic animals." At Victoria his ship took aboard hundreds of barrels of molasses to be traded to the Indians for hard-won furs and carried by canoe up remote glacial inlets to be distilled into hootch.

At Wrangell hootch struck at Muir himself, though indirectly. Toyatte, their steersman and captain of the year before, had gone out to stop an armed clash between a band of crazy-drunk Hootzenoos and the local Stickeens, who were fighting mad because their houses had been entered and their women insulted. Toyatte, unarmed except for his ceremonial spear, and Hall Young, who stood beside him, tried to reason with the invaders. A Hootzenoo shot the chief through the heart.

* Quoted by Linnie Marsh Wolfe in *Son of the Wilderness: The Life of John Muir*, p. 190.

Kadachan, their diplomat of the year before, was drinking so heavily as to be unreliable. Hall Young therefore arranged to charter the canoe of one of his parishioners, Lot Tyeen, whose seal hunting expeditions had given him experience among bergs; his son-in-law, Joe, went along as a rower; the third crewman, a young halfbreed known as "Smart Billy," was their interpreter.

As Young stood on the wharf saying a last goodbye to his wife, he suddenly decided to take along their little dog. The Wrangell Indians had given him their tribal name, "Stickeen," a great honor to bestow on a dog. He had the brown, black and white markings of a collie, though he was not half the size of the average member of that breed, and long, silky hair and a tail like a plume — a cool, independent little hunter, very selective in his choice of friends and impatient with caresses. Yet almost everyone who laid eyes on Stickeen became extraordinarily devoted to him. Tyeen the steersman had shot one of his valuable hunting dogs for worrying Stickeen.

Muir was not so readily enchanted. He called up from the canoe, which was tied up to the float at the pier's end, protesting that Stickeen was a useless bit of fluff and would be a nuisance. Mrs. Young also protested. Stickeen listened for a bit, then calmly trotted down the steep gangway to lie in the bow close to Muir. Everybody, including the Indians, laughed, and Stickeen went along.

The canoe was twenty-five feet long, ten feet shorter than Toyatte's and swifter and more maneuverable. But the strength of all five was often taxed, not only at times of contrary winds and currents, but because Muir was in a tearing hurry and he was paying for the expedition. Tyeen, a massive, powerful man, sat on the high stern wielding his broad steering paddle; Joe and Smart Billy manned the long oars amidships; Muir and Young, with paddles, sat side by side near the bow, just behind the twin masts on which they set square sails.

The voyage up the mainland coast was wild and exhausting. Muir, anxious about his wife (though he had left her in good health) and feeling obliged to be home by harvest time, was determined to catch the October mail boat at the latest. But he was even more determined to see all the ice mountains he had missed the year before. The frustration of having "lost" a glacier reported to lie up an arm of Sum Dum (now Holokham) Bay galled him particularly — almost intolerably. He therefore insisted on keeping the canoe going at a killing pace, no matter what the weather, and often until after dark.

Coming in through rock strewn shallows toward an unknown beach, wet to the skin and half-blinded by the driving rain was nobody's delight, nor in any way safe. Phosphorus in the waves that smashed over the rocks and reefs gleamed on the seaweed that waved like hair and made it seem as if the canoe were charging at a line of monsters with flashing teeth. When at last they reached the rock strewn sands, bulbs of a rockweed called "fucus" exploded under their feet as they groped their way to higher ground and began the weary business of finding by lantern light a spot dry enough for sleeping.

The interest of the voyage, however, and the sudden, bizarre beauty they encountered made the hard times seem a bargain price. One dark, rainy night at the mouth of a salmon stream well-known to Tyeen, where they meant to make camp, jets and streaks of silvery light began to flash around them. As the canoe advanced upstream the flashes became more numerous and more exciting and the Indians shouted with joy. *"Hiyu salmon. Hiyu mucha muck!"* ("Plenty of salmon. Lots of food!") While Billy and Joe made camp, Muir and Young paddled upstream with Tyeen. There seemed to be more salmon in the stream than water, which was beaten to gleaming froth by the thousands of phosphorus-churning fins.

From the tail of his eye, after a paddle stroke, Muir saw something that brought a startled exclamation from him. Behind them stretched a long, straight furrow of silver light as if some creature out of Tlingit mythology were following — and gaining.

The creature presently resolved itself into Stickeen who, as usual, had gone exploring as soon as they made camp, and — as usual — had made sure that he would not be left behind. In a whirlpool below some rapids, Tyeen caught half a dozen salmon in a few minutes, gaffing them with a hook on a pole, by the light the fish themselves furnished.

The following morning was sunny and to Muir a singularly wonderful example of the bounty of Alaska and the adaptation of the Indians. A family of amiable Hoonahs who had raced the voyagers to the salmon stream had not even bothered to put up their portable hut of cedar bark sheets. In the early light they were cheerfully drying out and admiring the uncountable multitude of salmon that filled the stream bank to bank — so many that those on the top layer had their backs out of the water. Gorged eagles sat somnolent on dead branches.On the beach, ducks and wading birds in flocks of thousands were getting a hearty breakfast, as were two babies in the Hoonah camp. Their mothers, seated on the ground, had set the carrying boards on end, so that the little prisoners' mouths were at breast level.

That night the voyagers camped beside some gold miners who had built wing dams and sluiceboxes on a stream just inside Sum Dum Bay. They woke to find a formidable army of bergs sweeping past on a furiously outgoing tide. At the turn the explorers got in front of the returning bergs and with their oars and paddles managed to keep ahead of the charging ice until stopped by a jam of bergs in the narrow mouth of the bay's longest arm — the Endicott — which they meant to follow.

Lot Tyeen had brought ice guards fashioned by himself with hand adze and pocket knife out of selected branches. They landed below the ice-jam to fit these to bow and stern — and to cook a hot meal. Wise precautions, both. Threading their way through the bergs, shoving aside the smaller ones with tent poles, avoiding the two hundred-footers which occasionally broke up with a thunderous roar and sent out waves that rocked their fellow bergs for half a mile around, proved time consuming and tiring, though Muir enjoyed it. Once beyond the jam, lanes of berg-free water opened up. But they passed headland after headland with no terminal glacier in sight. The Indians began to tease Muir, telling him that the Sum Dum Glacier did not care to show his face to the

Ice Chief.

When after fourteen hours they negotiated the last twist in the narrow fiord, they found themselves confronted with the loveliest glacier in Alaska, or so Hall Young thought; to Muir all glaciers were beautiful. This was actually a frozen cataract pouring wildly down a precipitous notch in granite mountains. The perpendicular base, about three-quarters of a mile across, was a deep, vitriol blue. Above it the slightly inclined face of pure debris-free ice rose nearly a thousand feet more. Great patches were dusty white with ice powdered by the glacier's ceaseless grind against the walls.

Between these striking bands of blue and white the front ranged through the entire top of the spectrum: sky-blue and sapphire, indigo, lilac, amethyst. As Muir stood up in the canoe to sketch, a couple of big pieces broke loose and came thundering down into the water. "The ice mountain thinks well of you," Tyeen said to Muir in Chinook. "He is firing his big guns to welcome you."

Paddling around a large, burnished rock on the west side of the channel, they came upon another large glacier pouring ice into the fiord. Late in the evening, when the sunset had faded and the dawn was still some way off, they looked for a camping place. But the granite came down so steeply to the water that there was no landing place. They finally had to scramble up two hundred feet of steep, smooth rock, dragging food and blankets with them, to a timbered ledge. It turned out to be the best campground of the trip — a garden of wild flowers and bushes bearing ripe berries. Sixteen cascades, falling four thousand feet from the ice cap atop a nearby mountain, sang them to sleep.

In the morning Muir and Stickeen — who was now his inseparable companion — went exploring on and above the walls of bare-seeming granite that rose three to four thousand feet on either side of the glacier. Actually they were not bare, but patched with the crimson, yellow, magenta and green of wildflowers and other hardy plants which grew wherever a little crumbled granite had collected in a depression or on a shelf. At the top the mountain ridge was forested. To Hall Young, seated on a great rock that jutted out in front of the glacier, the trees looked like a curtain parted to show the drama of descending ice.

After Young's near-tragedy on Glenora Peak he had promised his tearful young wife never to climb again beyond a few hundred feet of relatively safe scrambling. He envied Muir whom he could see now botanizing in a patch of vegetation, now disappearing into a crevasse of the upper glacier, now spread-eagled on a cliff with Stickeen dancing below and howling in protest at being left. But most of Young's attention was absorbed by the glacier itself which, by Muir's estimate, was flowing down at the rate of eighty to one hundred feet a day. As Young watched, the center, moving faster than the sides which were grinding against the walls, gradually became vertical, then began to lean outward. At this point two lines of deep, vivid blue developed from the top of the ice front to the water. The glacier's center became a leaning tower, shedding ice dust and fragments. The suspense became almost unbearable as the mass leaned farther, and Young found himself waving his arms and shouting, "Hurry up! Hurry up!"

The climax was astonishing. Instead of falling over, the ice pinnacle shot two hundred feet into the air, forced upward by the tremendous squeeze of pressure exerted on its base, which descended over nine hundred feet under water, according to Muir's estimate. As the majestic crystal rose, Hall Young cheered, and he could hear Muir cheering and Stickeen's bark high above.

When the new berg hit the water it sent out a wave that splashed half way up the one hundred and fifty-foot rock where Hall Young sat. The glacier put on this performance several times during the two days the voyagers spent in its presence. Muir named this glacier "The Young," for his friend and companion in discovery. But the name was later changed to "Dawes Glacier," just when and by whom is not known.

On the way back down the bay they ran a stretch of seething, swirling water where the tide rushed over a ridge of granite so hard that the glacier which had anciently dug out a side branch of the fiord had been unable to erode it. The branch with its domes and towers and pinnacles and leaping waterfalls was so like Yosemite Valley — excepting for its sea-water floor — that Muir named it "Yosemite."

Leaving Young to missionary work at the mining camp, Muir explored the other great arm of the bay. This also proved a tremendous experience of landscape being formed by ice, water and pioneer growth. Muir and Young together produced the first map of Sum Dum's octopus-like waterways.

Running north from Sum Dum the voyagers had a fair day with a following wind to fill their square sail. The Indians took advantage of the situation to overhaul and dry out their provisions and gear. Joe, the hunter, wanted to put a fresh charge into his old musket, so he stepped to the bow, forward of the mast, and fired — at a sea gull.

The bird came down beside the canoe in a dying glide, a ribbon of blood trailing from its beak. Muir gave Joe a severe lecture, but all the excuse the Indian could make was that he had learned from the whites to be careless about taking life.

Tyeen was also upset. He still clung to the old Tlingit belief that it is wrong and unlucky even to speak disrespectfully to the fishes and animals. Only the year before a young boy had gone into a decline because, the shaman said, a crab the lad had made fun of stole his soul. This belief that discourtesy is unlucky was one reason for the extraordinary politeness of these Alaskan Indians, and the remarkably good behavior of their children. Another cause, of course, was that they were a proud and touchy people and discourtesy might easily lead to killing.

Taking on a load of firewood at Pleasant Island, the voyagers headed straight up Glacier Bay to Muir Glacier. Its two-mile wall of deep blue ice was discharging bergs, Muir estimated, at the average rate of one every five minutes. The air was full of continuous roar and thunder, the water never calm. Tyeen refused to beach the canoe any closer than a mile and a half from the front. The best Muir could do was persuade the Indians to take him and his equipment by land for a one-man camp near the terminal moraine on the west side. They had barely landed the gear when a berg leaped from the depths, streaming water like hair, fell back and leaped again, sending waves far down the bay. The Indians got out of there fast, leaving Muir to find his own camp.

During the next six days Muir crossed and recrossed the glacier, delighted with the streams that ran sweetly singing in blue ice channels, to pour into lakelets with colored ice crystals like bright flowers along their sides. The glacier's surface, which looked so smooth from a distance, he found to be a bewildering network of ridges and blades of ice separated by yawning crevasses. It was a long day's work to cross and re-cross it. Stickeen's paws were so badly cut by the sharp ice that Muir made moccasins for him out of handkerchiefs.

From a twenty-five hundred foot mountain a few miles from the front he was able to see the whole panorama of apparently motionless, but slowly flowing, ice. It seemed more like a prairie than a river, with its seven main tributaries, each with many branches, so that the total, he estimated, was more than two hundred glaciers which drained at least eight hundred square miles. North and west the towering peaks of the Fairweather Range formed a magnificent frame.

This was not Muir's most spectacular sight during those days on the glacier and in camp at its foot. On a night of storm, the water turned phosphorescent and, with the luminous leaping bergs, the glowing waves that dashed against the glacier front and the rivulets of fiery drops dripping down, it seemed a wild celebration put on by Nature for Muir's especial delight.

Just before they left the vicinity of Muir Glacier, Joe the hunter went up a high mountain on whose green shoulders mountain goats grazed, appearing at this distance like white mice.

Joe returned to camp carrying a fine buck on his shoulders, explaining that the goats had eluded him. As the others admired his kill, Joe, looking pleased with himself, remarked that he had brought the fattest one.

"Did you shoot more than one?" Muir asked, giving him a stern look from under his formidable eyebrows.

Joe held up ten fingers plus one. "Eleven," he said, in Chinook. Muir turned as red as John Bull in England, blasted Joe with a burst of languages that would have burned the fur off a seal's back and went for Joe with his fists doubled and blue fire in his eyes. Joe was young and quick enough to scramble up the slope of jumbled rock back of camp, where Muir could find no footing for an attack. He refused to come down until promised safe conduct.

This was the first and only time Hall Young saw Muir truly angry in one thousand miles of voyaging cramped in a canoe and spending interminable nights in wet, miserable campsites. Muir was what athletes call a "bench jockey": he loved to jibe and harrass his friends, stir up arguments, pretend to be angry, as when he kicked at Stickeen, making sure to miss. He was impatient, and therefore often irritated, but never in a rage before the day Joe shot eleven deer and brought home only one.

Going down Glacier Bay and westward through Icy Strait toward Cross Sound, which leads to the open sea, they poked into every glacial fiord and inlet — all of them unmapped and unknown. The weather was foul; their clothes and blankets remained sodden wet for a week. The last twenty miles were the most gruelling. They were bucking a headwind that drove the rain into their faces like birdshot. The canoe mounted and slid down great swells driving in from the Gulf of Alaska. Amidships Joe and Smart Billy lifted their seats off the thwart with the effort they put into each stroke, with Tyeen urging them on like a coxswain. In the bow Muir and Young plied their paddles with all the power they could muster, heads bent except for an occasional glance at the black cliffs that towered dizzily above them. The waves were dashing up toward the ultimate splash line, which Muir estimated from the growth on the rocks to be seventy-five feet above the water. Only Stickeen, gazing over the side like a happy tourist, was pleased.

Chapter 42
Trapped on an Island of Ice

By the time they pulled into the sheltered waters of ice-rimmed Taylor Bay, the men were all exhausted. While the Indians made camp, Muir and Young pushed their way through tall, thick grass to the three-mile front of a very large glacier which had receded some distance from the water. But it was receding no longer.

Muir stopped suddenly and gestured toward the ice-front. "All the glaciers we've seen have been shrinking back. This one is advancing. Look at the great ice plough turning its furrow!"

The glacier had thrust its projecting forefoot under a sizeable hill and was carrying it seaward. Huge rocks had been shattered into fragments. Forest trees leaned crazily at all angles. Some had already been engulfed and were being chewed up by the grinding ice.

Close to the glacier wall the men picked salmon berries and strawberries as large and finely flavored as Muir had ever encountered. The weather was worsening ominously, but he planned to explore this glacier in the morning.

Hall Young fully intended to get up and make breakfast for his companion — in part as escape from his frustration because his vulnerable shoulder prevented him from going along. But he had been kept awake by the violent flapping of the tent and the rising voices of the storm. When the musical howling of a wolf finally put him to sleep he slumbered on, until — in the half dark that should have been dawn — he heard Muir arguing with Stickeen.

"Go back. Go back and get your breakfast!" Silence, and then "Go back, Stickeen! Go back, I say. In this storm the big glacier's no place for a wee beastie like you."

Again, silence. Hall Young chuckled to himself. There had been many such arguments, and Stickeen won them all.

Muir gave the little dog a crust of bread from the small supply he carried to see him through the day and set off against a wind that frequently made him stagger. The rain was not exactly falling; mixed with shreds of cloud it arrived horizontally in flat, thick sheets that took his breath. The world was an even, gray, structureless gloom. The wind, moaning through the nearby forest, snarling among the spires and chasms of the glacier, mingled its sounds with the roar from a network of streams and rivulets foaming across the low ground below the ice front. Muir, who had put on rubber boots, sloshed through this water net and made his way up the east side of the glacier through a peculiarly ragged woods along its edge. Taking shelter behind a tree, he removed his boots and his long, gray overcoat and laid them on a log to be recovered later, for he knew he would be wet to the skin no matter what he wore.

Tightening the laces on his mountain shoes and shouldering his ice axe, he continued up a newly-smoothed slope of granite encumbered here and there with the torn and broken remains of trees. The advancing glacier was steadily encroaching on the forest. In some places Muir looked down beneath the edge of the ice cataract and watched great logs being slowly ground into pulp.

Three or four miles up-glacier he cut steps and, climbing to its top, found it to be no longer a frozen cataract but a nearly level ice prairie stretching away indefinitely under the low sky.

The wind had moderated to a half gale though it was still raining and the clouds tended to sink close to the ice, further limiting visibility. Muir hesitated to cross to the western side, which he judged to be six or seven miles off, fearing that in a maze of crevasses he would have trouble finding his way back. Nevertheless he explored some distance out on the ice and found only narrow crevasses he could step across; also, occasional rifts began to appear in the dense canopy of clouds.

He started across, Stickeen sometimes following and sometimes ahead. The ice-prairie proved relatively smooth, and he made steady progress until the mountains beyond the western shore came into sight. Then Muir began to enjoy himself, stopping to admire a rill sliding through its ice bed with musical, tinkling sounds, or gaze into the depths of a rounded well from which came the grating and bumping of a boulder being polished. Here and there a mountain peak appeared, sunk to the throat in the plane of ice that stretched away toward the cloud-curtained heights of the Fairweather Range.

Nearing the western shore Muir encountered crevasses so wide that he had to range up and down the glacier searching for ice bridges he could cross. In places he had to walk five hundred yards to make fifty. He took compass readings at short intervals, hoping that they would help him find his way back.

But when he had explored a beautifully-curving torrent frozen into pinnacled waves — an ice cataract greater than Niagara Falls — and traced it to a lake filled with bergs, the afternoon had waned. At 5 p.m. he struck directly across the ice to traverse the fifteen miles to camp.

The first few miles were easy going, though he had frequently to take compass bearings. The low clouds that literally dragged across the ice obscured the mountains behind, and he was on a totally different track than the one he had so carefully marked in memory earlier in the day. He moved through a little world of beautiful ice, changing every few rods, but always closely curtained by the rain-filled mist through which Stickeen would disappear and emerge as he went about his own explorations. The moan of wind through unseen crevasses and the muffled grinding of great stones deep in the glacier's mills intensified the solitude and tinged it with foreboding.

About two hours out on the ice Muir found himself confronted by a labyrinth of crevasses of such depth and width that he was appalled. Ranging up and down, making ten times as much progress sidewise as forward, he found places where he could cross — perilously. Those that were no more than eight feet across, he jumped. Wider chasms he crossed on "sliver bridges" — narrow strands of melting ice that spanned the abysses. Their tops were sharp as knives and he traversed them by cutting off the upper edge with his axe, straddling the smoothed part and inching his way along. He was driven by the knowledge that if he could not cross in the fading light (for the incessant rain had changed to snow) he would have to spend the night jumping up and down and dancing to the mournful music of the wind. It would be the only way to keep from freezing — but he was sodden-wet, weary and hungry, in poor condition for a night on a glacier.

The more formidable the obstacles, the more determined Muir therefore became. When he and Stickeen were brought up short at the lip of a crevasse some eight feet wide, he hesitated. The opposite side of the chasm was lower than the side he stood on. He might get across, but if the crevasses beyond proved impassable, he could not get back. The ice on the far shore, however, looked smooth and inviting. Chopping a foothold on the chasm's lip, Muir coiled his legs and leaped. He made a safe landing and became worried about Stickeen. But the little dog, with scarcely a glance at the abyss, came flying across like a furry rocket.

Two hundred yards across level ice, Muir and Stickeen came to a crevasse forty feet wide at the narrowest and increasing up to seventy-five. It yawned to an incalculable depth. Man and dog explored for nearly a mile and found that it curved to join the chasm they had just crossed. In the gathering gloom they went a long mile down-glacier and found that here also the crevasse before them joined the one behind. They were trapped on an island of ice. The snow fell thicker and more blinding than before.

In spite of himself, Hall Young worried about Muir when his friend did not show his face before dark. Throughout the evening concern built up with unusual intensity because of the storm and the power of the advancing glacier, which made it strange to all previous experience. A Hoonah chief who had visited Young that afternoon thought it malign. He came with his three wives and a covey of children and grandchildren from his salmon camp on the stream that issued from beneath the great glacier. After an afternoon of silence he asked for a formal conference, which he began by comparing Hall Young to the sun and moon. When Young finally interrupted the speech by asking what the chief really wanted, he said: "I want you to pray to your God. Once I had the finest salmon stream on the coast; schools of King Salmon came — the fattest and best salmon among these islands. But the cruel spirit of the glacier grew angry and drove the ice mountain down and spoiled my salmon stream. A year or two more and it will be no more. I have prayed to my Gods. Last spring I sacrificed my best slaves — a strong man and his wife — but the glacier comes on. Now I want you to pray to your Gods."

When Hall Young exclaimed in horror at the human sacrifice, the chief was astonished.

"Why, they were *my* slaves," he said, "and the man suggested it himself. He was glad to die to help his chief."*

The only sliver bridge Muir could find in the whole length of the big crevasse hung like a sagging rope. It was badly weathered, with a knife-like upper edge. Worse, it was attached eight or ten feet below the lip of the chasm. Muir studied it, compared its dangers with the jump he would have to make if he retreated over the crevasse he and Stickeen had crossed to get into this trap and decided to risk the sagging sliver. While Muir was cutting a hollow for his knees on the chasm's lip, Stickeen came up, looked earnestly into his face and began to mutter and whine as if trying to ask Muir whether he really intended to go down on that awful bridge. Muir told him it was the only way to go and the little dog ran off wildly along the chasm's edge looking for a better crossing. Finding none he lay down behind Muir and cried louder than ever. It was the first time Stickeen had seemed to know what fear was.

By this time Muir had chopped out a step deep enough to balance upon while he reached down and chopped another. Thus slowly and perilously he descended to the sagging bridge. Calling on all the mountain training that had taught his nerves and muscles to keep him balanced in improbable situations, he cut a small platform, got astride it and, gripping with his knees as a cowboy grips his horse, inched his way across, cutting off the sharp edge ahead of him. It took a long time to traverse the seventy-five feet spanning the dark abyss, and even longer to cut steps and fingerholds up the ice wall on the other side. And all the time Stickeen was crying as if his heart would break.

When Muir called him in a reassuring tone he only cried louder, as if trying to say that he could never, never get down onto that bridge. Muir pretended to leave him. but he only cried louder and made no move. At last, as if responding dubiously to Muir's insistence that he could do it if he only tried, Stickeen hushed his cries, slid his little forefeet into Muir's top step, brought hind feet and body down and proceeded to the bridge with great caution but no hesitation. The top Muir had smoothed was only four inches wide. Stickeen moved along it one paw at a time, seeming to hold his breath, bracing himself against the snow and the moaning wind that whirled his silky hair and threatened to blow him off. He did not stop until he reached the farther wall. Here he paused as if to fix the steps in his mind. Muir was kneeling on the lip of the crevasse ready to help. But when Stickeen was ready he gave a spring that

* Eight years later the chief visited Hall Young at Wrangell and reported that the glacier had indeed stopped and the salmon had come back to the stream.

-223-

sent him scrambling swiftly up and onto the level ice where he whirled and rolled in a delirium of joy, barking as if to shout "Saved! Saved! Saved!"

Muir had to tell Stickeen severely that they must start at once if they were to get off the ice while there was still a little light. Soon a forested headland loomed faintly through the snow-filled mist; the ice proved good all the rest of the way and they got down the dangerous rocks they had climbed that morning before full dark settled down. Then reaction set in, and man and dog stumbled down the muddy moraine slopes and through the tangled brush toward the light of a signal fire the crewmen had made to guide them.

It was after ten when Muir and Stickeen dragged themselves into camp. Stickeen, too tired even to shake himself, lay down on his piece of blanket. One of the Indians helped Young strip off Muir's wet clothes, got him into dry underwear and sat him by the fire with a blanket around him, too worn out to say a word. Hall Young had cooked the best camp meal possible. Muir did not speak until he had eaten his way through clam chowder, fried porpoise, bacon and beans, rice and curry, "savory meat" made with mountain kid and camp bread. As he took his first sip of coffee and began on a bowl of wild strawberries, he looked over at Stickeen and said, lapsing into Scotch, "Yon's a brave doggie!" Stickeen opened one eye and thumped his tail on the blanket. But he neither ate nor rose until Muir — who, once he began to talk, had been holding Young spellbound with his narrative of the day's adventure — came to the desperate crossing of the big crevasse. Then Stickeen crossed the tent and crouched down, with his head on Muir's foot, murmuring what Young thought to be canine words of adoration.

To Young that day's travel was an astounding demonstration of endurance. In seventeen hours, without rest, man and dog had covered over thirty miles, including the most trying ice-work. Neither slept well, but started up from time to time imagining themselves once more on the sliver bridge. Yet they were both out on the glacier all the next day.

Muir's fascination with ice delayed their departure so long that the trip down to Sitka became a race against the sailing of the October mail steamer. Riding the flood tide up a narrow inlet, they dragged the canoe one hundred fifty feet over a little hill at its head and caught the ebb in a similar channel on the other side. In three days and two nights, they stopped only once.

Opposite the mouth of Peril Strait, the unmistakable beat of war-drumming came out to them from Angoon, the main village of the Hootzenoos. As they approached they saw that the whole tribe was dancing, the men painted and costumed for war. Hall Young insisted on landing, for he was greatly alarmed. The war of the previous winter, when Toyatte and several other Stickeens were killed, had been ended by an uneasy peace. Young felt certain that the Hootzenoos were working themselves up to attack Wrangell again.

As the canoe hit the beach he hurried up to the chief, who was directing the war dance, and asked him abruptly what the tribe was going to do. The chief gave him an odd look, then led the way into his house and pulled away the embroidered blanket that covered a human figure surrounded by totemic carvings, elaborate baskets and other symbols of power and wealth. The chief's eldest son lay there with one side of his head smashed.

He had recklessly fired at a *hootz*, the huge brown bear of Alaska. The animal, enraged by a superficial wound, had crushed the young man's skull with one swipe of his paw. The whole tribe had declared war on that *hootz*, and every man and every gun on the island would soon be on the warpath after him.

Before Muir boarded the mail steamer at Sitka, he sat on a coil of rope, took Stickeen's head in his hands and reasoned with the little dog, telling him to be brave; they would go exploring together again bye and bye. Stickeen thumped his tail as if he understood — but his cries came far over the water when the Indians had carried him struggling to the canoe and rowed away.*

---

* Muir and Stickeen never met again. The dog was stolen from Hall Young by a trader or a tourist.

Chapter 43
Mission to Arctic Seas

A mong the letters Muir found waiting for him at Sitka was one from Louie Wanda written a few weeks after he left home at the end of July. She had been desperately ill and, as she said, passed many nights among the strange shadows and wild wandering phantoms of delirium. Now that it was over, she wrote "I know that neither time nor space can ever separate us."*

He was greatly relieved when he reached the ranch to find her well and happily pregnant. But now it was Muir's turn to be ill in a totally unexpected and at that time unexplainable way — though his symptoms would suggest to a modern physician severe allergic reactions to influences in the ranch environment. He developed a bronchial cough which grew steadily more wracking; also what was then called "nervous indigestion." Muir had not been so ill since his near-fatal bout with fever in Florida fifteen years before. But he drove himself from dawn to dark nevertheless, setting out new fruit trees and vineyards in former hayfields, grafting grapes and pears to produce more profitable crops on land leased from his father-in-law as well as the acres he and Louie Wanda had inherited.

Neither work nor illness could dim Muir's delight in his baby girl, born on March 25, 1881, and named Annie Wanda for Muir's mother and her own mother. Ever since he had left home, Muir had sought substitute families wherever he could — from Canada to Florida, from Indianapolis to San Francisco, from Yosemite to Alaska. He fit into households so well that his friends felt privileged to have him. He made close friends with children of all ages and delighted them. But none of this borrowed warmth could satisfy his need for children of his own. To sustain his loved ones in such comfort and security as he himself had seldom known was the major reason why he drove himself without remorse.

One evening shortly after Annie Wanda arrived, Muir attended a dinner in Oakland honoring the officers of the U. S. revenue cutter, *Thomas Corwin*, due soon to sail in search of an exploring ship named *Jeannette* — unreported for over a year — and also to do whatever Arctic exploring became practicable. Muir was given the seat of honor beside C. L. Hooper, the *Corwin's*

---

* Letter from his wife to John Muir quoted in part by Linnie Marsh Wolfe in *Son of the Wilderness: The Life of John Muir*, pp. 220-221.

captain, whom he had known in Alaska. Hooper tried to persuade him to go along as scientific observer. Muir refused, but Hooper, not easily put off, told him to talk over the opportunity with his wife.

Muir dutifully reported the offer at breakfast next morning. Dr. Strentzel heartily agreed that a man with a wife and child had no right to go off on a high-risk adventure whose end could not be foretold. But later, in the privacy of their own room, Louie Wanda told Muir that he simply had to go. His cough continued to worsen; he had grown irritable; his appetite was not only poor, but so finicky that she and her mother were at their wits' end in devising ways to tempt him. Besides, the trip would stimulate him to write — and Louie Wanda considered his writing to be not only Muir's true vocation, but the expression of his essential self.

When the *Corwin* sailed from San Francisco on May 4, 1881, Muir was aboard, sharing the captain's cabin with Hooper and the ship's surgeon.

On May 15, twelve days out from San Francisco, the *Corwin* tried to buck her way into the Bering Sea between Unalaska and the next Aleutian island east. She had the help of a powerful tide pouring north through the narrow channel, but the Arctic sent its greetings in the shape of a fierce wind with snow in it which drove great combers in quick succession against the tide. The waves reared almost straight up; the wind carried their tops away in gray scud and the channel from side to side became — as Muir described it — one white, howling, rampant mass of foam.

The *Corwin* was only one hundred thirty-seven feet long (some present day fishing boats are larger), and though she still answered her helm well as the storm's violence increased, there was danger that some waves would sweep her decks and carry away lifeboat, steam launch and everything else that could be torn loose.

Corwin turned back and rode out the storm in the shelter of a red rock bluff. She reached Dutch Harbor, on Unalaska, on May 17. From there Muir sent five letters to his wife, some to be passed on to the *San Francisco Bulletin* when she had read them. The more personal letters were filled with warm affection and memories and thoughts of home; of being upstairs with his wife and baby and his longing to touch them; of the ripening cherries down the hill and the flocks of finches, each with a red beak from guzzling them. Through his wife he assured his mother-in-law — who had gone to great lengths to tempt Muir's failing appetite — that he felt fine, ate even those "slippery puddings" (no doubt custards) and was looking forward to seal, walrus and fishy-tasting birds.

But Muir was realistically frank with Louie Wanda about the prospects of the voyage. In searching for the *Jeannette*, or survivors from her, *Corwin*'s people would attempt to land on mysterious, unvisited "Wrangell Land," off the Arctic coast of Siberia. It was supposed to extend toward the North Pole and perhaps across the Arctic circle to Greenland on the Atlantic side. Lieutenant George W. De Long, *Jeannette*'s skipper, had meant to proceed along Wrangell Land. If the *Corwin* succeeded in reaching there, Muir wrote, they might very likely have to spend the winter. Or the ship might be frozen into the ice-pack and be unable to escape until the following summer. Muir did not add "if they got out of the ice at all," as he very well might. *Corwin* was also to search for two whaling ships that had disappeared at about the same time as the *Jeannette*, and in the same area off the Siberian coast. Nor at this time did Muir mention that in the summer of 1879 thirty-three whalers had been crushed between the ice pack and the shelf ice along the Alaskan shore near Point Barrow.

He reported instead a pleasant meeting with an old acquaintance to whom he gave six bottles of the Strentzel wine he had brought along. This elderly man was now doctor for a fur company that employed most of the Aleut men in Dutch Harbor as sea otter hunters.

The Aleuts both fascinated and saddened Muir. The hunters, in skin covered kayaks so light they could be carried under one arm, voyaged hundreds of miles among smashing seas and wicked volcanic rocks and brought in nearly six thousand sea otter pelts a year. Each hunter earned up to $800 per year, excellent wages at that time. But beyond a few pieces of poorly made furniture, cheap clocks and accordions, the Aleuts had nothing to spend it on except rum when they could get it, and the makings of *kvass*, a fermented alcoholic disaster as deadly as *hoochinoo* and easier to make. At the time of Muir's voyage the Aleuts were a vanishing people; like the sea otter they hunted, their births were fewer than their deaths. Some feeble protection for the otter was provided by a United States regulation which prevented anyone from killing sea otters who was not a North Pacific native, or married to one. But nothing could protect these shy and beautiful creatures from repeating rifles.*

Grass greened the roofs of the sod houses the Aleuts built for themselves, and goats (introduced by the Russians) were eating it. But the black mountains rising steeply around Dutch Harbor were mantled with snow. The forbidding panorama brought to life the geologist who was still a major part of Muir's complex make-up. The mountains had evidently been thrust up by volcanic action, but the shapes of the peaks, the conformation of the valleys, the deep fiords indenting this and other islands, recounted a history of grinding, sculpturing ice. The Aleutians, therefore, seemed to have been heavily glaciated, and he wondered why none of the previous observers had noted this, to him, very exciting phenomenon.

In late May the *Corwin* visited the Pribiloff Islands, far out in the Bering Sea. Here the seals would soon come to breed in such number that the rocky beaches would be closely carpeted with loving, fighting, nursing mammals. But the migration had not yet commenced, and Muir therefore saw no part of the slaughter which occurred here annually.

At St. Lawrence Island, the largest in the Bering Sea, the best dressed Indians Muir had ever seen came aboard. The *Corwin's* people traded for sealskin shoes, parkas made from the breasts of ducks, reindeer or sealskin

* John Muir, *The Cruise of the Corwin*, pp. 13 and 20.

trousers and light, waterproof sacques made of the intestines of sea lions. They would need this clothing if they became locked in the ice and had to spend the winter. Even Muir, who had slept comfortably in many a Sierra snowstorm, had already found himself cold in his overcoat. He also bartered for a small fur robe and some playthings carved from walrus tusks to take to Annie Wanda.

The *Corwin* then crossed to the Siberian side and steamed slowly northward. She was hunting for news of the movements of the ice farther north, news of the *Jeannette* and the two lost whalers. Her people were also hunting dog teams and drivers, for it was Captain Hooper's intention to land a party north of Bering Strait to search for survivors from the *Jeannette*. Only two of the deep, glacier-carved fiords in the rocky shore were free enough of floating ice to be entered. In the first they found a driver who agreed, after much persuasion, to hire himself and his six dogs. He spoke a little English and would be helpful as an interpreter among the Chukchis, to which tribe he belonged.

"Chukchi Joe," as they called him, took Muir and Captain Hooper to his village, which consisted of two large teepees with poles bent down at one end and elongated so that they seemed to be turning their backs to the prevailing wind. The ground here was boggy and the twenty-five-foot ellipse that served as common living quarters reminded Muir of a California corral.

But around the sides were tiny, clean, luxurious bedrooms with walls and ceiling of furs, carpets of reindeer skins several thicknesses deep, and heated by a wick of moss burning in a trough of whale oil. Looking into one of these cloisters — which the people called "pologs" — Muir found Chukchi Joe taking a bath. Had he not agreed to go on the search for the *Jeannette*'s people, he would have left off his clothes and lain down to rest away the weariness of the hunting trip he had been on when he met the *Corwin*'s captain.

His wife shed protesting tears at Joe's leaving; his little boy clung to his legs. The long trip, with the snow softening as the weather warmed, and the shore ice moving unpredictably, was undeniably dangerous.

Unable to procure additional dogs along the adjacent Siberian shore, *Corwin* steamed out to the Diomede Islands — those three barren lumps of rock sticking out of the water in the middle of Bering Strait. Muir had already made up his mind, on the basis of the ice-sculpture on both shores, that the Asian and North American continents had been connected by a land bridge of which the Diomedes were the only visible remains. This belief, generally accepted today, was not considered in the 1880s. It was supposed that the striking similarities between the peoples, plants and animals on both sides of the strait were the result of crossings by boat. Boat crossings there had surely been, for a long time. The traffic was still lively — people from both sides bringing out goods to trade for a different cargo to take back. The Diomede Islanders were the middlemen, eager to trade almost anything they had. Eskimo after Eskimo stood in his skin boat, pitching in the swell, and handed up wolf-like, snarling, snapping brutes until nineteen dogs were penned on the upper deck. Captain Hooper paid a sack of flour for each dog.

The western Diomede cliffs dropped abruptly to the sea with no beach, and the islanders on their return carried their boats up an extremely steep trail to the village atop the cliff. There they put them on frames of whalebone above the skin roofs of their stone houses. Otherwise the dogs would have eaten them.

With her twenty-five dogs howling protest against their confinement, *Corwin* steamed through the strait, rounded East Cape and proceeded slowly along the shore-ice edging Siberia's northwestward-trending coast. Another driver was needed, and when some Chukchis signalled from a comparatively narrow strip of shore-ice, Muir, Captain Hooper and Chukchi Joe landed and went to meet them.

Like all the Chukchis the *Corwin's* people had talked with, this group of hunters insisted that there was no use in searching for survivors of the *Jeannette*. If there were any, they would have heard of them. One man nevertheless consented to go on the search, and the whole group set off for their village so that he could get ready and say his farewells.

The ice here, jumbled in pinnacles, slabs and blocks ten to thirty feet high, made very difficult walking, especially for Muir and Captain Hooper, hampered as they were by overcoats and "civilized" boots. But they came presently to the party's eleven sleds with nearly one hundred dogs to pull them. Three teams were straightened out, and Muir embarked on his first sled trip behind one of them. Up one side of a crazily-tilted block and down the other with the sled slewing perilously sidewise around a fantastic ice pinnacle on one runner; through slushy snow and pools of crystalline water lying in blue ice. At every critical point the driver jumped off to steady the sled, but the dogs never varied their steady, businesslike trot, responding unhesitatingly to the driver's shouted commands. He used his whip seldom. And when they came to a stretch of smooth ice leading to the village he turned to entertain Muir, like a tourist guide, in pure Chukchi.

The habitation in which Muir and the captain were entertained was like Chukchi Joe's, except that the ground was dry; there was a welter of dogs, people, spears, nets and household gear. "Hair is everywhere," Muir wrote, "and strangely persistent smells that defy even the arctic frosts." Around the perimeter were the clean, luxurious pologs of reindeer skins and furs, and the people charmed Muir with their amiability and naturalness. When time came to feed her baby, the Chukchi mother simply slipped an arm from the loose sleeve of her parka, pulled the garment down and nursed the infant. Muir noted that these women's breasts were like those of the Tlingit women in Southwest Alaska: pendulous and cylindrical.

On the first of June, 1881, nearly one hundred fifty miles northwest of Bering Strait, the great polar pack joined the fixed ice along the Siberian shore. For a time the *Corwin* followed a sort of ice fiord — a "lead" of open water — into this barrier. But the lead began to close, and she backed out to cruise along the edge of the polar pack, which was restless and required constant watching.

About one in the morning Muir was wakened by unusual sounds from the stern. Dressing hastily he went on deck to find the crew hauling up the rudder. The pack had started to move, surrounding the *Corwin* with large, detached masses of ice and threatening to lock her in. In attempting to back clear, with her rudder hard over, the ship had run into a lump of ice sixty to seventy-five feet thick. The impact broke the rudder almost completely off.

The steadily rising north wind was filled with snow so thick they were almost blinded when they faced the blast. Snow encumbered the decks and ropes. There was, of course, light enough from the sun, which never set at that time, but an eerie sort of glow filtered through the storm. The sled dogs had gotten loose and ran howling about the ship. All the while the ice-pack inexorably moved southward to join the shore ice. If the ship were between these masses when they came together it would be *Corwin*'s end.

Yet Corwin's people worked coolly, steadily and efficiently, as if making jury rudders was an ordinary part of sailoring. They lashed and nailed four long spars together, weighted them, lowered them over the stern, attached lines to the steering winches — and by midmorning the ship had a helm to which she answered well.

This was obviously as far west as the ship could now go. The captain therefore asked the two Chukchi sled drivers what the chances were of an expedition crossing the shore ice at this point. The ice looked good to them. The landing made an extraordinary sight: the life boat in the lead took two of the Corwin's lieutenants and supplies for two months. She towed behind her a boatload of furious dogs, with a driver to keep them from killing one another and behind this a skin boat carrying the sleds. It struck Muir as remarkable that the dogs went wild with joy when they landed on the formidable ice.

The expedition would proceed westward as far as practicable, seeking news of the *Jeannette* and the missing whalers. *Corwin* planned to pick them up at the village where the second sled driver lived.

Corwin's *people were unaware at that time that the* Jeannette, *on the edge of the Arctic Circle and a third of the way to Sweden, was undergoing her final agonies. The ice which had imprisoned her for more than two years was beginning to break up and, in the process, was squeezing* Jeannette *like a wicker basket.*

Below decks she was a labyrinth of cross braces, but every time the enormous pressure came, her decks arched, to spring back when the constriction was released. On June 10 she sank, and the thirty-three survivors of her crew, having landed on the ice, made sleds for their boats and began to drag them toward Siberia, five hundred miles to the south.

Chapter 44
Mysterious Unknown Shores

By the time *Jeannette* sank, the *Corwin* was well on her way to the deep fiord where the Czar's navy had left a deposit of coal for the use of its own vessels. Shore ice made the fiord virtually impenetrable, but *Corwin*'s people blasted and sawed a sort of drydock for their wounded ship. They then brought out coal with dog teams, piled it on deck forward to raise the stern and completed repairs on her rudder.

Meanwhile Muir had some opportunity to explore. The general conformation showed that a great glacier had been here in the not-too-distant past. But the rock surfaces had been so much eroded by weathering that the details were hard to read. It was not until he had climbed the cliff that he found unmistakable glacier tracks — grooves, scratches and polished surfaces — the first he had seen on the shores of the Bering Sea. He also found anemones blooming in hidden gardens of dwarf plants among mountainous piles of loose stones that looked as if they had been dropped from the sky.

Recrossing the Bering Sea, *Corwin* put into St. Michaels, an old trading post established by the Russians near the delta of the Yukon river. The Eskimos of this town were famous for their skill in making fur garments, and Muir commissioned a woman to make a little parka for baby Wanda.

Furs were, in fact, the life of the town. Soon after Muir arrived, a small river steamer came down the Yukon towing three large skin boats loaded with Indians and at least $50,000 worth of furs from the interior. The Indians, grim and cruel-looking, of a totally different breed than the amiable maritime Eskimos and Aleuts, were painted and decked out as if for war and held themselves contemptuously aloof. They seemed wilder, even, than their catch of bears, wolves, and wolverines, skinned with open jaws, hair on end, and claws extended as if fighting for their lives.

Corwin had come to St. Michaels to take on provisions for the run back to the Siberian coast to pick up the search party. The weather turned lovely — the first days in a month without snow. Sun spangles made the calm water look to Muir as if it were strewn with lilies; water birds swam and flew in myriads. The sea and air at St. Michaels are warmed by the Yukon's waters. Indian children ran about naked, and Muir felt as if the ship's company had emerged from a gloomy, icy cave.

The happy weather did not last long. Around the Diomedes, where *Corwin* stopped to land a party assigned to measure tides and water temperatures, the fog was so blindingly thick that Muir wondered how the birds — whose flight in such weather guided the Eskimo and Chukchi voyagers to and from the Diomedes — knew how to come and go from the opposite shores.

On the way north *Corwin* ran through a furious storm, and when she reached the Siberian bay where the search party was to meet them, they found the way blocked by three miles of jostling ice against whose face the waves broke in savage surf.

Nevertheless the search party was readily retrieved, though by a procedure which in most times and places would be considered an extraordinary feat of seamanship. One of *Corwin*'s boats worked her way in perilously close and, while she pitched in the angry water, a seaman stood up to throw a line to one of the party waiting on the edge of the ice. The line was made fast to a skin boat the party had dragged over the three miles of rough ice, then launched and, with the party in it, was pulled back to the *Corwin*.

The search party had travelled to its assigned objective — far to the east — but had heard no word of the *Jeannette*. They had, however, gained definite proof of the fate of the *Vigilant*, one of the whalers *Corwin* was seeking. Some North Siberian Chukchis, far out on the ice on a seal-hunt, had boarded a ship with her masts broken off and four dead men in the cabin. Antlers at the end of her bowsprit identified her as the *Vigilant*, since no other whaling ship had this adornment. Binoculars and other articles the hunters brought away before drifting ice carried the ship into oblivion were traded to the search party for a few ounces of tobacco.

In addition to searching for lost ships and their crews and aiding those in danger, *Corwin* had revenue service duties, one of which was to enforce the regulations against trading alcoholic beverages and repeating rifles to the Eskimos. On St. Lawrence Island, where they stopped after returning Chukchi Joe to his Siberian home, Muir had a spectacular demonstration of the reason for prohibiting alcohol.

Drunk and happy, the islanders had failed to prepare for the extraordinarily severe winter of 1878-79. Starvation had reduced the population from fifteen hundred to five hundred. In seven villages everyone had perished. With E. W. Nelson, zoologist, photographer and ethnologist, who had joined the *Corwin* at St. Michaels, Muir visited a village where two hundred skeletons lay among rotting furs. The first to die had been laid outdoors; the survivors, now weakened, had piled the next against the walls of their huts; the strongest had died in bed.

Nelson calmly threw whitened skulls into piles as fast as he could select them, reminding Muir of how he used to gather pumpkins as a farm boy in Wisconsin. One hundred skulls were carried aboard the *Corwin* to be transported to the Smithsonian Institution, which had sent Nelson to the Arctic to observe and collect. He also brought away bone spears, harpoon points, bone armor, utensils and other artifacts. Muir took a box of children's toys and dolls, though he supposed that his wife would not let them in the house. In any case, he wrote her, he had plenty of other dolls as well as ducks, walruses, seals and bears carved by the living from walrus tusks.

Muir had thought alcohol to be the sole cause of these wholesale deaths, and it was certainly a major contributor. Drunken sprees, and the hope of them, made the Indians careless of the future; they neglected to fish and hunt for winter supplies, to make and mend boats, huts, weapons and fur clothing. Now that he was more familiar with these people, Muir understood that rifles and goods obtained in trade made them less efficient in the arts and crafts required to survive the hostilities of their environment, making them more dependent upon the outside world and less upon themselves.

The damage done by repeating rifles was borne in on Muir as the *Corwin* voyaged northward to visit the whaling fleet, busy with its lucrative and perilous work along Alaska's ice-rimmed shore. These weapons seemed to make the natives kill-crazy. The wild reindeer had been exterminated around St. Michaels; in the North the process was still going on. The Eskimos slaughtered every reindeer within rifle range, often leaving hundreds of slain animals to the wolves.

As *Corwin* worked her way north she now and then sent a boarding party to a trading schooner or whaler to look for contraband rifles and whiskey which the Yankee vessels traded for furs and walrus ivory when they could, not forgetting the tricks which made the Yankee trader notorious in his day. A favorite device was to give the strong man whom the Eskimos had selected as taster and tester a glass of straight alcohol. Delighted with the instant inebriation produced, the Eskimos were happy to part with valuable pelts for bottles and kegs of plentifully watered grog that disappointed them greatly.

Muir's admiration for these unlettered people who had learned so well how to deal with their environment grew throughout the leisurely voyage up the formidable coast. King Island, on Bering Strait, seemed fit only for seabirds and walruses as Muir and Nelson approached in one of *Corwin*'s boats. The winter huts looked like cliff dwellings — stones among stones. Guided by hand signals from the islanders, the boat threaded her way perilously between wave-washed boulders. She could not have made the rocky beach except that there was an almost flat calm. In stormy weather the islanders launched their kayaks by throwing them into the water and jumping into them just when a wave was on the point of receding.

It was now July, and the islanders were living in their summer houses made of skins stretched over driftwood poles. The only place flat enough for a bargaining session was the roof of one of these houses. Muir and Nelson came away with an unusually fine assortment of carved ivory and bone fishing and hunting gear. Muir was even more admiring of the King Island kayaks — the best he had seen. In really stormy weather the islanders lashed them together in side-by-side pairs to form catamarans. These would live in any sea.

The Chukchis and Eskimos were still making astonishing voyages with nothing between them and the icy water but a thickness of walrus hide. At the head of Kotzebue Sound, well north of Bering Strait, Muir found an annual fair in progress. Indians had come down the rivers from deep in the frigid interior: there were Eskimos from the Yukon Delta and Aleuts from the Diomedes. A party of Chukchis had brought bearskins in large skin boats called "umiaks" from Cape Yakán, hundreds of miles westward along Siberia's Arctic coast.

Muir was impressed with how much these people knew of their world and what went on in it. They were inveterate gossips and curious about all new things. One of the Chukchis who boarded the *Corwin* tried to buy a lock of a cabin boy's bleached-out blond hair.

Muir's short but frequent trips to study the geology and flora of the country back from the coast were a delight to him. The Arctic summer was now at its climax. Not far from the site of the Arctic Fair he found a strange region of dead-looking white hills (of calcareous slates) and between them garden-like valleys where some fifty different plants were in flower. The tundra — that strange layer-cake of lichened mosses a foot deep, resting on ice which rests on lava — he found lavishly in bloom. Ptarmigan, ducks, geese, songbirds and wading birds had their nests everywhere among the grassy hummocks.

On July 23 the *Corwin* reached Icy Cape, the bleakest, dreariest spot Muir had yet seen. He could find only four species of plants struggling for life on this windswept, gravelly promontory. Here they met the polar ice pack close inshore and moving restlessly. It would have been folly to enter the "lead" of open water by which they had hoped to reach Point Barrow on Alaska's northern shore. In this lead thirty-three ships had been trapped and all but one crushed in the summer of 1874. The pack, a seemingly limitless mass of blocks one hundred feet and more thick, moved inshore so abruptly that the whalers had no time to escape. Some were driven aground and others smashed to pieces against the shore ice.

Every year some ships were lost between Icy Cape and Point Barrow. Men took these grim risks simply because whales were still plentiful and the oil from each one was worth four to five thousand dollars. And when no whales were in sight they could land on the ice and shoot for oil and ivory. The whaler *Daniel Webster* was in trouble now, *Corwin* learned from a ship she met while cruising along the edge of the pack hoping for a wind shift that would enable her to get through.

The ice did not open up, and *Corwin*, mindful of her primary mission, turned south, paused while the crew mined thirty tons of coal from a sea bluff and carried it out to *Corwin* in boats, then set off for mysterious "Wrangell Land" where Commander George De Long, leader of the *Jeannette* expedition, had intended to leave records and reports under cairns of rocks.

De Long had also planned to leave cairns on Herald Island, near Wrangell Land, though previous expeditions had reported it to be inaccessible. This island came in sight on July 30 at 1 p.m. of a calm, sunlit day. It was still ten miles distant when *Corwin* came to the edge of the ice. The ship's bow was sheathed in boiler iron, and Captain Hooper used it as a ram to shove aside the cakes and blocks which were relatively light, being only about sixty-five feet thick with narrow waterways between. As they approached, Muir stood braced against the rail, his eye glued to a spyglass trained on the steep cliffs of crumbling granite which rose from a narrow beach. As evening came on, the light continued undiminished.

At ten in the evening *Corwin* came to anchor about three hundred yards from shore. Eight members of the crew swarmed down the bowsprit chains, jumped onto the ice and headed for shore, where they disappeared into a gulch with sides two hundred feet high.

Muir did not go with this party, but, with Nelson and a couple of others, angled northward across the ice, dragging a skin boat. Muir carried an axe, and when they had crossed a strip of water to reach the foot of a ravine choked with hard, compacted glacier-like snow, he began to cut steps. The face of the snow-cliff had an angle of fifty degrees, but when Muir had cut a stairway one hundred feet high, the men found themselves on an easy slope and quickly reached the top. The first party, meanwhile, had been stopped by a sheer thousand-foot cliff. When the leaders tried to climb it they sent down a shower of rocks that would have maimed or killed those below if the jagged missiles had not, fortunately, leaped over them.

Muir and Nelson ranged the entire six-mile length of the island. Small, white foxes followed at their heels like dogs and one made off with a notebook Nelson had left beside his burrow. A small, residual glacier, as well as glacial markings on the rocks, showed that a great glacier flowing from the Siberian mountains had covered this island in the (geologically) recent past. Muir collected specimens of fifteen different plants. But no cairns were to be found. Though they searched until two in the morning, they realized by midnight that *Jeannette*'s people had not been here. No one else had been here. They were the first men to walk on Herald Island.

As the sunlit night wore on, a strange feeling of loneliness compounded with awe and excitement grew in Muir. It climaxed at midnight. From the highest point of the island he gazed through incredibly clear air at the flowing frieze of Wrangell Land's mountains, blue against the infinite white of the ice. Somewhere out there lay the North Pole, one of earth's greatest wonders and (at that time) enticing mysteries. He felt its tug — more primitive than thoughtful — which had led many to their deaths and would lead many more.

In the morning *Corwin* set off to Wrangell Land itself. The approach was a nerve-wearing series of high hopes dashed. Fogs which Muir described as "reeking" made it so dangerous to move among the drifting ice masses that *Corwin* was forced to anchor just when the island's blue hills were only a few miles away.

One after another waterlane ended in hard, high, close-packed blocks or began to close, forcing *Corwin* to retreat to the edge of the pack. The only relief came from polar bears, which the *Corwin* chased wherever open water permitted. Three were shot from the deck, which upset Muir because the bears had no chance; it seemed a shame to kill for mere trophies these magnificent creatures — the kings of the ice, powerful enough to drag a thousand-pound walrus up onto a floe.

At last late one afternoon in mid-August, *Corwin* followed a wedge-shaped lead to within five miles of shore before coming up against huge blocks that seemed an impenetrable barrier. Captain Hooper decided to send a party over the ice next day. But when morning came the barrier appeared less formidable. Moreover there was a strip of open water between the shore and the ice. Under a full head of steam and wide open throttle, *Corwin* forced her way through the towering blocks and came to anchor a cable length from a dry gravel bar stretching across the mouth of a river.

This place struck Muir as indescribably lonely and untouched. On the beach lay the skeleton of a whale, an oak barrel stave, a piece of a boat's mast, a double kayak paddle with both blades broken and some driftwood. All the wood was well chewed by the ice and looked as if it had lain a long time where *Corwin*'s people found it. There were plenty of polar bear tracks on the beach and river bank, along with those of foxes, marmots and a dozen varieties of shore and sea birds, but no traces of human beings at all, either Chukchi or Caucasian.

Yet this was the most likely place to look for signs of the Jeannette's people, not only because wood and water were available, but also because De Long had written that he would try to reach the far end of this "land" over the ice in case he lost his ship. Muir and Captain Hooper and Nelson explored two miles upstream, Muir collecting such plants as he could find. A party of officers searched three or four miles up along the bluffs. They also set up an American

"They set up an American flag and claimed Wrangell Land for the United States...."

flag and claimed Wrangell Land for the United States, being reasonably sure by now that the *Corwin* party was the first to set foot here.

They would have stayed much longer and searched much farther, but the ice was drifting majestically past at a speed of fifty miles a day. The shore was studded with bergs so large they had stranded in sixty feet of water. To stay more than a few hours was to risk being locked in — in which case *Corwin* could neither search for *Jeannette* survivors elsewhere, nor assist endangered whalers.

Even though they left within a few hours, the ship took a severe beating before she got free, for the lane by which she came in had all but closed. A week after the landing on Wrangell Land, the *Corwin* lay anchored in the lee of Point Barrow, in the midst of half a dozen whalers. The *Daniel Webster* was not among them. She had been crushed. The crew got out onto the ice before she sank, but the Point Barrow Eskimos — who by now were proficient wreckers — made off with the supplies they had helped to salvage. When the crewmen asked for some of their own food, the wreckers offered to trade ship's biscuits for tobacco. The Eskimos remained on the ship while she was sinking, salvaging sails and everything else they could readily carry, including chronometers and sextants, which they dismembered for jewelry.

One of the whalers had letters for Muir. Joy and relief flooded him; this was his first word from home since May; Louie Wanda was well and getting along all right, though she missed him achingly; the baby was well and maturing; the baby's grandparents were all right. By a returning whaler Muir sent the

Herald Island surrounded by ice.

letter of a loving and romantic father and husband, dwelling on the little parka he had commissioned for Annie Wanda. But he also warned his wife that he might yet have to spend a year or more trapped in the ice, or on ice-beset Wrangell Land. On August 18 *Corwin* set out once more to search for the *Jeannette*'s people.

The sun now disappeared at eight o'clock to circle just below the horizon and create a gloomy twilight for the rest of the night. The weather was stormy, heavy fogs frequent. But they did not encounter serious frustrations until they came in sight of the ice that rimmed Wrangell Land. The pack extended a good twenty miles offshore, and as they skirted its edge to the eastward they found it piling up more and more heavily against the shore of Wrangell, which they now realized was no "land" at all, but a rather large island. They could see no way to approach. As evening came on with rising waves, a dull, lurid, purple light in the sky and the ice shifting southward toward them, Captain Hooper ordered *Corwin* hove to until the weather improved.

They were then off Herald Island, where the sea is so shallow that a mature redwood tree, rooted on the bottom, would have one hundred feet of its top above water — an area of steep, leaping waves that follow one another in very rapid succession. The wind rose to a howling gale filled with snow, and some time during the night the continual smash of combers against the bow broke the Corwin's boiler-plate armor at a riveted seam. There was nothing to do but cut the armor free and let it sink. For two days longer *Corwin* hung on, hoping for a break in the weather which would permit a return to Wrangell. Hove to, the ship still drifted thirty miles a day, wallowing and writhing wildly.

On the second of September one of the rudder chains parted. The crew made what repairs they could, but their search for *Jeannette* was over for that year.

Part VI

HUSBANDMAN

"A ranch that needs and takes the sacrifice of a noble life...ought to be flung away beyond all reach and power for harm."

Chapter 45
Dogged As An Animal in a Cage

In early December of 1881, Muir received word that survivors from the *Jeannette* had reached the Russian outposts roughly halfway across Siberia on the Lena River. Of thirty-three who left the sinking ship and began the five hundred-mile trek over ice and across treacherous waters of the coast, only thirteen reached land, and five of these were dying from the effects of privation and frozen flesh.*

It is logical to surmise that when the news came, Louie Wanda flung herself trembling and weeping with relief into Muir's arms. From the hour *Corwin* left San Francisco until its return, laden with a treasure of furs and carved ivory, she had lived in the anguish of repressed fear.

Muir himself felt not only joy at being able to touch his wife and baby, as he had longed to do throughout the voyage, but also an all-out desire to compensate, by his devotion, for the long and harrowing absences that had been, in a sense, his wedding gift.

He had bold plans for converting the farm into a highly profitable enterprise that would insure his family's comfort for life. But before he launched on this program he had, first, to oversee the grape harvest — and to him this meant being out all day in the vineyards showing his farm hands how he wanted the work done. Second, he had to get his arctic plant collection sorted and to ship duplicate specimens to Asa Gray at the Harvard Arboretum. There were over two hundred specimens, as Gray reported to the American Academy of Arts and Sciences: a truly valuable collection containing, as it did, plants from heretofore unvisited Wrangell and Herald Islands and a flower entirely new to science — a member of the lily family, whose showy flowers look like daisies. Gray named it *Erigeron muirii*. Muir also helped Captain Hooper write his report on the *Corwin's* expedition and wrote two reports of his own: one on the glaciation of the arctic and sub-arctic areas visited, the other on the flora of shores and islands visited by the *Corwin*. The report on glaciation was published as part of a senate executive document, the one on arctic flora as part of a treasury document — unlikely sources in which to look for scientific information. Both reports sank from

---

* For a dramatic and well-documented account of the *Jeannette* epic, see *Hell on Ice, the Saga of the Jeannette*, by Commander Edward Ellsberg, pp. 329 and 418.

sight of the scientific community, a fate which they scarcely deserved. The botanical report was undoubtedly the first to describe in detail the relation to soil, climate and topography of the flora of nine widely distributed locations, ranging from little known to totally unknown. The report on glaciation was probably the first ever made of the area covered. Considering that Muir was in the far north only four months, and the great difficulty of reading the signs left by glaciers long since vanished, his observations are remarkably in agreement with those of modern scientists.*

In the winter of 1881-82 Muir, at the urging of friends in the California Academy of Science, also drafted two conservation bills for submission to Congress: one to enlarge Yosemite Park (which was still under administration of the State of California), the other to make a public park of virtually the same area as the presently combined Sequoia and Kings Canyon National Parks.**

The latter was so large it did not receive the support of the citizens in and near Visalia in the San Joaquin Valley below the Giant Forest, who for some years had beeen fighting a rear-guard action against the sheep which consumed or trampled everything within reach, the recklessly ignited forest fires and the lumbermen who gained possession of great tracts of virgin timber by fraudulent means and left more than half the timber they cut lying on the ground.

Both these bills died in committee. As Muir wrote, "The love of nature among Californians (was) desperately moderate." Though briefly checked here and there, the plunder of the watershed went on.***

By this time Muir was completely committed to his program for turning the ranch into a money-maker. He was well-equipped to do so, both by botanical training and his upbringing by a father who had continued to use the talents of a successful Scotch merchant to make money for churches and missions.

Bartlett pears sold the best; Muir therefore grafted Bartletts to the sixty varieties of pears growing in Dr. Strentzel's experimental orchard. The

* The main points of disagreement are 1) that Muir considerably overestimated the amount of glaciation that had existed along the American shores of the Bering and Chukchi Seas and the Arctic Ocean, and 2) his belief that the Bering Sea was scooped out by a glacier. As Muir himself pointed out, the water around the Diomede Islands is extremely shallow. Modern glaciologists believe that it was frozen solid to the bottom, during at least one period. But the weight of this relatively thin ice sheet was not great enough to do much, if any, excavating. Moreover, the Bering Sea ice was not flowing as mountain-born glaciers do, grinding and carving as they inch their way downward.
** Linnie Marsh Wolfe, *Son of the Wilderness: The Life of John Muir*, pp. 277-278.
*** A favorite land-grabbing device was to hire stony-broke sailors and less reputable denizens of San Francisco's Barbary Coast to claim large chunks of redwood land under a loose law called the Timber and Stone Act. Once having gained title, they turned the land over to the lumber companies for the price of a weekend spree. The leader of the Visalia conservationists was Colonel George W. Stewart, publisher of a local newspaper, who also published official lists of persons who had filed claims on timber lands. When the editors going over these lists discovered fraud, they brought it to the attention of the U.S. Land Office. Large tracts of irreplaceable timber (for it takes thousands of years for a giant redwood to mature) were thus rescued in the usually-routine process of reading proof. Fry and White, *Big Trees*, p. 24.

region around Martinez was already famous for Tokay grapes sold for the table, not the wine press. Muir converted his father-in-law's experimental vineyards to Tokays. What Dr. Strentzel thought of these changes the record does not reveal. But he evidently did not object. He regarded Muir as a beloved son and now, in his declining years grew more and more dependent upon him for management. The ranch, in fact, became Muir's to do with what he liked, not only because Dr. Strentzel turned over the responsibility to him, but also because Muir steadily enlarged the acreage by lease and purchase.

Lumbering freight wagons hauled the tons of fruit to Martinez, where it was loaded into sidewheelers which carried it to San Francisco. The tempting, softly-gleaming loads, breathing perfumes, were lovely in themselves. But fruit was a commodity — thus the bone of contention between Muir and the commission merchants who bargained for it. With a contentious nature honed by a youth spent in arguing with his father, and with an ingrained Scotch pride in getting the best of the bargain, Muir was a formidable antagonist in these chafferings, which became legendary in the neighborhood. At least once, the commission men combined against him, refused to meet his price and departed, warning that his fruit would rot on the dock. "Let it rot!" Muir said, and sold all the produce he had available to the next day's boat, at his own figure.

Money quite literally piled up. Along the dusty main street of Martinez, the townsmen learned to expect Muir to drive up to the bank in work clothes, his frost-bitten foot dangling over the side of the buggy, and carry in a big laundry bag full of greenbacks.

The cost of prosperity ran high. Muir's bronchial cough, which always afflicted him in and around the fertile lowlands of Martinez, grew chronic. His body wasted away to bone and sinew. He grew increasingly irritable, for the conflict raging within him became at least as painful as his wracking cough. He felt an exile in this tamed docile environment, so near and yet so far from the unmodified wilderness, his chosen home. And all he was accomplishing was to make money — for which he could not wholeheartedly respect himself.

On one side of this internal war, love of his wife and child, and his compulsion to give them both security and luxury, became allied with his urge to prove himself a respectable, successful member of society. In depressed moments he felt (and sometimes said) that he had "made himself a tramp" to pursue his lonely studies, a judgment many erstwhile friends, and especially his Muir relatives, had strongly implied. On the other side fought the usually-suppressed knowledge that, in order to make money, he was deliberately altering the trees in his orchards and the vines in his vineyards, thus violating his deeply held principle that unchanged nature does most for man. As time went by, he felt increasingly alienated from himself.

The light in his life was Annie Wanda. When she was still very small, her mother or grandmother would bring her down to the orchard where Muir had been laboring all too long, and he would stop work to carry her back to the house and rest a while, talking to her and playing with her. When she got her chubby legs firmly under her, Muir took the child on walks. He taught her the botanical names of the flowers they stopped to admire, "...because," he said, "how would you like it if you were introduced to someone and he was never told your name?"

Louie Wanda worried about him increasingly, and in the summer of 1884 she persuaded him to take her to Yosemite on a camping trip. It did not turn out well. Brought up to be mistress of an estate in the cultivated out-of-doors, Louie Wanda, though thrilled, found herself a helpless and somewhat frightened stranger among the gigantic rocks, thundering falls and whispering forests that harbored snakes and bears. She could not follow Muir where he wanted to go, he was afraid to leave her and they both worried about Annie Wanda, though the child was well and happy in her grandparents' care. So they hurried home to immerse themselves more thoroughly than ever in domesticity and fruit-growing.

Muir's enterprise continued to develop very rapidly, but prosperity only made the tether that held him all the shorter.

He wished increasingly to visit his family in the midwest, whom he had not seen for eighteen years. "I could not come now without leaving the ranch to go to wreck, a score of workmen without a head, and no head to be found, though I have looked long for a foreman." Perhaps, he went on, after the grapes were pruned and sulphured and the cherry crop sold, he could get away. Dusting the grapes with sulphur to prevent mildew was a delicate operation over which Muir agonized — which suggests a reason why he could not find a foreman. Irascible from illness, impatient and intense, demanding of others the meticulous skill he devoted to every task, Muir could have been a very hard man to work for.

It took a premonition of his father's death to get him away from the ranch at that time. The elder Muir, then in his late seventies, had been living with his youngest daughter, Joanna, in Kansas City. At first restless and surly as an animal with a sore paw, he had mellowed remarkably after the birth of Joanna's first child. He adjured Joanna to rule her children "only with love" and confessed to her that he had been cruel to his "poor wandering son, Johnny."

One day in August, when John Muir was writing a letter, he abruptly put down his pen, went to find his wife, and told her that if he were to see his father again, he must go to Wisconsin immediately. Though she was three months pregnant at the time, Louie Wanda was no woman to argue against such a compelling presentiment. She urged him to make the trip, but for the health of his body and spirit, to go by way of Mount Shasta and Yellowstone National Park. The wild, flower-sprinkled meadows and deep, clear streams of Shasta set up in Muir an almost intolerable longing for the mountains. He wrote his wife that the temptation to give up everything and linger there had to be put aside as resolutely as a drunkard giving up whiskey.

To this Louie Wanda replied that she wished his good angel would keep him awhile where he found rest and peace; the ranch would be there when he got back; a few grapes more or less would make no difference; but it would make a world of difference whether he came back "shadowy and ghostly, or strong and well."*

John Muir had not fully recovered when he reached Wisconsin, but he had ample vitality to rally his family. His brother David, a prosperous small town merchant in Portage, near their old farms, was bent and older-looking than John himself. The elder sisters, Annie and Sarah, were wracked by recent grief and illness that originated in the years of farm slavery imposed by their father to support missions from Africa to central Canada. David's wife had recently died, and they made a sad household. Only his mother, erect and capable still, held them together until John came.

Together they went to Kansas City and were joined there by the others of the family, John Muir paying the way of those who could not afford the fare.

Mr. Muir had sunk into a semi-coma. John Muir, to rouse him, talked in "braid Scots," their native dialect. More often than not his father would only reply, "You're a Scotsman, aren't you?" But occasionally he would rise up and seize his eldest son's hand saying, "Is this my dear Johnny? Oh yes! My dear wanderer."

On October 6, 1885, Mr. Muir died with seven of his eight children in the house, but only John by his bedside.

John Muir's mother could not be persuaded to leave her familiar turf, even for a visit. But Sarah and Margaret came, to warm themselves in the California sun and enjoy the affectionate hospitality bountifully bestowed by Louie Wanda and her parents. The new Strentzel home — as unadorned as any Victorian could contrive, but with a fireplace in every room — seemed a palace to them.

Louie Wanda had been unwell during most of her pregnancy. The girl child she bore in January 1886 was a frail infant, vulnerable to the respiratory ills that made her father miserable. For a year and a half after her birth John Muir scarcely left the ranch for fear little Helen would fall critically ill and he would be needed. Some time during this period of intensive horticulture and overanxiety abut his family, he wrote on the flyleaf of a book: "Time partially reconciles us to anything. I gradually became content — doggedly content, as wild animals in cages."

Pressures from outside made it increasingly difficult to hold himself to the grind. Friends kept urging Muir to re-join the battle to halt the desolation of the forests, which were being laid waste from Maine to Southern California. Literary friends, particularly Robert Underwood Johnson, who had become a highly influential editor of *Century Magazine*, bombarded him with pleas to start writing again. When he got no response from Muir himself, Johnson urged Louie Wanda to work on her husband — which she was heartily glad to do. She had thought she was marrying a writer-scientist, not a money-grubbing fruit-grower.

---

* Linnie Marsh Wolfe, *Son of the Wilderness: The Life of John Muir*, p. 234.

Signs that the urge to write was beginning to stir in Muir began to appear, and in the same form as his earliest work — long letters to people who warmed his heart. One of them he wrote in January, 1887, to a girl named Janet Moores, whose letter out of the blue recalled the days twenty years before when he lay in a darkened room in Indianapolis, and she came with other children to read to him. Memory of darkness and despair set off an almost-poem in praise of the light that had since filled him with wonder and joy — liquid gold flooding California valleys, the spiritual colors of the alpenglow on high mountains, light passing prismatically through glaciers and waterfalls, the magical fields of stars and snow. In the light you could see God's fingers playing upon "every living thing, making all together sing and shine...in the one love-harmony of the Universe."

He and Janet would see one another soon, for she was cordially invited to visit the ranch. But she should come a little later, when the orchards were in bloom, making a "Dolly Vardenish beauty" not to be compared to the wild gardens of the Sierra, but more accessible.

Though her childhood look was living-clear in his mind, they might not know one another after twenty years. So he drew a cartoonist's sketch of the self he saw in the mirror: "...two eyes like small open spots in a hillside mostly overgrown with chaparral." Annie Wanda, now nearly six, was seated, as she often was, in his lap, decorating the margins of his notebooks with her drawings. She paused to look at the sketch. "Is that you, Papa? It looks just like you! Only the hair and beard aren't curly enough." Muir was photogenic, but this simple sketch of a broad-browed face dominated by his eyes may be the best likeness of him.*

"So he drew a cartoonist sketch of the self he saw in the mirror: 'two eyes...like small open spots in a hillside mostly overgrown with shaggy chaparral.'"

* See William F. Badè, *The Life and Letters of John Muir*, pp. 214 et seq.

A few months after he penned this letter with his eagle feather quill trimmed to the nub, Muir accepted an offer to write part of, and to coordinate all of, an elaborate illustrated publication called *Picturesque California*. This title is a misnomer: the volumes cover almost the entire West Coast, from Juneau, Alaska, to the Mexican border. Muir's first writing for this opus shocked Louie Wanda, who had an unusually good critical sense. The prose was so pedestrian, flat and weary that she was frightened that years of over-discipline and toil had quenched the blaze of inner life in her husband.

Muir, in fact, never was able to devote himself to this project with full enthusiasm and effectiveness. It never became anything more than a set of pictures loosely strung together. But the paintings and drawings, done by highly-regarded artists of the time, furnish a striking record of the way the West Coast looked during the last quarter of the 19th century — before man achieved complete domination over the landscape.

Coordinating the elements of a book such as *Picturesque California* is complex, and Muir found the task — in addition to managing his ever-growing ranch — almost too much for him. Exhausted physically and continually frustrated by trying to fulfill two demanding and antithetical responsibilities, he took no pleasure in either the beautiful fruit or the money it was bringing him.

One day in May, 1888, when he was down in the orchard supervising the pickers, he glimpsed among the cherry trees a light, agile figure totally foreign to this cultivated scene. Hurrying to meet him Muir saw that this was indeed Hall Young.

"You've come to take me on a canoe voyage, haven't you?" Muir said when still too far off to shake hands. "I'm so tired of this humdrum life it's like to crush me!" With a gesture toward the bushel baskets of cherries he grumbled on. "Penal servitude with these miserable little bald-heads. And for money! Man, I'm like to die of the shame of it!"

Young, on his part, was escaping *into* civilization, saying that if he did not get away from his Indians for a while he would never be able to speak proper English again. The two friends sat talking most of the night.

Reviving old adventures with Hall Young helped to loosen the chains that bound Muir to the ranch. Within a month he was coasting in a skiff along the shores of Lake Tahoe with a botanist friend. And in July Muir set out north with William Keith, to collect final material and make sketches for *Picturesque California*. Shasta proved depressing; Sisson's had become a shanty town of shingled tourist shacks pretending to be cottages; the forests and flowering "bee pastures" were rapidly disappearing. Perhaps Muir's most significant contribution to *Picturesque California* was his strong recommendation that Shasta be made a national park.*

Muir was ill when his party, the sixth to climb 14,000-foot Mount Rainier, began the ascent. But the hard climb revived him, though the last and steepest part was over ice. When he got back to Seattle he was ready to take to heart the

* It became a national forest in 1903.

-248-

wistful, selfless letter Louie Wanda had written as he was attacking the slopes of Rainier:

"A ranch that needs and takes the sacrifice of a noble life, or work, ought to be flung away beyond all reach and power for harm....The Alaska book and the Yosemite book, dear John, must be written, and you must be your own self, well and strong; there is nothing that has a right to be considered beside this except the welfare of our children."*

When Muir got back to the ranch he found Louie Wanda already planning which portions of the ranch to sell, which to lease and which to keep.

Picturesque California was published piecemeal during 1888 and 1889. Muir was relieved to get it off his hands, but these months were nevertheless sad for him; friends as well as relatives kept dying—as they will when one has lived past fifty. Muir accepted the pain, in part because he regarded death as simply going back to nature, and in part because he had for long depended upon absent friends for contacts no less sustaining because they were imaginary.

As has happened with many poets, death brought Muir's eloquence to an intensity it seldom otherwise achieved. Writing to General and Mrs. Bidwell on the death of a botanist friend he said:

"The Scotch have a proverb, 'The evenin' brings a' hame.' And so, however separated, far or near, the evening of life brings all together at the last. Lovely souls, embalmed in a thousand flowers, embalmed in the hearts of their friends, never for a moment does death seem to have had anything to do with them. They seem near, and are near, and as if in bodily sight I wave my hand to them in loving recognition."**

* William F. Badè, *The Life and Letters of John Muir*, Vol. II, p. 220.
** Ibid., p. 243.

Chapter 46
The Making of an Activist

A high, pleasant, but at the moment somewhat petulant voice came down one of the interminable corridors of San Francisco's Palace Hotel: "Johnson, Johnson! Where are you?"

Robert Underwood Johnson, associate editor of *Century Magazine*, who was not quite finished dressing for a formal dinner, called out to let his invited guest know his room.

Muir entered grumbling: "I can't make my way through these confounded artificial canyons. Now, if you were up in the Sierra, every tree and mound and scratch on the cliff would give you direction. Everything there is as plain as a signpost, but here how is one to know?" And so began a friendship whose consequences for the United States of America, and for both men, reached far beyond the perception of either.

Johnson had come out west to develop for *Century* a series of articles called "Gold Hunters," by and about men who had been part of the rush for California's precious sands and veined rocks during the wild period from 1848 to 1855. He was already acquainted with Muir through correspondence, having been on the staff of *Scribner's Monthly* when that magazine published his famous essays on the water ouzel and the Douglas squirrel. These articles had made Johnson a Muir devotee for life.

Johnson was something of an outdoor man and something of a poet. So when they had succeeded in locating the right men to produce the "Gold Hunters" series, Muir invited the editor on a trip to Yosemite. The quickest way was then a stage coach journey of a day and a half through clouds of choking dust — for it was midsummer — and along cliff-hanging roads so narrow that two vehicles could not pass except at turn-outs. Johnson was overcome with wonder, especially by the giant redwoods of the Mariposa Grove and the "incredible valley" itself — so bemused that he scarcely noted the devastation of Yosemite's meadows and groves by the "combine" that now ran the new and ugly hotels, or the fact that the falls were mere whispers of falling drops.

It was only when they were in camp at Soda Springs in the Big Tuolumne Meadows that Johnson realized that during Muir's earlier adventures this terrain had been different.

Beside one of their first evening campfires Johnson remarked that they had

Sketch of a giant redwood in Mariposa Grove.

FROM THE MUIR JOURNALS

seen none of the beautiful wild gardens Muir had written of so lovingly in his earlier articles: gardens with lilies up to the shoulders of a horse, and carpets of violets and daisies and gentians under foot.

It seemed to Johnson that there were tears in Muir's voice when he answered, "We don't see those any more. The hoofed locusts have wiped them out."

This was the first time Johnson had heard Muir's customary epithet for bands of domestic sheep, and it struck him with particular force. He urged Muir, who was glad for the opportunity, to explain the truly desperate situation in which Yosemite Valley and the drainage basins that supplied its beautiful river and spectacular falls had been placed.

The Federal Government had ceded to California only Yosemite Valley, with a mile-wide border around it; an area approximately nine miles long by two miles wide at its greatest. Sheepmen and lumbermen, by denuding the watershed of the trees and brush that normally caught the rains and snow-melt in a sponge of roots that released the life-giving fluid gradually, had created violent spring floods that left the upland parching, the falls of Yosemite gasping and, in time, would turn the San Joaquin Valley into a desert. To Johnson it immediately became obvious that a national park should be created around Yosemite, whose waters would thus be protected. Muir sadly explained that he had helped draft a bill creating such a park but that it had died because of complete indifference on the part of both Congress and the public. He felt that to make any further efforts toward preservation of the wilderness would prove futile and a waste of time.

Johnson thought otherwise, for he possessed precisely the equipment in lobbying skill, highly placed connections and the arts of public influence which Muir and his friends had lacked during their earlier effort.

Century Magazine owed much of its success to service by its senior editors on commissions and boards which had taken on important causes. The pages of the magazine itself were available for publicizing the findings and proposals of these groups. Johnson himself was secretary of a joint committee representing authors, illustrators, publishers, printers and others who greatly needed an international copyright law which would protect American publications abroad and foreign publications at home. But piracy was profitable, and the opposition therefore formidable.

Johnson had been spending nearly half his time in Washington fighting for the copyright bill on which all the proponents, representing a variety of interests, had reached an uneasy agreement. He was now a highly experienced lobbyist, with many useful contacts. And he had come fully to understand that great patience is often required to accomplish, by political means, some good that cries out to be done. For example, when Johnson and Muir sat talking by their campfire in Tuolumne Meadows, fifty-two years had gone by since Daniel Webster introduced the first copyright bill into Congress on behalf of himself and Henry Clay.*

Muir was not easily persuaded out of his discouraged unwillingness to expend his energies on a new campaign to protect Yosemite. He was much more intent on showing Johnson the Lake Tenaya region and Tuolumne Canyon. "But," as he wrote Louie Wanda, "how much we will be able to accomplish will depend upon the snow, the legs, and the resolution of the *Century.*"**

The "*Century's* legs" gave out at the foot of a rock wall a thousand feet high. Here — as Johnson wrote in his cultivated style, which reminds one of an old-time starched collar — "The debris of the wall...lay in a confused mass of rocks varying in size from a market basket to a dwelling house, and the interstices were overgrown with that objectionable shrub, the manzanita, the soft leaves of which concealed its iron trunk and branches.***

Muir, who (except for the bighorn sheep) was the best rock runner in the Sierra, had no problems, but Johnson, as he himself said, "foundered like a

* R.U. Johnson, *Remembered Yesterdays*, p. 241.
** William F. Badè, *The Life and Letters of John Muir*, Vol. II, p. 236.
*** R.U. Johnson, *Remembered Yesterdays*, p. 283.

bad swimmer" through the hostile brush. He was having such a hard time that Muir gave up teasing the tenderfoot and helped him to get down to a spot where he could watch the extraordinary Waterwheel Falls, made by the cascading Tuolumne striking a bar of granite which the ancient glacier was unable to remove. As it struck, the water was thrown upstream in a great arc.* Here he left Johnson while he went off for an hour's exploring alone. Johnson was ever after grateful for Muir's attention to his comfort that evening, for the editor was desperately tired when they reached camp, and showed it.

Neither manzanita nor exhaustion diminished Johnson's tendency to invent stratagems. Before they mounted their unwilling burros and rode down to Yosemite, he had developed a workable plan. If Muir would write two articles describing the park-around-a-park and showing its necessity, and would also collect a set of photographs illustrating the region to be set aside, Johnson would personally bring them to the attention of influential senators, congressmen and cabinet officers. Further, he would make sure that a bill creating the protective national park was not only drafted, but pushed.

Muir agreed and, once having committed himself, threw every unit of energy and minute of time he could muster into the effort. Throughout the fall of 1889 and the early months of 1890, through letters published in California newspapers, interviews and talks, he exposed the destruction going on throughout the Sierra, and especially the degradation of Yosemite Valley under the mismanagement of the State Commission: native vegetation ploughed under to grow hay that could have been more cheaply brought in from nearby farms; a swath cut through a beautiful grove to give guests of a minor hotel a view of Yosemite Falls, and the trees left where they fell; a hog-pen polluting the Merced and making a stink Muir thought must surely penetrate the very rocks.**

In March, 1890, Muir sent to Johnson, at the latter's request, a map on which he had drawn the outlines of three Yosemite Parks; in the middle was the existing state park, consisting of the valley and a frame around its edge; outside this was the national park which Muir thought there was some chance of bringing into existence — it included most, though not all, of the drainage systems of the Merced and Tuolumne. The third was Muir's ideal — a park that included the "higher fountains" — glaciers and snowfields along the backbone of the Sierra — and extended far enough west to include the Tuolumne, Merced and Mariposa groves of Big Trees.***

* According to Starr's *Guide*, the two spectacular falls upstream are not truly "waterwheels."
** When the United States Congress presented the Yosemite Valley to California in 1864, planning for the development and management of the park was entrusted to Frederick Law Olmstead, who later planned and developed a number of the nation's outstandingly beautiful and valuable parks. The most famous is Central Park in New York City. Olmstead spent nearly a year in developing a plan for Yosemite, but his report was suppressed by the State Legislature, and the future of Yosemite left to the whims of political appointees and the short-term ambitions of concessionaires. See *John Muir and the Sierra Club: The Battle for Yosemite*, Holway R. Jones, p. 29 et seq.
***Ibid. End papers show maps.

Shortly after he sent this map, Muir forwarded two articles: "The Treasures of the Yosemite," to attract general attention, and "The Proposed Yosemite National Park," to make their project specific.

Johnson got them into type at once and took the proof sheets to Washington, where he was trying to convince the House Committee on Public Lands that the park proposed in a bill offered by a congressman named Vandever was too small to protect either Yosemite Valley or the farmlands below in the valley of the San Joaquin.

Muir, suffering from a combination of exhaustion and bronchitis, was a shadow of himself. In early June, 1890, ensued the following dialogue:

Muir: "I'm planning to leave soon to explore Muir Glacier."

Doctor: "If you go on this journey in your condition, you'll pay for it with your life!"

Muir: "If I don't go I'll pay for it with my life."

Chapter 47
Alone on Muir Glacier

On June 23, 1890, Muir arrived in Glacier Bay on the steamer *Queen*, the first ship to carry tourists to this part of Alaska. She anchored close to the east wall of the Muir Glacier, where no bergs were falling, so that the sightseers could climb the moraine and photograph one another with the great ice river for a backdrop. It seemed to Muir that every one of the 180 passengers carried a Kodak.

The Muir was then about two and a half miles across and two hundred fifty feet high. The central portion, where ice masses — some several hundred feet high — were peeling off on the average of one every five minutes, was wildly pinnacled and broken, displaying a very beautiful spectrum of blues, for the day was unusually clear. The towering peaks of the Fairweather Range, though some thirty miles away, seemed close neighbors. Muir explored up the glacier to a rocky peak sticking up from the ice. Here he meant to plant markers to measure rate of flow. But also, in the first hours of his return to Glacier Bay, he found battered pieces of ancient wood. Had a forest once grown on this barren island in the ice?

This find proved to be the first paragraph of a scientist's mystery story — one that would occupy him throughout the entire trip and continue to occupy men and women for generations. Here on Glacier Bay the wonder of the ever-changing earth proceeds so rapidly one can almost watch it happen. But this only intensifies the mystery. If ice had destroyed the trees of which this wood was the battered remains, why had the glacier shrunk back? What had this landscape of sterile ice and barren, crumbling rock been like when forests grew here? What would it be like in another fifty or one hundred years?

The ship was just weighing anchor when Muir reached the glacier's brink, and when he waved his hat in a goodbye salute, dozens of handkerchiefs waved like little flags in reply. Muir hurried down to a rocky hollow less than a mile from the glacier front where the *Queen's* crewmen had deposited supplies and camp gear for himself and Henry Loomis, an old mountaineering companion.

Muir had walked twelve glacier miles that day, but — though he was still coughing — his energy had picked up remarkably, and he fell to work with Loomis building a windbreak by piling two cords of dry firewood bought in Juneau and laying a floor of planks brought all the way from Seattle. On this they set up a 9 x 9-foot tent. By the time they had stored their provisions and made their beds it was 11:30 p.m., and the strange twilight of northern midnight was just beginning to fall.

Muir spent the next several days in exploring the nearby portions of the glacier, finding more ancient wood, some in stratified moraines, and speculating on the sequence of events that had left this clue to the formation and re-formation of a landscape.

And Muir watched the falling bergs. During the time it took the tide to come in, he counted sixty-two; during an ebb, sixty-eight fell. The air was filled almost continuously with their thunderous impact on the water, for the larger ones leaped above the surface, sometimes disappearing and reappearing several times before they finally lay quiet.

On the seventh day of Muir's stay, another steamer arrived with tourists and a scientific party of seven headed by Professor Harry Fielding Reid, of Cleveland. They sought out Muir at once and made their camp beside his. He was very glad to have the company of professional colleagues, well-equipped with instruments for making studies of glacier flow and topography more precise than Muir's own explorer's estimates. He had found it extremely difficult to set sighting markers across the wildly broken surface of the glacier — nearly three miles wide at its brink, and with its sides flowing at different rates than its center.

During the early days of July, Muir busied himself with preparations for the lone-hand exploring trip on Muir Glacier which he still felt would cure his bronchitis completely. He made new, heavy soles for his hiking boots and built a wooden sled three feet long, with runners of strip iron. He also sewed a bearskin into a sleeping bag covered by a red wool blanket and a sheath of canvas. His only provisions were tea and hardtack.

Loaded, the sled weighed a hundred pounds. On July 11 Loomis helped drag it to a rocky peak — a *nunatak* sticking up from a great river of ice. Next day, having helped Muir as far as a peak on the eastern margin of the glacier, he went back to camp, as his friend wished.

Next day Muir, exploring eastward around the base of the peak, was delighted to discover the first trees he had seen on the shores of Glacier Bay or any of its ice rivers. The remnants of an old, well-established forest grew here on the only ground stable enough for the roots to hold. The rest of the crumbling mountain looked like a quarry being worked.

Leaving his sled on the ice, Muir climbed up among the trees, which were mountain hemlocks growing at an elevation of between two and three thousand feet. In openings were patches of flowering shrubs and, beneath the trees, plushy pillows of moss spangled with wild flowers. Bees, birds and small animals lived prosperously. Here, then, was one answer to the deposits of ancient wood and a sample of what Glacier Bay had been like at a kindlier period in the past.

From this mountain Muir looked down at the great, white, moraine-banded expanse of the Muir Glacier and three of its seven principal tributaries, each with its own set of smaller glaciers. Marking their boundaries rose dark, sharp, peaks and ridges, awesome in their abstract geometrical beauty. As lonely and lifeless a scene as one could conjure from the depths of imagination.

Yet life was here, and death followed like a shadow. At the edge of a muddy stream on the main glacier's back, Muir saw a raven devouring a large cod, still alive and flopping. As he made camp in an ice-coated cul-de-sac, he made out three mountain goats high on a brush-shaggy slope. They were standing motionless, as if at bay, and as he watched he heard the long, drawn-out howl of wolves.

In this unhuman place it sounded particularly dismal, and Muir was wary of wolves. The Indians were convinced that they attacked humans, whether hungry or not, and were very strong, the most cunning of animals, more to be feared than the great Alaskan brown bear.

In the morning only one goat was left. A short while later the howling commenced again, and several wolves appeared. Muir had no gun, but remembering the way goats defend themselves, he took up his ice axe and put his back against a boulder. The wolf-pack came quite close and stood for a considerable time staring at him. Then, as if deciding that this strange creature might prove too hard to handle, they trotted up the canyon and disappeared. Muir named this place "Howling Valley."

July 15 dawned clear and fine, and Muir, having eaten his breakfast of tea and hardtack and made the acquaintance of a handsome ptarmigan — tame as a barnyard fowl — climbed a 3,000-foot peak then (and still) known as "Snow Dome." His object was to plan his route across the main glacier. As usual he observed a good deal more, including two handsome, berg-filled lakes and a pass through the ridges dividing the ice-streams flowing down to Glacier Bay from those that flow toward the Lynn Canal in the country of the Chilcats. Toward evening a haze turned the light amethyst. The mountains lost their look of iron sculpture and appeared delicate and ethereal. Even the forever-reaching ice seemed tender.

Muir lingered late on Snow Dome. Then, thinking to get down in a hurry, he undertook to slide down a snow-filled, chute-like gulch. A fine slide — until he struck a place where the snow had blown away from a patch of blue ice. Here he lost all control and went tumbling wildly down at great speed until brought up by a deposit of small, loose stones.

As he picked himself up, unhurt but slightly dazed, he heard a demoniacal, graveyard scream as if spirits from the nether world had come for him and were exulting in his death. Looking toward the sound, he saw two ravens drop from the sky and light upon a jag of rock. Muir shook his fist at them and shouted "Not yet, you devils! You'll not have my body yet!"

The next day was as clear and lovely as any he had seen in Alaska. Lashing down his sack of hardtack and sleeping bag so firmly they could not fall off, no matter what the sled's position, he started across the glacier. His preparation proved a good thing, for his route lay across the confluence of a large tributary and the main ice river. The conflicting currents had thrown one another into a wild confusion of fantastic hummocks, sharp ridges, pot-holes and yawning crevasses. In some places Muir had to pick the sled up bodily and carry it through slots between hummocks. In others he crossed crevasses by sliver-bridges so narrow that he had to get astride them and inch his way across, shoving his precariously-balanced sled ahead of him. He had made no more than eight miles when, at 6 p.m., he found himself in a region so contorted and upheaved that he had not enough strength left to tackle it.

He made his smallest campfire yet, in a tin can, from matchstick size pieces of wood whittled from the bottom of his sled. On the can he set a teacup of water and brewed hot tea to wash down the hardtack. Then, feeling somewhat rested, he sat on his sled, writing up the day's observations while the sun dropped below the earth's rim, turning the horizon yellow and purple.

Against this glowing light, the bare mountains stood in a magnificent circle; close about him, the ice rose in a welter of wave forms like a wild, choppy sea. Some Alaskan explorers report a vast, almost overpowering, silence in such glacial surroundings. Muir was enchanted with the sounds: from deep below, solemn grinding and growling of big boulders being smoothed in the glacier mills and all around him the whispers and gentle songs from a network of little streams and rills. Snug in his bearskin bag, lying on his sled with feet and lower legs projecting onto the ice, Muir passed a tolerable night "neither warm," he wrote in his journal, "nor intolerably cold," in spite of a knife-edged wind.

When he got up next morning, his three-month cough had vanished — a marvel to Muir, and good evidence today that his miseries on the ranch were of allergic origin rather than microbial. It took him all day over ice ridges and across crevasses to reach the glacier's western edge. He was very tired, but pleased with his accomplishment and delighted with the new variations he had seen of earth's bounty of beauty.

He paid for the latter, for when he went out to sketch next day, July 18, he found that every mountain he looked at had above it a double. He was going snow-blind; the naked human eyes are not built to stand a succession of days when the sun falls unencumbered on a landscape of ice.

The next day, light was intolerable. Muir lay on his sled with snow poultices over his eyes until early evening, when clouds covered the sky. Fortunately the glacier hereabouts was not crevassed, and he was able to move down a few miles and make camp near one of the rocky peaks that stick up from the ice like islands. He could see the main camp five or six miles away.

In the morning his eyes were much better and, though still seeing double, Muir moved on down the glacier, observing how variations in the size of stones — from sand to great boulders —determined their distribution by water and ice. A hummingbird visited him twice, buzzing his sleeping bag to see whether the red wool lining would yield nectar.

Toward evening he changed courses and began to hurry toward another rocky island. The steamer *Queen* was due; no doubt with letters from home. A biting wind had come up, and the island would shelter him. Also he was getting pretty hungry, now having lived on tea and hardtack for nine days. He had covered forty miles of ice and rock so unfriendly that the new soles he had put on his boots were nearly worn out and his feet were continuously wet. Even the glacier conspired to make him a little less cautious than usual, for the surface appeared perfectly solid, without fissures or holes.

He had gone scarcely a dozen steps toward the island when ice gave way beneath his feet and he suddenly found himself under water. As he bobbed up again he realized that floating pieces of ice had frozen together just firmly enough to appear solid, but not enough to support his weight.

Hanging onto his ice axe and the sled rope, Muir floundered across the crevasse and managed to strike his axe deep enough into the margin to hold firm — a considerable feat considering that he had only water to tread on. It was even more difficult to haul himself up over the edge, but he managed to do so. Then he pulled his sled over at a spot where the ice was firmer, stripped off his clothes, which he flung into a sodden heap, crawled into his bearskin bag and shivered the night away.

It was miserable the next morning getting into his underwear, though he had wrung out the long johns as well as he could. But his eyes felt much better, and he spent a profitable day exploring the broken stumps of a spruce forest, destroyed by sand and gravel from the retreating glacier so recently that some of the trunks still had their bark on. He had meant to wait till next day to signal the camp. But in the early evening Reid and Loomis came and took him back to camp in the long boat.

It would be reasonable to suppose that this eleven-day, forty-mile trip alone on an unexplored glacier was enough of a scootcher to be Muir's final one. But he and the ice had another adventure in store.

A few days after his return, he set out with Professor Reid and his students to visit some of the other large glaciers. But the upper Bay was so choked with floating ice that Reid and his party returned to camp in the whaleboat, leaving Muir a small dugout canoe they had brought along. About sunset of a trying day, Muir reached the mouth of the inlet leading to Hugh Miller Glacier. He could find no place on the steep, boulder-strewn shore where he could drag the canoe up out of reach of the tide. Remembering a place where he had camped in 1879, Muir set off for the opposite shore. For two hours he picked his cautious way among a host of bergs and accomplished almost two of the four miles to his destination. A pack of very large bergs then barred his path, and he hesitated, paddling to right and left, in search of an opening. The only channel he could find was about four feet wide and two hundred feet long, evidently made when a very large berg split in two.

The dangers ahead seemed no greater than those he had passed. He entered the faintly starlit corridor with the breath of ice on either cheek. But he had gone only sixty yards or so when the glimmer on the ice cliffs told him that the gap was beginning to close. A dugout canoe is more eggshell than icebreaker. He backed water with a desperate fury, and as his prow cleared the gap, the ice masses came together with a growling, savage crunch.

Terrified for one of the few times in his life, Muir retreated across the inlet, found a reasonably safe place for the canoe and spent the night wrapped around two boulders like a sleeping seal, except that he did not sleep. For a while he watched the stars, then upright bars in all the clear colors one sees when light passes through a prism began to march across the northern horizon from west to east. These "soldiers of light," as he called them, kept up their parade until almost dawn.

Near the end of July the *Queen* brought pre-cut lumber for a cabin which Muir and Loomis, with the help of the Reid party, put up in a few days. The last weeks of Muir's stay were pleasant and relaxed except for one day when a camp helper named York, who had come with the Reid party and remained to work for "the Professor," took out after Muir with a rifle.

York would have had more success hunting a mountain goat. Professor Reid says in his notebook that Muir returned to camp fifteen hours before his would-be murderer. York then disappeared into Chilcat country and was never heard of again. Muir himself never mentioned this episode at all.

Part VII

ACTIVIST

"*Saving these woods from the axe and the saw, from the money changers and the water changers is in many ways the most notable service to God and man I have heard of since my forest wanderings began.*"

Chapter 48
Creating the
National Forest System

When Muir got home in early September, he was no longer a private citizen, but a standard bearer in the true meaning of the term — one who provides a fighting force with a presence around which to rally and who shows the way. "Treasures of the Yosemite," published by *Century* in August, 1890, and "Features of the Proposed Yosemite Park," which followed in September, had been reprinted in part and in whole over the length and breadth of the country, and commented upon and discussed. Muir had already published some sixty-five articles, and to his established readership were now added thousands who were ready for someone to show them that, if they wanted the country they loved to remain habitable, they had best do what was necessary to keep it so.

The opposition was, naturally, furious. In California its chief hatchet-man was John P. Irish, the living portrait of an old-time ward politician and, from 1889 to 1893, secretary and treasurer of the State Park Commission. Irish helped to launch the campaign of whispers and innuendos accusing Muir of every sin from marital infidelity to nature faking and sentimental ignorance. He deluged newspapers with scurrilous letters. Muir's friends defended him indignantly and capably, but the poison persisted long beyond Muir's lifetime and even prevented Kings Canyon National Park from being named in his honor when it was created in 1940.

Muir himself made no public reply, except to a letter published in the *Oakland Tribune* on September 8, 1890. In this slanderous screed, Irish accused Muir not only of cutting live trees in Yosemite Valley, but of selling the lumber he sawed from them.* The Noble Park Commission, Irish said, had expelled Muir from the park in the nick of time. The gist of Muir's cool reply, published in the *Tribune* September 16, 1890, is as follows: "...twenty-five

---

* Irish had been incensed by a piece Muir wrote which seemed to favor the return of Yosemite Valley to the Federal Government. Muir had no such objective at that time. On March 4, 1890, he had written to Johnson: "For my part, I should rather see the Valley in the hands of the Federal Government. But what a storm of growls and howls would rend our sunny skies...at the outrage of...snatching the diadem from California's brow! A man may not appreciate his wife, but let her daddie try to take her back!" See William F. Badè's *The Life and Letters of John Muir*, Vol. II, p. 238. Holway Jones takes great pains to be fair to Irish. See *John Muir and the Sierra Club: The Battle for Yosemite*, note 35, pp. 62-63.

years ago I was employed to saw lumber from fallen timber . . . I never cut down a single tree in the Yosemite, nor sawed a tree cut down by any person there...or sold a foot of lumber there or elsewhere....While I lived in Yosemite, Galen Clark was guardian. He is guardian now, and to that gentleman I would refer you for further information, should you require it."

At this time during the closing weeks of September, 1890, mysterious events were taking place in Washington. The House Committee on Public Lands was still supposed to be debating Vandever's bill for a national park around Yosemite Valley, when the Committee itself introduced a substitute measure into Congress. This new bill proposed a "forest reservation" of 1,512 square miles — five times as much land as in the park proposed by Vandever. Its boundaries were almost exactly the same as the "ideal" Yosemite Park Muir had mapped for Johnson the previous spring. The act calling for this larger park was passed by both House and Senate on the last day of the session, September 30, 1890, without even being printed, as is customary.*

At about this time, bills introduced by Congressman Vandever made Grant Grove a national park of 3.9 square miles and created a Sequoia National Park of 604 square miles — minute beginnings, but a start toward saving at least some of the giant redwoods for posterity.

John Muir's time for good feeling about Yosemite proved to be only a month. On the last day of October Dr. Strentzel died, "as one falling asleep." John Muir took his death as hard as did his wife and daughter, for Dr. Strentzel had in many ways been more of a father to him than his own physical progenitor. To make it easier to care for Mrs. Strentzel, the Muirs moved down to the "big house," leaving the old ranch house to John's eldest sister, Margaret, and her husband, John Reid. Fortunately for John Muir, who now had the burden of managing Dr. Strentzel's estate added to the ranch and the fight to preserve the wilderness, Reid had at last given up the unending struggle against the natural difficulties of farming on the high, dry prairie and become his brother-in-law's manager.

Among the events of the 1890s that had consequences larger than their apparent size was the meeting of Robert Underwood Johnson and John Noble, Secretary of the Interior (1889-1893), at the Yale commencement where both men received honorary degrees in June of 1891. Noble had already become effectively interested in conservation, and when Johnson explained Muir's idea that the whole roof of the Sierra should be made a national park or forest,

*Holway Jones, a scholar so meticulous that he provides 601 footnotes in a book of 169 text pages, says there is some evidence that the Southern Pacific Railway's Washington lobby played a part in getting the bill for the "ideal" Yosemite Park drafted and passed. He presents indisputable evidence that the Southern Pacific went to considerable lengths to promote the scenic wonders which brought tourists to California — especially Yosemite, to which its rail-stage connection provided the most convenient method of travel for many years. However, Jones comes to no firm conclusions concerning this matter, saying: "The circumstances surrounding the introduction and passage of these bills to establish Yosemite National Park are lost in the passage of time and insufficient documentation." See *John Muir and the Sierra Club: The Battle for Yosemite*, p. 43 et seq.

to preserve the watershed and provide unmodified environments where people could return occasionally to man's original habitat, the Secretary responded not only enthusiastically, but more energetically than the editor foresaw.*

On the same day, March 4, 1891, when Congress finally passed the Copyright Act in a legislative cliff-hanger that kept Johnson and others rushing around all night, the legislature also passed a Civil Sundry Bill which contained a most extraordinary amendment.**

The epoch-making amendment to the Sundry Bill of March, 1891, was conceived and drafted by Edward A. Bowers, an official in the Department of Interior whose name has been honored by preservationists ever since. It gave the President the breath-taking power to reserve, by proclamation, forest lands and scenic areas which were still part of the public domain.

Advised by Secretary Noble, who in turn was influenced by Muir's articles, President Harrison lost no time in using this newly-granted authority to preserve our forests for the benefit of all Americans. Less than a month after the act was passed, he set aside, in Wyoming, the Yellowstone Reserve of 1,239,040 acres.***

On May 13 Muir went to San Francisco and bought the best map he could find of the Sierra, south of Yosemite. On this he drew the boundaries of a greatly enlarged Sequoia National Park, which included most of the remaining stands of giant redwoods. He sent this map to Johnson, who passed it on to Noble with an explanatory letter. Noble did not reply until some weeks after their conversation at Yale during commencement time. Then Johnson received the first in a series of letters in which he and the Secretary exchanged ideas and kept one another informed concerning the progress of conservation and the threats to it. Muir was actually a third party to this exchange, supplying first-hand knowledge of both the wilderness to be preserved and problems arising in California. He supplied many of the ideas reaching the President through Johnson and Noble and, most importantly, provided the inspiration which sustained their belief in what they were doing and stimulated them to action.

Replying to Johnson's letter accompanying Muir's Sequoia Park map, Noble wrote:

*Among other powerful men who welcomed and supported the idea of preserving the higher regions of the Sierra Nevada was Senator George Hearst, one of the most acute and successful mining men of his time — father of the flamboyant newspaper publisher, William Randolph Hearst, who as early as 1889 was fighting Muir, Johnson and the whole conservation movement. See R. U. Johnson, *Remembered Yesterdays*, p. 292.

** At that time it was customary at the close of each session to enact a piece of legislation, "making," in the language of H.R. 15, first session, 55th Congress, "appropriations for the fiscal year . . . and other purposes," — in brief, a catch-all containing everything Congress had forgotten or neglected to do during the session, and, thus, excellent concealment for measures which might arouse formidable opposition if examined individually.

*** These lands are now in the Shoshone and Teton National Forests. See U.S. Department of Agriculture, Forest Service, *Highlights in the History of Forest Conservation*, p. 5.

"It will greatly please me to bring the additional reservation for the Sequoia National Park before the President...the necessary legislation will also be asked...."

Secretary Noble goes on to mention difficulties with a group formed to cut giant redwoods within the already-established Sequoia National Park. Then he says: "There are also communications coming on against even the Yosemite reservation. There seems to be opposition (of more than ordinary magnitude) brewing to the policy of these reservations and there will be an attack, I think, next winter.

"But I am preparing a general system of reservations of our headwater forests under the Act of March 3, 1891,* because I believe the great body of our public timber is in danger."

In the late spring of 1891, Muir made another lone-hand journey through the magnificent South Fork Canyon of the Kings River to refresh his observations for a *Century* article in support of the Sequoia project. Johnson, no doubt, got the proof sheets to Noble in early fall, and the Secretary made Muir's plan his own recommendation in a report to Congress. The best President Harrison could do that fall was to reserve the White River National Forest of 1,198,000 acres in Colorado.

Nevertheless the National Forest System was well launched. Commenting upon that eventful period, R. U. Johnson wrote, "Muir and Noble were the two salient leaders and pioneers of forest conservation, and Noble's torch, like those of most of us, was kindled at the flame of Muir's enthusiasm."

"Enthusiasm" seems an inadequate word here. Muir had an incandescent quality perceived even by enemies of wilderness preservation, a quality fed by his passionate love of unaltered nature, his understanding of its miraculous dynamics and, above all, his faith that man — since he cannot escape being part of nature — must live with it in harmony.

At no time was this quality in Muir more effective than during the intense months of 1890 and 1891 when an important portion of the nation's public opinion was as ready to be touched off as a forest during drought. This is, no doubt, why the events of this period gave rise to the often-repeated and seldom-understood statement that Muir was "the father of the American National Forests."

* Most sources give the date of this act (actually an amendment), giving the President power to set aside national forests by proclamation, as March 4, 1891. Noble's letter quoted above appears in *Remembered Yesterdays*, by R. U. Johnson.

Chapter 49
Sierra Club Born to Battle

Because of Secretary Noble's well-informed warnings, R. U. Johnson became acutely aware of the dangers to the enlarged Yosemite Park and frequently urged Muir and his friends to form a "defense association." Though Muir and Johnson had gotten this park-around-a-park created almost entirely by their own efforts, it would take organized power to protect its vegetation and its boundaries.

The threats came from interests — people — who wished to use some of the new park's 1,512 square miles for private purposes and were, therefore, antithetical to its reservation for use by the public and to the protection of its beauty and resources by U. S. Cavalry under singularly tough and unyielding officers. As Muir and his supporters clearly recognized, many private holdings had been acquired before the park's enlargement. The cavalry officer sent out in 1890 to guard the reservation estimated that more than sixty-five thousand acres had been claimed as homesteads or preempted under the timber laws, and that there were approximately three hundred mining claims in addition.

Many of the land claims were, of course, fraudulent, and most of the mining claims barren. But the claims had, nevertheless, to be "extinguished" — to use the technical word for getting the land back into government hands — either by buying it or proving the claim invalid.*

Moreover, public land had been freely used by rugged individualists under a somewhat extraordinary interpretation of democratic rights: the land belonged to the United States, they were U. S. citizens, therefore they had the right to use the land as they saw fit. Alternatively, it was often assumed that since public land belonged to everyone in general, it belonged to no one in particular, and the fellow who got there first and was tough enough to hold a given area was entitled to use it as he chose. Under these theories, which were products of custom and often held simultaneously, stockmen, particularly sheep-growers, exploited the grazing lands destructively and set devastating fires, lumbermen plundered national resources, hydraulic miners filled

---

* In 1875 the Supreme Court had declared the Yosemite Valley claims of James M. Hutchings, John Lamon (the gigantic pioneer who planted fruit trees) and two others to be invalid because they were filed before Yosemite was surveyed. The State of California reimbursed Hutchings in the amount of $24,000 and gave lesser amounts to the others.

streambeds with silt and gravel to create flood conditions and railways burned and slashed huge areas along their rights of way.

It should be borne in mind that not all of these enterprisers were exploiters. For example, Hale Tharp, whose home on his summer range was a fifty-two-foot redwood log hollowed by fire, actually protected the Giant Forest for many years. Railway companies occasionally helped to preserve some parts of the environment even while destroying others. Perhaps the most curious anomaly was the behaviour of the Boone and Crockett Club, organized by Theodore Roosevelt in 1887 "to promote manly sport with the rifle" and "to work for the preservation of the large game of this country."

Hunters usually did not care much for national parks, where hunting was prohibited or strictly limited. Nevertheless the Boone and Crockett Club was active in the preservation of Yellowstone Park and helped to induce Congress to pass the legislation which created the first forest reservations.*

Several other clubs to foster climbing and enjoyment of the out-of-doors existed or were being formed in several parts of the country, and the idea of organizing such an association locally had been discussed for some time between Muir and some specially interested friends, many of whom were on the faculties of the University of California and Stanford. By March, 1892, they had already found a name for the projected club and were ready to hold preliminary meetings when disaster once more struck the Muir family in Wisconsin.

Parry and Muir, the once-prosperous mercantile firm in which David was the working partner, had failed because of the recklessness and poor judgment of Parry, David's associate. In that time and place, a bankruptcy was traumatic. David, at home in Portage, found himself backed against the wall in trying to pay farmers and other creditors — for Parry and Muir bought and sold local produce as well as a general-store variety of merchandise.

When the firm's insolvency became public knowledge, the community was furious. Friends of a lifetime turned against David, and there was even talk of lynching him. David himself was near collapse with "brain fever," at that time a catch-all designation for most disorders of the mind. At first John Muir thought that David's interest in the firm might be saved by an infusion of money. But when he reached Portage, he found the firm too deeply compromised to be saved. The best he could do was stiffen the spines of the family members so they kept their heads up and their pride intact.

David agreed to pay off all of his share of the firm's debts — a promise he was able to keep by working some of John Muir's land on shares and, as his farming prospered, by leasing still more acreage.

John Muir was now free to give the most of his energy and his talents to wilderness projects, the most important and pressing of which was formation of the Sierra Club. On May 28, 1892, he met informally with some friends in the office of an influential lawyer named Warren Olney to draft the articles of incorporation. Olney put the consensus in proper legal form, and, on June 4,

* Holway R. Jones, *John Muir and the Sierra Club: The Battle for Yosemite*, pp. 4-5.

twenty-seven prominent men, meeting once more in Olney's office, signed the articles of incorporation and approved the by-laws. The most important provisions were Section II of the Articles, "That the said . . . corporation is formed, not for pecuniary profit," and Section III, "That the purposes for which this Corporation is formed are as follows, to wit: to explore, enjoy and render accessible the mountain regions of the Pacific Coast; to publish authentic information concerning them; and to enlist the support and cooperation of the people and the government in preserving the forests and other natural features of the Sierra Nevada Mountains...." John Muir was elected president.

According to a college-age guest at the ranch, Muir came home jubilant and regaled them all with an account of the meeting. The young man had never seen Muir let go when delight overcame him. "He seemed hilarious with joy, as if this were the happiest day of his life."

The new club was tested as soon as it was formed. Representative Anthony Caminetti of California introduced into the House a bill intended to strip away nearly half of the newly-created Yosemite Park. Muir and most of the Sierra Club's charter members felt that the Caminetti Bill was "in favor of sheepmen and timbermen" and began opposing it at once by letter, telegram and interview. But the Sierra Club was not ready to go into action as a whole until fall. By that time it had some 160 members, for the most part prominent professional and business men, a considerable proportion of them university presidents and professors who were accorded a great amount of respect. The Sierra Club had also made honorary members of such personages as John Tyndall, head of England's Royal Institution; John W. Noble, Secretary of the Interior; John Wesley Powell, explorer of the Grand Canyon of the Colorado and Director of the U. S. Geological Survey; and Robert Underwood Johnson of *Century Magazine*. The Club's voice was thus far more powerful than its numbers suggest. It was credited with an important role in defeating both Caminetti's original bill and a second which would also have stripped away vital lands from Yosemite Park. The Sierra Club thus established itself almost from the start as a potent force in shaping U.S. conservation policies.

Not that the Club was monolithic in the sense that everyone subscribed to the same ideas and supported the same policies and the same programs of action. From the start its members were persons of strong individual opinions and intense feelings. The wilderness is very likely to create passionately-held beliefs acted upon with stubborn vigor and at times expressed intemperately. But 1893 began in relative calm and with encouraging progress.

In the early spring, President Harrison took a long step toward making real Muir's dream of saving the entire roof of the Sierra. By proclamation he created the great Sierra Forest Reserve of more than four million acres of magnificent forest and canyon country, extending from the southern border of Yosemite Park to the latitude of Bakersfield. In other parts of the West, Harrison created additional reserves totalling some nine million acres.

Chapter 50
A Mountain Social Lion

When Muir went to San Francisco, which was often, he usually stopped in at William Keith's spacious, cluttered studio on Montgomery Street. Here among a select few of the city's illuminati, Muir looked like a farmer. He did not act like one, but at once attacked Keith's art and opinions as if he meant to demolish the man himself. Keith gave back as good as Muir gave him. It was a grown-up version of the combative games they had played in the schoolyards of Scotland. "I'm Scotch," Keith said to an amused but puzzled spectator, "and he's Scotch, and so we always fight." But when they were together for long stretches, the game sometimes grew too rough for comfort. "Muir," Keith once remarked, "is an awful cross fellow to travel with."

One result was that the trip to Europe, which they had been planning for ten years, turned into a pursuit race. One May morning in 1893, Muir received a telegram from Keith saying that he and his wife could not wait any longer; they would meet Muir at the world's fair in Chicago. But when Muir got there, Keith had already gone on, and they never got together. Though they were both in New York at the same time, Keith had fallen into the hands of party-loving art promoters and art buyers, and Muir promptly surrendered to the program which Robert Underwood Johnson had laid out for him.

Johnson's major objective was to extend Muir's reputation and influence, which would help both the cause of conservation and the *Century Magazine*. He well knew that his man was even more effective in face-to-face situations than through his printed words. And influential friends they were going to need if the forests were to be saved. By the time Muir reached New York, Grover Cleveland was in the White House; there were many new faces in Congress; Secretary Noble's place in the Interior Department had been taken by a man named Hoke Smith. Persuasion would have to begin all over.

By now Muir's reputation had grown to the point where a great many people wanted to meet him. Johnson therefore had no trouble in carrying out his design to give Muir as much "exposure" as possible to the great and powerful. At elaborate dinners, where the courses followed one another in fantastical succession, with a different wine for each (unless one preferred to stick to champagne), and luncheons, only less stomach-stretching and impressive, Muir talked with the elite of New York and Boston: the mayors of both these cities; prominent judges and legislators; editors of the largest and most influential newspapers and magazines; Mark Twain, George W. Cable, and other authors; scientists such as Nicola Tesla; and specialists such as the superintendent of Central Park.

Through all this exotic eating, drinking and talking, Muir's stomach, as he wrote Louie Wanda, "behaved like a gentleman." There were other diversions Muir enjoyed more. One was a sight-seeing ride with Johnson on the elevated railway which then ran up Ninth Avenue and turned west at 110th Street to cross the top of Central Park.

Just after the cars had screeched their way around the turn, Muir suddenly jumped up, exclaiming, "Let's get out of here! We've got to get out of here!"

Puzzled but indulgent, Johnson followed him out at the next stop and, as they ran down the long flight of steps to the sidewalk, Muir explained that he had seen a big boulder which they simply must examine. From ground level it lay out of sight in a vacant lot, behind a high board fence which the two gentlemen proceeded to climb in their elegantly tailored suits, spats and high starched collars swathed in dark silk cravats. Arriving at the boulder, which was really a half-exposed outcropping, Muir brushed the dust away from some deep, parallel scratches, explaining that these marks could only have been made by hard stones on the underbelly of a glacier. Manhattan Island, therefore, had been overswept by ice.

Johnson was delighted, more by the quaintness of the adventure than by his new knowledge, and they spent the afternoon walking down through Central Park and finding rocks with glacial signatures most of the way.*

When Johnson took him to Cambridge, Muir also noted that glaciers had lived and died at Walden Pond. The lovely mixed forest around the little lake was growing on the crumbled granite remnants of moraines. Within these low, encircling hills the bush-and-briar-fringed lake gleamed like a dark eye. Muir well understood Thoreau's contentment there. But, as he wrote Louie Wanda, he was puzzled that the people of Concord thought Thoreau lived as a hermit, when the town was only a "simple saunter" of two miles from his cabin.

When he and Johnson called at the home of Emerson's son, Muir had the most heart-warming experience of the trip. On the porch sat an elderly man whom Johnson recognized as young Emerson's father-in-law, Judge Keyes, who had been a college mate of Thoreau and his lifelong friend. When Johnson introduced himself, the Judge responded with frosty indifference. But when Johnson said, "This is John Muir," the old man sprang up and seized him by the shoulders as if he were a long-lost son.

"John Muir?" he said. "Is this John Muir?" and went on to explain that Muir's articles and essays had made him feel that he had known the author for a lifetime. Indoors, Mrs. Keyes — whom Muir described in a letter home as a "charming old-fashioned lady" — served them cider and other summer refreshments and said that she, too, felt as if a son had unexpectedly come home.

* R. U. Johnson, *Remembered Yesterdays*, pp. 313-314.

From Cambridge, Muir and Johnson went to stay for several days at the Brookline estate of Charles Sprague Sargent, the foremost authority of his time on trees and forests. He developed the Arnold Arboretum at Harvard into a living museum of world renown and was active and influential in both regional and national affairs. At the time of Muir's visit, Sargent was engaged upon his monumental *Silva of North America*, in fourteen volumes, published at intervals between 1891 and 1902.

Friendship developed rapidly between Muir and Sargent, and they no doubt had a great deal to say to one another about trees and forests. But Muir seems to have thought that his family would be more interested in the Sargents' life-style and his own surprising (to him) social success; at least these form the substance of his long letter home. The house was two hundred feet long, with piazzas in proportion, set in a park of fifty acres — much of it still native groves and meadows, but many acres in lawns surrounded by cultivated flowers. The Sargents made Muir feel entirely at home — free to do what he liked. But the servants wore liveries and the dinners were "occasions."

At each of them Muir was required to tell the story of Stickeen and their hair-raising adventure on Brady Glacier. The audiences, which included servants listening from behind screens and through partially open doors, were unfailingly enthralled. Stickeen, as Muir knew him, was a canine personality capable of linking man, in spirit, to the biological world of which man is a part. And through empathy with Stickeen, Muir's listeners were able to place themselves on a wildly-crevassed glacier and comprehend a little of what it meant to be there, whether one is man or beast. Perhaps no other animal ever did so much as this little dog to help change a nation's attitudes toward nature.

Another home that Muir visited during this summer of 1893 was "Wing-and-Wing," the house of Henry Fairfield Osborne on the Hudson opposite West Point.*

Osborne, almost twenty years younger than Muir, had not yet achieved the international eminence he reached as president of the American Museum of Natural History, but he was, as the saying goes, doing all right as professor of biology and dean of the faculty of pure science at Columbia University. There was a natural affinity between Osborne and Muir, whose warm friendship endured until Muir's death.

Muir reached Europe in early July and had a good time doing exactly what he liked. In Dunbar he stayed in his old home, which had become the Lorne Temperance Hotel, so that he could have a look at the dormer window out of which he had climbed one wet, dark night onto the steep slate roof. He looked up relatives and playmates, including the woman who had been the only child who could outrun him. From Dunbar he went to the north of Scotland to

* A curious example of both Muir's contradictory nature and his understanding of women is a letter home in which this outdoorsman, who was perfectly willing to sleep curled up on a boulder with no covering at all, makes favorable reference to the embroidered, lavender-scented bed linen at Wing-and-Wing.

wander over hills and vales of blooming heather; across to Ireland for a look at the bogs; to the glaciers of Switzerland and the glacier-carved fiords of Norway; back to England to visit Sir Joseph Hooker, the botanist, on his country estate which seemed wilder than the Martinez ranch, though only twenty-five miles from London; and, finally, back to Dunbar for a last visit. Less concerned with remembered people than before, he perceived the misery of the many poor so poignantly that, afterward, he sent money each Christmas for distribution among them.

When Muir reached New York in mid-September of 1893, he found a telegram from Louie Wanda — who had been in close touch with conservation affairs through R. U. Johnson and the Sierra Club — suggesting that he go to Washington and accomplish what "forest good" was possible. Muir spent a busy week visiting new members of Congress and Cleveland's new Cabinet officers, as well as old allies such as Edward Bowers, the obscure civil servant whose pen produced the legal mechanism by which the national forests were created. Then Muir went home to plunge into the task of writing the book on the Sierra Nevada which he had promised Johnson to produce.

For all his impulsiveness and tendency to "lean and loaf at (his) ease, observing a spear of summer grass," Muir attacked a job of writing as if he were working for wages. By the time the sun rose, he was in the kitchen cooking the eggs and heating the coffee the Chinese cook had left ready for him. Before he and Louie Wanda left the table after ten o'clock family breakfast, Muir read her what he had accomplished during the four preceding hours. Often he made the changes she suggested then and there. He labored again until lunch time and, if he were up against a deadline, into the night.

Muir worked in an upstairs room beside a window looking over orchards and down the valley to Carquinez Strait. Over the mantle hung a large landscape by Keith and the skull and horns of a mountain goat he had found on Muir Glacier. He had dragged them back to the base-camp on his sled, though snow-blinded during the whole time and, at the end, chilled to the soul by his plunge into an ice water-filled crevasse. Framed photographs of friends crowded the mantlepiece.

Bookcases to the ceiling kept his scientific library in reasonable order. One section was reserved for his favorite poets. Another was for the unsystematic philosophers, especially Thoreau, who had become the most congenial to him of them all. When he read he sat in an oak rocking chair with a sagging bottom and smoked a clay pipe through the long stem of a thistle. When a special friend was invited in to talk, Muir cleared the books and manuscripts from this chair, since there was no other besides the one at his desk.

No one else was allowed to touch the extraordinary clutter of notes, sketches, manuscripts, pamphlets, letters and opened reference books. To do so would derange Muir's non-filing system, for he knew (approximately) where every item resided at any given time.

The clutter originated in necessity rather than indolence or caprice. Muir understood very well that the material benefits of conservation (which would accrue mainly to future generations) were not likely to motivate either the public or legislators, no matter how logically and cogently they were presented. If the wilderness was to be saved, people must come to love it. His task, then, was to enable his readers to re-live the experiences through which his own love had been created: complex experiences, embodying not only sights and sounds and taste and smell — all the sensory elements — but the

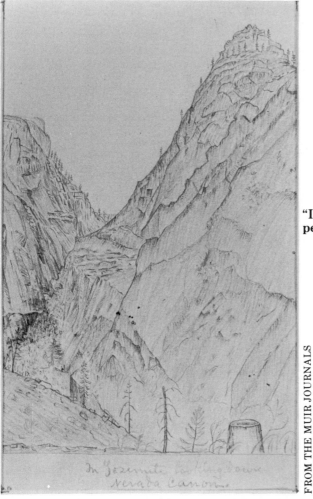

"If the wilderness was to be saved, people must come to love it."

FROM THE MUIR JOURNALS

feelings aroused and his thoughts, including scientific observations and his efforts to understand Nature's continuing labor of re-creation. He must therefore use description, narrative and devices of poetry such as Whitmanesque passages of sequential images, recounting some apparently commonplace but truly marvelous trains of events such as raindrops falling on and through a forest.

To do all this he must select subtly from voluminous notes and journals and hundreds of on-the-spot sketches, each item expanding fantastically in memory so that it had to be restrained before he could use it. Even the considerable amount of material he lifted from his published articles did not make his work much easier. Outlines and file cards were of no use. He must hold the whole complex in his mind, trimming and expanding, moving each element until it found the place where it would best illuminate its context and be illuminated by it.

With good editorial help from Louie Wanda and R. U. Johnson, Muir created *The Mountains of California*, a most extraordinary feat — the book book delighted scientists as much as it did the public. The first printing sold out within weeks of its publication by the Century Company in the autumn of 1894. Charles Sprague Sargent wrote Muir, "I have never read descriptions of trees that so picture them to the mind as yours do....I believe you are the man who ought to have written a *Silva of North America*. Your book is one of the great productions of its kind and I congratulate you on it." From Britain, Sir Joseph Hooker wrote, "I do not know when I have read anything I have enjoyed more. It has brought California back to my memory with redoubled interest and more than redoubled knowledge...."

It appears that in this letter Sir Joseph was attempting to express his gratitude for Muir's ecological perceptions — insights which science understands systematically today and for which we have developed language which we use familiarly and sometimes glibly. Taken as a whole, *The Mountains of California* is a general ecology of the Sierra Nevada, presenting in one grand panorama the interwoven, dynamically interacting environments reaching from the summits where glaciers linger to the burning foothills where the hour of beautiful life is over almost as soon as it begins.

Starr King Group from the S.W.

Illustrating Dome forms and combinations — The arrows indicate the direction of the over sweeping ice current —

Sketch indicates Muir's focus—the ecological system of the Sierra Nevada, "...the summits where glaciers linger...."

Chapter 51
Roses and Rattlesnakes

In January of 1895, the rains which had threatened a prolonged, gloomy winter suddenly gave way to a succession of bright days that made the Martinez ranch and everything around it seem new and lovelier than ever. Muir was writing an article about Alaska and, thus, working with memories he enjoyed. His health was better than it usually was on the ranch.

He was happy — which meant that his family was happy. As one of his nieces put it, "Uncle John was not an easy man to live with. But Aunt Louie knew how to keep everything smooth."

Louie Wanda went to considerable lengths to achieve this tranquillity and still preserve not only her identity and self respect but to live according to her lights. For example, Muir never had been able to endure piano practice since the months he tried to write in competition with John Swett's children struggling against the piano in the room below his own. Louie Wanda's talent was so considerable that professional musicians had urged her to train for the concert stage. To her it was unthinkable that her daughters should grow up without music lessons. Her solution was a soundproof room in the ranch house where Annie Wanda and Helen could practice without disturbing their father.

Louie Wanda somehow managed to give the girls enough conventional education so that her eldest daughter had no difficulties when she entered the University of California. "More wild knowledge and less book knowledge" was John Muir's prescription for the girls. Yet he insisted that they learn his favorite poets, including some passages from the Bible, as well as the Latin names of the plants they encountered. That they loved to walk with him when Helen was nine and Annie Wanda fourteen is the best evidence that he gave himself as fully to intimate relationships as to the wilderness causes which absorbed an increasing proportion of his time. He was especially pleased with Helen, who seemed to have outgrown the respiratory illnesses which had worried her parents so much during her early childhood.

Helen was a quick, imaginative, impulsive child, in some ways very much like John Muir himself. She flung herself enthusiastically into the "pretend games" he promoted. In one which they played for years, she was "momma" to grizzled William Keith, who was a frequent house guest, and to greying John Muir.

Wanda was more like her mother: constant, thoughtful, observant of the needs of others, quietly reserved — yet responsive to enjoyments. She had a fine sense of rhythm and, from early childhood, joined her father in rhyming sessions. Both the girls insisted that John Muir tell a "Paddy Grogan Story"* after dinner no matter how august the company at table. Instead of a horse, Paddy rode a kangaroo and had wild west adventures in the outback of Australia. Not only the family, but guests of all ages, pressed Muir to make a book (or several) of the Paddy Grogan series.

He promised to do so — sometime. Meanwhile he was very much occupied with his writing: his increasingly heavy correspondence with members of the Sierra Club and other conservationists, and minor but important concerns such as a campaign to protect the meadowlarks from pot-hunters. He wrote in a newspaper article (published in the *San Francisco Call*, March 24, 1895): "Better far, and more reasonable it would be, to burn our pianos and violins for firewood, than to cook our divine midgets for food."

Muir was especially happy on the seventeenth of April, when three dozen Cherokee rose bushes arrived ". . . to be planted along the new fence by the roadside . . . to bless with their blossoms thousands of passengers to come.

"What a hedge I shall have — fifty rods (825 feet) long, six feet high, with millions of lovely white blossoms . . . lasting more than a month, and the leaves forever."**

Century published Muir's Alaskan article in June, 1895, and he immediately embarked on a more ambitious project — a book on the Yosemite region. To refresh his memories, he descended alone on August 7 into the cyclopean furrow where the Tuolumne River rushes in silver and irised spray. Here the thickest, most powerful ice stream in the Sierra ground its way through monolithic granite, forming a V-shaped canyon 4,000 to 5,200 feet deep, but only two miles wide in its amplest sections.

Muir, then fifty-seven, claimed that he could climb as well as ever. But his pack seemed very heavy as he made his way down the higher part of the gorge through heavy underbrush. He kept shouting to warn the bears of his coming, for though many were away preying on flocks of sheep, he saw one eating raspberries and saw also fresh bear signs such as a newly ruined wasp nest. He followed bear trails down the gorge, though they often led among huge earthquake-tumbled boulders and over bare granite ridges hundreds of feet high, for he knew there was no easier way than the lumbering animals had found.

Muir was also bothered more than ever before by rattlesnakes, though he thought two of the several he saw were very beautiful. Another, as he noted in his journal, "was a common dull grey fellow, thick and muscular, that I came

---

* Paddy Grogan stories were the original adventures of an Irish youth and his kangaroo steed. According to those who heard them, "The world has lost a great juvenile classic" because they were not written down. See Linnie Marsh Wolfe's *Son of the Wilderness: The Life of John Muir*.
** The Cherokee rose is very close to its wild forebears and no longer cultivated by sophisticated growers, except for breeding stock. See Linnie Marsh Wolfe, *John of the Mountains*, p. 339.

Sketch illustrating the formation of the upper Tuolumne Valley and its tributaries.

upon suddenly. Toward night in pushing through brush and rocks, I threw my bundle ahead of me. It fell plump on the rattler. He, highly indignant, crawled away a few feet and coiled and thundered. I cautiously withdrew my bundle and passed him a few feet away, he...striking at me."*

Muir did not trust that snake. He slept the night on top of a fifteen-foot high boulder with nearly vertical sides, which he climbed with the aid of a leaning tree-trunk that he managed to kick away when he reached the top. This camp, if it can be dignified by such a name, was at the head of Muir Gorge, the narrowest, most twisting and difficult section of the Tuolumne's Grand Canyon.

It took him three more days, until August 12, to reach the flower-waving meadows and friendly groves of Hetch Hetchy, which looked at that time like a miniature Yosemite Valley. He washed himself and his clothes in the river which here flowed calmly, but went supperless to sleep beneath a filigree of oak leaves, iron black against the moon. Breakfast next morning was his last handful of crackers, for his pack had become too much for him coming down Muir Gorge, and he had discarded over half of his supplies.

Early on the fourteenth he started for the nearest settlement, but had been on the trail only a short while when he met two men with pack animals and an

* Linnie Marsh Wolfe, *John of the Mountains*, p. 345.

outfit so complete that they breakfasted in the middle of Hetch Hetchy on a portable table loaded with dishes. The expedition had been undertaken expressly in the hope of meeting Muir. The leader, T. P. Lukens, was a banker and developer from Pasadena. He had joined the Sierra Club and was already committed to the cause of wilderness preservation. The meeting eventually proved one of the more important in Muir's fight to save Yosemite.

Meanwhile Lukens had no trouble in persuading Muir to go back up the Tuolumne as far as the pack animals could make it, thence to the upland, where Muir was delighted to encounter a bevy of "short-skirted girl mountaineers," their faces radiant with happiness as they strode through the forest arches.

Muir remained in the Yosemite area visiting old haunts until early September. Then, once more settled at home, he wrote two significant letters. The first, to his mother, contains a highly perceptive insight into the ways in which, to extend an old saying, the boy fathers the man: "How much I enjoyed this excursion, or indeed any excursion, in the wilderness, I am not able to tell. I must have been born a mountaineer and the climbs and 'scootchers' of boyhood days about the old Dunbar Castle made fair beginnings....I am trying to write another book but that is harder than mountaineering."*

The second letter was to R. U. Johnson and pre-figured Muir's activities during much of the ensuing ten years. "The sheepmen are more than matched by the few troopers in this magnificent park, and the wilderness rejoices in fresh verdure and bloom," he wrote, speaking of the newly-created Yosemite National Park. "Only the Yosemite (Valley) itself is . . . like an abandoned backwoods pasture....

"I have little hope for Yosemite, as long as the management is in the hands of eight politicians (the State Park Commission) appointed by the ever-changing governor of California; there is but little hope. I never saw the Yosemite so frowsy, scrawny, and downtrodden as last August, and the horsemen have begun to inquire, 'Has the Yosemite begun to play out?' "**

The fight to save Yosemite Valley from the laxness, venality and myopia of people who collaborate in the ruin of the beauty they control was, so to speak, in the backyard of John Muir and the Sierra Club.

But from many quarters were coming reports that the nation was losing a bigger fight without putting a single designated defender in the field. The mills were still moaning "like bad ghosts" among the giant redwoods which had been set aside as forest reserves; great bands of sheep were chewing and trampling mountain pastures into wasteland. Everybody, it seemed, from careless campers to the engineers of spark-belching locomotives, were setting fires that could destroy a thousand acres of timber at a gulp. Much of this wanton waste was going on illegally and without hindrance, for no provisions had been made to guard the forest reserves. The contrast between the condition of the reserves, and Yosemite and Yellowstone, the only National

* William F. Badè, *The Life and Letters of John Muir*, Vol. II, pp. 290-1.
** Ibid. pp. 294-5.

Parks then in existence, was both heartbreaking and infuriating.

In the West, John Muir and his Sierra Club friends became increasingly disturbed. In the East, Charles Sprague Sargent and R. U. Johnson — who by a major effort had induced New York's legislature to protect that state's remaining forests — determined that action on a national scale must begin at once. They asked Congress to appoint a commission to investigate the condition of the American forests, especially those in the reserves. But Congress was too much influenced by persons and companies which preferred that the public did not learn what was happening in the forests.

The National Academy of Science, as Sargent well knew, is legally obliged to undertake investigations when requested by the executive branch of government. Sargent therefore asked R. U. Johnson, in whose powers of persuasion he had great confidence, to ask the Secretary of Interior to appoint an investigative forest commission. Johnson met with Hoke Smith, the Secretary of Interior, at 11 p.m. one evening — by one in the morning he had convinced him that such a commission should be formed.*

Charles Sprague Sargent was chairman of the commission of six distinguished scientists which finally set out on its travels in the summer of 1896. Its secretary was young Gifford Pinchot, who had spent several years studying the methods which had developed during generations of forest management in Western Europe. John Muir had been invited to become a member, but had declined because of fatigue and ill health. He even declined to attend the Harvard commencement, where he had been invited to receive an honorary master of arts degree.

Muir's plans were abruptly changed by the third of his extraordinary premonitions, for which he could find no rational explanation but still refused to ascribe to the occult. Science, he believed, would one day find the correct answers.

One morning in June of 1896 it came to him that, if he were to see his mother once more in this life, he must go to Wisconsin at once.

When he opened the gate of Sarah's home in Portage, she rushed down the path crying, "God must have sent you! Mother is terribly ill." Mrs. Muir had been stricken only a few hours earlier with what appears to have been a heart problem. But she rallied under her son's affectionate jollity and the love of the other children whom he had brought with him. Daniel Muir, the physician brother, and the local doctor agreed that it was safe for Muir to go on to Cambridge to receive his degree.

* The main arguments Johnson used — and which he later employed to get from Congress $25,000 for the commission's expenses — came from *The Earth As Modified by Human Action*, a book in which George P. Marsh, diplomat, linguist and scientific observer, showed that the dessication of lands bordering the Mediterranean was largely due to overgrazing by goats and wanton cutting of trees that once clothed the slopes. This book has been called one of the greatest productions by an American. It was certainly an awakener — of Muir as well as of Johnson and a number of other pioneer conservationists. The final U. S. edition was brought out posthumously in 1885. For Johnson's use of Marsh's exposition, see *Remembered Yesterdays*, pp. 292, 298.

Mrs. Muir died while he was absent. John Muir returned for the funeral and spent a few days in visiting old friends: in Indianapolis, the Merrills and Moores who had been so kind to him; in Milwaukee, William Trout, for whose broom-handle and rake mill he had made his first productive inventions thirty years before. Then, in early July, he joined the Forest Commission for its zig-zag journey into the West.

Chapter 52
The Split

By every kind of transportation available — sail, saddle, mule, carriage, ranch wagon, river boat and their own feet, the commissioners traveled northwestward from the Black Hills, across Wyoming to the Big Horn Mountains, thence to the Flathead Reserve in Montana, the Cascade Range of Washington and Oregon, down the length, almost four hundred miles, of the Coast Redwood belt, up through the remaining stands of *Sequoia gigantea* in the Sierra Nevada and on to the Grand Canyon. For Muir especially, it was a journey of ever-changing delights, which made the areas of wanton destruction all the more sickening.

Around Crater Lake in Oregon, sheep had stripped the earth so thoroughly it seemed the ground would be naked forever.* The Commission passed through thousands of acres of charred forest where only the ashes stirred, and hundreds of acres of stumps and other even larger areas littered with trunks that had proved too difficult to get to the mills. Mines were being worked on the floor of the Grand Canyon, and the erosion-checking forests chopped and sawed from the rim.

Sargent and the others went east by way of the new forest reserves in Colorado, to the labor of analyzing their data and developing recommendations. Muir returned to the ranch, but the Commission kept in close touch, sending him memoranda and rough drafts "for criticism and inspiration." Muir in turn consulted frequently with respected members of the Sierra Club. One result of this collaboration was the creation of the Stanislaus National Forest, north of Yosemite.

The main recommendations of the Commission reached President Cleveland in February, 1897, though the formal report was withheld from the general public for several months by Cornelius N. Bliss, Secretary of the Interior. The principal recommendations of the Commission were:

1. The creation of thirteen new reservations distributed among eight western states,
2. The repeal or modification of timber and mining laws leading to fraud and robbery,

---

* Some kinds of plants which had grown there were still absent in the 1930s — twenty-five years after this jewel among mountain lakes had become a national park. See Linnie Marsh Wolfe, *Son of the Wilderness: The Life of John Muir*, p. 271.

3. The scientific management of forests to maintain a permanent timber supply and

4. The creation of two new national parks: the Grand Canyon and Mount Rainier, with adjacent areas.

President Cleveland, whose term of office was nearly over, acted at once. On Washington's birthday, 1897, he created the thirteen new reservations the Commission suggested. They totalled twenty-one million acres. Congress was thrown into a state which William Badè, Muir's friend and literary executor, called a "rogues' panic." During a wild and stormy weekend session in which the "dreamy Harvard professors" and the "nature fakers" who had engineered this dastardly deed were reviled in language smelling of barnyard and corral, the Congress tried to impeach Grover Cleveland. Failing to muster enough votes for this, the legislators tacked onto the Civil Sundry Bill an amendment which annulled all the reserves Cleveland had created.

In May under William McKinley, the new president, a special session of Congress voted to suspend creating the reserves of Cleveland's executive order until March, 1898. There was one exception: at the request of California's senators, the forest reserves in that state were left untouched. The senators in making this request reflected the attitude of their constituents, for Californians had begun to understand that, in their situation, the relation between trees and water was a life and death matter. The Sierra Club sent a memorandum of thanks to the senators. Elsewhere, mining, lumbering and stock-grazing interests rushed in to grab land in the suspended reserves while the grabbing was good.*

Most of the nation's conservationists were extremely discouraged. Yet on the West Coast the Sierra Club was still growing rapidly, and here and there throughout the country new friends of the wilderness were adding their influence to the fight to save it. One of these was Walter Hines Page, editor of the *Atlantic Monthly*, which, at the time, seems to have been the most influential publication in the United States. Page asked Muir to write some articles on the wilderness, its values and its preservation.

The first of these pieces, "The American Forests," was finished in time for Muir to attend commencement at the University of Wisconsin, where he received the degree of Doctor of Law. He then joined Sargent and a companionable botanist named Canby for a tour of the forests of western Canada and a run up to Alaska where the rush to the Klondike gold fields was in full hysteria.

They went on the *Queen*, famous in her day as the first steamer to approach Muir Glacier. Aboard the *Queen*, Muir encountered Hall Young on his way with a party of missionaries to attend the spiritual needs of the gold rushers.

* Holway R. Jones thinks that this legislation not only gave limited permission to exploit, but also accomplished some necessary good: 1) it established the principle that land in national forests could not be sold, though trees might be, 2) set forth a statement of purposes of the forest reserves and 3) authorized the Secretary of the Interior to protect the national forests. See *John Muir and the Sierra Club: The Battle for Yosemite*, p. 172.

The two tramped the decks late each night, reminiscing and renewing acquaintance. At Wrangell the "Sky Chief" and the "Ice Chief" were warmly remembered.

The Chilcats had been overwhelmed, and the *Queen* took her passengers fifteen miles farther up the Lynn Canal than they had dared venture in their canoe voyage of 1879, to that "new, chaotic camp in the woods called Skagway" — to use Young's words.

While the *Queen* discharged her cargo, the tree botanists explored the woods. Muir had reluctantly decided that, by advising prospective gold-seekers of the difficulties that lay ahead and the need to conserve their energy for the harder going, he might do some good. The sight of men by the hundreds, sliding, falling and crawling up the muddy and rocky pass leading to the Yukon's headwaters, was much more like Charlie Chaplin's "The Gold Rush" than Jack London's hero tales.

Muir therefore wrote a few short articles at the earnest request of the Hearst publications. But he was not too occupied to eat a last meal, a delicious one such as Hall Young delighted to cook, in the missionary's lonely camp under a hemlock tree.

In August, 1897, the botanists arrived in Seattle, which was now swollen by the gold rush to twice its previous size. Here in a hotel lobby Muir encountered Gifford Pinchot, a few minutes after reading in a newspaper Pinchot's statement that sheep did no harm in the mountains where they were taken to graze. Not realizing that the men standing near Pinchot were reporters, Muir strode up to him with his finger marking the offending item.

"Have they quoted you correctly here?" The ears of every reporter were hanging well out, and Pinchot could not deny his words. He admitted that the quotation was correct.

"Then," Muir said, and the blaze in his eyes told far more of his feelings than his words, "I don't want any more to do with you. Last summer when we were in the Cascades you agreed that sheep do a great deal of harm!"

This episode was the small fracture which widened into a serious division among people engaged in the effort to save the forests. Some writers, notably Holway Jones, have found it useful to distinguish them into "conservationists," i.e., those who followed Pinchot in believing that the resources of trees, water and minerals in the national forests were the only reasons for government protection, and "preservationists," those who believed with Muir that a wilderness is worth saving for itself. The very words express a different outlook. A "conservationist" in the Pinchot sense was concerned with the material utility of the earth, the "preservationist" with the earth as environment. These differences inevitably produced a divergence in attitude. The "conservationist" assumed that man is destined to be master of the earth — perhaps the universe — and thus is entitled to use it in any way he thinks will benefit him. The "preservationist" felt himself to be a mere citizen of the earth, entitled only to share it with other living things permitted to dwell here.

When Muir reached the ranch at Martinez he was distressed to find Louie

Wanda's mother very ill and sinking rapidly toward her death two weeks later. Muir had never feared death and did not fear it now. But the passing of his loved ones depressed him and he investigated the psychic research which was then being vigorously pursued by some able minds. These studies simply took him back to the beliefs he had held since early manhood. "At the bottom (of psychic phenomena under whatever names) there is . . . a basis of truth, founded on natural laws which perhaps some day we may discover."*

The *Atlantic Monthly* published Muir's "The American Forests" in the August, 1897, issue. Linnie Marsh Wolfe says "He performed the remarkable feat of sublimating a government document (the Forestry Report) into literature," and in doing so went over the heads of congressmen to get the message to the "common people."**

In this instance Mrs. Wolfe forgot that relatively few of the "common people" could read in 1897, and that of the literate only the intellectual elite and their imitators were likely to read the *Atlantic*. But Muir's article had a "ripple effect" that went far beyond its immediate audience. It has been much praised for its eloquence, and indeed there are some passages that read like hymns to forest trees. There are passages of eloquent anger, such as the one in which he suggests that the railroads, instead of advertising that a route is the most scenic, should claim that its route is the blackest, ashiest and most burned out — "the route of superior devastation." Some passages are almost apocalyptic.***

It seems likely, however, that, more than his eloquence, two other qualities made "The American Forests" extraordinarily effective. One is the balance he maintains throughout. Of course, he says, the railroads have to cut passageways through the forest — but they should use the timber they cut rather than leaving it on the ground to feed fires set by the spark-belching engines. "No place is too good for good men," he says. "Let them be free to use the American earth for homes and bread. Nor will the woods be the worse for this use, or their benign influence be diminished any more than the sun is diminished by shining. Mere destroyers, however, tree-killers — let the government hasten to cast them out and make an end of them."****

The second quality that gave "The American Forests" special effectiveness was the clear and cogent use of both statistical and physical evidence. Muir shows, for example, that the United States had sold for $2.50 an acre

---

* From a paper called "Mysterious Things," quoted in *Son of the Wilderness: The Life of John Muir*, by Linnie Marsh Wolfe, p. 277.

** Ibid., p. 273

*** "Thoreau...said that the country would soon be so bald that every man would have to grow whiskers to hide his nakedness, but he thanked God that at least the sky was safe. Had he gone West he would have found out that the sky was not safe: for all through the summer months, over most of the mountain regions, the smoke of mill and forest fires is so thick and black no sunbeams can pierce it, the whole sky with clouds, sun, moon and stars is simply blotted out. There is no real sky and no scenery." See *Our National Parks* by John Muir, pp. 356-357.

**** Ibid., p. 363.

thousands of square miles of land covered by trees worth up to one thousand dollars each. Yet in spite of this prodigality the nation still had some seventy million acres of timberland in the public domain. In support of his contention that railroads were outrageously reckless along their rights of way, he recalls seeing with his own eyes five fires along a stretch of three miles.

"The American Forests" re-animated the friends of the wilderness and greatly extended their base of public support. Giffort Pinchot, who was an even better politician than he was a forester, was very rapidly achieving great influence among the decision-makers in Washington. In spite of their unpleasantness in Seattle, Pinchot wrote Muir in December, 1897, asking his help and that of the Sierra Club in planning new forest reservations. He wanted Muir to draw on an official map the outlines of any areas of government forest land not yet reserved, but which should be included. Devastated lands should be included "because the government alone can protect them and secure their return to usefulness."*

Muir complied, but less than a month later the *Atlantic Monthly* published a second piece by him entitled "The Wild Parks and Forest Reservations of the West." From this distance in time it seems a benign invitation to enjoy one's self as a natural human being.

"Thousands of tired, nerve-shaken, over-civilized people are beginning to find out that going to the mountains is going home, that wilderness is a necessity and that mountain parks and reservations are useful not only as fountains of timber and irrigating rivers, but as fountains of life. Awakening from the stupefying effects of the vice of over-industry and the deadly apathy of luxury, they are trying as best they can to enrich their own little outgoings with those of Nature and to get rid of dust and disease.... This is fine and natural and full of promise. So is the growing interest in the care and preservation of forests and wild places in general, and in the half-wild parks and gardens of towns. Even the scenery habit in its most artificial forms, mixed with spectacles, silliness and Kodaks, its devotees arrayed more gorgeously than scarlet tanagers — even this is encouraging...."**

When this piece came out, people interpreted it as a "bold attack" on Pinchot's utilitarian policies toward the forest reserves. Cooperation between the two men ceased, though nearly ten years were to pass before their differences reappeared to fuel one of the most furious fights in the embattled history of conservation.

Meanwhile Muir had his hands full with the fight to secure recession of Yosemite Valley to the United States in order to save it from neglect and exploitation under the California State Park Commission. He scarcely had time to feel happy that the "Wild Parks" article had been enthusiastically received and had increased *Atlantic's* circulation "enormously" according to its editor, who later became U. S. Ambassador to Britain. For the nation it is more important that the article was an effective influence upon the House of

---

* Holway R. Jones, *John Muir and the Sierra Club*, p. 18.
** John Muir, *Our National Parks*, pp. 1, 2.

Representatives, which voted (in effect) to restore permanently to the public the twenty-one million acres of forest reserves set aside by Grover Cleveland. The vote was 100 to 39.

Muir was never able to grind away at his desk for more than a few months at a stretch without becoming fed up, weary and irritable from bronchial attacks. In early June, 1898, he took off for Mt. Shasta to look for the blossoms of the red cedar. Sargent needed them for *Silva of North America* illustrations and could find none in any known collection. In a week of floundering through deep snows Muir failed to find the flowers; bitter frost the year before had killed both cones and leaf buds. But Muir had an informal network of forest friends who kept him informed of what was going on up and down the Sierra. A few weeks later he got perfect specimens from the summits above Lake Tahoe.

Sargent was delighted. He had finished the eleventh volume of his *Silva of North America*, which he dedicated to Muir. (Muir was gratified and praised the work but added that a line or two of Mother Earth poetry in no way

"...floundering through deep snows."

weakens or blurs the necessarily dry, stubbed, scientific description.)

Sargent now proposed that they ramble southward through the Appalachians, surveying the forests as they went. Canby, the botanist who had been in Alaska with them and who had addressed Muir as "Old Streak-of-Lightning-on-Ice," planned the trip, enticing Muir with promises of beautiful views.

They set out in September of 1898, travelling through a rippling wonder of fall foliage. Muir was definitely feeling his age; he wrote home proudly that he could walk ten miles and not be tired, a comedown from the Muir who walked a thousand horizontal Sierra miles and nearly that many vertical miles in one short summer. Nevertheless he felt free and happy, exulting in the experience. Reminiscing about a climb to the summit of a commanding peak, he reported his defense against the reserved scientific friends who were put off by his uninhibited enthusiasm:

"I couldn't hold in, and began to jump about and sing and glory in it all. Then I happened to look around and catch sight of Sargent, standing there as cool as a rock, with a half-amused look on his face at me, but never saying a word.

" 'Why don't you let yourself out at a sight like that?' I asked.

" 'I don't wear my heart on my sleeve,' he retorted.

" 'Who cares where you wear your little heart, mon!' I cried. 'There you stand in the face of all Heaven come down to earth, like a critic of the universe, as if to say, 'Come, Nature, bring on the best you have. I'm from Boston!' "

The trip ended in Florida when Muir spent a couple of days finding and reminiscing with the family that had nursed him when he lay at death's door, at the end of his thousand-mile walk from Indiana to the Gulf of Mexico.

Returning to the ranch in December, 1898, he plunged into the effort to sort out and synthesize his Yosemite notes for a book. He had sent off one article to the *Atlantic* and gotten the rest of the material almost in hand when he was diverted by an invitation he was unable to resist.

Chapter 53
Harriman and Roosevelt Become Muir's Allies

$\boxed{A}$ transportation magnate named Edward Henry Harriman — one of the wealthiest and most powerful men of his time — had fallen ill. To complete his recovery, he was advised to forget business for a while. It occurred to Harriman to accomplish this by surrounding himself with scholars and scientists whose main interests were in truth and the well-being of mankind, rather than in making money. They would divert his mind (a very good one) and provide unusual educational opportunities for his children and young relatives.

He selected a small, seaworthy passenger steamer from the fleet of one of the lines he owned and invited a large party of savants, many of them first rate, to go on a cruise in Alaskan waters. He had the ship fitted up with a library and laboratories and equipped with such instruments as the scientists wanted. One objective was scientific observation of little-known areas, another was big-game hunting.

Muir left his Yosemite book reluctantly but, as he wrote to friends, some day before he died he would have to see Kodiak Island and the wild, deeply-fiorded coast north of the entrance to Glacier Bay.

When the *George W. Elder* left Seattle on the last day of May, 1899, she had 126 souls aboard, including crew: 23 assorted scientists, an already-famous photographer and three artists; Mr. and Mrs. Harriman and the latter's sister, Mrs. Averill, with her husband; four teenage girls — two of them Harriman daughters, one an Averill, and a friend named Dorothea Draper; two preschool children and seven-year-old Averill Harriman, the future ambassador and expert on the Soviet Union, U. S. cabinet officer and governor of New York. In addition, the ship carried a few cronies of Mr. Harriman who planned to hunt big game with him.

The hunting, however, began with setting ninety small traps in which the scientists caught five mice and one toad at a Taku Indian Village on the Lynn Canal. At Skagway Muir found Hall Young, who was spending a laborious month transporting supplies over the mountains to Lake Bennett. From here Young's party of missionaries planned to voyage, in a thirty-foot open boat, some two thousand miles down the Yukon River to the Pacific.

At Muir's suggestion Harriman urgently invited Young to come on the *Elder* expedition. But Young's conscience would not permit him to abandon his professional enterprise.

The *Elder* steamed to Glacier Bay, and a party immediately went off to hunt the wolves Muir had seen at "Howling Valley" eleven years earlier. He did not accompany the hunters, but took three of the older girls up Muir Glacier to a nunatak. The youngsters, already awed by the majestic ice river and enchanted by the shimmering blue grottoes, were emotionally overwhelmed when a "rampart" two hundred feet long fell from the glacier's face, disappeared beneath the flock of floes, then leaped one hundred fifty feet into the air. Muir had hurried the girls to a high slope, safe from the surging berg waves.

Next morning the *Elder*'s scientists broke up into specialized parties: some to collect birds' eggs and bird skins to be stuffed at leisure, some to dredge the chill waters for minute marine life, some to trap animal specimens and others to botanize. Henry Gannett, chief geographer of the U. S. Geological Survey, mapped the positions of the glaciers as they found them, and Edward S. Curtis, the famous photographer of Indians, photographed the termini of many of these ice rivers. Together with data and photographs obtained by Muir and the small group he led, Gannett's maps and Curtis' pictures proved the most definite scientific accomplishments of the expedition. But their importance was not realized until some weeks after everyone had gone home — and then only because of a totally unexpected and dramatic cataclysm of nature.

Meanwhile the *Elder* had worked her way northward for nearly a month. Though she dropped off parties on uninhabited islands and desolate shores and picked them up again at agreed-upon times, not very much of scientific importance was accomplished. The only discovery was Muir's, and that was geographical.

The *Elder* had been poking around in Prince William Sound, a complex body of water with many fiords, which indents the south-facing segment where the Alaskan coast trends out toward the Aleutians.* Some of the fiords. were, of course, occupied by glaciers still in the act of carving them.

Just inside the mouth of one that seemed to be open, the *Elder*'s way was abruptly blocked by a wall of rock and ice. The Alaskan captain they had taken on as pilot refused to go farther, saying that he was not about to take the ship into every frog pond, and this was too dangerous.

From the pattern of ice and rock, Muir judged that they would find a passage farther west. Harriman therefore displaced the pilot, and Muir conned the ship into a heretofore undiscovered fiord which proved to be fifteen miles long. Five glaciers never before seen were discharging bergs into it. Harriman was greatly excited, both by the adventure and by being a party to the discovery of a new segment of the earth.** Muir, exercising his right of discovery, named both the fiord and one of the glaciers for the expedition's

* One of the termini of the Alaskan pipeline is on Prince William Sound, at Port Valdez.
** For Muir's account of the discovery of Harriman Fiord, see George Kennan's *Edward Henry Harriman*, Vol. I, p. 450.

patron, thus furthering his developing friendship with Harriman and putting that powerful man somewhat in his debt.

Women and girls, from "two-year-old philosophers" to "lily grandmothers," delighted John Muir most of all earth's creatures. And at sixty-one Muir had not lost his attraction for those whom the Victorians called "the fair sex." It was inevitable that strong ties of affection would develop between Muir and the Harriman-Averill females, who were a vigorous, high-spirited, adventurous lot, well endowed with fortitude. It was a familial sort of relationship of the kind that often develops through sharing rugged outdoor experiences. Plenty of such were to be had as the *Elder* zig-zagged northward through the Bering Sea.

At the trip's northernmost reach, they touched on the Siberian coast just below Bering Strait, then crossed over to Port Clarence on the Alaskan side. Here the ship's boats went ashore for water, and the women and children decided to come also to stretch their legs on land. As Muir tells the story in his journal:

"Had a hard surfy landing, and to get into the boat again the ladies and children had to be carried through the surf. It was a sight to see the demolishment of dignity and neat propriety....It was difficult getting aboard; the ladies and children had to climb a rope ladder on the lee side, the boat dancing and wobbling awfully for landlubbers....*

From Port Clarence the *Elder* headed for Seattle, accomplishing some minimal investigations at points along the way. Muir was considerably disappointed with the results of so elaborate an effort. On July 19 he wrote in his journal:

"We had a long talk about book-making, with much twaddle about a grand scientific 'monument' of the trip, etc....Much ado about little....Game hunting, the chief aim, has been unsuccessful. The rest of the story will be mere reconnaissance."** After Muir reached home, he wrote Hall Young that he wished he could have escaped the elegant steamer and gone on a canoe trip with his old companion. (Young had wintered at Nome, fifteen hundred miles from the nearest post office. He received Muir's letter in June, 1900, some eight months after it was mailed.)

It seems probable that the "reconnaissance" of the *Elder* and her great variety of scientists provided a necessary basis for the more intensive studies in Alaska that have been made since and are still continuing. A more dramatic justification occurred only a few weeks after Muir reached home. On September 10, 1899, an earthquake of unusual and lethal violence racked the Glacier Bay area. All of the adjacent ice masses were altered and Muir Glacier was changed beyond recognition. Glacier Bay was so filled with floating ice that no boat could enter it for two weeks. Muir Glacier is still

* Linnie Marsh Wolfe, *John of the Mountains*, p. 409.

** The "monument" turned out to be a set of twelve volumes entitled *The Harriman Alaska Expedition*, in which Muir's contribution is entitled "Pacific Coast Glaciers." The quotation is from *John of the Mountains*, p. 413.

wondrous, still beautiful, but it will never again look the same as when Muir saw it.

Muir's final observations in 1899, together with Henry Gannett's precise maps of the glacier fronts and the documentary photographs taken by G. K. Gilbert and Edward Curtis, provide a precise reference point for the studies which are still going on of the havoc wrought by glaciers when they advance and the land life that follows them in ecological succession when they retreat.*

Important friendships begun on the expedition were soon cemented by visits to the ranch. C. Hart Merriam, Chief of the U. S. Biological Survey, was a house guest; Henry Gannett, Chief Geographer of the U. S. Geological Survey, spent a couple of days. Captain Doran of the *Elder* came with his wife for a pleasant visit, unmarred by any presentiment that the Captain would shortly be drowned at sea.

In June of 1900 Muir sent off his contribution to the "monument," recounting the adventures and scientific gatherings of the Harriman expedition. He was pushing along toward completion of the ten *Atlantic* articles, published in 1901 as *Our National Parks*. The development of the Sierra Club, which now had almost five hundred members, gave him considerable relief and a great deal of pleasure. At the board meetings, it frequently happened that Muir and George Davidson would fall to reminiscing about their Alaskan experiences, with the result that the members who were present listened, simply enthralled, and no work got done.**

Muir and Davidson did not always see eye to eye. One important matter on which they disagreed was the recession of Yosemite Valley to the United States government. Both Muir and his allies were gradually winning over most of the Sierra Club's members to the necessity of making all the Yosemite region one national park. In 1897 a resolution empowering the governor of California to return the Valley to federal control had been introduced in the state legislature at the insistence of Theodore P. Lukens, the Pasadena banker who, several years earlier, had packed into Hetch Hetchy purely in the hope of meeting Muir.

This resolution got nowhere, but Lukens in the south and other Sierra Club members in the San Francisco region organized associations to bring pressure to bear on the legislature. Moreover, in 1900, William Colby was elected recording secretary, a post he was to hold for forty-six years. He has been described as "indefatigable," and the record makes this seem an understatement. He was in the forefront of every battle the Sierra Club fought — Muir's trusted and indispensable lieutenant until the latter's death. Colby

---

* See Dave Bohn, *Glacier Bay*, pp. 71-72, and comments on Glacier Bay ecology scattered throughout the book.

** In 1867 George Davidson made the survey of Alaskan resources which was largely responsible for the purchase of that territory by the United States. From 1867 to 1887 he was in charge of all the work of the survey on the Pacific Coast, including Alaska. His directing mind resulted in the classic *Pacific Coast Pilot* and the *Alaska Pilot*. He was also an astronomer of note.

also greatly expanded the Sierra Club's function as disseminator of vital information through the respected *Bulletin* and special publications, including those calling members' attention to legislation requiring support or opposition.

Among the most important of the friendships Muir developed during the Harriman Alaska expedition was that of C. Hart Merriam, whose studies of life zones made him an important contributor to the development of ecology. It was Merriam who first told Muir — in October of 1901, barely a month after the assassination of McKinley had elevated Theodore Roosevelt to the nation's highest office — that the new president wanted to talk with men who knew at first hand how America's forests were being wiped out by sheepmen and other exploiters. Roosevelt was the archetype of the romantic outdoorsmen of his time; he had spent a number of years on his ranch in North Dakota; he owed his popularity not a little to having organized and led a regiment of cowboys called the "Rough Riders" during the Spanish American War. He was also intellectually gifted and dedicated to vigorous reform.

Very early in his administration, Roosevelt backed his secretary of interior against formidable opposition in opening a very smelly can, not exactly of worms, but an octopus-like organization whose tentacles were fraudulent operations, greedily grasping mining rights, grazing lands and, most of all, timber throughout the western states. Among those eventually indicted were senators, congressmen and judges, as well as prominent bureaucrats and executives of lumber, livestock and mining syndicates, giving proof of Muir's ironical report of the situation in "The American Forests," which appeared in the *Atlantic Monthly* for August, 1897. "The outcries we hear against forest reservations come mostly from thieves who are wealthy and steal timber by wholesale. They have so long been allowed to steal and destroy in peace that any impediment to forest robbery is denounced as a cruel and irreligious interference with 'vested rights.' "*

In the spring of 1902, the President himself wrote, saying that he would be in San Francisco in May and wished to go camping with Muir. "I want to drop politics absolutely for four days," he said, "and just be out in the open with you."**

Though the politicians and hangers-on who had tagged Roosevelt to Yosemite wished to prevent them, Muir and the President spent three nights together in the open, the first under the giant redwoods of the Mariposa Grove. The next night they camped on Glacier Point, high above Yosemite Valley, lying on the fern and flower and cedar bough beds Muir loved to make. When they had cooked and eaten their supper of beefsteak, Muir, who loved spectacular campfires as much as he hated forest fires set by the careless and the greedy, lit off a dead pine standing in safe isolation on rocky ground.

Roosevelt was as uninhibited an enthusiast as Muir. As the great torch blazed against the dark, he shouted, "This is bully! Hurrah for Yosemite!" And

* Linnie Marsh Wolfe, *Son of the Wilderness: The Life of John Muir*, pp. 290 et seq.
** John Muir, *Our National Parks*, pp. 360-361.

in the morning, when they found themselves blanketed with four inches of snow, he jumped up exclaiming once again, "This is bullier!"

Late next afternoon they entered the Valley from the upper end. A celebration with fireworks and lights playing on Yosemite Falls had been prepared for the President and a photographic studio converted into an elegant bedroom. He refused all artificial entertainment and camped with Muir in the open at the foot of El Capitan, where the fading light turned the granite into a palette of pastels.

Muir had done most of the talking, filling in the President on the grim realities of wilderness destruction which Roosevelt knew about only at second and third hand, spelling out the critical need to protect the watersheds, doing his best to convert Roosevelt from thinking of the mountains and prairies as hunting preserves, turning him toward a fuller realization of their healing

"Muir had done most of the talking, filling in the President on the grim realities of wilderness destruction...."

peace-giving, spirit-lifting values for man.

This trip was the beginning of a friendship between the two which was to prove somewhat undependable, though it lasted the rest of Muir's life. Its immediate effect was to convince Roosevelt that measures to preserve the wilderness must be undertaken at once. Before leaving the state, he said in a speech in Sacramento: "No small part of the prosperity of California...depends upon the preservation of her water supply.... We are not building this country of ours for a day. It is to last through the ages."*

Roosevelt was, above all, a man who acted on his convictions: during the remaining years of his presidency, he set aside 148 million acres of new national forests, more than three times the territory reserved by the three preceding presidents. His influence pushed Congress into doubling the number of national parks (by creating five new ones) and passing the "Monuments and Antiquities Act," which authorizes the President to create national monuments by proclamation. Roosevelt created twenty-three, including the Grand Canyon of the Colorado.

To camp with Roosevelt, Muir had postponed the start of a long-planned trip around the world with Charles Sprague Sargent and his son. They left in May, 1903, exhausted themselves in the museums of Paris and Moscow, toured the forests of Russia and Finland and crossed to the Pacific on the trans-Siberian railway — a long, hard journey in the coaches of that day. Muir had been desperately ill in western Russia and arrived in Manchuria suffering from a serious case of ptomaine.

At Shanghai he left the Sargents. They wanted to visit inland China, then hurry home. Muir set out alone and happy, for he always became restless when forced to conform to the wishes and necessities of travel companions. He began a zig-zag journey with a look at the Himalayas which then took him to Egypt, Australia, New Zealand, the Philippines, Japan, Hawaii and home on one of Harriman's ships, where he was treated like royalty. He had been gone a year. In spite of his illnesses during the trip, the sea had restored him. He arrived so well-filled out that his family teased him, though he still weighed less than one hundred fifty pounds.

He needed all the health and strength he had accumulated. Mismanagement of Yosemite Valley had become a national scandal, and the sentiment for returning it to the federal government, so that it would be integrated with the National Park which now surrounded it, had gathered effective strength.

The Sierra Club was the spearhead. Muir therefore asked young William Colby, who was a lawyer, to draw up an appropriate measure.

Colby's bill was introduced to the state legislature in January, 1905. Opposition was ferocious — both by people who genuinely felt that California would lose prestige by giving up Yosemite, as well as by lobbyists for interests entrenched in the Valley, who were enriching themselves by exploiting it. So formidable was the reaction in the legislature that it appeared the bill might

* Linnie Marsh Wolfe, *Son of the Wilderness: The Life of John Muir,* pp. 293-294.

lose, even though most Californians were in favor of it. Muir and Colby made nine trips to appear before legislative and committee sessions, and the Sierra Club promoted a barrage of letters. Muir as a last resort asked the help of Harriman who, as president of the Southern Pacific Railroad, was the most potent political force in the state. Harriman's behind-the-scenes influence was decisive. In February, 1905, the bill passed the senate by one vote, having already cleared the assembly by a comfortable margin.

Muir wrote immediately to R. U. Johnson when news of the narrow victory arrived. He credited Johnson with being the "commanding general," though he and Colby had carried most of the burden and endured the boredom of opposition oratory — "fluffy, nebulous, howling, threatening like sand storms in the desert."

"I am an experienced lobbyist," he claimed. "My political education is complete....And now that the fight is finished...I am almost finished myself."*

Neither the fight nor Muir were anywhere near finished. Though the United States Senate promptly and enthusiastically agreed to accept the return of Yosemite Valley to federal control, some curious maneuvers in the House precipitated a wrangle that continued fitfully, month after month throughout 1905, with no resolution in sight.

* William F. Badè, *The Life and Letters of John Muir*, Vol. II, p. 355.

Chapter 54
Death, Disaster, Discovery

I n the spring of 1905 Muir's daughter, Helen, suffered one of her recurrent bouts with pneumonia. Her recovery was so slow that a specialist insisted that she must live on the desert for some time.

In May Helen's father and elder sister, not realizing that Louie Wanda, whose health had been precarious for some years, was in greater peril, took Helen to the high desert of eastern Arizona. They had expected to camp out on a large ranch near the town of Wilson, but arrived in a driving rain and the rancher insisted that they make themselves comfortable in his large, Mexican-style ranch house, surely one of the most hospitable kinds of dwelling ever developed.

Muir with Louie Wanda and their two daughters, Annie Wanda (left) and Helen, on the porch of their Lower Ranch home in Martinez.

In the dry, bracing air, free of the allergens that made both Helen and John Muir so miserable at home beside Carquinez Strait, both gained health and strength rapidly. But they had been in Arizona barely a month when a telegram brought them home to Louie Wanda's bedside.

She died of lung cancer on August 6, 1905. They laid her beside her parents in the generous soil of the ranch in Alhambra Valley.

Muir was devastated far beyond the ordinary grief which his associates recognized. Louie Wanda, career wife and mother, had been so retiring that few appreciated her excellent mind and strength of character upon which he had leaned throughout their married life of twenty-five years.

For more than a year after her death, he scarcely wrote a line for publication, though he was greatly pressed for articles and books.

His usual good fortune, together with his insatiable desire to know, reprieved him. After Louie Wanda's death he returned to the Arizona desert with Helen, and with Annie Wanda, the eldest daughter, to take care of them. The girls, both superior horsewomen, spent a great deal of their time riding in the beautiful environment which is a continuation of the Painted Desert. When Muir could muster the strength, he rode with them.

On one of these rides, he came to a plateau where the loose, tawny desert soil was strewn with large tree trunks with no apparent business being there. No forest grew within many miles. Besides, the trunks had turned to solid stone of a spectacular shade of blue. Exploring the vicinity Muir also found what are now called the Black Forest, the Rainbow Forest, the Crystal Forest and the Jasper Forest. These stone logs gave Muir a new and absorbing interest. He nevertheless returned to the ranch to keep up his correspondence and maintain contact with associates in the never-ending struggle to save some of the wilderness.

Congress was still wrangling as to whether to accept Yosemite Valley, now that California wished to return it. There were other threats: a railway was being built up the Merced Canyon to Yosemite; in 1905 the Yosemite Park boundaries had been changed to cut out some twenty thousand acres, most of them from the southwest corner; Mount Ritter and the Minarets were also eliminated. It appeared that if everyone got the land he wanted, there would be no park left.

For months Muir escaped his worries, his grief and his loneliness by burying himself in the geologic past when the stone trees had been a living forest. He spent several days each week in Berkeley at the University of California library.

"I sit silent and alone," he wrote Helen, "from morn to eve in the deeper silence of the enchanted old forests of the coal age. Glorious for the imagination...but tough for the old paleontological body now nearing seventy...."

But there was really no way to escape from the present. At 5 a.m. of April 18, 1906, San Francisco was rocked by the most damaging earthquake the United States had felt since the first settlers arrived in our country from Europe.

Stoves had been lighted in the cheaply and poorly constructed wooden homes of the manual laborers' families who made up the bulk of the city's 400,000 people. The houses collapsed into kindling which caught fire and in many cases trapped the occupants amid the flames. The gas works exploded, and the dislocated water mains burst. When the fire finally burned out three days later, 315 bodies were recovered from the debris, but 352 persons remained unaccounted for. The center of the city, made up of 28,188 buildings, was now rubble.

John Muir lost neither property nor friends; the earthquake altered the shape of his life because of San Francisco's need for water. Since the Gold Rush the frantically growing city on its sandy peninsula had lived in fear of going thirsty and in anger against the Spring Valley Water Company, a monopoly which gouged the citizens remorselessly.

In 1901 a financier named James D. Phelan, who was mayor of San Francisco, had surveys made and filed claims for the rights to make reservoirs of the beautiful Tuolumne Meadows above and slightly northeast of Yosemite Valley, along with Hetch Hetchy Valley, a natural reservoir site where the Tuolumne Gorge widens out to form a smaller version of Yosemite Valley, as well as Lake Eleanor on the Tuolumne watershed northwest of Hetch Hetchy, but still inside Yosemite National Park.

To Muir the plan to drown Hetch Hetchy beneath 175 feet of water was an outrage against the people of the nation. From his explorations he was certain that there were several other sources from which San Francisco could get plenty of water and that it was cruelly unnecessary to obliterate one of Nature's loveliest creations. Moreover to use these areas for utilitarian purposes would violate not only one major national park, but endanger all national parks by setting a precedent contrary to the basic objective for which Congress had founded them: to retain unmodified, beautiful wilderness areas in which Americans could meet Nature face to face.

Phelan's application had been denied by E. A. Hitchcock, Theodore Roosevelt's first Secretary of Interior, in early 1903, on the grounds that it violated the law reserving the park for public enjoyment and recreation. Hitchcock denied it again in December, 1903, and once more in 1905, though Phelan had turned over to the city and county of San Francisco the rights that might be secured on the renewal of his application.

In the days following the earthquake, when citizens were straining at the herculean task of clearing away the debris of the city they had loved, and were still looking for the remains of their loved ones, San Franciscans were on the verge of hysteria concerning water. Taking advantage of the emotional situation, Phelan made a public declaration that there would have been plenty of water to fight the earthquake fire if his application had been approved promptly. Secretary Garfield sent the head of the U. S. Patent Office to San Francisco, where he learned what nearly everyone who had actually fought the fire already knew: the supply of water had been adequate, but most of it flowed uselessly off to make mud when the pipes were ruptured by the violent movement of the earth. Moreover, a Hetch Hetchy water system, even if construction had started the day Phelan's application was first received, could not have delivered water until many years after the earthquake.

Muir was aware that Pinchot was encouraging Phelan and his associates in San Francisco to press for permission to dam Hetch Hetchy, and that Pinchot, now Chief Forester and head of the Forest Service (created in 1905 out of the former Bureau of Forestry), had achieved great power — partly because the organization he was developing to manage the forests had grown increasingly effective, and partly because of his belief that wilderness resources should be made to yield all the material benefits possible, while still conserving their ability to produce. This philosophy was politically advantageous because it won the support of all who saw profit in exploiting the resources within the national forests.

Pinchot was a force to be reckoned with. Moreover, Phelan and his associates had managed very quietly to slip through Congress a law permitting the building in national parks of aqueducts, pipelines, tunnels, dams — all the devices necessary to the impounding and transportation of water. Muir, however, was not yet particularly worried about the fate of Hetch Hetchy. Other problems demanded the immediate use of his strength.

Congress had now been wrangling for more than year over the simple matter of taking back Yosemite Valley. There was increasing risk that the debates would go on so long that the agreement to recede the Valley would lapse. Muir and his associates were unable to muster enough votes to accomplish acceptance.

In the late spring of 1906, Muir again called upon Harriman for help; Harriman's influence proved to be as great in Washington as in California. Theodore Roosevelt and some influential senators also leaned on their Capitol Hill colleagues. On June 11, after a struggle of seventeen years, Yosemite Valley became a part of Yosemite National Park.

Muir had also been writing to his influential friends, including President Roosevelt, urging the passage of a bill (introduced by Congressman John F. Lacey) empowering the President to set aside, for preservation and public use, "American antiquities" and features of scientific or historical interest situated upon land owned or controlled by the federal government. Ever since Roosevelt signed the Antiquities and Monuments Act on June 10, 1906, it has been enormously useful in preserving our national heritage.

Muir was incensed that, on hearing of his discovery of the petrified forest, certain predatory railroad interests began hauling away the gem-like logs, shipping them by carloads to workshops where they were hacked and carved into gewgaws to sell to tourists. He began urging Roosevelt to make a national monument of the petrified forest, a move the President seemed in no hurry to make.

Helen's health had improved greatly, and Muir began dreaming about the happy life he and his daughters could lead together in "the big house." He had not reckoned with Wanda's popularity, nor understood that she was one of those girls who hesitate to be put "into their mother trade."

One of Wanda's sorority sisters was Angeline Stansbury, daughter of a pioneer physician in Chico, the town that had developed upon a piece of General Bidwell's ranch up the Sacramento. The two girls visited frequently in one another's homes. Angeline Stansbury told her nephew, Frederick Stansbury Clough, that, in the lingering light of early evening, eligible young men of Chico ("swains," in the usage of that time) gathered in front of the Stansbury home, calling politely but loudly, "Wanda! Wanda!" They would not give up until she had appeared at an upstairs window for a session of small talk.

In any case, Wanda did not intend to become a career daughter and sister-caretaker. In June, 1906, she returned abruptly to the ranch and married Thomas Rae Hanna, a young engineer to whom she had become engaged at the University of California. They set up housekeeping in the venerable adobe dwelling built by the original grantee of the ranch.*

Helen's health had improved more rapidly than expected. She came home in August. With her companionship to cheer him, together with the devotion of Wanda and Muir's sister Margaret, now living in the house where John and Louie Wanda had begun their married life, and with a remarkably capable Chinese houseman to take care of the ordinary routines of living, Muir's life became more cheerful. To further conserve his energies for the effort to save the forests, he employed a business manager. For further companionship he also had John Swett, the most stable and perceptive of his old friends, who had bought the ranch just up the Alhambra Valley from Muir's own.

Though Helen's impulsive and unconventional ways shocked her Aunt Maggie, she played the hostess well. Visitors came from far and near as before her mother's death, and candlelit dinners and evenings in the light of an open fire glowing in the semi-darkness of the living room (the house had no electricity) became once more memorable as Muir rambled from one enthralling yarn to the next.

From babyhood Helen had been Muir's good companion. For the sake of her delicate breathing apparatus, he had taken her out of doors whenever he could. She shared his uninhibited delight in nonsense and imaginative games, which they often improvised on the spur of the moment. When he teased her, she was flattered by the attention rather than hurt.

Helen learned to type so that she could help her father keep up with his heavy correspondence, the bulk of it concerning Hetch Hetchy, and notes and outlines for books he intended to write. They broke off the day's work early enough to roam the hills, discover which of their friends the wildflowers were showing themselves and whistle up the birds by imitating their calls. Sometimes they went down to Muir Station on the Santa Fe line, which ran

* It is said that the valley in which the ranch is situated was first called "Valley of Hunger" (*Valle de Hambre*), which reminded Louisiana Strentzel too much of their trip by wagon from Texas in 1849. She therefore named the valley "Alhambra."

just below the ranch on a trestle and twined west into a tunnel.

Helen was crazy about railroads, a passion with which Muir sympathized because of his own attraction to mechanics. He bought books, subscribed to technical magazines and provided the chaperonage required for her to make friends with the train crews. The Muirs were made free to ride in the cab, and Helen learned to operate the engine well enough to make the run from Stockton, down in the San Joaquin Valley, to Muir Station.

The railroaders also played Helen's games. When a train came by, the engineer made the whistle crow like a rooster, and Helen came out to wave, even when at dinner with guests.

When the cherries and grapes were ripe, Muir and Helen brought baskets of them down to the train crews; once they fastened a big bough laden with cherries above the entrance to the tunnel. A fireman picked it off as the engine entered the tunnel.

In December President Roosevelt gave Muir and the nation a Christmas present. Using his authority under Congressman Lacey's Act, he made part of the Arizona Petrified Forest into the nucleus of a national monument.

Chapter 55
The Drama of Muir Woods

By 1907 preservation of the wilderness had become a highly emotional issue. Newspapers east and west* had joined the struggle for the minds of the voters who, in the long run, would decide the fate of our national parks.

In the short run the battle over Hetch Hetchy had become like a courtroom trial, in that every twist and turn of the law and every device of procedure was used to full advantage by each side as opportunity offered.

For example, in the winter of 1907, Congress passed a law making itself the primary authority in creating or enlarging national forests in a number of western states, thus depriving the president of the power to protect forests in these states by proclamation. Theodore Roosevelt signed the Agricultural Appropriations Bill, to which Congress attached the rider limiting his powers. But in signing, he made the law effective March 4, 1907; and on March 1st and 2nd Roosevelt signed thirty-three proclamations creating new national parks and increasing some already existing, adding a total of 15,645,631 acres to the National Forest system.**

In September, 1907, the Sierra Club sent a resolution to the Secretary of the Interior formally stating the Club's opposition to the damming of Hetch Hetchy. It was drafted by a committee of directors, Muir acting as chairman *ex officio*. The gist and intention of this rather long document is clearly stated in a communication to the membership from William Colby:

"Since there are other adequate sources of water supply available for San Francisco, it is only just to the nation at large, which is vitally interested in preserving the wonders of Yosemite National Park, that their destruction or alteration should be avoided if it is possible to do so, as it most certainly is when the question resolves itself into one of mere expense."***

Muir and his supporters encountered considerable opposition, not only from San Francisco newspapers, politicians and "practical" people to whom

---

* Almost the only major papers which favored the damming of Hetch Hetchy Valley were in San Francisco; elsewhere the scheme became known as the "Hetch Hetchy Grab."

** U. S. Department of Agriculture, Forest Service, *Highlights in the History of Forest Conservation.*

*** Holway R. Jones, *John Muir and the Sierra Club: The Battle for Yosemite*, pp. 95-96.

profits* were more important than the future of their country, but from fellow members of the Sierra Club. These opponents were neither stupid nor selfish; their number included such men as Benjamin Ide Wheeler, the influential president of the University of California, and Warren Olney, the attorney in whose office the Sierra Club was founded. They simply believed that San Francisco needed Tuolumne water and Hetch Hetchy must therefore be dammed.

In October Muir went with William Keith for a badly-needed respite in Hetch Hetchy itself, though Helen's cough had returned, and he worried about her. They camped in the Valley for only a week, but it was a supremely happy and tranquil time. In the two-volume revision of the *Mountains of California*, published in 1911, Muir wrote: "The leaf colors were then ripe, and the Great Godlike rocks seemed to glow with life. The Artist...after making about forty sketches declared...in picturesque beauty and charm Hetch Hetchy surpasses even Yosemite!"

They returned to find Helen seriously ill and her physician insisting that she must live on the desert for at least two years. Muir lingered only long enough to put his affairs in order and help prepare a brief memorandum protesting the drowining of Hetch Hetchy. It was intended to suggest the sort of personal letters Sierra Club members were urged to write to the President or the Secretary of the Interior. In December Muir took Helen to the California desert near Dagget, northeast of San Bernardino.

Here Muir built her a comfortable cabin and engaged a Miss Safford, whom he persisted in calling "Miss Sassafras," as nurse-companion. He returned shortly to the ranch and the unending crisis of the conflict over Hetch Hetchy. But the memory of Helen's woebegone look haunted him, and he sent down not only her saddle horse, "Sniffpony," but also "Stickeen," their big companionable shepherd dog.

Some members of the Sierra Club had been incensed by the memo suggesting letters to the President or Secretary of Interior. One prominent attorney vigorously voiced a suspicion which plagued the preservationists for years.

"I most earnestly protest against the Sierra Club being used as a catspaw to pull chestnuts from the fire for the Spring Valley Water Company or for the grafters who have taken up the Sierra water rights with the object of selling (them) to San Francisco."**

This suspicion, that the Spring Valley Water Company was funding the effort to save Hetch Hetchy, came naturally to people familiar with that firm's history of ruthless and shady dealings. Moreover, it was true that speculators

---

* New transportation facilities to Hetch Hetchy, which would be required to build a dam, would make available some beautiful stands of timber currently protected by the park. There is also considerable evidence — including Phelan's original request for the right to develop Hetch Hetchy and the observations of R. U. Johnson — that the dam promoters envisioned handsome profits from hydro-electric power generation.

** Holway R. Jones, *John Muir and the Sierra Club: The Battle for Yosemite*, p. 97.

had filed claims on several water rights outside the park. But neither Muir nor his supporters had anything to do with these operations. No evidence has ever been produced that they desired anything beyond preserving one of the nation's most beautiful wilderness areas and protecting the integrity of the national parks. Muir and a few of the more dedicated Sierra Club board members paid, out of their own pockets, the costs of telegrams, postage, printing and other expenses necessary to win support, often at considerable sacrifice, for most of them were in quite unremunerative professional situations — e.g., William Frederick Badè, one of the most able and devoted preservationists, was a professor of literature and languages at a theological seminary.

The growing division in the Sierra Club depressed Muir increasingly, for the opposition newspapers and speakers lost no opportunity to attack and ridicule the preservationists as not being able to convince even their own associates. But Muir had more friends and supporters than he knew.

At that time, late 1907, one of these was about to see his own preservationist's dream drowned by a reservoir. William Kent, originally a Chicagoan, had inherited wealth and large land-holdings in Marin County across the Golden Gate from San Francisco. Near the family's second home at Kentfield was an almost-hidden ravine on the southern flank of 2,571-foot Mt. Tamalpais. Here flourished a virgin forest so lovely that San Franciscans gladly made the fifteen-mile trip by boat and buggy or saddle horse for the delight of wandering in it. It was then called "Redwood Canyon" because the Coast Redwood predominated in the dense, mixed forest.

In 1905 Kent bought this canyon of some five hundred acres for $45,000, saying to his dissenting wife, "If we lose all the money and save the trees it will have been worthwhile." Except for Kent's purchase, the woods would surely have been logged off after the earthquake, when San Francisco was desperately hungry for lumber.

Ever since his purchase Kent, a lifelong outdoorsman who responded so deeply to Muir's writings that he felt compelled to act, had been trying to find some governmental body to whom he could give "Redwood Canyon" and so protect and preserve it for all the people.

He had been unable to find anybody willing to accept the priceless gift when, late in 1907, a local water company sued to condemn "Redwood Canyon" for a reservoir, as was allowed under a law giving local water systems priority in the use of suitable sites.

In this dark hour Kent was reminded of the National Monuments and Antiquities Act. He was experienced in politics, having served as a reform alderman in Chicago. Therefore he began his campaign to have "Redwood Canyon" made a national monument through Gifford Pinchot. He had become aware of the situation Roosevelt described so graphically to Robert Johnson: "In all forestry matters I have put my conscience in the keeping of Gifford Pinchot.*

* Robert U. Johnson, *Remembered Yesterdays*, p. 307.

Perhaps Pinchot considered "Redwood Canyon" in a different category from Hetch Hetchy; more likely Roosevelt was not so much under Pinchot's thumb as he suggested. In any case Roosevelt made Kent's piece of untouched wilderness a national monument on January 9, 1908. He wanted to name it Kent Monument, but Kent insisted that it be called Muir Woods, for he admired Muir above most other men, though the two had never met.

In his letter of acknowledgment Muir said: "This is the best tree-lovers' monument that could be found. You have done me a great honor and I am proud of it....Saving these woods from the axe and the saw, from the money changers and the water changers is in many ways the most notable service to God and man I have heard of since my forest wanderings began...."*

* See *Muir Woods*, by Jim Morley, p. 6. Very probably Muir would be even more gratified and delighted today. The only changes in the woods are those made by nature, except for foot paths which keep the thousands of visitors who come each year from trampling the undergrowth out of existence (and being made miserable by poison oak). To make the short trip across the Golden Gate bridge and wander in this flowering, seeding, ever maturing, ever aging cooperative, enriching and renewing itself as the earth takes back its offspring, is to experience a true forest.

Chapter 56
Women and Other Allies

Muir's pleasure in the national monument that bears his name armored him somewhat against the blow which shortly fell. Pinchot had advised the dam promoters that the newly-appointed Secretary of Interior, a friend of Pinchot's named James R. Garfield, might be sympathetic to a renewed request for the right to dam Hetch Hetchy. The promoters promptly applied.

It took Garfield several months to make up his mind, thus giving the preservationists some opportunity to make their case. Muir wrote a letter to Roosevelt. After correcting some errors of fact put forward by the promoters, he said: "I am heartily in favor of a Sierra or even a Tuolumne water supply for San Francisco, but all the water required can be obtained from sources outside the park, leaving the twin valleys . . . (to be) passed on unspoiled to those who come after us, for they are national properties in which every man has a right and interest."

Apparently both Roosevelt and Secretary Garfield had made heavy commitments to political supporters, and on May 11 Garfield issued to San Francisco a permit to dam Hetch Hetchy and Lake Eleanor. But Garfield, in response to a suggestion by Roosevelt which was practically an order, ruled that Hetch Hetchy could not be dammed until the resources of Lake Eleanor and its sub-watershed had been fully developed. Moreover, Hetch Hetchy could not be dammed until the city of San Francisco proved conclusively that it could not obtain sufficient water of the necessary purity from other sources.

Muir was not invited to the widely publicized "Conservation Conference" called by the President. It was Pinchot's show. Only Charles Evans Hughes, then governor of New York, later Chief Justice of the Supreme Court, and Dr. J. Horace McFarland, president of the American Civic Association, spoke for preservation of parts of America in their natural state.

Muir probably could not have attended had he been invited. He was confined to home much of the time by exhaustion complicated by his racking bronchial cough and savage migraine headaches. But his spirit was an inexhaustible reserve of strength and rational optimism to sustain his followers. To Colby he wrote: "...the Phelans, Pinchots and their hirelings will not thrive forever.... We may lose this particular fight, but truth and right will prevail at last. Anyhow we must be true to ourselves...."

Colby had activated the Sierra Club's intention "to explore, enjoy and render accessible the mountain regions of the Pacific Coast" by organizing periodic camping trips into the Sierra. Muir usually went with these groups, and the mountain air never failed to diminish his cough and revive his spirits. Sometimes he was brooding and remote, sometimes a clowning, teasing boy who amused the party, made up largely of prominent men and their wives, as he had amused his own family. Beside the campfire, when a question or two got him started, he became the master teacher whose discourse was a treasured experience to all who heard him.

In the summer of 1908, a group went to the Kern River. In this party was Harriet Monroe of Chicago, the founder and editor of *Poetry, a Magazine of Verse*, a major influence in the surge of literary creativity during the first one-third of this century.

Monroe wrote a theatrical sketch in which Muir was persuaded to play the part of an intruder into a forest where the non-human inhabitants welcomed him. He suffered agonies of embarrassment but he forgave Monroe because of both the sensitivity and acuteness of her perceptions, and the clarity and force of both her mind and her discourse. He enjoyed her company, and she seemed a person who might do the preservationist cause some good.

Not long after returning from the Kern, Muir visited the Harriman family at their ranch on Klamath Lake, Oregon. On fine evenings the family and guests sat around a big outdoor fireplace, dropping politics, baseness and small talk to listen to Muir when they could get him started.

One night when Muir had been reminiscing about his early days in Scotland and Wisconsin, Harriman was struck by the fact that his guest's discourse was natural, spoken literature; whereupon he ordered his stenographer to dog Muir's footsteps and take down every word. Though the discourse was patched with profane complaints of the situation, which Muir called "beneficent bondage," and comments on birds, animals, trees and flowers they met in walks about the ranch, the resulting manuscript was the rough draft of an autobiography covering Muir's boyhood and youth.

Muir had no chance to work on the manuscript when he returned to the ranch. On November 12 the city of San Francisco voted a bond issue of $600,000 to develop the Hetch Hetchy water supply. (It should be borne in mind that a dollar was a day's wage for a western coal miner in 1908.) It appeared that Yosemite's twin valley was about to be drowned.

The preservationists made their fight at hearings on a proposal by the dam promoters that the federal government accept certain camping sites (some virtually unreachable, others without water) in exchange for the floor of Hetch Hetchy, which Muir and Colby estimated to be worth one thousand times as much.

A reprint of Muir's article on Hetch Hetchy, which had appeared in *Century Magazine*, and some photographs and eloquent letters caused the House and Senate committees responsible to postpone the hearings for almost a month, until January, 1909. During the lull the Sierra Club published a pamphlet bearing Muir's name as author.*

It was distributed to congressmen and other influential persons, including members of the General Federation of Women's Clubs. Hundreds of letters poured in on the committees asking that San Francisco's proposal be dismissed. The responsible House committee issued one majority and two minority reports. Harriet Monroe, the poetess and editor,** ably presented the preservationist cause at the hearings before the Senate committee, which decided not to report at all. The land-exchange bill died.

Muir and his fellow preservationists scarcely knew what to expect from William Howard Taft, who was inaugurated in March, 1909. Roosevelt thought that he had boosted Taft into the presidency, and that the big, slow-seeming man would keep Roosevelt's own cabinet officers and continue his policies. But Taft had several elephantine characteristics beside his bulk. He moved well, both physically and mentally, and he pursued his own determined purposes with little regard for opposition. One of his first acts on becoming president was to get rid of Garfield and replace him with a Seattle attorney named Ballinger, as Secretary of Interior. Pinchot was furious, accused Ballinger of reversing Garfield's policies and called him a "yellow dog." John Muir and his people saw opportunity and began to organize a campaign to accomplish exactly what Pinchot feared — to get the permit to dam Hetch Hetchy revoked.

The preservationists now had the necessary connections with other organized groups for a national campaign.

One of their foremost and most active supporters was J. Horace McFarland, a gifted organizer, imaginative as well as knowledgeable, and one of the first to insist on enlisting the help of women. In a letter summing up the members of various groups on which the preservationists could count, he wrote: "Suppose, for instance, that someone . . . like Miss Harriet Monroe . . . was to go to the next meeting of the general federation (of Women's Clubs) and there to talk as she talked before the Senate committee. It would mean that five or six thousand women from all over the country would be 'on the job.' "***

The attacks on the preservationists had been especially personal and savage during the land-exchange hearings. Phelan had the effrontery to revive the long-disproved lie that Muir had cut living trees for Hutchings' Yosemite sawmill. "Verily the lover of the tree destroyeth the tree," Phelan proclaimed and went on in a burst of sleazy rhetoric, "(Muir) is a poetical gentleman...he would sacrifice his own family for beauty. He considers human life very cheap...the works of God superior...."

Muir shrugged off this kind of thing as behavior to be expected from people who had left decency behind them in pursuit of office and wealth. But it was a

* Muir had approved all the contents, though Colby, Badè and E.T. Parsons of the Sierra Club Board had written parts of the pamphlet.
** Her way to Washington had been paid by subscriptions from the Chicago Saturday Walking Club and the Chicago Geographical Society.
*** See Holway R. Jones, *John Muir and the Sierra Club: The Battle for Yosemite*, p. 106.

bitter disappointment that Warren Olney, a long-time director of the Sierra Club, had appeared at the hearings to urge the damming of Hetch Hetchy.

Muir could understand opinions different from his own (though he did not tolerate them very well), but the apparent defection of Olney and other members was making it impossible for the Sierra Club to present a united front.

San Francisco newspapers exaggerated the slightest sign of dissension in their all-out effort to keep the city's voters fully and emotionally committed to the Hetch Hetchy water supply. Muir began to fear that his own zeal was doing more harm than good. He decided to resign both the Sierra Club presidency and his membership.

Colby persuaded him that if he resigned the entire campaign would fall apart and went on to flesh out a suggestion made by a Boston lawyer: that a separate organization should be formed to take some of the heat and act as a unified force.

By April, 1909, Muir, Colby and their most active associates had organized "The Society for Preservation of National Parks, California Branch," John Muir, President.

This society was actually national from the beginning, through an advisory council made up of influential preservationists representing a number of different organizations and many different sections of the country. Shortly after this society's formation, J. Horace McFarland made the Washington offices of the American Civic Association available as a clearing house and headquarters for representatives of the various groups dedicated to the national parks. The preservationists thus had the means to coordinate their efforts and also (for the first time) an outpost overlooking the "political quag" of Washington.

Chapter 57

The Conversion of President Taft

I n September, 1909, President Taft spent a day in Yosemite with Muir as his guide. Taft had Muir's own pleasure in unsmiling remarks calculated to "get a rise" out of the respondent. Coming with Muir down the four-mile trail from Glacier Point on foot, sweat pouring in rivulets down his beet-colored face and neck, Taft paused to remark that the majestic rock gateway by which the Merced leaves Yosemite would be a fine place for a dam. Muir exploded appropriately. "The man who would do so would be damning himself!" and he went on to compare those who sought to commercialize the magnificence of the Sierras to the money changers whom Christ scourged from the temple.

Reporters for San Francisco papers, which never missed an opportunity to demean Muir, wrote that the President showed "tolerant amusement" and "twitted Muir on his sentimentality." Actually the two men enjoyed one another's company, and in the afternoon Taft arranged a time for them to be alone in order to go over the maps and charts Muir had drawn to illustrate his plan for the development of the park. One major project was a system of roads and trails linking the outstanding features — including Hetch Hetchy — into one great scenic route.

Taft was delighted and left with Muir a letter for Richard Ballinger, the Secretary of Interior, who was due the next day with George Otis Smith, head of the U.S. Geological Survey, and two engineers. Taft's letter asked Ballinger to accept Muir as their guide through Hetch Hetchy. Their report motivated Taft to appoint a board of government engineers to determine whether Lake Eleanor would be sufficient to meet San Francisco's need without exploiting Hetch Hetchy.

Meanwhile the preservationists continued their efforts to enlist as much public support as possible. In November a second pamphlet, largely written by Muir and issued in his name, went out with help from the Federation of Women's Clubs and the American Civic Association to a large distribution list. Nationally it was very successful, but in San Francisco it stirred up the dam promoters like a nest of yellow jackets. Some newspapers went to great lengths to bring the contention to the point of fury.

The result was that on December 18 the Sierra Club asked its members to declare (using an enclosed ballot) whether they desired that Hetch Hetchy remain intact and unaltered, or favored using it as a reservoir. After a very considerable amount of both intelligence and emotion had been expended on the public argument, the result was 589 votes for retaining nature's Hetch Hetchy, to 161 for making it a reservoir.

The dam faction had called for a general meeting to discuss the issue, but this gathering was delayed by the curse of all volunteer organizations — absenteeism — until February 18, 1910, when the vote had already been counted. Next day some papers accused Muir of packing the meeting. "I had only packed about eighty stomachs," Muir wrote to friends. "The long flowery table (at the Poodle Dog restaurant) flanked with merry mountaineers looked something like a Sierra Canyon, so they called it 'the Muir Gorge,' and after dinner...we entered the hall in a triumphant rush, fairly overwhelming the poor, astonished Hetch Hetchy dammers."

The "dammers" never again offered collective opposition to the preservationist board of directors. Fifty members resigned.*

On the basis of what he had seen for himself and the reports of his expert investigators, Secretary Ballinger called on the dam promoters (usually referred to by the name of their stalking horse, the "City of San Francisco") to appear at a hearing in May and show cause why Hetch Hetchy should not be removed from the permission to exploit National Park Water Sources granted by Garfield, the previous secretary.

This hearing turned out to be first in a long series of postponements granting the city more time to comply with the order to "show cause." The struggle over Hetch Hetchy remained in a virtual stalemate during most of Taft's remaining years in office. During this period Muir and his fellow preservationists were striving to get the government to provide an adequate budget for the parks; to get a national park service established;** and to have the wonderful wilderness which is drained by the three branches of the Kings River joined to an enlarged Sequoia National Park.*** But none of these caused a seemingly endless succession of crises as did Hetch Hetchy during its periods of intense activity. Muir was not so frequently called upon to write pamphlets and material for the press; to urge influential friends to action through letters and telegrams; to advise, edit and plan. More of his energy was left for his own writing. And his health and strength both profited by spending a good deal of time away from the home ranch. He frequently visited Helen, who had married the son of a cattle man and still lived near Dagget on the desert. He was also very welcome to stay with any of half a dozen families in and near Los Angeles. One of the wealthier of these had fitted up a pleasant work room which Muir called his "Palace Garret." Here he converted forty-

* In 1956 William Colby told Holway R. Jones that many who favored the dam stayed on "because they thought they could do us more harm by saying they were members."

** William Kent, donor of Muir Woods, got himself elected to Congress in 1910. He helped to draft and, in 1916, introduced the bill establishing the National Park Service.

***Muir's dream of "one great national park embracing the Sequoia/Kings River areas" was not consummated until 1965.

year-old notes into a book called *My First Summer in the Sierra*. Ellery Sedgewick, editor of the *Atlantic Monthly*, where this account of Muir's extraordinary and beautiful adventures as a supervising sheepherder ran briefly as a serial, wrote to Muir: "When I first read it I felt as if I had found religion."

During the summer of 1910 Muir was called back to Martinez by the terminal illness of his much loved elder sister, Margaret. He returned to Los Angeles, and by the spring of 1911 had cut and edited into nearly publishable form the one thousand pages of random notes he had dictated to Harriman's secretary.

Muir had been pressured by the feeling that he might not live long enough to write all the books which lay unrealized in his journals. Having completed two books in good time, he felt at liberty to fulfill his life-long dream and told his friends that he was going to South America.

Some thought he must have left his senses, and all feared for him. To spare their feelings he forbore to mention that he also intended to go to Central Africa.

Chapter 58
Kind Mother Calling

As soon as Muir reached New York, Robert Underwood Johnson carried him off to Washington for a chat with President Taft, three conferences with Walter C. Fisher, the new Secretary of Interior, and visits with several influential legislators, including the Speaker of the House.

In late June he went to New Haven to accept a degree from Yale. To march in the solemn procession of black-robed scholars "shining like crow blackbirds" amused him, and he was vastly entertained by the alumni, each class in its own special costume, "cavorting all over the campus more wildly than autumn leaves in a hurricane."

Until he took ship in mid-August Muir stayed in a guest cabin on the wooded estate of Henry Fairfield Osborne, refining two books: *The Yosemite* and *The Story of My Boyhood and Youth*. The Osbornes were more than kind to him; they afforded the mutual exchange of affection and understanding response that is possible only among intimate friends. At this time Muir needed such friends very badly. Relatives and associates were dying in such quick succession that he wondered, in a letter to Helen, whether leaves feel lonely when they see their fellows whirl away on the wind. His letters to the Osbornes, mailed from stopping points on his ambitious journey, are as eloquently affectionate as any he ever wrote.

His first objective was a huge white flower called *Victoria regia*. Muir pursued this vision for a thousand miles up the Amazon and into a backwater of its Rio Negro tributary. The final part of the search was made, first in a skiff, then on hands and knees under and through the looping, writhing vines which interlace the jungle trees. The liana barrier at last became so impenetrable that Muir gave up and returned with his companions to the tug that had brought them from the river town of Manáos. Muir was not much disappointed. The majesty of the Amazon and the all-but-unbelievable fecundity of the growth along the banks were experience enough for the time. He wrote to Los Angeles friends saying he was glad that their scientifically inclined daughter (who had thought to accompany him) had not done so, "on account of yellow fever and the most rapidly deadly of the malarial kinds."

Muir miraculously remained untouched, and everyone, it seemed, was kind and solicitous. In part this attention was due to President Taft, who had sent word out through the State Department's network of consular officers that this old man was special and should be given every consideration. In part it was due to Muir's frail and venerable appearance. But for the most part it was due to his own gift for winning friends.

On the boat going down to Rio de Janeiro he fell in with some lumbermen who took him another thousand miles up a South Brazilian river called the Iguacú. His objective was a curious geometrical pine tree called the *Araucaria braziliana,* which one finds today in old gardens and parks in California, where it was much planted early in this century for its spectacular silhouette. He found whole forests of them, their tops towering like gigantic umbrellas above the surrounding jungle.

His next quarry was a relative of this tree — *Araucaria imbricata* — the "monkey puzzle tree" whose rope-like branchlets interlace and are set with stiff, sharp-pointed leaves like bayonets. Cats injudicious enough to climb these trees have to be rescued by means of ladders. One of the few things then known about this tree was that it grew in Chile. Muir crossed the continent by rail to Santiago. Though he was warmly welcomed by the U.S. Minister, who introduced him to the Chilean scientific community, Muir found no one who could tell him where the monkey-puzzles were to be found.

He accepted the challenge willingly; putting together what little he knew of the tree's needs for soil, moisture and temperature, he made a scientist's enlightened guess as to where they ought to be.

With two companions he journeyed five hundred miles south, hired a carriage in which they mounted into the Andes until the road petered out, then continued on horseback into the higher region. On a ridge just below the snow line, they came to a great stand of monkey-puzzle trees stretching as far as the eye could reach. Muir's companions slept in a tent but Muir slept out under the canopy of constellations entirely new to him and familiar stars in new places, all seen through the silhouettes of the strange trees, like a fantastic tracery of wrought iron.

Muir next went in search of the baobab, a tree with smooth bark like hippopotamus hide and trunks so massive the African tribesmen sometimes hollowed them out for homes. To reach them he journeyed from Montevideo to Capetown, and thence by rail to the vicinity of Victoria Falls. "Baobabs?" said the manager of his hotel. "Nobody has ever asked for baobabs. I don't know what they are." So Muir went out into the street and asked every English speaker he met until he found a black boy who led him to a grove of baobabs a mile from the head of the Falls. Muir wandered here all day, through a continual shower of spray which rises like smoke from the great plunge of water and drifts over the surrounding countryside. Muir was especially delighted with this display of nature's economy: in the spray from Yosemite Falls and Bridal Veil grew some of his favorite wild gardens, but Victoria waters a whole woods.

From here Muir went by ship and rail to Lake Nyasa to watch the Nile's waters start their journey to the sea half a continent north. He came back to the United States via the Red Sea and the Mediterranean and headed straight for the ranch. He had been gone seven months; he had now completed all the journeys of his boyhood dreams and fulfilled his ambition to see all of earth's major mountain chains and all of her greatest forests.

Comparing nature's great displays as he had seen them, Muir decided that his best love was his first — the sun-drenched, shower-refreshed Sierra Nevada, with its friendly, open forests and flowering meadows, and its stupendous rocks carved by glaciers into a matchless display of natural sculpture.

Annie Wanda had borne her third son while he was away; Helen bore her second son shortly after his return. This "growth of the boy underbrush," as he called it, somewhat compensated for the inevitable loss of old friends. Two of his most compatible Los Angeles hosts had died during his absence. There was thus less incentive to leave the ranch, and the Hetch Hetchy battle had been resumed so that he was continually on call. He therefore remained in the big ranch house inhabited by himself, his Chinese houseman and a few hungry mice. He despaired of making it a home, though the exotic trees and shrubs he and Louie Wanda had planted were flourishing and his hedge of Cherokee roses was a snowbank of blooms.

In spite of advancing age, this period of Muir's life was far from grim. Each morning at an appointed hour he met his old friend, John Swett, at the fence dividing their two ranches. Each meeting started with a ritualistic quarrel about the weather; if Swett said it was fine, Muir said the sun would parch the crops; if Swett said it was foul, Muir said it was just what the crops needed. When they got this ritual out of the way they sat on the porch of Swett's ranch house and discussed the presidential campaign, which was a seething cauldron because Theodore Roosevelt had formed the Progressive ("Bull Moose") Party and was running against Taft and Woodrow Wilson, seeking a third term.*

Muir also had the companionship of Wanda's little boys, who delighted in such games as putting a basket over their grandfather's head and shrieking with laughter because he looked like a tall, lean bird peering bright-eyed from its cage. One of Muir's nieces who was a spectator of these antics said that Muir, at the age of seventy-four, was the most alive man she ever knew.

In the summer of 1912, Muir made his first trip by automobile from Santa Barbara to the Giant Forest, thence to Yosemite and home to the ranch. Later that year he attended a conference on national parks held in Yosemite. To his considerable disappointment the main topic was whether automobiles should be admitted to Yosemite. "All signs indicate automobile victory," he wrote, "and doubtless, under certain precautionary restrictions these useful, progressive, blunt-nosed mechanical beetles will be allowed to puff their way into all the parks and mingle their gas breath with the breath of the pines and waterfalls...."

* Taft had dismissed Gifford Pinchot from his post as chief forester because of the savage public attacks Pinchot had launched against the Secretary of the Interior, Ballinger. Pinchot then became one of Roosevelt's principal campaign supporters and financial backers.

There was no way to foresee the many millions who would come to inhabit California, nor the numbers automobiles would bring within reach of the fragile environments of the High Sierra. Muir therefore thought the automobile would mean little good or harm to the true mountaineer.

On May 14, 1913, John Muir and John Swett, their hair like snow above black robes, sat waiting their turn to receive honorary doctorates from the University of California. This was Muir's third such degree, in addition to his M.A. from Harvard. The universities could not, of course, give him an academic degree. He was a drop-out, lacking even a B.A., and had never committed himself to a career in any one science. On the other hand, he was a fellow of the American Association for the Advancement of Science, and his contributions to geology, botany, geography, and ecology are more significant than many which have been rewarded by doctorates.

He is still called an amateur — and perhaps this is correct. An *amator* is a lover. Muir above all loved the world he studied, and loved studying it. Degrees cannot be given for love, and so the savants rewarded him for something vaguely known as "public service."

From today's perspective it seems as if Muir's memory should be honored for two intangibles. The first is particularly convincing because of the downright commonplaceness of its statement in a letter from a woman in Yokohama.

"More than twenty years ago ... I read a short sketch of your own in which you pictured your sense of delight in listening to the wind, with its many voices, sweeping through the pines. That article made a lifelong impression on me, and shaped an inner perception for the wonders of nature which has gladdened my entire life ever since.... It has always seemed that I must some time thank you."

Muir was pleased though in his reply he made one of his favorite points. "Written descriptions of fire or bread are of but little use to the cold or starving....Nature's tables are spread and fires burning. You must go to warm yourselves and eat."*

Muir did not seem to realize that his articles and books had "shaped the inner perceptions" of thousands besides Mrs. Swain, and that through their children and grandchildren an impressive proportion of Americans would come to see their country with new eyes.

He also gave to hundreds in his time — and through the intervening years to many thousands — a "moral equivalent of war," if one takes William James' phrase to mean the all-out commitment to a worthy cause which is commonly given to one's country or faction in war.** There is no doubt that Muir inspired a great many to just such a commitment during his lifetime and after.

The dam promoters lost little time in getting an already-prepared

* William F. Badè, *The Life and Letters of John Muir*, Vol. II, pp. 336-337.
** This interpretation is the creation of Elliot Richardson, the versatile and distinguished public servant who resigned his position as attorney general because Richard Nixon dismissed the special prosecutor, Archibald Cox, during the notorious "Saturday Night Massacre."

campaign to influence Congress under way. The struggle degenerated to the level of intrigue in which the preservationists were at a great disadvantage because of lack of both money and cynicism. Pamphlets illustrated with pictures of lovely Swiss lakes were brought out to show what a fine thing it would be to change Hetch Hetchy from a grove-dotted meadow to a reservoir.*

There came to light an engineering report which apparently had been suppressed by San Francisco officials because it showed that water sources other than Hetch Hetchy were adequate and available. But the House Committee considering the so-called Raker Bill, designed to give the dam promoters their way, refused to consider it, saying that the hearings (of July, 1913) were closed to new evidence.

At the time of the fall recess it was announced that the Raker Bill would not be considered until December. Many congressmen therefore left Washington. Suddenly in early September the Raker Bill was brought to the floor and passed by a vote of 183 to 43, with 205 not voting because of absence.

To Mrs. Henry Fairfield Osborne Muir wrote, "The Raker Bill has been meanly skulked and railroaded and logrolled through the House, but we are hoping it will be checked in the Senate." What Muir and the preservationists most needed at this point was the Harriman clout in Congress. But Harriman had died in 1909. The Senate passed the Raker Bill in December, 1913. Woodrow Wilson, under great political pressure, signed it a few weeks later.

Muir had spent most of the vitality he brought back from the Araucaria and the baobab woods. Visitors who found him sitting exhausted and listless in his cobwebby study, while echoes chased one another through the silent, high-ceilinged rooms of the big, empty house, were overcome with the pathos of the scene. They thought him about to leave this life, for his cough was now chronic and the infection had entered his right lung. Their reports fostered the idea that the Hetch Hetchy defeat killed John Muir.

But on January 4, 1914, he wrote to Henry Fairfield Osborne: ". . . wrong cannot last; soon or late it must fall back home to Hades, while some compensating good must surely follow.

"With the new year to new work we will gladly go — you to your studies of God's lang syne people in their magnificent Wyoming-Idaho mausoleums, I to crystal ice...."

"Crystal ice" was the substance of the book on Alaska at which he had worked for several years when the "everlasting Hetch Hetchy business" permitted. Muir made poor and difficult progress until Marian Randall Parsons, widow of a preservationist colleague, came out from Berkeley several times each week — an intelligent, perceptive woman with genuine editorial ability. She provided just the help he needed, and the work

** The dam promoters must certainly have been aware that the reservoir would fluctuate with the seasons and for much of the year have around the water's edge a twenty-foot ring of mud with stumps protruding from it like teeth from a dead man's jaw. See Hetch Hetchy picture sections in Holway R. Jones' *John Muir and the Sierra Club: The Battle for Yosemite.*

prospered. She found his mind and spirit unimpaired. Only his intense fatigue suggested that he might be failing.

Like every man and woman who has lived a long time (and Muir was now seventy-six) he knew he had contracted the one inevitably terminal disease — old age. But since he could not predict his time of departure, he decided that there was no point in living miserably in the past. In the summer of 1914, he startled his friends and relatives by installing electricity in the old house. He bought new curtains, rugs and furniture. With the help of his Chinese houseman — who seems to have been a remarkable character — he built new bookcases and cupboards, and had the whole place cleaned up and touched up. He made it a house for the future, though whether his own or one of his daughters he did not know.

That fall of 1914 Muir went down to Wanda's home in the old adobe for all his meals, and it was Wanda who in early December packed his bag for a trip he insisted on making to visit Helen on the desert. The morning after he arrived he and Helen walked a mile across the desert. That evening he sat by the fire making corrections on the manuscript he had brought with him. But when he tried to get up, he staggered.

The diagnosis was pneumonia, which (in those days before antibiotics) was called "the old man's friend." They rushed him to a Los Angeles hospital and in a day or two he seemed to be himself, joking with the doctor and nurses and planning to finish his book. But he was not so sanguine as he seemed, for on a fugitive scrap of paper he wrote: "Death . . . is a gracious mother calling her children home."

He died peacefully on Christmas Eve, with proof sheets of *Travels in Alaska* spread out on his bed.

Appendix A — On Reading John Muir

The delight Muir gave his readers and the influence he had upon them are likely to seem mysterious to modern readers. He wrote in the idiom of his times — Victorian — which was adapted to courtesies and pomposities, beliefs and sentiments forgotten or rejected in our own day. But Muir, like his favorite poet Robert Burns, was a Scottish plowman, equipped with a native humor and earthiness to save him from the rigidity and mawkishness which make many of his contemporaries all but unreadable today. Muir's writing, though excellently attuned to readers of his own day, nevertheless presents certain difficulties after the lapse of a century. I have, on occasion, been at considerable pains to translate Muir's meaning out of its Victorian expression into a modern idiom.

The decline of the "literary magazines" has also made it much more difficult for an author to influence a wide public. In Muir's time such magazines as *Dial*, *Scribner's* and *Century* flourished along with *Harper's* and *Atlantic*. Most well-educated people read one or several of them, in leisure and with great enjoyment; and the well-educated, by and large, were the opinion makers. Today we are all but drowning under a deluge of news and other information reported as fast as it comes to light. The situation of the professional man and the executive is complicated by the paper river of specialized information in his field — and perhaps in his hobby as well. He has little time to read pleasant writing in which facts are not laid out with the "angular factiness" — to use Muir's term — which enables the initiate to grasp them on the fly.

Muir's intense desire to share his experiences resulted in remarkably rich and varied rewards that are only to be obtained at a price. The phenomenon is familiar, since many of the greatest writers (Tolstoy and Milton are prime examples) require their readers to pay the same dues. They require of us unremitting and complete response. To the extent to which any reader fails to respond fully he misses a proportional amount of the experience the author is trying to share with him.

After "living" with Muir for five years and finding it one of the happiest and most lastingly-satisfying experiences of my life, I conclude he is best read as he was read by our grandparents — in small segments at a sitting. Otherwise the effort to respond becomes fatiguing, the Victorianness irritating. The discontinuity of the books (which are made up of revised articles and letters) is often frustrating. Reading in relatively short "takes," from a paragraph to an essay, one is able to respond to some of the most exciting, beautiful and revealing stimuli in American literature.

It may be that Muir's contemporaries found it easier to respond to him than we do. Wilderness experience was far easier to come by. It was inevitable that many of Muir's readers had journeyed through wilderness without realizing how greatly the hours so spent could enrich them, until he taught them how to understand the value of Nature's offerings and open themselves to receive them. In uncounted cases men and women, who had adopted this most natural way of enlightenment, passed on to their children and grandchildren this understanding.

As Frederic Gunsky and others have pointed out, Muir's articles and notes are the best reading because they are the freshest and least cramped by revisions undertaken in an effort to meet conventional standards. Consequently, I like best *My First Summer in the Sierra*, which is alive with Muir's youthful wonder and delight — not only with what he saw and experienced in the course of his first journey across the Sierra Nevada, but also the intellectual adventure of his geological discoveries.

I think most readers today will also find great pleasure in *South of Yosemite*, which consists of articles and essays collected and edited by Frederic Gunsky, who knows the Sierra Nevada very well, basically in Muir's way, as a human being informed by science. Also, I find the photographic illustrations in this book splendid in themselves and as representations of the sights to which Muir responded so fully.

Beyond these, my personal favorites are *Travels in Alaska* and *The Cruise of the Corwin*, which describes an Arctic voyage. The scenes, even now, are novel to most readers. And in these books, for the first time, Muir applied his remarkable powers of observation and his capacity for sympathetic understanding to his fellow man.

Muir's letters and notes are, naturally, the most personal expressions of his experiences and his response to them. Consequently they are the least inhibited, the most completely revealing of the man. Both are set here and there with astonishing passages — some gem-like descriptions, others view-windows into the nature of Nature and the future of man.

The best browsing is thus to be found in two books of short pieces selected and placed in the context of Muir's life with great affection and intellligence: *The Life and Letters of John Muir*, by William Frederic Badè, and *John of the Mountains*, edited by Linnie Marsh Wolfe.

Appendix B — On Reading about John Muir

Some readers may wish to know more about areas of John Muir's life which I have not presented in detail. Others may wish to know more of the backgrounds against which Muir's adventures of body, mind and spirit must be seen. For such readers I offer the following annotations of books which I especially enjoyed or found particularly illuminating.

In 1937 Muir's daughters, Wanda and Helen, asked Linnie Marsh Wolfe to put in order the chaotic collection of letters and other memorabilia. Two years later the sisters asked her to write John Muir's biography.

Wanda wanted particularly to have her father rescued from the plaster-sainthood to which some of his admirers seemed determined to consign him. She and Helen wanted Muir to be remembered as a warm-hearted, original and complex human with the normal human complement of faults. Mrs. Wolfe's way of satisfying this requirement was to go into considerable detail concerning Muir's intimate relations with his family and other people among whom he grew up, and in his adult life his relations with his wife, children and close friends.

Mrs. Wolfe also went to great pains to drag every derogatory report and rumor concerning Muir into the light and trace it to its source, "only to find that they melted into thin air when brought face to face with attested facts." (See *Son of the Wilderness*, preface, page vii.)

Mrs. Wolfe was a good researcher in the field as well as in the study. She lived nearly a year in the Muirs' "Hickory Hill" farmhouse in Wisconsin and made extended visits to Portage, Prairie du Chien and the University of Wisconsin. Many of the people who had known John Muir were still living and of course were eager to tell all they could remember or invent. She was also able to find out a great deal concerning Muir's ancestral roots in Scotland and the circumstances of his earliest years. In California Mrs. Wolfe had not only the advantage of her own extensive knowledge of the Sierra Nevada, but the memories of many of Muir's younger associates, such as William Colby and other active figures in the Sierra Club. Her biography of Muir, *Son of the Wilderness: The Life of John Muir*, was published in 1945, six years after she undertook to write it.

Wanda Muir told Mrs. Wolfe it was better that the biographer had not known John Muir personally. "You would have seen only one side of him, and he had many sides. No two people ever had the same idea of him."

Up to a point, Wanda's judgment seems correct. Like many brilliant, complex men, Muir was analogous to a gem stone cut into many faces, each of which throws back the light in its own particular way.

Moreover, Wanda had no way of understanding how a man's character can be revealed in the course of three months spent in a thirty-six-foot canoe with only one English-speaking companion. S. Hall Young, who accompanied Muir on his two voyages of discovery from Wrangell Island to Glacier Bay, was an insightful, highly responsive man who had a great deal in common with his companion. Young was enthusiastic about people he admired — in particular Toyatte, steersman and canoe captain on their first voyage, and John Muir. His hero worship, however, did not dim his perceptions. The living portrait which emerges from *Alaska Days with John Muir*, Young's narrative of their adventures and discoveries, seems to me as complete and true a representation as one human is likely to make of another.

Hall Young wrote well, and the sidelights he shines upon Alaska when it was still effectually possessed by its original settlers, the Indians, are especially interesting in conjunction with the observations Muir made at the same time. Together, *Travels in Alaska* and *Alaska Days with John Muir* give one a stereoptican view of a remarkable culture just before it was overwhelmed.

William Frederic Badè's introduction to John Muir's *The Cruise of the Corwin* is also very good reading, and helpful in placing the Corwin's voyage in the context of Arctic exploration. Badè's research was painstaking, and the glimpses he gives of both nautical detail and the bureaucratic in-fighting that confused publication of Muir's report, are illuminating.

Glacier Bay: The Land and the Silence, text and photographs by Dave Bohn, also helps to place Muir's explorations in the sequence of discovery, adventure, and scientific study of a landscape which is being made, unmade and remade again more rapidly than almost any other area of earth where nature's forces are free to work their will.

For a modern understanding of the Sierra Nevada — hence a more complete and correct account of its geology than Muir was able to develop with the knowledge and instrumentation available in his day — *The Incomparable Valley* is the indispensable book. It was a project of Dr. François E. Matthes, who spent most of his professional lifetime in studying the Sierra Nevada. His *Geologic History of Yosemite Valley* is regarded as a classic. But he hoped also to make his knowledge of the mountains he loved more readily available to the public in a book less burdened with scientific documentation.

When Dr. Matthes died in 1948, his long-time friend and associate, Fritiof Fryxell, took on the task of selecting from Matthes' notes, lectures, published works and unfinished manuscripts, the relevant materials — and welded them into the book his friend had envisioned. Dr. Matthes had intended it to be a book for the general reader, and so it is. But it is not "popular" in the sense of readability at the expense of true understanding. It is as lucid as a Sierra lake, but so informative that the reader must be willing to spend the effort required to assimilate a great many facts marshalled in the uncompromising formulations of scientific discourse. No question that such effort is well spent on this book.

Among the specialized books available to the reader who has fallen under the spell of the *Sequoia gigantea*, my favorite is *Big Trees* by Walter Fry and John R. White. Judge Fry, formerly U. S. Commissioner of Sequoia National Park, knew the great trees from 1887 onward for over fifty years. For eighteen years, John R. White was Superintendent of Sequoia and General Grant National Parks, which for a long time were separate.

This book is intimate, parochial (to the extent of ignoring John Muir's part in saving the still existing stands of Big Trees), at times crotchety, and highly informative. To me the most useful part is the map showing the location of seventy-one groves of redwoods over ten feet in diameter at six feet above the ground. This map is keyed to a list of these groves by name and location, with a very brief description of each.

Of the many publications on the Coast Redwoods (*Sequoia sempervirens*) my favorite is a pamphlet, *Muir Woods*, text and pictures by Jim Morley. For all its brevity it is highly informative, and by taking the reader through the four seasons of the year, the author provides the added attraction of narrative. The pictures are lovely.

Two of Shirley Sargent's brief, specialized publications cast fascinating sidelights upon the people among whom Muir lived in Yosemite Valley, and his relations to a number of them. Both of these books are adequately described by their titles: *John Muir in Yosemite*, and *Pioneers in Petticoats*. The photographic illustrations are splendid, both for their intrinsic interest and as supplements to the text.

The stories of Muir's part in the fight to get Yosemite National Park created and the "incomparable valley" made a part of it, and the overlapping fight to save Hetch Hetchy Valley from becoming a reservoir, are tangled beyond hope of revealing a complete, coherent, lucid, balanced account.

In *John Muir and the Sierra Club: The Battle for Yosemite*, Holway R. Jones has made a heroic attempt. It appears that no relevant letter or document, however obscure, has been left unexamined. Every rumor, innuendo and clue has been traced to its origins in truth, falsehood or vanished evidence. I have the feeling that Holway Jones has given most of the true story; I harbor no need to know any more about it. But I must also confess that R.U. Johnson's account in *Remembered Yesterdays*, of his part in the struggle as Muir's comrade in arms, is much easier reading and has also the advantage of being a first-hand report.

The photographs in the Sierra Club's edition of *John Muir and the Sierra Club* show Hetch Hetchy before the dam was built — and after. The contrast chills the blood. The "before" photographs show that Hetch Hetchy was as beautiful as Muir and others described. These are the only good pictures of the original Hetch Hetchy which I have seen. The "after" pictures showing tree stumps sticking out of the mud like the stubs of a dead man's teeth exemplify the typical fluctuating reservoir whose water level decreases in every dry season.

Many picture books of Yosemite and the Sierra Nevada have been published. Some of the photographs are excellent and in various ways fascinating to look at. But in the back of my mind John Muir's complaint against all pictures of the wilderness — even his own word-pictures — inevitably stirs: "You cannot feed a hungry child with pictures of bread, or warm a shivering man by showing a picture of a fire."

Bibliography

Asbury, Herbert. *The Barbary Coast: An Informal History of the San Francisco Underworld.* Garden City: Alfred A. Knopf, 1933.

Badè, William Frederic. *The Life and Letters of John Muir.* 2 vols. Cambridge: Houghton Mifflin, 1924.

Bohn, Dave. *Glacier Bay: The Land and the Silence.* Edited by David Brower. New York: Ballantine Books, 1967.

Bowen, Ezra. *The High Sierra.* New York: Time-Life Books, 1972.

Chapman, Royal N. *Animal Ecology.* New York and London: McGraw-Hill, 1931.

Dosch, Arno. "The Mystery of John Muir's Money." *Sunset Magazine,* Vol. 36, No. 2. February, 1916.

Ellsberg, Edward. *Hell on Ice, The Saga of the Jeannette.* Dodd, Mead, 1938.

Fry, Walter, and White, John R. *Big Trees.* Stanford: Stanford University Press, 1930.

Gunsky, Frederic R., ed. *South of Yosemite: Selected Writings by John Muir.* Garden City: Natural History Press, 1968.

Hoopes, Penrose R. *Connecticut Clockmakers of the Eighteenth Century.* New York: Dover Publications, Inc., 1974.

Johnson, Paul C. *Sierra Album.* Garden City: Doubleday and Co., 1971.

Johnson, Robert Underwood. *Remembered Yesterdays.* Little, Brown, 1923.

Jones, Holway R. *John Muir and the Sierra Club: The Battle for Yosemite.* San Francisco: Sierra Club, 1965.

Kennan, George. *Edward Henry Harriman.* 2 vols. Houghton Mifflin Co., 1922.

Kent, William. *Reminiscences of an Outdoor Life.* San Francisco: A.M. Robertson, 1929.

Leighly, John. "John Muir's Image of the West." *Annals of the Association of American Geographers,* Vol. 48, No. 4. December, 1958.

Matthes, François E. *Geologic History of the Yosemite Valley.* Professional Paper No. 160, U.S. Geological Survey. Washington, D. C.: Government Printing Office, 1930.

_____ . *The Incomparable Valley, A Geologic Interpretation of the Yosemite.* Edited by Fritiof Fryxell. Berkeley: University of California Press, 1970.

Morley, Jim. *Muir Woods.* Berkeley: Howell-North Books, 1968.

Muir, John. *The Cruise of the Corwin.* Edited by William F. Badè. Boston and New York: Houghton Mifflin Co., 1917.

_____ . *The Mountains of California.* New York: Doubleday and Co., 1961.

_____ . *Our National Parks.* Cambridge: Houghton Mifflin and Co., 1902.

_____ . *Picturesque California: The Rocky Mountains and the Pacific Slope.* New York and San Francisco: J. Dewing and Co., 1888.

_____ . *Stickeen.* Boston: Houghton Mifflin Co., 1909.

_____ . *Studies in the Sierra.* San Francisco: The Sierra Club, 1950.

_____ . *A Thousand-Mile Walk to the Gulf.* Edited by William F. Badè. Boston: Houghton Mifflin Co., 1917.

_____ . *Travels in Alaska.* Boston and New York: Houghton Mifflin Co., 1915.

_____ . *The Yosemite.* New York: Doubleday and Co., 1962.

Sargent, Shirley. *John Muir in Yosemite.* Yosemite: Flying Spur Press, 1971.

_____ . *Pioneers in Petticoats.* Los Angeles: Trans-Anglo Books, 1966.

Shepherd, Jack. *The Forest Killers: The Destruction of the American Wilderness.* New York: Weybright and Talley, 1975.

Starr, Walter A., Jr. *Guide to the John Muir Trail and the High Sierra Region.* San Francisco: The Sierra Club, 1962.

Studdard, Gloria J. *Common Environmental Terms: A Glossary.* Washington, D. C.: U.S. Environmental Protection Agency, 1974.

U. S. Department of Agriculture, Forest Service. *Highlights in the History of Forest Conservation,* Agriculture Bulletin No. 83. Washington, D. C.: Government Printing Office, 1958.

Voge, Hervey, ed. *A Climber's Guide to the High Sierra.* San Francisco: The Sierra Club, 1954.

Walker, Franklin. *San Francisco's Literary Frontier.* New York: Alfred A. Knopf, 1939.

Wurm, Ted. *Hetch Hetchy and its Dam Railroad.* Berkeley: Howell-North, 1973.

White, Lynn, Jr. "The Historic Roots of Our Ecologic Crisis." *Science Magazine,* Vol. 155, No. 3767. March 10, 1957.

Wolfe, Linnie Marsh, ed. *John of the Mountains.* Boston: Houghton Mifflin Co., 1938.

_____ . *Son of the Wilderness: The Life of John Muir.* New York: Alfred A. Knopf, 1945.

W.P.A. in Northern California, American Guide Series. *San Francisco: The Bay and its Cities.* New York: Hastings House, 1947.

Young, S. Hall. *Alaska Days with John Muir.* New York: Fleming H. Revell Co., 1915.

Index